Police Pass OSPRE Part 1 Revision Cramm

Contents

Section 1 – Evidence & Procedure

Unit 1	PACE 1984 Authorities	Page 1
Unit 2	Designated Police Stations & Custody Officers	Page 2
Unit 3	Rights of Detainees	Page 6
Unit 4	Conditions of Detainees	Page 26
Unit 5	Searches of Detainees	Page 32
Unit 6	Charging Detainees	Page 42
Unit 7	Delaying Rights to Legal Advice & Interviewing in the Absence of a Solicitor	Page 45
Unit 8	Detention Periods	Page 56
Unit 9	Reviews	Page 69
Unit 10	Identification Procedures	Page 77
Unit 11	Samples, Fingerprints & Footwear Impressions	Page 91
Unit 12	Photographs	Page 109
Unit 13	Silence, Cautions, Interviews & Excluding Solicitors	Page 113
Unit 14	Bail	Page 142
Unit 15	Cautions, Reprimands & Warnings	Page 163
Unit 16	Facts in Issue, Sources of Evidence, Presumptions & Burden of Proof	Page 169
Unit 17	Hearsay, Character, Opinion, Corroboration & Judicial Notice	Page 175
Unit 18	Disclosure	Page 199
Unit 19	Excluding Confessions & Other Evidence	Page 208
Unit 20	Summonses & Warrants	Page 215
Unit 21	Court Procedure	Page 223
Unit 22	Witnesses	Page 230
Unit 23	Sentencing	Page 244
Unit 24	Youth Justice & Youth Crime & Disorder	Page 249

Section 2 – Crime

Unit 1	Actus Reus & Mens Rea	Page 259
Unit 2	Incomplete Offences	Page 267
Unit 3	General Defences	Page 270
Unit 4	Homicide	Page 273
Unit 5	Misuse of Drugs	Page 281
Unit 6	Offences Against the Person	Page 301
Unit 7	Sexual Offences	Page 316
Unit 8	Offences Against Children & Vulnerable Persons	Page 351
Unit 9	Theft (1) – Basic Theft, Burglary & Robbery	Page 358
Unit 10	Theft (2) – Fraud & Other Dishonesty Offences	Page 371
Unit 11	Criminal Damage	Page 385
Unit 12	Offences Against the Administration Of Justice	Page 395

Section 3 – General Police Duties

Unit 1	Police	Page 403
Unit 2	Extending the Police Family	Page 418
Unit 3	Human Rights	Page 421
Unit 4	Police Powers & Trespass	Page 428
Unit 5	Harassment, Anti Social Behaviour & Communication Offences	Page 462
Unit 6	Public Order	Page 476
Unit 7	Firearms	Page 489
Unit 8	Weapons	Page 502
Unit 9	Civil Disputes	Page 511
Unit 10	RIPA 2000	Page 515
Unit 11	Sporting Offences	Page 528
Unit 12	Licensing Offences	Page 540
Unit 13	Information Offences	Page 558
Unit 14	Diversity, Discrimination & Equality	Page 563
Unit 15	Terrorism	Page 570

Blue Light Publishing Limited – 4th Edition 2008

Evidence & Procedure
Unit 1: Rank of Authorising Officers for Powers Exercisable Under PACE 1984

PACE 1984 Authorisations

- There are over 40 different authorities exercisable under PACE 1984.

- Differing authorities have differing ranks of authorising officer.

- Instead of revising each of the authorities in turn – just revise the following mnemonic.

- All of the powers **contained** in this **mnemonic** require the authorisation of a **Superintendent.**

- Any power is **not specified** within the mnemonic require the authorisation of an **Inspector.**

36	-	Extending the detention period from 24 to **36 hours.**
R	-	**R**oad checks.
U	-	**U**rgent Interviews in the absence of a solicitor, appropriate adult, or interpreter, or urgent interviews of persons unfit for interview.
D	-	**D**elaying notification of a solicitor.
E	-	**E**xcluding solicitors from interviews.
Terrorist	-	**Terrorism offences.**

Evidence & Procedure
Unit 2 – Police Station Procedure (1)
Designated Police Stations & Custody Officers

A - Defining A Designated Police Station – Section 35 PACE 1984

- A **designated police station** is a **station designated** by the **Chief Officer of Police** within a force.

- The **Chief Officer of Police** must designate **sufficient police stations to deal with prisoners.**

- Once the **Chief Officer of Police** chooses to designate a station the **details of designation** are **published**.

- A designated station will commonly possess **adequate facilities to detain arrested persons**.

B - How Long Can A Police Station Be Designated For? – Section 35 PACE 1984

- A police station:
    - *Can* be **designated** either:
        - **Permanently**; or
        - For a **specified period.**
    - *Cannot* be **designated part of a day.**

C – Action To Be Taken Following An Arrest - Section 30 PACE 1984

- As soon as practicable following arrest;
- The suspect **must be taken to** a **police station;**
- **Unless;**
- The suspect has been **street bailed** under section 30A PACE 1984 prior to their arrival at the police station.

D - Which Type Of Police Station Must The Suspect Be Taken To?

- A suspect who either:
    - **Will** be detained; or
    - Is **likely** to be detained;
- For **more** than **6 hours;**
- **Must** be taken to a **designated police station.**

- Therefore if:
    - **Detention** either:
        - **Will not**; or
        - Is **unlikely** to;
    - **Exceed 6 hours**;
    - The suspect **can** be taken to a **non designated police station**.

E – Custody Officers

1 - The Role Of Custody Officers – Section 36(5) PACE 1984

- The role of the **Custody Officer** is:
    - To act **independently**;
    - Ensuring the **protection** of the **detainee's**:
        - **Welfare**; and
        - **Rights**.

2 - Prohibited Activities Of The Custody Officer – Code C Paragraph 3.4

- The **Custody Officer** must **not**:
    - **Ask** the detainee any **questions** in relation to their suspected **involvement** in the offence;
    - Make **value judgments**;
    - Make **comments** that cast doubt on their **impartiality**.

3 - Custody Officers In Designated Police Stations – Sections 36(3) & (4) PACE 1984

(i) - The General Rule

- In **designated police stations**:
    - **One** or **more**;
    - **Designated Custody Officers**;
    - *Must* be appointed who must:
        - **Not be involved** in the investigation of the offence; and
        - Be **at least** the rank of **Sergeant**.

Exam Trip Up

- In the case of *Vince v Chief Constable of Dorset* [1993] 1 WLR 415:
- It was established that:
    - The **Chief Constable** for each force:
        - *Must* appoint **1 designated Custody Officer** for each designated police station; and
        - *May (discretion)* appoint **further designated Custody Officers** for each designated police station.
- The case also established that here is **no requirement** that:
    - There be **sufficient designated Custody Officers**;
    - To ensure that the functions of **Custody Officer**;
    - Were **always performed by designated individuals.**

(ii) - The First Exception To The General Rule

- If a **designated Custody Officer is not readily available,** the role may be performed by:
    - A **Sergeant** or **above**;
    - **Not involved** in the investigation of the offence.

(iii) - The Second Exception To The General Rule

- If such a **Sergeant is not readily available,** the role may be performed by:
    - Any **constable**;
    - **Not involved** in the investigation of the offence.

Exam Trip Up

- A **Constable**;
- **Cannot** act as a **Custody Officer** in a **Designated Police Station** if:
    - There is a **Sergeant** in the **Designated Police Station**;
    - Who is *not* otherwise engaged.

4 - Custody Officers In Non Designated Police Stations – Section 36 (7) PACE 1984

(i) - The General Rule

- In a **non-designated police station** the role of **Custody Officer** may be performed by:
    - An **officer** of **any rank**;
    - **Not involved** in the investigation of the offence.

(ii) - The Exceptions To The General Rule

- **If no such person is available** any of the following may perform the role:
    - The **arresting** officer;
    - **Any other officer involved in the investigation;**
    - Any officer who **granted street bail.**

- In such circumstances:
    - An **Inspector** or above;
    - At a **designated police station;**
    - *Must* be **informed.**

Summary Table

Who May Perform The Role Of Custody Officer?

Designated Police Stations	Non Designated Police Stations
A **designated Custody Officer** of the rank of **Sergeant** or above; or	**Any officer not involved** in the investigation of the offence; or
If the **designated Custody Officer** is **not available**: • A **Sergeant** or above **not involved** in the investigation of the offence; or	If **no such officer is available:** • The **arresting** officer; • Any **officer involved in he investigation**; or • The officer who **issued street bail.**
If the above are **not available**: • **Any other officer not involved** in the investigation of the offence.	If above – an **Inspector** or above **must be notified** at the **designated police station.**

Evidence & Procedure
Unit 3 – Police Station Procedure (2)
Rights Of Detainees In Police Detention

A – The Definition Of Police Detention – Section 118 PACE 1984

- A person will be in **police detention** when:
    - They have either been:
        - **Taken to a police station** after being **arrested**:
            - For an offence; or
            - A terrorism offence under section 41 Terrorism Act 2000; or
        - **Arrested at a police station** after having initially attended the station voluntarily; and
    - Are **detained** there under the **charge of a constable**.

B - Dealing With Detainees Expeditiously – Code C Paragraph 1.1

- All persons held in custody must be:
    - Dealt with **expeditiously**; and
    - **Released** as soon as the **need for detention no longer applies**.

C - Bringing The Suspect Before The Custody Officer - Code C Paragraph 2.1A

1 – Persons In Police Detention

- When a person is **bought to a police station** either:
    - Under **arrest;**
    - **Voluntarily** but is **subsequently arrested**; or
    - To answer **bail;**
- They shall be **brought before the custody officer as soon as practicable,** following either:
    - Their **arrival** – if under **arrest** or answering **bail;** or
    - Their **arrest** - if they initially attended **voluntarily.**

2 - Persons Attending The Police Station Voluntarily Who Are Not Under Arrest – Code C Paragraph 3.21

- Persons attending the police station **voluntarily**:
    - **Need *not* be brought** before the **Custody Officer** as they are **not under arrest**;
    - Are **free to leave** until they are arrested;
    - If they are interviewed under **caution**, the person administering the caution must **inform** them that:
        - They are *not* under arrest;
        - They are *not* obliged to remain in the station;
        - That they are **entitled to free and independent legal advice** including speaking to a solicitor via telephone.
- If they are **prevented from leaving** – they must be:
    - **Informed** that they are under **arrest**; and
    - Be **brought before** the **Custody Officer** as soon as practicable who will **notify** them of their **rights.**

What About The Rights To Legal Advice Of A Person Attending A Police Station Voluntarily Who Has Not As Yet Been Cautioned? – Code C Paragraph 3.22

- If a person attending a police station voluntarily **asks about their right to legal advice** they must be provided with a **copy** of the **notice** explaining the arrangements for obtaining legal advice.

3 - The Timing Of The Custody Officers Duties – Code C Paragraph 1.1A & Note 1H

- The **Custody Officer** *must* perform their functions **as soon as practicable**.
- The **Custody Officer** will **not breach** the **Codes of Practice** if:
    - The **delay** is **justifiable** e.g:
        - A large number of suspects being brought simultaneously into custody;
        - All interview rooms being used; or
        - There are difficulties contacting:
            - A **solicitor**;
            - **Appropriate adult**; or
            - **Interpreter**; and
    - **Reasonable steps** are **taken** to **prevent unnecessary delay**.

4 - Recording Delays – Code C Paragraph 1.1A

- A **note** must be made in the **custody record** of:
    - **When** a delay occurs;
    - The **reasons** for any delay.

D – The Custody Record

1 - Opening A Custody Record - Code C Paragraph 2.1

- A separate **custody record** *must* be opened **as soon as practicable** by the **Custody Officer** for each person brought before them.

- All information *must* be **recorded** in the custody record **as soon as practicable** unless otherwise stated.

2 - Duties Of The Custody Officer In Relation To The Custody Record - Code C Paragraphs 2.3 – 2.7

- The **Custody Officer** is responsible for:
    - Ensuring the **accuracy** and **completeness** of the **custody record**; and
    - Ensuring the **record accompanies any detainee transferred** to another station.

3 - Entries In The Custody Record – Code C Paragraph 2.2 & 2.6

(i) - The General Rule

- In circumstances where any **authorisation** is required, an entry *must* be made in the custody **record** of the **authorising officers**:
    - **Name**; and
    - **Rank.**

- All **entries** in the custody record *must* be:
    - **Timed**; and
    - **Either:**
        - **Signed** by the **maker** – paper custody records;
        - Contain the **operator's identification** – electronic records.

(ii) - The Exception To The General Rule – Code C Paragraph 2.6A

- It is **not necessary** to enter an officer or police staff's details where either:
    - The **officer** or **police staff reasonably** *believes* that **recording** or **disclosing** their **name** may **place them in danger**; or
    - The enquiries relate to an act of **terrorism.**

- In such circumstances they should **instead enter:**
    - Their **warrant** or other **identification number**; or
    - The **name** of the **police station.**

4 - Detainee's Refusal To Sign The Custody Record - Code C Paragraph 2.7

- Any **refusal** by the **detainee** to **sign** the **custody record** when asked to do so *must* also be:
    - **Timed;** and
    - **Recorded.**

5 - Who Is Permitted To Gain Access To The Custody Record During Detention? Code C - Paragraph 2.4

- Either a:
    - **Solicitor;** or
    - **Appropriate Adult;**
- *Must* be permitted to **inspect** the detainee's **custody record;**
- Either:
    - As **soon as practicable after their arrival** in the police station; or
    - At **any other time thereafter** during the suspect's detention.

Exam Trip Up

- Whilst this is a **mandatory obligation** to permit them access **as soon as practicable** following their arrival, their access is **qualified** to the extent that:
    - **Access** must be **agreed** with the **Custody Officer;** and
    - **Access** must **not unreasonably interfere** with the **Custody Officer's duties.**

- Watch out for questions involving a Custody Officer who is busy dealing with processing detainee A when the solicitor or appropriate adult of detainee B arrives and immediately demands to see the custody record.

- In such circumstances an **unilateral demand** will **not automatically trigger access** to the custody record as:
    - The Custody Officers **agreement** is **required;** and
    - The Custody Officer is already **preoccupied with another task.**

6 - Who Is Permitted To Obtain A Copy Of The Custody Record Following Detention? Code C Paragraph 2.4A

- Either:
    - The **detainee;**
    - Their **solicitor;** or
    - Their **appropriate adult;**
- *Must* be **given** upon **request;**
- A **copy** of the **custody record;**
- For **up to 12 months after** the detainee's **release** from custody.

7 - Who Is Permitted To Inspect The Original Custody Record Following Detention? – Code C Paragraph 2.5

- **Following** the **detainee's release** from custody either:
    - ☐ The **detainee**;
    - ☐ Their **solicitor**; or
    - ☐ Their **appropriate adult**;
- Shall be permitted to **inspect** the *original* **custody record**;
- Provided they give **reasonable notice** of their request.

- Any **inspection** must be **noted** in the **custody record**.

E - Informing The Custody Officer Of The Reasons For Arrest - Code C Paragraph 3.4

- Either:
    - ☐ The **arresting officer** – if they are **present**; or
    - ☐ If the **arresting officer** is **not present**:
        - The **arresting officer remotely**; or
        - A **3rd party** on the **arresting officer's behalf**;
- *Must* inform the **Custody Officer** of:
    - ☐ The **nature** of the offence;
    - ☐ The **grounds** for the arrest.

F - Recording Obligations In Relation To The Reasons For Arrest – Code C Paragraph 3.4

- The **Custody Officer** *must* make a **record** in the **custody record** of:
    - ☐ The **offence** for which the detainee has been arrested;
    - ☐ The **reasons** for their arrest;
    - ☐ Any **comments** made by the **detainee** in respect of the arresting officer's account.

G - Recording Obligations In Relation To The Grounds For Detention – Section 37(4)-(6) PACE 1984 & Code C Paragraphs 3.4 & 3.23

- When **detention is authorised**, the **Custody Officer** *must:*
    - ☐ **Inform** the **detainee** of the **grounds** for authorising their detention:
        - **As soon as practicable**; and
        - **Before** they are **questioned** about any offence;
    - ☐ Make a **written record** of the **grounds for detention** in the custody record;
    - ☐ In the **presence** of the **detainee**;

- □ Unless;
  - □ **At the time** the record is made the **detainee** is either:
    - **Violent** or likely to become violent; or **V**
    - **Incapable** of understanding what was said; **I**
    - In urgent need of **medical** attention. **M**
  - □ **Record** any **comments** made by the **detainee** in respect of the **decision to detain them**.

Exam Trip Up – Prohibited Activities By The Custody Officer – Code C Paragraph 3.4

- The **Custody Officer** must **not**:
  - □ **Invite comment** - they must merely record any gratuitous comments;
  - □ Put any **specific questions** to the detainee in relation to their **comments**; or
  - □ Put **specific questions** to the detainee regarding their **involvement in the offence**.

H - Authorising Detention

- Where a person has been arrested the **Custody Officer** *must* determine whether they have **sufficient evidence before them to charge**.
- The **Custody Officer** can **authorise detention** where there is either:
  - □ *Sufficient* evidence to charge;
  - □ *Insufficient* evidence to charge.

1 – Sufficient Evidence To Charge

(a) Options Available To The Custody Officer Where There Is Sufficient Evidence To Charge - Section 37(7) PACE 1984

- If the **Custody Officer** determines they have *sufficient* evidence to charge, they may either:
  - □ **Release** the person arrested either:
    - Without charge on bail for the purpose of enabling the CPS to make a decision whether to charge;
    - Without charge on bail but not for that purpose;
    - Without charge and without bail; or
  - □ **Charge**.

(b) - Action To Be Taken By The Custody Officer Where The Detainee Is Bailed To Allow Consultation With The CPS – Section 37B PACE 1984

- The **officer involved in the investigation** *must* send the requisite information to the DPP as soon as possible.

- The **DPP** must **decide** if there is **sufficient evidence to charge**.

- If they decide that there is **sufficient evidence to charge** they *must:*
    - Determine whether to:
        - **Charge**; or
        - **Caution**.
    - Provide a **written notice** of their decision to the **officer involved in the case**.

- The **Custody Officer** *must* provide the person with a **notice in writing** stating that they will **not be prosecuted** if the **DDP** decide that either:
    - There is **insufficient evidence to charge**; or
    - There is **sufficient evidence to charge** but they will instead be **cautioned**.

(c) - Action To Be Taken By The Custody Officer To Charge - s37(1) PACE 1984

- Where there is *sufficient* evidence to charge:
    - The person may be detained at the police station for **such period as is necessary to enable the custody officer to charge**.
    - In *D v HM Advocate (2000)* The Times, 14th April, an **unreasonable delay in bringing charges** was deemed in **contravention of Article 6 ECHR**.

2 – Insufficient Evidence To Charge

Action To Be Taken By The Custody Officer Where There Is Insufficient Evidence To Charge – Section 37(2) PACE 1984

- Where there is **insufficient evidence to charge**:
    - The person shall be **released** either **with** or **without bail**;
    - **Unless**;
    - The **Custody Officer** has **reasonable grounds** to *believe* that **detention** without charge is **necessary** to either:
        - Secure or preserve evidence; or
        - Obtain such evidence by questioning.

I - Informing The Detainee Of Their Rights - Code C Paragraph 3.1

- The **Custody Officer** *must* inform a person:
    - Brought to a police station under **arrest**; or
    - **Arrested** at a police station having attended initially voluntarily;

- Of the following **continuing rights** exercisable throughout the period of custody:
    - ☐ The right to have **someone informed of their arrest** (s56 PACE 1984);
    - ☐ The right to **consult privately** with a **solicitor** (s58 PACE 1984)
    - ☐ The right to consult the **Codes of Practice.**

Exam Trip Up - Code C Note 3D

- The **right to consult** the **Codes of Practice** is **qualified** to the extent that exercising the right must **not delay unreasonably** any:
    - ☐ **Investigative** action; or
    - ☐ **Administrative** action;
    - ☐ Including:
        - Taking **non intimate samples, fingerprints** or **footwear impressions**;
        - Conducting **searches**; or
        - **Blood, breath** or **urine** for traffic offences.

J - Providing The Detainee With Written Notices - Code C Paragraph 3.2

- The **Custody Officer** *must* give the **detainee** a **written notice** setting out:
    - ☐ The aforementioned rights;
    - ☐ The arrangements for obtaining legal advice;
    - ☐ The right to a copy of the custody record;
    - ☐ The caution;
    - ☐ A list of their entitlements whilst in custody.
- The **detainee** will be **asked to sign the custody record** to **acknowledge receipt** of the **notices.**
- Any **refusal to sign** must be **recorded.**

K - Additional Notification Obligations For Foreign Nationals – Code C Paragraph 3.3

- Citizens of:
    - ☐ An **independent Commonwealth country**; or
    - ☐ A **foreign national**;
- *Must* be **informed as soon as practicable** of their **rights of communication** with their:
    - ☐ **High Commission;**
    - ☐ **Consulate**; or
    - ☐ **Embassy.**

Exam Trip Up

- Watch out for questions involving Irish citizens:
    - ☐ If they are from the **Republic of Ireland** – the notification obligation **will** be **triggered**.
    - ☐ If they are from **Northern Ireland** – the notification obligation will **not** be **triggered**.

L - Risk Assessments – Code C Paragraphs 3.6 – 3.10

1 – Purpose Of The Risk Assessment

- The **Custody Officer** *must* determine whether the detainee is either:
    - ☐ In need of **medical treatment** or **attention**; or
    - ☐ Requires:
        - An **appropriate adult**;
        - Help checking documentation;
        - An **interpreter**.

2 - Responsibility For The Risk Assessment

- The **Custody Officer** is responsible for initiating a **risk assessment** to determine whether the **detainee** presents any **specific risks** to:
    - ☐ **Custody staff**; or
    - ☐ **Themselves**.
- The **Custody Officer** must always **check the PNC computer as soon as practicable** to check for any risks highlighted in relation to the detainee.
- The **reason** for any **delays** *must* be **recorded** in the **custody record**.
- The **Custody Officer** *may* **consult** others - e.g. health care professionals.

3 – Recording The Results Of The Risk Assessment

- The **results** of the **risk assessment** *must* be **recorded** in the **custody record**.
- The **Custody Officer** *must* ensure that **others responsible** for the detainee are appropriately **briefed** about any **risks**.

4 - Implementing The Response To The Risk Assessment

- The **Custody Officer** is responsible for **implementing** the **response** to the **risk assessment** which may include:
    - ☐ Reducing opportunities for self harm;
    - ☐ Calling a health care professional; or
    - ☐ Increased monitoring.
- Risk assessment is an **ongoing process**.

M - Determining Whether The Detainee Wishes To Exercise Their Rights - Code C Paragraph 3.5

- The **Custody Officer** *must* ask the **detainee** whether they:
    - Want **legal advice**;
    - Want **somebody informed** of their detention.
- The **detainee** will be **requested to sign the custody record** to confirm their decision.
- Any **refusal to sign** *must* be **recorded**.

N - The Detainees Rights

1 - The Right To Have Someone Informed Of Their Whereabouts - Code C Paragraph 5.1

(i) - Exercising The Right To Intimation

- Section 56 PACE 1984 provides the **right not to be held incommunicado**.
    - Any person **arrested**; and
    - Held at a **police station** or **other premises**;
    - May request to have a person:
        - **Known to them**; or
        - **Likely to take an interest in their welfare**;
    - **Informed** of their whereabouts;
    - **As soon as practicable**;
    - At the **public expense**.

(ii) - Contacting Alternative Persons - Code C Paragraph 5.1

- If the person initially requested **cannot be contacted** the detainee can choose up to **2 alternatives**.
- If they **also cannot be contacted**:
    - Either:
        - The **Custody Officer**; or
        - The **officer in charge of the investigation**;
    - Retain the *discretion* **to allow further attempts** until contact is made.

(iii) - Intimation Is a Continuing Right

- The right to intimation is **continuous** throughout detention.

(iv) - Intimation Where The Detainee Is Moved To Another Station - Code C Paragraph 5.3

- If the **detainee is moved** to another police station:
    - ☐ The right to intimation will **arise again**;
    - ☐ **Even if** the suspect has **previously exercised** their right at a prior station.

(v) - Delaying The Right To Intimation - Code C Paragraph 5.2

- The right to intimation can only be **delayed** in accordance with **Code C Annex B**.

2 - The Right To Write Or Telephone - Code C Paragraph 5.6

(i) – Exercising The Right To Write Or Telephone

- A **detainee** will have the **right to request**:
    - ☐ **Writing materials to send a letter**; or
    - ☐ **To telephone one person** for a reasonable period of time.
- This is a **separate right** which exists **in addition** to the **right to have a person informed of their detention**.

(ii) - Privacy and The Communication – Code C Paragraph 5.7

- The **detainee** *must* be informed by the **Custody Officer** *before* writing or calling that:
    - ☐ The communication can be **read** or **listened to**; and
    - ☐ Its contents may be **given in evidence**.

(iii) - Delaying The Right To Write Or Telephone

- The right can only be **delayed** if the circumstances in **Code C Annex B** are satisfied.

3 - Enquiries About The Detainees Whereabouts – Code C Paragraph 5.5

- If either a:
    - ☐ **Friend**;
    - ☐ **Relative**; or
    - ☐ Person with an **interest** in the **detainee's welfare**;
- Makes **enquires** about the detainees **whereabouts**;
- The detainees whereabouts shall be **disclosed** if:
    - ☐ The **detainee agrees**; and
    - ☐ **Code C Annex B** does *not* apply.

4 - Visitors - Code C Paragraph 5.4 & Note 5C

- The detainee *may* receive **visits** at the **Custody Officer's** *discretion.*
- Visits should be allowed **when possible**, subject to:
    - Having **sufficient personnel** to **supervise** the visit; and
    - Any **possible hindrance caused to the investigation** that the visit may cause.

Recording Obligations – Code C Paragraph 5.8

- A **record** should be made of:
    - Any **requests** to exercise either right;
    - The **actioning** of any subsequent:
        - Letters;
        - Telephone calls;
        - Messages; or
        - Visits.
    - Any **refusal** by the **detainee** to have **information given** about their whereabouts to an outside **enquirer.**

5 - Contacting A Solicitor - Code C Paragraph 6.1

(i) – Exercising The Right To Contact A Solicitor

- **Section 58 of PACE 1984** provides the **right to legal advice**.
    - All detainees *must* be **informed** by the **Custody Officer;**
    - That they may **at any time;**
    - **Consult and communicate privately with a solicitor either:**
        - **In person;**
        - **In writing; or**
        - **By telephone**
    - And that **free independent advice is available from the duty solicitor;**
    - **Unless Code C Annex B applies.**

(ii) - Action To Be Taken In Respect Of A Request For Legal Advice - Code C Paragraph 6.5

- Whenever **legal advice is requested:**
    - The **Custody Officer** *must* contact the solicitor without delay;
    - **Unless;**
    - **Code C Annex B** applies.

(iii) - Prohibition On Interviewing The Suspect Prior To The Arrival Of A Solicitor Requested – Code C Paragraph 6.6

- The detainee who has **requested legal advice**:
    - **May not be:**
        - **Interviewed;** or
        - **Continue** to be **interviewed;**
    - **Prior** to the **solicitor's arrival;**
    - **Unless;**
    - The conditions in **Code C Paragraph 6.6** apply (see later).

(iv) - Action To Be Taken When The Detainee Declines Legal Advice - Code C Paragraph 6.5

- If the **detainee declines legal advice** the **Custody Officer** must point out that the right **includes speaking to a solicitor on the telephone.**

- If the **detainee continues** to decline legal advice the **Custody Officer** must:
    - **Record** the **reasons for refusal** in the custody record (the **detainee** is **not obliged** to give their reasons); and
    - **Remind** the **detainee** of their right **prior** to any subsequent:
        - Interview;
        - Review;
        - Decision to extend detention;
        - Post charge comments being made by a detainee;
        - Post charge interviews;
        - Intimate searches;
        - Intimate samples;
        - X-rays or ultrasound scans;
        - Identification procedure.

(v) - What If A Solicitor Arrives At A Police Station Who Has Not Been Requested By The Detainee? – Code C Paragraph 6.15

- Where a solicitor arrives at a police station;

- The detainee **must be informed of their presence** (unless Code C Annex B applies);

- Irrespective of whether the detainee is being interviewed at the time of the solicitors arrival; and

- The detainee must be **asked if they wish to consult** with the solicitor.

- The **solicitor's attendance** and the **detainee's decision** must be **noted** in the custody record.

Exam Trip Up

- The **obligation of notification continues to apply** even if the detainee has **previously** either:
    - **Declined** the offer of legal advice; or
    - **Took up** the offer of legal advice but **subsequently agreed to be interviewed without receiving the advice.**

Exam Trip Up

- It is the **detainee's choice** whether to speak to the solicitor.
- The **solicitor has no automatic right to consultation** with the detainee.
- This is still the case even if the solicitor is attending at the request of a relative of the detainee.

(vi) - Privacy When Obtaining Legal Advice – Code C Note 6J

- Code C Note 6J states that whenever a detainee exercises their right to legal advice by either:
    - **Consulting** a solicitor in person; or
    - **Speaking** to a solicitor over the **telephone;**
- They must be allowed to do so **in private;**
- **Unless** it is **impractical** to do so because of either:
    - The **design** and **layout** of the custody area; or
    - The **location** of the **telephones.**

O - Additional Procedural Obligations

- There are **additional procedural obligations** where the detainee is:
    - **A juvenile;**
    - **Mentally disordered or mentally vulnerable;**
    - **Deaf;**
    - **Unable to speak English;**
    - **Blind;** or
    - **A foreign national.**

P - Juveniles And Mentally Disordered And Vulnerable Witnesses

1 - When Will A Detainee Be Treated As A Juvenile? – Code C Paragraph 1.5

- A detainee will be treated as a **juvenile:**
    - If they **appear** to be **under 17;**
    - In the **absence** of **clear evidence** to the **contrary.**

2 - When Will A Detainee Be Treated As Mentally Disordered Or Mentally Vulnerable? – Code C Paragraph 1.4

- A detainee of **any age** will be **treated** as either:
    - **Mentally disordered;** or
    - **Mentally vulnerable;**
- If either:
    - The **officer has any suspicion** that this is the case; or
    - Is **told in good faith** that this is the case.

3 - Juveniles: Ascertaining The Identity Of The Person Responsible For The Juveniles Welfare - Code C Paragraph 3.13

- Where the **detainee** is a **juvenile**, the **Custody Officer** *must:*
    - If it is **practicable**;
    - **Ascertain** the **identity** of the **person responsible** for the **juvenile's welfare**.
- The person *may* be either:
    - Their **parent** or **guardian**;
    - If the juvenile is **in care** – a **person appointed** by the **local authority** or **voluntary organisation** to have responsibility for their welfare; or
    - Any other person, who **for the time being has assumed responsibility** for their welfare.

Exam Trip Up

- A person will have **assumed responsibility for a child** where they are looking after the child in the **ordinary lay sense**.
- It is **not necessary** for them to have obtained a **Parental Responsibility Order** from court.

Exam Trip Up

- Note that whilst there is a **presumption** that the person responsible for the child's welfare will be contacted, the presumption can be **displaced** where it is **not practicable to do so.**
- It is therefore **not** a **mandatory obligation**.

4 - Notifying The Person Responsible For The Juveniles Welfare - Code C Paragraph 3.13

- Once their identity is ascertained they *must (no discretion)* be **informed, as soon as practicable:**
    - That the juvenile **has been arrested;**
    - **Why** they have been **arrested**; and
    - **Where** they have been **detained.**

Exam Trip Up

- This right exists *in addition* to the right to **intimation.**

Exam Trip Up

- This **action** *must* be taken **(no discretion) regardless** of whether the **juvenile:**
    - **Wishes to have a person informed;**
    - **Has contacted some other person already.**

Exam Trip Up

- The notification provisions **continue** to apply even if the detainee is being held **incommunicado** under the provisions of **Code C Annex B**.

5 - Notification Where The Juvenile Is Subject To A Court Order - Code C Paragraph 3.14

- If the **juvenile** is **subject** to a **court order** under which:
    - Either:
        - A **person**; or
        - An **organisation** (e.g. YOT);
    - Is given **statutory responsibility** to **observe** or **monitor** the juvenile;
- *Reasonable steps* must be taken to **notify** the:
    - **Person** - "The Responsible Officer"; or
    - **Organisation**.

Exam Trip Up

- These notification provisions **continue** to apply even if the detainee is being held **incommunicado** under the provisions of Code C Annex B.

6 - Securing The Attendance Of An Appropriate Adult - Code C Paragraph 3.15

- The **Custody Officer** *must* secure the **attendance** of an **appropriate adult, as soon as practicable** where the detainee is either:
    - A **juvenile**;
    - **Mentally disordered**;
    - **Mentally vulnerable**.

7 - Juveniles: Defining Appropriate Adults - Code C Paragraph 1.7

- An **appropriate adult** *may* be:
    - A **parent**;
    - A **guardian**;
    - Where the juvenile is **in care** – a **person representing the local authority or voluntary organisation caring for them**;
    - A **social worker**;
    - Failing the above - some other:
        - **Responsible adult**;
        - Aged **18 or over**;
        - Who is **not a police officer** or **employed by the police**.

8 - Mentally Disordered Or Vulnerable Persons: Defining Appropriate Adults – Code C Paragraph 1.7

- An **appropriate adult** for a **mentally disordered** or **mentally vulnerable** person may be either:
    - [ ] A **relative**;
    - [ ] A **guardian**;
    - [ ] A person **responsible** for their **care** or **custody**;
    - [ ] Someone who:
        - Is **experienced** in dealing with mentally disordered or mentally vulnerable people; and
        - Is **not** a **police officer** or **employed by the police**;
    - [ ] Failing the above - some other:
        - **Responsible adult**;
        - Aged **18 or over**;
        - Who is **not** a **police officer** or **employed by the police**.

9 - Arranging For The Attendance Of An Appropriate Adult - Code C Paragraph 3.15

- The **Custody Officer** *must* as soon as practicable:
    - [ ] **Inform** the **appropriate adult** of:
        - The **grounds** for detention;
        - The detainee's **whereabouts**; and
    - [ ] **Request** the appropriate adult to **attend the police station**.

10 - Informing The Detainee Of Their Rights In The Appropriate Adults Presence - Code C Paragraph 3.17

- If the **appropriate adult** is **in attendance** at the time the detainee is booked into custody:
    - [ ] They must be **allowed to be present** when the **detainee** is **read their rights**.

- If the **suspect has already been read their rights** prior to the arrival of the appropriate adult:
    - [ ] The **rights** must be **repeated** to the **detainee** in the **presence** of the **appropriate adult**.

11 - Advising The Detainee Of Their Rights In Relation To The Appropriate Adult – Code C Paragraph 3.18

- The detainee shall be **advised:**
    - That they can **consult privately** with an **appropriate adult at any time;**
    - The **function** of the **appropriate adult** is to provide:
        - **Advice;** and
        - **Assistance.**

12 - Assessing Mentally Disordered / Vulnerable Detainees - Code C Paragraph 3.16

- A **mentally disordered** or **mentally vulnerable** detainee must be **assessed as soon as possible.**
- The **Custody Officer** *must* as soon as practicable secure the attendance of:
    - An **approved social worker;**
    - A **registered medical practitioner.**

13 - What If The Juvenile Wishes To Decline Legal Advice But The Appropriate Adult Wishes A Solicitor To Attend To Provide Legal Advice? – Code C Paragraph 6.5A

- Code C Paragraph 6.5A states that:
    - Even if a **juvenile** indicates that they **do not want legal advice;**
    - The **appropriate adult has the right to ask for a solicitor to attend** if it would be in the **juvenile's best interests.**
    - However, the **juvenile cannot be forced to see the solicitor** if they are adamant that they do not wish to do so.
- Therefore whilst there is **nothing to stop the appropriate adult securing the solicitors attendance** at the police station, the **juvenile cannot be forced to speak to the solicitor** once they have arrived.

Exam Trip Up

- A juvenile can speak to a solicitor privately in the absence of their appropriate adult if they expressly request to do so.

Q - Calling Interpreters - Code C Paragraph 3.12

- Where the **Custody Officer** is **unable to establish effective communication** because the detainee is:
    - ☐ Deaf;
    - ☐ Unable to hear;
    - ☐ Unable to speak; or
    - ☐ Unable to understand English;
- The **Custody Officer** *must:*
    - ☐ Call an **interpreter**;
    - ☐ **As soon as practicable**;
    - ☐ To **assist** in the notification steps in Code C Paragraphs 3.1 – 3.5.

R - Assisting Blind Detainees - Code C Paragraph 3.20

- If the detainee is:
    - ☐ **Blind**;
    - ☐ **Seriously visually impaired**; or
    - ☐ **Unable to read**;
- The **Custody Officer** shall ensure that one of the following is available to **help check and sign documentation**:
    - ☐ Their **solicitor**;
    - ☐ **A relative**;
    - ☐ **Any appropriate adult** (if a juvenile or mentally disordered); or
    - ☐ Some other person likely to take an interest in their welfare who is not involved in the investigation.

S - Addition Procedural Obligations In Relation To Citizens Of Independent Commonwealth Countries And Foreign Nationals - Code C Paragraphs 7.1 – 7.4

- Any **citizen** of:
    - ☐ An independent Commonwealth country;
    - ☐ A foreign country;
- *Must* be **informed as soon as practicable** of their right to:
    - ☐ **Communicate at any time** with their **High Commission, Embassy or Consulate**; and
    - ☐ Have their **High Commission, Embassy or Consulate** informed of:
        - Their **whereabouts**; and
        - The **grounds** for their detention.

- Any **request** must be **acted on as soon as practicable** by the **Custody Officer**.

- If the detainee is a **national** of a country specified in **Code C Annex F**:
    - Their **High Commission, Embassy or Consulate** must be **notified** of their **arrest as soon as practicable**;
    - **Unless**;
    - The detainee is either:
        - **A political refugee**; or
        - **Seeking political asylum.**
    - If this is the case:
        - Their **Consular Officers** shall *not:*
            - Be **informed** of their **arrest**; or
            - Given **access** to any **information** concerning the detainee;
        - **Unless**;
        - The **detainee expressly requests** that the information be divulged.

Recording Obligations – Code C Paragraph 7.5

- A **record** must be made of:
    - The **detainee** being **informed** of their rights; and
    - Any **communications** with a **High Commission, Embassy or Consulate**.

Exam Trip Up – Code C Note 7A

- These **rights** will **continue** to apply even where the **detainee** is being held **incommunicado** under the provisions of **Code C Annex B.**

Evidence & Procedure
Unit 4 – Police Station Procedure (3) Conditions Of Detainees Whilst In Police Detention

A - The Number Of Detainees To Be Held In Each Cell – Code C Paragraph 8.1

- So far as *practicable* not more than 1 detainee should be detained in **each cell**.

B - The Condition Of Police Cells - Code C Paragraph 8.2

- Cells *must* be *adequately:*
    - ☐ **Heated;**
    - ☐ **Cleaned;**
    - ☐ **Ventilated;** and
    - ☐ **Lit** and **dimmed** to allow **overnight sleep**.

C - Placing Juveniles In Police Cells – Code C Paragraph 8.8

1 - The General Rule

- A **juvenile** shall *not* be placed into a **police cell**.

2 - The Exceptions To The General Rule

- A **juvenile** *may* be placed into a **police cell** where:
    - ☐ There is *no* **secure accommodation available**; *and*
    - ☐ The **Custody Officer** considers that *either:*
        - It is *not* **practicable** to **supervise** the juvenile if they are **not placed in a cell**; or
        - A cell provides **more comfortable accommodation** than other secure accommodation in the station.

- If a juvenile is placed in a cell they must *not* be placed in a **cell with an adult**.

Recording The Reasons For Placing A Juvenile In A Cell – Code C Paragraph 8.10

- A **record** *must* be made of the **reasons** for placing a juvenile in a cell.

D - Bedding – Code C Paragraph 8.3

- Any:
    - Blankets;
    - Mattress;
    - Pillows; or
    - Bedding;
- Supplied *must* be of a **clean** and **sanitary** condition.

E - Toilet And Washing Facilities – Code C Paragraph 8.4

- The detainee *must* be afforded access to:
    - The **toilet**; and
    - **Washing** facilities.

F - Replacement Clothing – Code C Paragraph 8.5

- A detainee whose **clothing** has been **removed** for reasons of:
    - **Hygiene**;
    - **Health**;
    - **Investigation**; or
    - **Cleaning**;
- *Must* be provided with **replacement clothing** of a **reasonable standard** of:
    - **Comfort**;
    - **Cleanliness**; and
- They may *not* be **interviewed** unless adequate **clothing** has been **offered**.

Recording Obligations – Code C Paragraph 8.9

- A **record** *must* be made of **replacement clothing**.

G - Meals And Drinks – Code C Paragraph 8.6

- In any **24 hour period** the detainee should be **offered** at least:
    - **2 light meals**; and
    - **1 main meal**.
- **Drinks** should be provided:
    - At **meal times**; and
    - Upon **reasonable request between meals**.

Recording Obligations – Code C Paragraph 8.9

- A **record** *must* be made of **meals offered**.

H - Exercise – Code C Paragraph 8.7

- The detainee will be **offered**:
    - **Daily**;
    - **Brief outdoor exercise**;
    - If it is *practicable*.

I - Restraining Detainees In Cells – Code C Paragraph 8.2

- **Approved restraints** can only be used in a **locked cell** where their use in the circumstances is:
    - **Absolutely necessary**; and
    - **Reasonable**;
- Having regard to:
    - The **detainee's demeanour**; and
    - The need to **ensure** the **safety** of:
        - The **detainee**; and
        - Others.

Recording Obligations - Code C Paragraph 8.11

- If a **detainee** is **restrained** in their cell a **record** *must* be made of:
    - The **reason** for the **restraint**;
    - Any **arrangements** for **enhanced supervision**.

J - Checking Detainees – Code C Paragraph 9.3

1 - The General Rule

- Detainees *must* be **visited** at least **every hour**.

2 - The Exception To The General Rule

- Those who are:
    - **Intoxicated**;
    - Whose **level of consciousness causes concern**;
- *Must* **subject** to any clinical **direction** by an **appropriate health care professional**:
    - Be **visited** and **roused** at least every **half hour** to have their **condition assessed**; and
    - Shall if appropriate have any **clinical treatment** arranged.

K - Mandatory Obligations To Arrange Clinical Attention For Detainees

1 - Action Initiated By The Custody Officer – Code C Paragraph 9.5

- The **Custody Officer** *must* ensure that a **detainee receives appropriate clinical attention as soon as practicable** if they appear to be either:
    - [ ] **Physically ill;**
    - [ ] **Injured;**
    - [ ] **Mentally disordered;**
    - [ ] In need of **clinical attention.**

- If the need for attention is **urgent** the **Custody Officer** *must* **immediately call** either:
    - [ ] The **nearest available health care professional;** or
    - [ ] An **ambulance.**

2 – Action Initiated By The Custody Officer – Mandatory Obligation To Contact An Appropriate Health Care Professional Where The Detainee Suffers From A Serious Medical Condition – Code C Paragraph 9.12

- An **appropriate health care professional** *must* also be **contacted** for advice by the **Custody Officer** even though the detainee does **not appear** to be either:
    - [ ] **Physically ill;**
    - [ ] **Injured;**
    - [ ] **Mentally disordered;**
    - [ ] In need of **clinical attention.**

- When the **detainee** either:
    - [ ] Has **in their possession;** or
    - [ ] **Claims to need;**

- **Medication** relating to:
    - [ ] **A heart condition;**
    - [ ] **Diabetes;**
    - [ ] **Epilepsy;** or
    - [ ] A **condition of comparable seriousness.**

Exam Trip Up – Code C Paragraph 9.5A

- The **obligations continue to apply** even where either:
    - [ ] The **detainee** does *not* **request** clinical attention; or
    - [ ] They have **already received** clinical attention **elsewhere.**

3 - Action Initiated By The Detainee – Code C Paragraph 9.8

- If a **detainee** requests:
    - [ ] An **appropriate health care professional**;
    - [ ] *Must* be **called**;
    - [ ] **As soon as is reasonably practicable**;
    - [ ] To **assess** their **clinical needs**.

L - Detainees On Medication – Code C Paragraph 9.9

- Before a detainee is permitted to take any **prescription medication** the **Custody Officer** *must* **consult** with an **appropriate health care professional**.
- A **record** shall be made in the custody record of:
    - [ ] The **consultation**; and
    - [ ] The **outcome** of the consultation;
    - [ ] The **medication** the detainee had in their **possession** on arrival;
    - [ ] Any medication that the detainee **claims to need** but does **not have with them**.
- The **Custody Officer** is responsible for:
    - [ ] **Safekeeping** any medication; and
    - [ ] Ensuring the detainee is given the **opportunity** to **take their medication**.

M - The Custody Officer's Obligation To Disclose Information To Any Appropriate Health Care Professional Called – Code C Paragraph 9.4

- The **Custody Officer** *must* ensure that **all relevant information** that might **assist** in the **treatment** of the detainee's condition is **made available** to the **health care professional**.

N - Seeking The Opinion Of An Appropriate Health Care Professional Called – Code C Paragraph 9.13

- Whenever an **appropriate health care professional** is called to attend a police station the **Custody Officer** shall **ask** their **opinion** on:
    - [ ] Any **risks** to be considered when exercising decisions to **continue detention**;
    - [ ] **When** to carry out **interviews**;
    - [ ] The need for **safeguards**.

Recording Obligations – Code C Paragraph 9.15

- A **record** shall be made in the custody record of:
    - Any **request** by the **detainee** to be **examined**;
    - The **reasons** for their request;
    - Any reasons for the **Custody Officer initiating** the **examination** of the detainee;
    - The **arrangements** made in response; and
    - Any **clinical directions** and **advice** provided.

O - Complaints By Detainees – Code C Paragraph 9.2

- If either:
    - A **complaint** is made:
        - By a **detainee**; or
        - **On behalf** of a **detainee**; or
    - It comes to **notice** that a detainee may have been **treated improperly**;
- A **report** must be made **as soon as practicable** to:
    - An *Inspector* or above;
    - **Not connected** to the investigation.
- If the matter concerns a possible:
    - **Assault**;
    - **Unnecessary force**; or
    - **Unreasonable force**; and
- An **appropriate health care professional** *must* be called as soon as practicable.

Recording Obligations – Code C Paragraph 9.15(a)

- A **record** shall be made in the custody record of:
    - The **complaint**;
    - The **arrangements** for **examination** by an **appropriate health care professional**; and
    - The **comments** of the **Custody Officer**.

Evidence & Procedure
Unit 5 – Police Station Procedure (4)
Searches Of Persons In Police Detention

A - Searching Detained Persons – Section 54(1) PACE 1984

- The **Custody Officer** shall ascertain what **property** a person held **in custody** has **on their person** - i.e. Whenever they are:
    - ☐ Brought to a police station **under arrest**;
    - ☐ **Arrested at** a police station;
    - ☐ Detained at a police station after **surrendering to bail**;
    - ☐ Are **arrested** for a **failure to answer bail**;
    - ☐ Brought to a police station by **order or sentence of a court**.

B - The Extent Of The Search

- There are **3 forms** of searches:
    - ☐ **Searches not exceeding the removal of outer clothing (An Ordinary Search)**;
    - ☐ **Strip Searches**;
    - ☐ **Intimate Searches**.

C - Searches Not Exceeding the Removal of Outer Clothing – Ordinary Searches

1 - Definition Of An Ordinary Search

- An **ordinary search** involves any search that is *not* an:
    - ☐ **Intimate** search; or
    - ☐ **Strip** search.

2 - When Is It Necessary To Conduct An Ordinary Search? - Code C Note 4 A

- This form of search *must* **always be conducted** in respect of detainees where it is clear that:
    - ☐ The **Custody Officer** will have **continuing duties** in relation to the detainee;
    - ☐ The alleged **offence** makes a search appropriate; or
    - ☐ The detainee's **behaviour** makes a search appropriate.

Memory Aid

- Remember:
    - *Continuing duties* - **C**
    - *Offence* - **O**
    - *Behaviour* - **B**

- Just think of a *"cob"* loaf of bread.

3 - When Is It Not Necessary To Conduct An Ordinary Search? - Code C Note 4 A

- An ordinary search will *not* be **necessary** when the suspect will:
    - **Not** be placed in a **cell**; and
    - Only be detained for a **short period.**
- If this is the case the **Custody Officer** must **endorse** the **custody record** - "not searched".

4 - Conducting An Ordinary Search - Section 54 (8) & (9) PACE 1984

- The **Custody Officer** *must:*
    - **Authorise** the search;
    - Specify the **extent** of the search authorised.
- The search shall be **conducted** either by:
    - A **constable** upon the authority of the Custody Officer; or
    - The **Custody Officer** themselves.
- The **searching officer** *must* be the *same sex* as the person searched.

5 - The Extent Of The Ordinary Search - Code C Annex A Paragraph 9

- The detainee will be asked to:
    - **Empty their pockets;** and
    - **Remove their jewellery.**
- Searches of other areas *may* be conducted provided they do **not** involve **more** than the **removal of outer clothing** including:
    - **Coats;**
    - **Hats;**
    - **Jumpers;**
    - **Shoes;**
    - **Socks.**

6 - Need The Search Be Conducted In Private?

- No.

7 - Can Force Be Used If The Detainee Resists An Ordinary Search? – Section 117 PACE 1984

- *Yes* - **reasonable force** may be used where necessary.

8 - Recording Obligations Following An Ordinary Search - Sections 54 (2) & (2A) PACE 1984

- The **Custody Officer** is *no longer obliged* to **record** the items removed following a search.
- The provisions of sections 54 (2) & (2A) PACE 1984 merely provide a *discretionary* power for the **Custody Officer** to **record** the items in the **custody record**.

D - Strip Searches

1 - Definition Of A Strip Search - Code C Annex A Paragraph 9

- A **strip search** is a search involving:
    - The removal of *more* than *outer clothing*; or
    - The search of the *mouth*.

NB - The search of **any other orifice** would amount to an **intimate search**.

2 - When Will A Strip Search Be Appropriate - Code C Annex A Paragraph 10

- A **strip search** may only take place where:
    - The **Custody Officer** reasonably considers that:
        - The detained person might have **concealed**;
        - An **article**;
        - That they would **not be permitted to keep**; and
        - That if such items were found it would be **necessary to remove them**.

3 - The Definition Of Articles That A Detainee Would Not Be Permitted To Keep

- The **articles** that the detainee would "**not be permitted to keep**" include:
    - Items that are **evidence** in relation to an offence; or
    - Items that the **detainee may use to:**
        - Cause **injury** to **themselves** or **others**;
        - **Damage property**;
        - **Interfere** with **evidence**;
        - **Assist** their **escape**.

Memory Aid

- Remember this simple mnemonic – **"PIE":**
    - ☐ **P** - **P**roperty
    - ☐ **I** - **I**njury & **I**nterfere
    - ☐ **E** - **E**vidence & **E**scape

4 - Conducting A Strip Search - Code C Annex A Paragraph 11

- The **Custody Officer** *must:*
    - ☐ **Authorise** the search;
    - ☐ Specify the **extent** of the search authorised – i.e. What parts of the body may be searched.
- The search shall be **conducted** either by:
    - ☐ A **constable** upon the authority of the **Custody Officer**; or
    - ☐ The **Custody Officer** themselves.
- The **searching officer** *must* be the **same sex** as the person searched.
- Persons of the **opposite sex:**
    - ☐ May *not* be **present;**
    - ☐ **Unless;**
    - ☐ The person is an **appropriate adult** specifically **requested** by the detainee.
- The search must **not** take place in an **area** where the **search can be seen** by any **person who does not need to be present.**
- The detainee must be allowed to **re-dress ASAP** following the search.

5 - Strip Searches Where Genitals Are Exposed

(a) - The General Rule - Code C Annex A Paragraph 11(c)

- If the search involves **exposure of intimate body parts** as a **general rule:**
    - ☐ There must be at least **2 persons** present in addition to the detainee.
    - ☐ In the case of **juveniles** or **mentally disordered or vulnerable persons:**
        - The second person must be the **appropriate adult;**
        - **Unless;**
        - The **juvenile** signifies in the **presence of an appropriate adult** that they **do not wish for them to be present** and the **adult agrees.**
        - If so – a **note** must be made in the custody record of the decision which must be **signed by the appropriate adult.**

(b) - The Exception To The General Rule - Code C Annex A Paragraph 11(c)

- There is **no need** for at least **2 persons** to be present in addition to the detainee:
    - In cases of **emergency** when there is a **risk of** *serious* **harm** to:
        - The **detainee**; or
        - **Others**.

6 - Conducting The Strip Search - Code C Annex A Paragraphs 11(e) & (f)

- The detainee can be required to:
    - **Hold their hands in the air**;
    - **Open their legs**;
    - **Bend over**.
- *No* **physical contact** is permitted with a body **orifice**.
- A **request** must be made to **remove items** found in:
    - **On** the detainees **person**;
    - **In** their **mouth**; or
    - **In** any other **orifice**.

7 - Can Force Be Used If The Detainee Resists Being Strip Searched? – Section 117 PACE 1984

- *Yes* - **reasonable force** may be used.

8 - Recording Obligations Following A Strip Search - Code C Annex A Paragraph 12

- A **note** shall be made by the **Custody Officer** in the **custody record** of:
    - The fact a **strip search took place**;
    - Those **present**;
    - **Why** a strip search was **necessary**;
    - The **result** of the search.

E - Intimate Searches

1 – Definition Of An Intimate Search - Code C Annex A Paragraph 1

- An **intimate search** is a search which consists of the physical examination of **any orifice other than the mouth**.

2 - Grounds for Conducting An Intimate Search - Code C Annex A Paragraph 2

- An **intimate search** will only be permitted where:
    - An *Inspector* or above has **reasonable grounds** for *believing* that:
        - A person may have **concealed** on themselves:
            - Anything that they could or might use to cause **physical injury** to:
                - **Themselves**; or
                - **Others** at the station; or
            - A **Class A drug** which they *intended* to:
                - **Supply** to another; or
                - **Export**; and
    - An intimate search is the **only means** of removing the items.

3 - Providing The Detainee With The Opportunity To Hand Over The Item Prior To Conducting An Intimate Search - Code C Annex A Paragraph 2A & Note A1

- **Before** authorising the search the *Inspector* must:
    - **Explain why** an intimate search is **necessary.**
    - Make **every reasonable effort to persuade the detainee to hand over the item** *voluntarily* **without a search.**

- If the detainee **agrees**, a **Registered Medical Practitioner or Registered Nurse** should:
    - **Assess** any **risks;** and
    - **Assist in the removal of the item** where necessary.

4 - The Conduct And Location Of The Search - Code C Annex A Paragraphs 3 - 4

(a) - Class A Drugs

- An **intimate search** for a **Class A drug** *must:*
- Take place in either a:
    - **Hospital;**
    - **Surgery;**
    - **Other medical premises**;
        NB – *Not* in a Police Station.
- Be carried out by either a:
    - **Registered Medical Practitioner;** or
    - **Registered Nurse.**
        NB – **Not** by a Police Officer.

(b) - Other Items That May Cause Physical Injury

(i) - The General Rule

- An **intimate search** for **other items that may cause physical injury** must as a **general rule** take place in either a:
    - ☐ **Hospital;**
    - ☐ **Surgery;**
    - ☐ **Other medical premises**; or
    - ☐ *Police station;* and
- Be carried out by either a:
    - ☐ **Registered Medical Practitioner;** or
    - ☐ **Registered Nurse.**

(ii) - The Exception To The General Rule Permitting The Search To Be Conducted By A Police Officer

- Where an **Inspector** or above considers that it is **not practicable** for the search to be conducted by a:
    - ☐ **Registered Medical Practitioner;** or
    - ☐ **A Registered Nurse;**
- Because the **risk** of allowing the detainee to **remain** with the item **outweighs** the **risk** of **removing** the item;
- The search can be conducted:
    - ☐ By a **police officer of the same sex as the detainee;**
    - ☐ In a **police station;**
    - ☐ Provided a *minimum* of 2 people other than the detainee are present;
    - ☐ Who are of the *same sex* as the detainee (unless they are a registered medical practitioner or nurse).
- This is always a **last resort.**

5 - Intimate Searches Of Juveniles, Mentally Disordered & Vulnerable Persons - Code C Annex A Paragraph 5

- In the case of **juveniles** or **mentally disordered** or **mentally vulnerable persons** at a police station:
    - ☐ The intimate search **must** take place in the presence of an **appropriate adult** of the **same sex;**
    - ☐ **Unless;**
    - ☐ The **detainee** specifically **requests an adult of the opposite sex** to act who is readily available.

6 - Rejection of Appropriate Adult's Presence By A Juvenile, Mentally Disordered Or Vulnerable Person - Code C Annex A Paragraph 5

- A search may proceed in the **absence** of an **appropriate adult** where:
    - The **detainee signifies** in the **presence of an appropriate adult** that they **do not wish for them to be present**; and
    - The **adult agrees.**
- If so – a **note** must be made in the **custody record** of the decision which must be **signed** by the **appropriate adult.**

7 - Can Force Be Used If The Detainee Resists? – Section 117 PACE 1984

- *Yes* - **reasonable force** may be used.

8 - Recording Obligations Following An Intimate Search - Code C Annex A Paragraphs 7 & 8

- A **note** shall be made by the **Custody Officer** in the **custody record** of:
    - The fact an intimate search **took place**;
    - The **parts** of the detainees body searched;
    - Those **present**;
    - Why an intimate search was **necessary and why the item could not otherwise be removed.**
    - The **result** of the search.
    - If the search was conducted by a **police officer – the reasons why it was impracticable for a registered medical practitioner or registered nurse to conduct the search.**

Summary Table
Searches Of Persons In Police Detention

Type Of Search	Authorising Officer	Grounds For Search	Parties Present	Sex of Searcher
Ordinary Search	Custody Officer	Standard procedure	Searcher & detainee	Same sex as detainee
Strip Search	Custody Officer	Reasonable belief of concealment of prohibited item & removal necessary	Detainee and 2 others	Same sex as detainee
Intimate Search	Inspector	Reasonable belief of concealment of: Item that could cause physical injury; or Class A drug.	Registered Medical Practitioner; or Registered Nurse NB – If exceptionally searched by police officer, the detainee and 2 others	If by a RMP or RM then the sex of the searcher is irrelevant. If in exceptional circumstances they are searched by a police officer for an item likely to cause harm – the officer must be the same sex as the detainee

Type Of Search	Search Conducted By	Extent Of Search	Location Of Search	Reasonable Force Permitted?	Recording Obligations
Ordinary Search	Constable	Empty pockets Remove jewellery Remove outer clothing	In a station – Need not be in private	Yes	No Discretion Of the Custody Officer
Strip Search	Constable	Mouth Removal of more than outer clothing	In a station – Must be in private	Yes	Yes
Intimate Search	Registered Medical Practitioner Registered Nurse Exceptionally a constable for items that may cause harm	All orifices other than the mouth	Hospital Surgery Medical premises Exceptionally at a station	Yes	Yes

F - Seizure of Items Following A Search

1 – Circumstances In Which Items May Be Seized - Section 54(4) & (6A) PACE 1984

- **Clothes** and **personal effects** may only be **seized** if the **Custody Officer** has **reasonable grounds** to **believe** that:
    - The items are **evidence** in relation to an offence; or
    - The person may **use the item** to:
        - Cause **injury** to **themselves** or **others**;
        - **Damage property**;
        - **Interfere** with **evidence**;
        - **Assist** their **escape**.

Memory Aid

- Remember this simple mnemonic – **"PIE":**
    - **P** - **P**roperty
    - **I** - **I**njury & **I**nterfere
    - **E** - **E**vidence & **E**scape

2 - Action To Be Taken Following A Seizure – Section 54(5) PACE 1984

- The detainee *must* be **told** of the **reason** for the **seizure**;
- **Unless**;
- They are:
    - **Violent or likely to become violent**; or
    - **Incapable of understanding** what is being said.

Evidence & Procedure
Unit 6 – Police Station Procedure (5)
Charging Detainees

A - Informing The Custody Officer That There Is Sufficient Evidence To Charge – Code C Paragraph 16.1 & Note 16A

- Once the **Officer In Charge of the Investigation** reasonably **believes** that there is **sufficient evidence** to provide a **realistic prospect of conviction**;

- They shall **without delay inform** the **Custody Officer** that this is the case.

- The **Custody Officer** shall then be **responsible** for **considering** whether to:

    - **Charge**;

    - **Warn** or **reprimand** detainees aged **under 18**;

    - **Caution** offenders aged **18 or over**.

B - Referring Charging Decisions To The CPS – Code C Paragraph 16.1B

- Where **charging decisions** are **referred** to the **CPS**, **consultation** should take place **as soon as is reasonably practicable**.

- Where the **CPS** is **unable** to make a **charging decision** on the information available at that point:

- The detainee **must**:

    - Be **released without charge on bail** (**conditions** may be attached); and

    - Be **informed** that that they are being released to enable the **DPP** to make their decision whether to charge.

C - Charging Procedure

1 - Cautioning - Code C Paragraph 16.2

- When the detainee is either:

    - **Charged**; or

    - **Informed** that they may be **prosecuted** for an offence;

- They shall be given the **standard caution**;

- **Unless**;

- A **restriction** applies on the drawing of **adverse inferences** under **Code C Annex C.** – If so they will be given the **modified caution**.

2 - Recording Obligations – Code C Paragraph 16.8

- A **record** shall be made of any comments made by the **detainee** when **charged**.

3 - Issuing A Notice - Code C Paragraph 16.2

- Upon charge the detainee will be given a **written notice** detailing:
    - The **offence**; and
    - The **officers name**; and
    - The **case reference number**.

- The **notice** should be **given** to the **appropriate adult** if the detainee is:
    - A **juvenile**;
    - **Mentally disordered**; or
    - **Mentally vulnerable**.

4 - Post Charge Interviews – Code C Paragraph 16.5

- A detainee may **not** be **interviewed** about an offence **after** they have been:
    - **Charged**; or
    - **Informed** that they may be **prosecuted**;
- **Unless** the interview is **necessary**:
    - **To prevent** or **minimise harm** or **loss** to:
        - Some other **person**; or
        - The **public**;
    - To **clear up** an **ambiguity** in a **previous**:
        - **Statement**; or
        - **Answer**;
    - In the **interests of justice** for the detainee to have **put to them** and the **opportunity to comment** on, **information** concerning the offence that has **come to light since** they were:
        - **Charged**; or
        - **Informed** that they might be **prosecuted**.
- **Prior** to any such **interview**, the interviewer *must*:
    - Administer the **modified caution**; and
    - **Remind** the detainee of their **right to legal advice**.

5 - Recording Obligations – Code C Paragraph 16.9

- All **post charge:**
    - **Questions**; and
    - **Answers;**
- Shall be **recorded** in full.
- The record will be either:
    - **Signed** by the **detainee** if they **agree;** or
    - If the detainee **refuses** – **signed** by:
        - The **interviewer;** and
        - Any **3rd party present.**

6 - Special Considerations When An Appropriate Adult Is Present – Code C Paragraph 16.6

- The aforementioned procedures must:
    - Take place in the **presence** of the **appropriate adult** if they are **already at** the police station; or
    - Be **repeated** in the **presence** of the **appropriate adult** when they **subsequently arrive** unless the detainee has been released.

D - Juveniles Refused Post Charge Police Bail – Section 38(6) PACE 1984

1 - The General Rule

- The **Custody Officer** must try to make arrangements for the **juvenile** to be taken into the **care of the local authority** pending their appearance in the Magistrates Court.

2 - Exception To The General Rule

- Where it is **impracticable to do so**; or
- Only in relation to those **aged 12 and over:**
    - Where there is **no secure accommodation available**; and
    - There is a **risk of serious harm to the public** from the juvenile.

Recording Obligations – Code C Paragraph 16.10

- If it is **not practicable** to place a **juvenile** refused police bail into the **care of the local authority** – the **Custody Officer** must:
    - **Record** their **reasons;**
    - Complete a **certificate** to be produced before the court.

Evidence & Procedure
Unit 7 – Police Station Procedure (6) Incommunicado Delays & Interviewing Detainees In The Absence Of A Solicitor Requested

A - Detainees Rights Whilst In Police Detention

- The detainee is prima facie entitled to **4 free standing rights** whilst **detained** in a police station:
    - ☐ To free and independent legal advice;
    - ☐ To have the Custody Officer inform a nominated person of their whereabouts (intimation);
    - ☐ To have the Custody Officer respond to enquiries in relation to the detainees whereabouts;
    - ☐ To telephone or write a letter.
- These rights may be **delayed** in certain circumstances to keep the detainee **incommunicado**.

B – Incommunicado Delays

- When dealing with **incommunicado delays** – think in the context of **gangs**.
- You have **arrested** a **gang member**; and
- You wish to **delay** their **rights**; and
- Keep them **incommunicado**;
- To **prevent** them from **tipping off gang members at large** of their whereabouts;
- Because if the **gang members** are **tipped off** they will cause one of a number of **undesirable R.A.P.E. consequences**.

C - Differing Provisions For Terrorism And Non Terrorism Offences

- There are subtly **different provisions** for:
    - ☐ **Non Terrorism Offences**; and
    - ☐ **Terrorism Offences**.

D – Non Terrorism Offences

1 - Delaying The Detainee's Rights In Non Terrorism Offences – Code C Annex B Paragraph 1 & Code C Paragraphs 5.5 & 5.6

- The rights of a **detainee** who has **not** as yet been **charged**;

- In connection with an *indictable* offence to request either:

    - **Legal advice**; or
    - **Notification of a person of their arrest (intimation)**;
    - **Have a person enquiring informed about the detainees whereabouts**; or
    - **Telephone or write a letter**;

- May be *delayed* where either:

    - A *Superintendent* in relation to **delaying legal advice**; or
    - An *Inspector* in relation to **delaying**:
        - **Intimation**;
        - **Informing a person enquiring about the detainees whereabouts**;
        - **Telephone or write a letter**;

- Has **reasonable grounds** to *believe* that exercising the right will either:

    - Hinder the **recovery** of property obtained as a consequence of the commission of an indictable offence;

    For example: Gang members at large being tipped off to hide the proceeds of a theft.

    - Lead to either:
        - **Alerting** other people suspected of having committed an indictable offence but are not as yet arrested;

        For example: Alerting gang members to go into hiding.

        - Interference with, or physical harm to other **people**;

        For example: Gang members at large being tipped off to threaten witnesses with violence.

        - Interference with, or harm to **evidence** connected with an indictable offence.

        For example: Gang members at large being tipped off to destroy evidence.

Memory Aid

Remember:

- R - Recovery
- A - Alert
- P - People
- E - Evidence

2 - Additional Specific Grounds To Delay The Rights – Code C Annex B Paragraph 2 & Code C Paragraphs 5.5 & 5.6

- All of the rights can also be **delayed** in **two additional specific instances**:
    - ☐ **Drug Trafficking;** and
    - ☐ Offences to which **confiscation orders** apply.
- They both relate to hindering the *recovery* of proceeds ("R" of "R.A.P.E")
- Again the appropriate authorising officer will be:
    - ☐ A *Superintendent* (in relation to **delaying legal advice**); or
    - ☐ An *Inspector* (in relation to **delaying the other rights**).

(i) – Drug Trafficking - Code C Annex B Paragraph 2(i)

- Firstly where:
    - ☐ The offence is the *indictable* offence of **drug trafficking**; and
    - ☐ The **authorising officer** has **reasonable grounds** to *believe*:
        - The detainee has **benefited** from **trafficking**; and
        - The *recovery* of the detainee's **proceeds** would be **hindered** by the exercising of either right.

    For example: Exercising either right will result in the notification of a person at large who is aware of the location of proceeds from the import of drugs to either hide or dispose of the cash.

(ii) – Confiscation Order Offences - Code C Annex B Paragraph 2(i)

- Secondly where:
    - ☐ The offence is an *indictable* offence to which a **confiscation order** may apply; and
    - ☐ The **authorising officer** has **reasonable grounds** to *believe:*
        - The detainee has **benefited** from the offence; and
        - The *recovery* of any **property or pecuniary advantage** derived by the detainee in connection with the offence would be **hindered** by the exercising of either right.

3 - Additional Consideration If Contemplating Delaying Access To Legal Advice - Code C Annex B Paragraph 3

- The *Superintendent* must have **reasonable grounds** to *believe;*
- That the **solicitor** the detainee wishes to consult would:
    - ☐ **Either:**
        - **Inadvertently** or **intentionally pass on a message** from the detainee; or
        - Act in some other way that would result in one of the aforementioned consequences in **Code C Annex B Para's 1 or 2.**
- If the belief is established – the detainee must be **allowed to choose** *another* solicitor.

4 - The Duration Of The Delay For Non Terrorism Offences - Code C Annex B Paragraph 6

- The **delay** of the rights may **only last for as long as the ground justifying a delay exists.**
- Once the **ground ceases to exist:**
    - The detainee must be **asked as soon as practicable** if they wish to exercise their rights; and
    - Their **response** must be **recorded**; and
    - Any **request** must be **actioned.**
- The delay cannot last beyond *36 hours* after the **relevant time** if the **grounds** justifying the delay are **continuing.**

For example:

- If a gang member's rights are delayed on the basis that exercising their rights would lead to the **alerting of fellow gang members at large** who are also suspected of having committed an indictable offence; and
- **All of the gang members at large** are **subsequently arrested** before the expiration of 36 hours from the relevant time;
- Then the **premise for delaying the rights no longer exists**; and
- Therefore:
    - The detainee must be **asked** as soon as practicable if they wish to exercise either rights;
    - Their **response** must be **recorded;** and
    - Any **request** must be **actioned.**

- If however the **fellow gang members continue to remain at large beyond 36 hours** from the relevant time;
- Whilst the **premise for the delay continues to exist;**
- The **delaying of either right cannot continue beyond the permitted maximum period** and the detainee must:
    - Be **asked** as soon as practicable if they wish to exercise their rights;
    - Their **response** must be **recorded;** and
    - Any **request** must be **actioned.**

E - Terrorism Offences

1 - Delays For Terrorism Offences - Code C Annex B Paragraph 8 & Code C Paragraphs 5.6 & 5.6

- The rights of a **detainee** who has **not** as yet being **charged**;
- In connection with an offence under the **Terrorism Act 2000** to request either:
  - ☐ **Legal advice**; or
  - ☐ **Notification of a person of their arrest**;
  - ☐ Have a person enquiring informed about the detainees whereabouts; or
  - ☐ **Telephone or write a letter**;
- May be *delayed*;
- Where a *Superintendent* (for *all* of the rights);
- Has **reasonable grounds** to *believe* that exercising any of the rights will either:
- Hinder the **recovery** of property:
  - ☐ Obtained as a consequence of the commission of an indictable offence; or
  - ☐ In respect of which a **forfeiture order** could be made; or
- Lead to either:
  - ☐ **Alerting** other people suspected of having committed an indictable offence but are not as yet arrested;
  - ☐ Interference with, or physical harm to other **people**; or
  - ☐ Interference with, or harm to **evidence** connected with an indictable offence.

Memory Aid

- Remember:
  - ☐ R - Recovery
  - ☐ A - Alert
  - ☐ P - People
  - ☐ E - Evidence

2 - Additional Grounds For Terrorism Offences - Code C Annex B Paragraph 9

- The rights can also be **delayed** where:
  - ☐ The *Superintendent* has **reasonable grounds** to *believe:*
  - ☐ A **confiscation order** may be applied to the offence; and
    - The detainee has **benefited** from the offence; and
    - The exercise of either right would hinder the *recovery* of the value of the **benefit**.

3 - Additional Grounds For Terrorism Offences – Code C Annex B Paragraph 8

- The rights can also be **delayed** where:
    - The **Superintendent** has reasonable grounds to **believe** that exercising the right would either:
        - **Lead to interference in the gathering of information about terrorism;**

        For example: Tipping off fellow terrorist at large that they are under surveillance.

        - By **alerting** any person, **make it more difficult to:**
            - **Prevent** an act of **terrorism;** or
            - **Secure** the **apprehension, prosecution** or **conviction** of any person connected with **terrorism.**

            For example: The police have gathered intelligence that several bombers planned to detonate bombs at a variety of locations.

            The police plan to arrest each bomber on the way to each location.

            If any one bomber is arrested and detained they could tip off their fellow bombers, alerting them to either:
            - Abort their plans and flee; or
            - Alternatively bomb another venue.

4 - The Duration Of The Delay For Terrorism Offences - Code C Annex B Paragraph 11

- The **delay** of either right may only **last for as long as the ground justifying a delay exists.**
- Once the **ground ceases to exist:**
    - The **detainee** must be **asked as soon as practicable if they wish to exercise either right; and**
    - Their **response** must be **recorded; and**
    - Any **request** must be **actioned.**
- The delay cannot last beyond **48 hours** after the time of arrest (relevant time) if the **grounds** justifying the delay are **continuing.**

Exam Trip Up

- Note that there are **differing durations** that the rights can be delayed for terrorism and non-terrorism offences:
    - **Terrorism** offences – **48 hours** from the **relevant time;**
    - **Non-terrorism** offences – **36 hours** from the **relevant time.**

F - Recording The Grounds For Any Delay - Code C Annex B Paragraph 13

- Where the authorising officer delays either right:
    - The **detainee** must be **informed** as soon as practicable; and
    - The **decision** shall be **recorded.**

G - Prevention Of Adverse Inferences For Interviews Taking Place When Access To Legal Advice Has Been Delayed - Code C Annex B Paragraph 15

- Where a **detainee** has been **interviewed** during any period when access to **legal advice** has been **delayed** a court will be **unable to draw any adverse inferences** from any silence exercised during such interviews.

- In simple terms, whenever a detainee says *"I want legal advice"* and they are told against their wishes *"No you cannot"* – it will **not be possible to draw adverse inferences**.

H - Detainees Requiring The Presence Of An Appropriate Adult And Code C Annex B Note B1

- If the provisions of **Code C Annex B** apply to a:
  - **Juvenile**;
  - **Mentally disordered person**; or
  - **Mentally vulnerable person**;

- Whilst the following rights may be **delayed**:
  - **Legal advice**;
  - **Intimation**;
  - **Write or telephone**;
  - **Respond** to **queries** of their **whereabouts**;

- The following **must still be contacted**:
  - The **person responsible for the juvenile's welfare**; and
  - Their **appropriate adult**.

I - Foreign Nationals And Citizens Of Independent Commonwealth Countries And Code C Annex B

- If the provisions of **Code C Annex B** apply to a:
  - **Foreign National**; or
  - **Citizen of an independent Commonwealth Country**;

  - specified in Code C Annex F;

- Whilst the following rights may be **delayed**:
  - **Legal advice**;
  - **Intimation**;
  - **Write or telephone**;
  - **Respond** to **enquiries** of their **whereabouts**;

- Their **High Commission, Embassy** or **Consulate must still be contacted** and **notified** of their **arrest as soon as practicable**;

- **Unless** the detainee is either:
  - A political refugee; or
  - Seeking political asylum.

Summary Table

Right	Authorising Rank Non Terrorism Offences	Authorising Rank Terrorism Offences	Reasonable Grounds To Believe	Duration Of The Delay For Non Terrorism Offence	Duration Of The Delay For Terrorism Offences
Legal Advice	*Superintendent*	Superintendent	**Both Terrorism & Non Terrorism Offences** ■ Hinder **recovery** of property from an indictable offence; ■ **Alerting** fellow suspects of indictable offence at large; ■ Harm to **people**; ■ Harm to **evidence** in connection with an indictable offence; ■ Drug Trafficking - Hinder the **recovery** of proceeds; ■ Confiscation Order applies – Hinder the **recovery** of proceeds; --- **Terrorism Offences Only** ■ **Alert** terrorists; ■ **Interfere** with terrorist **intelligence**	Until the ground ceases to exist or a maximum **36 hours** from the relevant time	Until the ground ceases to exist or a maximum **48 hours** from the relevant time
Notification Of Arrest (Intimation)	Inspector	Superintendent			
Write or Telephone	Inspector	Superintendent			
Respond To Enquiries Concerning The Detainees Whereabouts	Inspector	Superintendent			

I - Proceeding With An Interview In The Absence Of A Solicitor Requested

- The detainee who has **requested legal advice**;
- **May not be:**
  - ☐ Interviewed; or
  - ☐ Continue to be interviewed;
- **Until** they have **received the advice**;
- **Unless the** conditions in either:
  - ☐ **Code C Annex B apply;**
  - ☐ **Code C Paragraph 6.6(b) apply;**
  - ☐ **Code C Paragraph 6.6(c) apply;** or
  - ☐ **Code C Paragraph 6.6(d) apply.**
- If any of the conditions apply it is possible to proceed with the interview before the solicitor requested arrives.

1 - The Conditions Of Code C Paragraph 6.6(b)

An interview will be permitted to proceed in the absence of a solicitor requested where:

- A *Superintendent* or above has **reasonable grounds to** *believe* that either:
  - ☐ Waiting for the arrival of a solicitor who has been contacted and has agreed to attend would cause an **unreasonable delay** to the investigation; or
  - ☐ Any consequent **delay** might either:
    - Lead to the **alerting** other suspects who are not yet arrested;
    - Lead to serious loss, or damage, to **property**;
    - Lead to interference with, or physical harm to other **people**;
    - Lead to interference with, or harm to **evidence** connected with an offence; or
    - Hinder the **recovery** of property obtained as a consequence of the commission of an offence.

Memory Aid

Remember:

- D   -   Delay (unreasonable)
- A   -   Alerting
- P   -   People
- P   -   Property
- E   -   Evidence
- R   -   Recovery

Just think that you want to proceed in the absence of a very well dressed **(DAPPER)** solicitor!

An Example Of Code C Paragraph 6.6(b) In Operation

- A gang are planning to carry out an **armed robbery** of a bank. Police surveillance has revealed that the robbery will take place later **today**. However, the police are **unaware** of the **specific bank targeted**. Officers **arrest one** of the gang members who **requests legal advice**.

- A **Superintendent** or above;

- Will be permitted to authorise the interview to **proceed immediately prior to the arrival of the solicitor requested**;

- As officers **urgently** need to interview the detainee in order to **ascertain** the **whereabouts** of the planned robbery; and

- Any **delay** in obtaining the information might lead to either:
    - Serious loss, or damage, to **property**; or
    - Interference with or physical harm to other **people**.

Prevention Of Adverse Inferences For Interviews Taking Place In The Absence Of A Requested Solicitor Under Code C Paragraph 6.6(b)

- If the interview is permitted to proceed in the absence of the solicitor requested;

- For any of the aforementioned grounds;

- **No adverse inferences** will be permitted at trial;

- In respect to any silence exercised during the interview.

- In simple terms, whenever a detainee says *"I want legal advice"* and they are told against their wishes *"No you cannot"* – it will **not be possible to draw adverse inferences**.

2 - The Conditions Of Code C Paragraph 6.6(c)

- Where a detainee has **selected a solicitor**; and

- The solicitor selected either:
    - ☐ **Cannot be contacted**;
    - ☐ **Has indicated previously they do not wish to be contacted**;
    - ☐ **Has declined to act**; and

- The **detainee**:
    - ☐ Has been **advised** of the **Duty Solicitor scheme**; and
    - ☐ Has **declined** to request the **Duty Solicitor**;

- An *Inspector* can authorise the interview to proceed.

Allowing Adverse Inferences To Be Drawn Where An Interview Takes Place In The Absence Of A Requested Solicitor Under Code C Paragraph 6.6(c)

- If the interview proceeds in such circumstances in the absence of a solicitor the **courts will be able to draw adverse inferences** from any silence exercised.

3 - The Conditions Of Code C Paragraph 6.6(d)

- Where a **detainee initially requests legal advice;**
- But **later changes their mind;**
- **The interview can be started without delay, provided:**
    - The **detainee agrees** to do so either:
        - **In writing;** or
        - **On tape;** and
    - An *Inspector* or above:
        - Has **enquired** into the **reasons** for their **change of mind;** and
        - Has **authorised** the **interview to proceed.**
- The Inspector **can** provide their **authorisation over the phone. (Code C Note 6I)**

Recording Obligation Following Authorisation Under Code C Paragraph 6.6(d)

- Once authorisation is provided the following information must be **recorded** either:
    - **On tape;** or
    - **On any written interview record:**
        - The **detainees agreement** to proceed without a solicitor;
        - The **reasons** for their change of mind; and
        - The **name** of the **authorising officer.**

Allowing Adverse Inferences To Be Drawn Where An Interview Takes Place Where The Detainee Has Revoked Their Request For A Solicitor Under Code C Paragraph 6.6(d)

- If the interview proceeds in such circumstances in the absence of a solicitor the **courts will be able to draw adverse inferences** from any silence exercised.

Summary Table

Power	Authorising Officer	Inferences Allowed From Silence At Interview?
Code C Para 6.6(b)	*Superintendent*	*No*
Code C Para 6.6(c)	*Inspector*	*Yes*
Code C Para 6.6(d)	*Inspector*	*Yes*

Evidence & Procedure
Unit 8 – Police Station Procedure (7)
Relevant Time & Detention Periods

A - The 2 Separate Clocks

- Throughout police detention there will be **2 separate clocks** ticking:
    - ☐ The *detention* **clock**; and
    - ☐ The *review* **clock** (see next unit).

- Both clocks invariably **start from different points** and have **different purposes.**

- The *detention* **clock** tracks the duration a suspect may be detained.

- The *review* **clock** tracks the periodic intervals at which the review officer must determine whether there continue to be sufficient grounds to detain the suspect (see next unit).

B - The Detention Clock – Section 41 PACE 1984

- There are limits to how long a person may be detained.

C - Differing Provisions

- The **detention clock** provisions differ for:
    - ☐ Non Terrorism Offences; and
    - ☐ Terrorism Offences.

Non – Terrorism Offences

D – Starting The Detention Clock - Relevant Time

- The **detention clock** starts to tick from the **"relevant time"**.

- The **relevant time** is determined by the provisions of **section 41 PACE 1984.**

- The **relevant time** will depend on the circumstances of the detained person.

1 - Persons Attending A Station Voluntarily Who Are Later Arrested At The Station – Section 41(2)(c) PACE 1984

- The **relevant time** will be the time of their *arrest*.

- It will **not** be the **time** that the person initially **arrived** at the station **voluntarily** – as at this juncture they are **not in police detention.**

- Once the subsequent **arrest** takes place at the police station they are being **detained** and therefore the **detention clock** starts ticking

2 - Persons Brought To A Police Station Under Arrest From Within A Force - The General Rule – Section 41(2)(a) PACE 1984

- The relevant time will be their time of *arrival* at the <u>first</u> police station in the police <u>area</u> where the offence is being investigated.

    i.e. As soon as the arrested person **crosses the boundary** of the <u>first</u> **station** that they are brought to **within the force that the offence is being investigated** the clock starts ticking.

    NB – It is irrelevant whether the suspect is interviewed at that first police station – as soon as they cross the boundary of that first station the clock starts ticking.

The Definition Of "At A Police Station" – Code C Paragraph 2.1A

- Code C Paragraph 2.1A states that a person is **at a police station** where they are:
    - **Within the boundary** of:
        - Any **building**; or
        - **Enclosed yard**;
    - Which forms **part** of that **police station**.

Exam Trip Up

- Watch out for questions where the detainee:
    - Is **kept in a police van**;
    - In the **enclosed yard** of a police station;
    - **Without entering the building**;
    - **Before being taken to another station for interview**;

    – as soon as they **cross the boundary** they **will be at a police station**.

Exam Trip Up

- Watch out for questions where the detainee:
    - Has been **brought into the police station**;
    - But there is a **delay in entering the custody suite**;

    – as soon as they **cross the boundary** they **will be at a police station**.

3 – Persons Arrested Outside Of The Force In Which They Committed The Offence

- The rules governing the relevant time are determined by the *sooner* of 2 variables:
    - ☐ The time of <u>arrival</u> at the <u>first</u> police station in the police <u>area</u> where the offence is being investigated; or
    - ☐ 24 hours <u>after</u> the *triggering event*.

- There are **3 different triggering events** for 3 different sets of circumstances.

Memory Aid

- ☐ **Enter** - **E**
- ☐ **Arrest** - **A**
- ☐ **Leave** - **L**

(i) - Persons Arrested Outside Of England and Wales – Section 41(2)(b) PACE 1984

Trigger - ENTRY

- The relevant time will be the **earlier** of:
    - ☐ The time of <u>arrival</u> in the <u>first</u> police station in the police <u>area</u> where the offence is being investigated; or
    - ☐ 24 hours after their <u>entry</u> into England and Wales.

- Therefore:
    - ☐ From the moment the person arrested *enters* England and Wales;
    - ☐ **Add 24 hours**.
    - ☐ The detention clock will begin to tick from this time;
    - ☐ Unless;
    - ☐ The person arrested **arrives sooner** at the **first police station** in the **police area** where the offence is being **investigated**.
    - ☐ If that is the case the clock will begin to run from the time of their **arrival**.

Exam Trip Up

- The following are **not** parts of **England and Wales**:
    - ☐ Isle of Man;
    - ☐ Channel Islands;
    - ☐ Scotland;
    - ☐ Northern Ireland.

(ii) – Persons Arrested By Force 1 On Behalf Of Force 2 And Force 1 Does Not Question Them – Section 41(3) PACE 1984

Trigger - ARREST

- The relevant time will be the **earlier** of:
    - The time of <u>arrival</u> at the <u>first</u> police station in the <u>area</u> they are wanted (Force 2);
    - 24 hours after their <u>arrest</u> by Force 1.

- Therefore:
    - From the time of *arrest* by **Force 1**
    - **Add 24 hours.**
    - The detention clock will begin to **tick from this point;**
    - **Unless;**
    - The person arrested **arrives sooner** at the **first police station in the police area where the offence is being investigated (Force 2).**
    - If that is the case the clock will begin to run from the time of their **arrival.**

(iii) - Persons Arrested By Force 1 For An Offence Committed In Force 1; And Is Also Wanted By Force 2 For An Unrelated Offence Committed In Force 2; And Force 1 Has Dealt With The Suspect For Their Own Offence; But Force 1 Has Not Questioned The Suspect In Relation To The Unrelated Offence Committed In Force 2; And Has Instead Handed The Suspect To Force 2

Trigger – LEAVING

- The relevant time will be the **earlier** of:
    - The time of <u>arrival</u> at the first police station in the area they are wanted for the unrelated offence (Force 2); or
    - 24 hours after <u>leaving</u> the police station in Force 1.

- Therefore:
    - From the time of *leaving* **Force 1;**
    - **Add 24 hours.**
    - The detention clock will begin to **tick from this point;**
    - **Unless;**
    - The person arrested **arrives sooner** at the **first police station in the police area where the offence is being investigated (Force 2).**
    - If that is the case the clock will begin to run from the time of their **arrival.**

Exam Trip Up

- Please note that the rules governing the **triggers** of:
    - ☐ **Arrest**; and
    - ☐ **Leave**;
- Is dependant upon <u>*no questioning*</u> taking place within **Force 1 in relation to the offence committed in Force 2.**
- If **questioning concerning Force 2's offence** *does take place* in **Force 1**:
    - ☐ You revert back to the **"General Rule"**; and
    - ☐ The relevant time will be the **time of <u>arrival</u> at the <u>first</u> police station in Force 1.**

Exam Trip Up - British Transport Police

- Watch out for questions where:
    - ☐ A person is arrested in **Force 1** for an offence committed in **Force 2**; and
    - ☐ The detainee is transferred by train to **Force 2** for questioning; and
    - ☐ Having arrived at the train station in **Force 2**;
    - ☐ The detainee is handed over to the custody of **British Transport Police** who take the detainee to the **British Transport Police Station** located within **Force 2**;
    - ☐ Pending the arrival of ordinary officers from **Force 2**;
    - ☐ Who collect the detainee and take them to an **ordinary police station in Force 2.**
- The **time of arrival at the first police station in the police area for which the offence is being investigated:**
    - ☐ Will be the time of **arrival** at the **British Transport Police** station in Force 2; and
    - ☐ Will **not** be the subsequent time of **arrival** at the **ordinary police station** in Force 2.

4 - Persons Answering Street Bail – Section 41(2)(ca) PACE 1984

- The **relevant time** for a person attending a police station to answer **street bail** is the time of their *arrival* at the police station specified in their street bail notice.

Exam Trip Up

- Watch out for questions involving persons who turn up at the police station earlier than the time specified on the street bail.
- The relevant time will be the time that they arrive at the police station and not the time specified in the street bail.

Exam Trip Up

- Watch out for questions where the person mistakenly answers street bail at a **different police station to that *specified* in their street bail** before turning up at the correct specified station.
- The relevant time will be the time that they **arrive at the police station *specified* in the street bail** and **not** the time of **arrival** at the initial **mistaken police station**.

Summary Table

Circumstance	General Rule	Triggering Event	Which Will Apply
Attending voluntarily and later arrested	NA	NA	Time of **arrest**
Arrested within force that the offence was committed	NA	NA	Time of **arrival** at the 1st station within the police area
Arrested outside England and Wales	Time of arrival at the 1st station within the police area	Time of **entry** into England and Wales plus 24 hours	Whichever is **sooner**
Arrested by Force 1 on Force 2's behalf and not questioned by Force 1	Time of arrival at the 1st station within the police area	Time of **arrest** by Force 1 plus 24 hours	Whichever is **sooner**
Arrested and questioned by Force 1 and passed onto Force 2 for a different offence	Time of arrival at the 1st station within the police area	Time of **leaving** Force 1 plus 24 hours	Whichever is **sooner**
Answering street bail	NA	NA	Time of **arrival** at the police station specified in their street bail notice

E - Stopping The Detention Clock

- The **detention clock** will **stop** whenever either:
    - The detainee is being **transported to or from hospital,** or is **attending hospital** provided **no questioning** has taken place at the time;
    - The detainee is **bailed back** to the police station.

Exam Trip Up

- If **questioning** takes place either:
    - ☐ **To**;
    - ☐ **From**; or
    - ☐ **At**;
- **Hospital**;
- The **detention clock will run for the duration of the questioning**; and
- The **Custody Officer** must be **informed** that questioning took place.

F – Re-Starting The Detention Clock

- The clock will **re-commence** upon the detainees **re-arrival** at the police station.

G - Time Limits On Detention For Non Terrorism Offences – Section 34 PACE 1984

1 – The Grounds For Detention Must Be Continuing

- The **decision to authorise detention** is **continuing**.
- The **Custody Officer** must **release** the detainee if at any point the **grounds for detention cease to exist**.

    i.e. If there are **no longer reasonable grounds to *believe*** that detention without charge is necessary to either:
    - ☐ **Secure or preserve evidence**; or
    - ☐ **Obtain such evidence by questioning.**

2 - The Basic Detention Period – Section 42 PACE 1984

- The basic detention period is **24 hours** from the **relevant time**.
- If an **extension is not sought by this point**:
    - ☐ The detainee must be either:
        - ■ **Released**; or
        - ■ **Charged**.
    - ☐ **Cannot be re-arrested unless new evidence comes to light.**

Definition Of New Evidence

- **New evidence** will include either:
    - ☐ Evidence that was **not available** at the time the suspect was detained; or
    - ☐ Evidence which **would not have been available even if all reasonable enquiries had been attempted.**

Exam Trip Up

- NB – The **detention clock** does **not** run from the time detention was **authorised**.
- That starting point applies to the **review clock** (see later).

3 - Extending The Detention Period To 36 Hours - Section 42 PACE 1984

(i) – Criteria For Extending The Detention Period To 36 Hours

- The detention period for an *indictable* **offence**;
- Can be **extended**;
- **Up to** a **further 12 hours**;
- To a maximum of **36 hours**;
- Provided a *Superintendent* or above who is **responsible for the station at which the suspect is detained** is satisfied that:
    - There is **insufficient evidence to charge**; and
    - The **grounds** for detention are **still present**; and
    - The investigation is being conducted **diligently and expeditiously**.

(ii) – Duration Of The Superintendent's Extension

- Note that the extension can be for a further period of *up to* **12 hours**.
- It is **not necessary** to extend by the **full 12 hours in one go**.
- Several **shorter incremental repeat extensions** can be made by the **Superintendent** or above up taking detention up to **36 hours**.

(iii) - The Timing Of The Superintendent's Authorisation For Further Detention - Section 42(4) PACE 1984

- The **Superintendent** must **authorise** a further detention:
    - **Within 24 hours** of the **relevant time**; but
    - **Not before the second review** has been carried out.

(iii) - Procedural Steps To Be Taken By The Superintendent Prior To Deciding Whether To Authorise Further Detention

(a) - Representations - Code C Paragraphs 15.3 & 15.3A

- The **Superintendent must** give any of the following the opportunity to make **representations**:
    - The **detainee**;
    - The **detainee's solicitor** – if they are available;
    - The **appropriate adult** – if they are available;
    - Any other **person having an interest in the detainee's welfare** (at the **Superintendent's discretion**).

(b) - Method Of Making Representations - Code C Paragraph 15.3B

- The **representations** may be made either:
    - ☐ **Orally** in **person**;
    - ☐ **Orally** by **telephone**;
    - ☐ **In writing**.

- The **Superintendent** may **refuse** to hear **representations** from the detainee if they are **unfit** to make representations because of either their:
    - ☐ **Condition**; or
    - ☐ **Behaviour**.

(c) – Reminders Of The Rights To Legal Advice - Code C Paragraph 15.4

- Prior to exercising the decision to extend detention the **Superintendent** must:
    - ☐ **Remind** the detainee of their **right to legal advice**;
    - ☐ **Unless**;
    - ☐ The rights can be **delayed** under **Code C Annex B**.

Exam Trip Up

- If the detainee is **asleep** – they **must** be **awoken** to enable the authorising officer to **remind** them of their **rights before** the decision to **extend detention** is taken.

- Note how this **differs** to **reviews** – where if the detainee is **asleep** there is **no need to wake them up** to **remind** them of their **rights**.

(d) - Recording Obligations Following A Decision Whether To Extend The Initial Detention Period

- A **record** shall be made in the **custody record** of:
    - ☐ The **reminder** of the right to **legal advice**; (Code C Para 15.12)
    - ☐ Any **comments** made by the **detainee**; (Code C Para 15.5)

        NB - The **Superintendent** shall also be **informed** of the **comments** made as soon as practicable.

    - ☐ The **outcome** of the **decision** whether to **extend** or apply for a warrant to extend detention (Code C Para 15.16).
    - ☐ When the **detainee** was **informed**; and
    - ☐ **Who informed** them (Code C Para 15.16).

4 - Warrants For Further Detention By The Magistrates

(i) - Timing Of The Application For A Warrant For Further Detention To The Magistrates Court – Section 43(5) PACE 1984

- The application for a warrant for further detention to the Magistrates Court may be made either:
    - Before the **expiry** of the **basic detention period** of **24 hours** (**by passing** the **Superintendent's authorisation** to extend for a further 12 hours);
    - Before the **expiry** of **36 hours** (as extended by the **Superintendent);** or
    - **Following** the **expiry** of **36 hours** where it has **not been practicable for the court to sit within the 36 hour period.**

(ii) - What Happens If Before Reaching The Authorised Detention Limit The Magistrates Are Of The Opinion That The Grounds For A Warrant Of Further Detention Are Not Satisfied?

- If the **Magistrates** *believe* that there are **not grounds to grant an extension** to the detention period they may either:
    - **Adjourn** up until the expiry of the current authorised period; or
    - **Refuse** the application.

- If the **Magistrates refuse** the application for a warrant of further detention:
    - They will **not** be obliged to hear any **further applications;**
    - **Unless;**
    - **New evidence** comes to light since their refusal.

- If the **Magistrates refuse** the application for a warrant of further detention:
    - Before the **expiry** of the **authorised detention period** of:
        - 24 hours – basic detention period; or
        - 36 hours – detention period extended by a Superintendent;
    - The suspect may **still be detained until the expiry of the authorised detention period.**

(iii) - The Dangers Of Lodging An Application For A Warrant For Further Detention Out Of Time – Section 43(7) PACE 1984

- If the Magistrates are of the opinion that it **would** have been **practicable** to make the application **within the 36 hour period;**
- Then they *must* **refuse** the application;
- **Regardless** of its **merits.**

- In determining the **practicability** of making an application Code C Note 15D states that applications for warrants for further detention should be made:
    - ☐ Between **10am – 9pm**; and
    - ☐ **If possible – within normal court hours**.

(iv) - The Initial Application For A Warrant To Extend Detention By The Magistrates – Section 43(1) PACE 1984

- A **warrant** can be issued by the **Magistrates** for a **further period** of detention of **up to 36 hours**.
- The **Magistrates** will only grant an **extension** if they are satisfied that:
    - ☐ The offence is an **indictable offence;** and
    - ☐ There is **insufficient evidence to charge**; and
    - ☐ The **grounds** for detention are **still present**; and
    - ☐ The investigation is being conducted **diligently and expeditiously**.

Exam Trip Up

- Note that the extension can be for a further period of **up to 36 hours**.
- It is **not necessary** to extend by the **full 36 hours in one go**.
- Several **shorter incremental repeat extensions** can be made by the Magistrates taking detention up to **72 hours**.

(v) - Subsequent Applications For A Warrant To Extend Detention By The Magistrates – Section 44 PACE 1984

- A further **application** for a **warrant extending** detention can be sought from the **Magistrates** taking the overall period of detention up to the **maximum of 96 hours**.
- The **grounds** for granting the **subsequent warrant** to extend are **identical** to the **grounds** for the **initial warrant** to the Magistrates;
- The application must be **lodged before the expiry of the previous extension** granted by warrant.

(vi) - Additional Recording Requirements In The Event Of An Extension Being Granted - Code C Paragraph 15.16

- If an **extension** is **granted** by the **Superintendent** – the **period of the extension** must be **recorded** in the custody record.
- If a **warrant for extension** is granted by the **Magistrates** – the **period of the extension** and the **date** and **time** it was granted must be **recorded** in the custody record.

(vii) - Procedure For Obtaining A Warrant To Extend Detention – Section 43 PACE 1984

- Both the **detainee** and the **police** must attend.
- An **information** must be laid before the **magistrates**.
- A **copy of the information** must be **provided** to the **detainee** before the hearing.
- The detainee is entitled to **legal representation**.
- If the detainee **rejects legal representation**:
    - The detainee should be **reminded** of their right prior to the hearing; and
    - This fact should be **recorded** in the custody record.

(viii) - The Content Of The Application To Extend Detention - Section 43 PACE 1984

- The application must be made **on oath** outlining:
    - The **nature of the offence**;
    - The general **evidence** forming the **grounds for arrest**;
    - The **enquiries made to date**;
    - The **proposed enquiries** to be made following the grant of an extension;
    - **Why it is necessary to continue detention** for the proposed enquiry.

H - Further Arrest Of Detainees Released Without Charge Following The Expiration Of Their Detention Period - Section 41(9) PACE 1984

- Section 41(9) PACE 1984 states that:
    - A **detainee**;
    - **Released without charge**;
    - After the **expiry** of their **detention period**;
    - Shall **not** be **rearrested** without a warrant for the **same offence**;
    - **Unless**:
        - **New evidence** has come to light;
        - In relation to the **same offence**;
        - **Since** their **release** from detention.

- In such circumstances a **new detention clock** will **start afresh**.

I – Terrorism Offences

1 - Relevant Time For Terrorism Offences – Section 41 Terrorism Act 2000

- The **relevant time** for terrorism offences is always the time of **arrest**.

J - Time Limits On Detention For Terrorism Offences

1 - The Basic Detention Period For Terrorism Offences

- The **basic detention period** for terrorism offences is **48 hours** from the **time of arrest** (relevant time).

2 - Applications To The Magistrates Court To Obtain A Warrant To Extend Detention In Terrorism Offences

(i) - Who Makes The Application? – Code C Paragraph 15.8

- The **application** to the **Magistrates Court** to **extend** the **detention period** must be made by either:
    - A **Superintendent** or above;
    - A **Crown Prosecutor**.

(ii) - When Must The Initial Application Be Made?

- The **first application** must be made **before the expiry of the initial 48 hour detention period**.

(iii) - The Duration Of Extensions In Terrorism Cases

(a) - Initial Extensions Taking Detention Up To 7 Days

- The **initial application to extend detention** can be made for a period of **up to 7 days**.
- This is an **initial** proscribed **maximum period**.
- The initial extended period may be **shorter** if either:
    - The request in the warrant to extend is for a shorter period; or
    - The court deems a shorter period to be more suitable.

(b) Further Extensions In Terrorism Cases – After The Initial 7 Days Of Detention Have Elapsed

- Further applications are permitted to take the **total period of detention up** to a maximum of **28 days**.

(iv) - When Can This Application Be Made?

- Such an application can only be made at a time where the **current warrant extending detention takes the period of detention up to the 7 day maximum**.

Evidence & Procedure
Unit 9 – Police Station Procedure (8)
Reviews

A - The 2 Separate Clocks

- Throughout police detention there will be **2 separate clocks** ticking:
    - The *detention* clock (see next unit); and
    - The *review* clock.

- Both clocks invariably **start from different points** and have **different purposes.**

- The *detention* clock tracks the duration a suspect may be detained (see last unit).

- The *review* clock tracks the periodic intervals at which the review officer must determine whether there continue to be sufficient grounds to detain the suspect.

B - The Function Of The Review Officer

- The **Review Officer** is responsible for determining periodically whether the **grounds for detention continue to be present**.

- i.e. That detention continues to be necessary to either:
    - **Secure or preserve evidence;** or
    - **Obtain such evidence by questioning.**

C - Differing Provisions

- The review clock provisions **differ** for:
    - **Non Terrorism Offences;** and
    - **Terrorism Offences.**

D – Reviews For Non Terrorism Offences

1 - The Rank Of The Review Officer - Code C Note 15A

- The **rank** of the **Review Officer** depends on **when** during detention a review takes place:
    - Review Officer *before* charge – **Inspector.**
    - Review Officer *after* charge – **Custody Officer (Sergeant).**

2 - The Review Clock

- The **review clock** starts from the time that **detention** is first *authorised*.

Exam Trip Up

- The **review clock** does *not* run from the **relevant time.**

- Only the **detention clock** runs from the **relevant time** (see last unit).

3 – Intervals At Which Reviews Before Charge Must Take Place – Section 40(3) PACE 1984

(i) – Maximum Time Limits For Reviews Before Charge

- In relation to **reviews before charge:**
    - The **first review** shall **not** take place *later* than **6 hours after detention** was **first authorised;**
    - The **second review** shall **not** take place *later* than **9 hours** after the **first review;**
    - **Subsequent reviews** shall **not** take place *later* than **9 hours after the last review.**

(ii) - Bringing Forward Reviews Before Charge

- The review limits are proscribed *maximum* periods.
- It is therefore possible for the **review officer** to:
    - *Bring forward* a review; and
    - Conduct the review *before* reaching the *time limit.*

By Which Point Must A Subsequent Review Take Place After A Prior Review Is Brought Forward?

- If the review:
    - Is **brought forward**; and
    - Takes place *before* the **maximum permitted point** is reached;
- The **next review** must take place **within 9 hours** of the **time** that the **prior review:**
    - *Actually took place*; and
    - *Not* from the **maximum point** at which it *could* have taken place.

3 - Delaying Reviews Before Charge – Section 40(4) PACE 1984

- A **review** may be **delayed** where either:
    - It is **not practicable** to conduct a **review;**
    - **No review officer** is readily **available**; or
    - The detainee is in the process of being **questioned** and the **review officer** is satisfied **interrupting** the questioning would **prejudice the investigation.**

By Which Point Must A Subsequent Review Take Place After A Prior Review Is Delayed?

- If the review:
    - Is **delayed**; and
    - Takes place *after* the **maximum permitted point** is reached;
- The **next review** must take place **within 9 hours** of:
    - The **maximum point** at which the **prior review** *should* have taken place; and
    - *Not* from the time the **prior review** *actually* took place.

4 - Post Review Recording Obligations - Code C Paragraph 15.14

- A **record** must be made of:
    - The **grounds** for a delay in conducting a review;
    - The **length** of any delay.

Summary Table
Reviews Before Charge For Non Terrorism Offences

Review	Time	Triggering Event	Authorising Officer
1st	**Not more** than 6 hours	From the time that detention was first *authorised*	Inspector
2nd	**Not more** than 9 hours	After the *first* review	Inspector
Subsequent reviews	**Not more** than 9 hours	After the *last* review	Inspector

5 - Stopping The Review Clock

- If the detainee is **released on bail** the **review clock** will **stop** at the time of their **release** from custody

6 - Restarting The Review Clock

- The **review clock** will **recommence** on the return date when the **Custody Officer** re-authorises detention.

Exam Trip Up

- Remember – it is *not* the time of the **arrival** of the detainee on their **return** to the police station.

D - Reviews For Terrorism Offence

1 - The Review Clock For Terrorism Offences

- The **review clock** will run from the time of **arrest.**

Exam Trip Up

- The review clock will *not* run from the time that detention is *authorised.*

2 - The Review Officer For Terrorism Offences

- The **rank** of the **Review Officer depends** on *when* the review takes place.

Summary Table
Reviews – Terrorism Offences

Review	Time	Triggering Event	Rank of Review Officer
1st	As soon as **practicable** after arrest	Arrest	Inspector
Subsequent Reviews	At least every 12 hours	After the last review	**Inspector –** If the review takes place *within* 24 hours *Superintendent* – If the review takes place *after* 24 hours
After a warrant for further detention is obtained	No reviews	-	-

Exam Trip Up

- Note the **shift in rank of the authorising officer** to a *Superintendent* for reviews carried out from **24 hours** after the review clock starts ticking.

- Note that once a *warrant for further detention* has been obtained **review obligations** *cease*.

3 - The Grounds Upon Which The Review Officer May Authorise Continued Detention In Terrorism Offences

- The **Review Officer** may only **authorise** a persons **continued detention** where they are satisfied that it is **necessary**:
    - [ ] In order to **obtain evidence** by:
        - **Questioning**; or
        - **Otherwise**;
    - [ ] To **preserve** relevant **evidence**;
    - [ ] Pending a **decision whether to apply** to the Secretary of State for a **deportation notice**;
    - [ ] Pending the making of an **application** to the Secretary of State for a **deportation notice**;
    - [ ] Pending **consideration** by the **Secretary of State** whether to **serve** a **deportation notice**;
    - [ ] Pending a **decision** whether the detained person should be **charged**;
    - [ ] Pending the **result** of the **examination** or **analysis** of:
        - Any relevant evidence; or
        - Anything that may result in relevant evidence being obtained.

E - Steps To Be Taken By The Review Officer Prior To Conducting A Review For Both Terrorism And Non Terrorism Offences

1 – Representations - Code C Paragraphs 15.3 & 15.3A

(i) – Who Can Make Representations?

- The **Review Officer** must give any of the following the opportunity to make **representations**:
    - [ ] The **detainee (unless** they are **asleep)**;
    - [ ] The **detainee's solicitor** – if they are **available**;
    - [ ] The **appropriate adult** – if they are **available**;
    - [ ] Any other **person having an interest in the detainee's welfare** (at the **Review Officer's discretion)**.

(ii) – Method Of Making Representations

- The **representations** may be made either:
    - [ ] **Orally** in **person**;
    - [ ] **Orally** by **telephone**;
    - [ ] In **writing**.

(iii) - Refusal To Hear Representations Prior To Exercising The Decision To Review - Code C Paragraph 15.3B

- The **Inspector** may **refuse to hear representations** from the detainee;

- If the **detainee** is **unfit** to **make representations** because of either their:
    - ☐ **Condition;** or
    - ☐ **Behaviour.**

2 - Reminder Of The Right To Legal Advice - Code C Paragraph 15.4

- Prior to exercising the decision to continue detention the **Review Officer** *must:*
    - ☐ **Remind** the detainee of their **right to legal advice;**
    - ☐ **Unless;**
    - ☐ The rights can be **delayed** under **Code C Annex B.**

F - Recording Obligations Following The Decision Whether To Continue To Detain

- A **record** shall be made in the **custody record** of:
    - ☐ The **reminder** to the right to **legal advice** and **intimation**; (Code C Paragraph 15.12)
    - ☐ Any **comments** made by the **detainee**; (Code C Paragraph 15.5)
    - ☐ The **outcome** of the **decision** whether to **continue to detain.** (Code C Paragraph 15.16).

- **If the detainee is awake** they must be:
    - ☐ **Present** when the **grounds** for continued detention are **recorded;**
    - ☐ **Informed** of the **grounds;**
    - ☐ **Unless** the **Inspector** considers that the person is:
        - **Incapable of understanding what is said;**
        - **Violent, or likely to become violent;** or
        - **In urgent need of medical attention.** (Code C Note 15C)

    - ☐ **If the detainee was asleep** at the time of authorisation – they must be **informed** as soon as practicable of the:
        - **Decision** to continue to detain; and
        - **Grounds** for doing so. (Code C Paragraph 15.7)

    - ☐ Also a **record** must be made in the **custody record** of:
        - **When** the person was **informed;** and
        - **Who** informed them. (Code C Paragraph 15.16)

G - The Review Officer Conducting A Review By Video Conferencing Or Telephone – Sections 40A & 45A PACE 1984 & Code C Paragraphs 15.9, 15.9A & 15.9B

1 – Methods Of Conducting Reviews

- The **Review Officer** can **conduct the review** either:
    - ☐ **At** the police station in person; or
    - ☐ **Away from** the police station via either:
        - **Video conferencing;**
        - If **video conferencing** is **unavailable** or it is **not practicable** to use it – Via **telephone.**

Exam Trip Up - Code C Note 15F

- Video or **telephone reviews** *can* only be used for:
    - ☐ **Pre charge reviews;**
    - ☐ Conducted by a **Review Officer;**
    - ☐ For **non terrorism offences.**

- Video or **telephone reviews** *cannot* be used for:
    - ☐ **Terrorism offences;**
    - ☐ **Post charge reviews** by the **Custody Officer.**

Exam Trip Up

- Remember **video** and **telephone** facilities may **only** be used for **reviews.**
- They **cannot be used** by the **Superintendent** or above to **extend the detention period** from 24 to 36 hours.

2 - Procedural Steps To Be Taken After A Video Or Telephone Review - Code C Paragraph 15.10

- After a **video** or **telephone review** is conducted:
- All of the aforementioned **procedural steps;**
- Must be conducted by an **officer in the station** in which the review takes place;
- In the **presence** of the **detainee;**
- On the **Review Officer's behalf.**

H - Reviews Following Charge – Section 40 PACE 1984

- **Following** the decision to **charge:**
    - ☐ **If bail is refused;**
    - ☐ The **Custody Officer** must:
        - Continue to **comply** with the **Codes of Practice** whilst the defendant is detained pending their appearance in the magistrates court.
        - **Review** the detention within **9 hours** of the **last decision to refuse bail.**

Exam Trip Up

- Note the point of **charging doubles up** as a **review.**
- Hence the subsequent review must take place **within 9 hours following charge.**

Exam Trip Up

- **Post charge reviews** by the **Custody Officer cannot** be conducted via:
    - ☐ **Video Link;** or
    - ☐ **Telephone.**

Evidence & Procedure
Unit 10: Police Station Procedure (9) Identification Procedures

A – First Description By Witnesses

1 - Recording the First Description By Witnesses - Code D Paragraph 3.1

- A record *must:*
    - Be made of the **first description** provided by a witness of the suspect;
    - **Before** the witness takes part in any **identification procedure.**

- The **record** *must:*
    - Be made in a **visible** and **legible** form;
    - That can be **given** to the **suspect** or their **solicitor.**

2 - When Must The Record Of The First Description Be Taken From The Witness?

- The **time since the incident** when the record is made is **irrelevant.**
- Provided the first description is recorded **before the witness engages in an identification procedure.**

3 – Supplying A Copy Of The First Description To The Suspect Or Their Solicitor - Code D Paragraph 3.1

- A **copy** of the **record** shall, *where practicable,* be given to:
    - **The suspect;** or
    - **Their solicitor.**
- *Before* engaging in an **identification procedure** for **known suspects.**

Exam Trip Up

- Whilst it is *good practice* for the **Identification Officer** to **serve a copy of the first description with the notice to the suspect** explaining the identification procedure – there is **no mandatory obligation** to do so at this point.

B - Known and Unknown Suspects

- The **rules** for identification **differ** depending on whether the suspect is:
    - **Known.**

    Code D, Paragraph 3.4 states:

    "…A suspect is **known** where there **is sufficient information known to the police to justify the arrest** of a particular person for the suspected involvement in an offence."

    - **Not Known.**

An Example Of An Unknown Suspect

- Janet and John are in their bedroom. They both look out of their bedroom window down to the street and see a youth vandalising their car parked on the road. They bang on the window and the youth runs off across open fields to an area where local youths are known to congregate. Janet phones the police who attend their house.

- At this point the suspect is **unknown** as they are **at large,** they have **not** as yet been **readily identified** and the police do **not have sufficient information to arrest them.**

- The officer will be required to take **separate first descriptions** of the suspect from **both** Janet and John.

C - Identification of Unknown Suspects – Code D Paragraph 3.2

- If a suspect is **unknown**:
    - A **record** should be made of the **witnesses' first description**; and
    - The witness can either be:
        - **Shown visual images;** (videofit's etc)
        - **Taken to a particular place;**
    - to see whether they can identify the suspect.

1 - Procedure Where Witnesses Are Taken To A Place To Look For An Unknown Suspect – Code D Paragraph 3.2

- The following steps must be taken to ensure that the identification of the **unknown suspect** is **not compromised:**
    - Where there are **more than one witnesses** they should:
        - Be taken **separately;**
        - To make an **independent** identification.
    - Care must be taken **not to draw the witness' attention** to any person unless this cannot be avoided.

- Once there has been a **positive identification:**
    - The identification rules for **known suspects** must be followed; and
    - The officer must **record** in their pocket book:
        - The **date, time** and **place** the witness **previously saw** the suspect;
        - **Details** of the **subsequent identification** including:
            - **Where** it was made;
            - **How** it was made;
            - The **quality of the conditions** at the time of identification;
            - Whether the **witnesses attention was drawn** to the suspect;
            - Anything **said by the witness** or **suspect** in relation to the **conduct of the procedure.**

An Example Of Witnesses Being Taken To A Place To Look For An Unknown Suspect

- Janet and John have provided their **first descriptions** to the officer of the unknown suspect who has vandalised their car.

- Both Janet and John can be taken **separately** in police vehicles to the area where youths congregate to attempt to make **independent identifications** of the **unknown** suspect.

- If Janet was taken first in the police vehicle and was able to make a **positive identification,** then the suspect would become **known** at that point, as the police would have a **readily identified suspect** who they would be **able to arrest.**

- If so, John would **not be permitted** to be taken to the scene to also make an identification. He would be required to make his identification via one of the appropriate methods for **known** suspects.

Exam Trip Up - Suspect Arrested Following The Circulation Of Their Description By An Officer – R v Lennon (unreported 28 June 1999)

- Watch out for questions where:

    - An officer initially witnesses an unknown suspect committing an offence; and

    - The unknown suspect flees the scene; and

    - The witnessing officer circulates a description of the suspect; and

    - The suspect is subsequently arrested by another officer who recognised the suspect from the description.

    - In such circumstances the suspect will have become a known suspect as soon as they are arrested.

- Care should be taken by the officer who initially witnessed the incident, to **avoid confronting** the now known suspect in the back of a police van, etc.

- The witnessing officer should **only be shown the known suspect during an identification procedure for known suspects** under Code D.

2 - Procedure For Showing Photographs Of Unknown Suspects - Code D Annex E, Paragraphs 1-10

- An officer of the rank of **Sergeant** or above must be **responsible** for the **showing** and **directing** of photographs (**The Supervising Officer**).

- The **actual showing** of photographs can be done by **another officer** or **police staff**.

- The **Supervising Officer** must ensure that the identification is **not compromised** by checking that:

    - The **viewing of photographs is postponed** until the **first description** has been **recorded** by the witness;

    - That only **one witness** is shown photographs **at a time** in as much **privacy** as possible;

    - Witnesses are **unable to communicate** with each other;

    - **No less than 12** photographs are displayed **at a time;**

    - All photographs shown are as far as possible of a **similar type**.

- The **witness** must be **told** that:
    - The photograph of the perpetrator **may or may not be present**;
    - If they **cannot** make a **positive identification** they **must say so**;
- The witness should **not make a decision until** they have **seen at least 12 photographs.**
- The witness must **not be prompted.**
- If the **witness** makes a **positive identification**:
    - **Other witnesses** must <u>**not**</u> be **shown** the photographs; and
    - **All witnesses** (including the witness who made the positive identification) will be required to attend an **identification procedure** for **known** suspects;
    - **Unless** either:
        - There is **no dispute** about the suspects identification (The suspect **acknowledges their presence**); or
        - The suspect is:
            - **Eliminated**; or
            - Is **not available.**
- **Irrespective** of whether a **positive identification** is made, the photographs used:
    - Shall be **numbered**;
    - Shall **not be destroyed**;
- A **separate photograph** shall be made of **any frame or part of the album** from which a **positive identification** was made.

Recording The Photograph Procedure - Code D Annex E, Paragraphs 11-12

- A **record** shall be made containing:
    - The **name** and **rank** of the **Supervising Officer**;
    - Anything **said** by the **witness** about:
        - Any **identification**; or
        - The **conduct** of the procedure;
    - Any **reasons** why it was not practicable to comply with the procedures;
    - The **Supervising Officer** must as soon as practicable:
        - **Inspect** the record; and
        - **Sign** the record.

3 - Subsequent Obligations Following A Positive Identification Of An Unknown Suspect – Code D Annex E, Paragraph 9

- When a witness:
    - **Later attends** an **identification procedure** for **known suspects;** and
    - Has **already been shown** photographs or other visual images;
    - The **officer in charge** of the investigation must ensure that:
        - The **Identification Officer is made aware** of this; and
        - The **suspect** and their **solicitor** are **made aware** of this fact before the identification procedure takes place.

D - Known Suspects

1 - When Must An Identification Procedure Take Place - Code D Paragraph 3.12

- An **identification procedure** *must* take place where:
    - A **witness** has **identified** a suspect; or
    - There is a **witness available** who:
        - Has expressed the **ability to identify** a suspect; or
        - Who has a **reasonable chance of identifying** a suspect; and
    - The **suspect disputes being the person** that the witness claims to have seen;
    - **Unless** an identification procedure:
        - Would **not be practicable** (e.g. An albino Eskimo, or unavailability of a witness); or
        - Would **serve no useful purpose** in proving the suspect committed the offence (e.g. where the suspect is already known personally by the witness or the suspect acknowledges their presence at the scene).

Exam Trip Up - Need There Always Have Been A Dispute By The Suspect Before The Mandatory Obligation To Conduct An Identification Procedure Arises?

- Despite the wording of **Code D Paragraph 3.12:**
    - The **mandatory obligation** to conduct an identity procedure does not only arise in circumstances where the **suspect** has **already disputed their identification.**
    - The **mandatory obligation** to conduct an identity procedure also arises where a **dispute by the suspect might reasonably be anticipated** – *R v Rutherford [1993] 89 Cr App R 191*

Exam Trip Up

- The case of *R v Forbes [2001] 2 WLR 1* established that:

- The mandatory obligation to hold an identification procedure still applies even where there has already been a:

    - **Fully satisfactory;**
    - **Actual and complete**; or
    - **Unequivocal;**

    - Identification of the suspect.

- Watch out for questions where there may be other identification evidence such as **forensic evidence** or **video evidence** that **already implicates the suspect.**

- An **identification procedure must still be held** in such circumstances if the suspect disputes the identification or a dispute by the suspect might reasonably be anticipated.

2 - Known Suspects - When May An Identification Procedure Take Place – Code D Paragraph 3.12

- An **identification procedure** *may* take place (discretionary power) where:

    - The **officer in charge** of the investigation;
    - Considers it to be **useful**.

3 - Identification Procedures of Known Suspects - Code D Paragraph 3.4-3.23

- There are **4** possible methods:

    - **Video identification;**
    - **Identification parades;**
    - **Group identification;**
    - **Confrontation.**

4 - Selecting The Method Of Identification - Code D Paragraph 3.14

- The following must **consult** to determine which procedure is to be offered:

    - **Identification Officer;** and
    - **Officer In Charge Of The Investigation.**

5 - The Rank Of The Identification Officer – Code D Paragraph 3.11

- The **Identification Officer** must be:

    - An **Inspector;**
    - **Not involved** in the investigation.

6 - Delegation By The Identification Officer - Code D Paragraph 3.11

- The **Identification Officer** may allow:
    - ☐ **Another officer;** or
    - ☐ **Police staff;**
- To make arrangements to **conduct** identification procedures;
- Provided the **Identification Officer** is able to:
    - ☐ **Supervise** the procedure;
    - ☐ Effectively **intervene;** or
    - ☐ **Be contacted** for advice.

7 - The Pecking Order - Code D Paragraph 3.14

- The suspect will **initially be offered** a Video Identification;
- **Unless** either:
    - ☐ A **Video Identification** is **not practicable;** or
    - ☐ An **Identity Parade** is **practicable** and **more suitable** than a Video Identification; or
    - ☐ A **Group Identification** is **practicable** and the officer in charge considers it to be **more suitable** than both **video identification** or an **identity parade.**

8 - Recording The Reasons For Departing From Video Identification - Code D Paragraph 3.26

- If the **Identification Officer;**
- Considers either a **Video Identification** or an **Identification Parade** to be **impractical;**
- Their reasons shall be:
    - ☐ **Recorded** on the custody record; and
    - ☐ **Explained** to the **suspect.**

9 - Providing The Suspect With An Oral Explanation Of The Procedure - Code D Paragraph 3.17

- Prior to the identification procedure taking place, the following must be **explained orally** to the **suspect:**
    - ☐ The **purpose** of the procedure;
    - ☐ Their entitlement to **free legal advice;**
    - ☐ The **procedure** to be adopted;
    - ☐ The right to have a **solicitor** or **friend** present;

- ☐ That they **do not have to consent**, but if they refuse:
  - ■ Their **refusal** may be given in **evidence at trial**; and
  - ■ The police may **proceed covertly without their consent**; or
  - ■ **Other forms** of identification may be chosen.
- ☐ If a **video identification** is adopted:
  - ■ Whether **images** of them **already exist**; and
  - ■ If so – that they may **co-operate** in providing **further images**.
- ☐ If appropriate the **special arrangements** for:
  - ■ **Juveniles;**
  - ■ **Mentally disordered or vulnerable persons.**
- ☐ If they have **significantly altered their appearance** since being offered the procedure:
  - ■ This may be **given in evidence** at trial; and
  - ■ The investigating officer may consider an **alternative procedure**;
  - ■ It may **not** be practicable to **hold** the procedure **that day**.
- ☐ **Moving pictures or photographs** may be taken during the identification procedure;
- ☐ Whether **before** the suspect became **known** the **witness** was **shown photographs or other images;**
- ☐ Any **initial description** given by the witness of the suspect must, **where practicable**, be provided to the suspect or their solicitor.

10 - Providing The Suspect With A Written Notice of the Procedure - Code D Paragraph 3.18

- ■ The information **must** also be **recorded** in a **written notice:**
  - ☐ The notice must be **handed to the suspect**;
  - ☐ The suspect must have a **reasonable opportunity to read** the notice;
- ■ They should be asked to **sign a second copy of the notice** to **confirm** whether they **consent** to the procedure;
- ■ This **copy** is **retained** by the **Identification Officer**.

11 - Who Provides The Notification? - Code D Paragraph 3.19

(i) - General Rule

- ■ The **Identification Officer (Inspector)** must notify.

(ii) - Exception

- ■ The **Custody Officer** or **another officer not involved** in the investigation may notify where:
  - ☐ The procedure will be held on a **later date (bailed back for the ID procedure)**; and
  - ☐ An **Inspector** is **not available** to act as the **Identification Officer**.

12 - Taking Pre Emptive Images Prior To Notification - Code D Paragraph 3.20

- If either the:
  - ☐ **Identification Officer**;
  - ☐ **Officer In Charge of the Investigation**;
- Have **reasonable grounds** to **suspect** that:
  - ☐ If the suspect is provided with notification;
  - ☐ They will **avoid all procedures**;
- **Video images may be obtained** prior to issuing the notice.
- If this method is used, the suspect may **subsequently be offered the opportunity to co-operate** in providing suitable **new images**.

13 - Advice Available To The Suspect Prior To Exercising Their Decision - Code D Paragraph 3.15

- The suspect may **obtain advice** before exercising their decision from any:
  - ☐ **Legal representative** present; or
  - ☐ **Appropriate adult** present.

14 - Representations Prior To Exercising The Procedure - Code D Paragraph 3.15

- The following may make **representations** on the appropriate identification method **before** relaying their **decision:**
  - ☐ The **suspect;**
  - ☐ Any **legal representative** present;
  - ☐ Any **appropriate adult** present (if applicable).
- A **record** will be made of any **representations.**

15 - A Refusal Of An Identification Procedure By The Suspect - Code D Paragraph 3.15

- If a **suspect refuses** an identification procedure offered:
  - ☐ They shall be asked for their **reasons for refusing**.
  - ☐ A **record** will be made of any reasons for refusal and any representations made.
  - ☐ The suspect's **refusal** may be **given in evidence** at trial.

16 - Considering Alternatives Following A Refusal - Code D Paragraph 3.15

- The **Identification Officer** shall **if appropriate:**
  - ☐ Offer the suspect an **alternative** method;
  - ☐ Which they consider to be **suitable** and **practicable.**

- If the officer decides that **no alternative** is **suitable** and **practicable** the **reasons** for their decision will be **recorded**.

17 - Definition Of Availability - Code D Paragraph 3.4

- **Available** means the suspect
    - Is either:
        - **Immediately available**; or
        - Will be **immediately available** within a **reasonably short period of time**; and
    - **Is willing to take part** in either a:
        - **Video identification**;
        - **Identification**; or
        - **Group identification**.

18 - Options Available To The Identification Officer Where The Suspect Is Known But Is Unavailable - Code D Paragraphs 3.21 & 3.23

- Where a **suspect**;
    - Is **not available**; or
    - Has **ceased** to be available;
- The **Identification Officer** may arrange a **video identification** using either **moving** or **still** images which may be obtained **covertly if necessary.**
- Alternatively the **Identification Officer** may arrange a **group identification**.
- The **Identification Officer** may arrange for a **confrontation without** the suspects **consent** where the aforementioned options are not practicable.

Exam Trip Up - Can Force Be Used In Conducting An Identification Procedure Without The Suspects Consent?

- **No** – The Court of Appeal in the case of *R v Jones* [1999] *The Times*, 21 April, confirmed that it is **not permissible to use force** in such circumstances.
- Code D Annex D, Point 3 also confirms this point.

E - Video Identification Procedure - Code D Annex A

- An **Identification Officer** with **no connection** to the case must:
    - **Arrange**;
    - **Supervise**;
    - **Direct** the video.

- The **images** must include the **suspect and at least 8 other people** who as far as possible **resemble** the suspects:
    - ☐ **Age;**
    - ☐ **Height;**
    - ☐ **General appearance**; and
    - ☐ **Position in life.**
- Only **1 suspect will appear at a time;**
    - ☐ **Unless;**
    - ☐ There are **2 suspects of roughly the same appearance.**
    - ☐ If so:
        - Both suspects may be **shown together;**
        - With **at least 12 other persons.**
- The suspect and other persons shall **as far as possible** be filmed:
    - ☐ In the **same position**; or
    - ☐ Carrying out the **same activity**; and
    - ☐ In **identical conditions;**
    - ☐ **Unless** the **Identification Officer** (recording their reasons) reasonably **believes:**
        - It is **not practicable** because of the suspects **refusal to co-operate**; or
        - Any difference would **not alert a witness.**
- Each person shown must be **identified by number.**
- If a **prisoner** is filmed, **all or none** of the persons should be in **prison uniforms.**
- **Before the film is shown** to the witness:
    - ☐ The **suspect;**
    - ☐ Their **solicitor;**
    - ☐ Their **friend;**
    - ☐ Any **appropriate adult;**
    - Must be given a **reasonable opportunity to view** the film.
- If there is an **objection** to:
    - ☐ The **images**; or
    - ☐ Any of the **participants;**
    - ☐ **Reasonable steps** should be taken by the **Identification Officer** to **remove the grounds for objection.**
    - ☐ If this is **not practicable**:
        - This should be **explained** to the suspect; and

- The **objection** and the **reason for not removing** the ground should be **recorded** by the **Identification Officer**.

■ Details of the **initial description** provided by the witness must be provided to:
  □ The **suspect**; or
  □ Their **solicitor**.

■ If the **media have broadcasted images** of a description of a perpetrator:
  □ The **suspect**; or
  □ Their **solicitor**;
  □ Must be **provided with copies of such images**;
  □ **Unless** it:
    ■ Would be **impracticable**; or
    ■ Would cause an **unreasonable delay**.

■ The suspect's **solicitor** must be provided with **reasonable notification** of the **time** and **place** of the Video ID to enable them to attend.

■ If there is **no solicitor**, the same information will be given to the **suspect**.

■ The **suspect** is **not permitted to be present** when the images are shown to the witness.

■ The **solicitor** is **allowed to be present**.

■ If there is **no solicitor**, the **viewing** of the images must be **recorded**.

■ **No unauthorised persons** must be **present** at the viewing.

F - Conducting The Video Identification

■ The **Identification Officer** must ensure the following:
  □ **Witnesses** are **unable** to:
    ■ **Communicate** with each other;
    ■ **Overhear** each other discussing the video.
  □ The **Identifications Officer** must **not discuss** the contents of the video.
  □ **Witnesses** must **not be told** whether other witnesses have made **positive identifications**.
  □ Only **1 witness** should view the video **at a time**.

■ The **witness must be told** that:
  □ The suspect **may or may not** be on the video shown;
  □ If they **cannot** make a positive ID they should **say so**;
  □ They can **ask** to see a **part of an image** or a **frozen image**;
  □ There is **no limit** on the number of times they can view an image;
  □ They should view the **whole set** of images **at least twice** before reaching a decision.

G - Making The Identification

- Once:
    - All of the images have been shown **at least twice**; and
    - The witness indicates that they **do not wish** to see the images again;
    - The **Identification Officer** will **ask the witness to identify** the perpetrator **by number.**
- The **image** will then be **shown again** to enable the witness to **confirm** their decision.
- Care must be take **not to direct the witnesses attention** to any one image.

- Where the witness:
    - Has made a **previous identification by "photofit"** etc
    - When the suspect was **unknown;**
    - They must **not be reminded** of:
        - The **image;** and
        - Any **previous description** provided;
    - Once the suspect is available by other means.

H - Steps To Be Taken Following The Identification Procedure

- After the procedure:
    - Each **witness** will be **asked** if the have **seen** any:
        - **Broadcast;**
        - **Films;**
        - **Photographs;**
        - **Descriptions;**
        - Relating to the offence; and
    - Their **reply** shall be **recorded.**

I - Tape Security and Destruction

- The **Identification Officer** must ensure that:
    - All tapes are **kept secure** and their **movements accounted** for.
    - Nobody involved in the investigation may view the tape prior to it being shown to any witness.
    - The film must be **destroyed** if either:
        - **No further action** is taken against the suspect;
        - The suspect is **cleared;**
        - The suspect is **not prosecuted** (unless they admit the offence and are cautioned).

J - Recording Obligations Following The Video Identification

- A **record** must be kept on the appropriate forms of:
    - ☐ The **names** of all **witnesses** who view the video;
    - ☐ Anything **said** by the **witnesses** in respect of:
        - **Identifications** made; or
        - The **conduct** of the procedure;
    - ☐ Any **reasons** why it was **not possible to comply** with the provisions governing video identification.

Evidence & Procedure
Unit 11: Police Station Procedure (10) Samples, Fingerprints & Footwear Impressions

A - Samples

- Samples can be sub divided into **2 categories**:
    - ☐ Intimate Samples;
    - ☐ Non Intimate Samples.

B - Intimate Samples

1 - Definition Of Intimate Samples

(i) - "BUD STOP" - Section 63 PACE 1984 & Code D Paragraph 6.1

- An **intimate** sample means any:

☐	B	Blood
☐	U	Urine
☐	D	Dental Impressions
☐	S	Semen
☐	T	Tissue Fluid
☐	O	Orifice Swabs (other than mouth swabs)
☐	P	Pubic Hair

Memory Aid

Think of somebody walking past a pub and they **"STOP"** for a bottle of **"BUD"**.

Exam Trip Up

- Watch out for questions involving the taking of <u>swabs</u> from the:
    - ☐ **Anus**;
    - ☐ **Vagina**;
    - ☐ **Ears**; and
    - ☐ **Nostrils**.

- They are **all intimate in nature** - as they are **taken from orifices other than the mouth**.

Exam Trip Up

- Watch out for questions involving the taking of a **nostril or ear hair samples**.

- Such samples of hair may be **taken from an orifice other than the mouth** – but they are:
    - ☐ **Not by a** <u>swab</u>; and
    - ☐ Therefore are **not intimate samples**.

- Also as the samples of **hair are non-pubic** – they constitute a **non intimate sample**.

Exam Trip Up

- Watch out for questions involving **blood**.

- If the blood is **drawn from inside the body via a syringe** then it is an **intimate** sample.

- If a swab of blood is **taken from the surface of the detainee's skin** then it will be a **body swab** and will be a **non intimate** sample.

(ii) - Additional Definition Of Intimate Samples – Section 65 PACE 1986 & s119 SOCPA 2005

- **Intimate samples** also now include:
    - In **males swabs** from:
        - The coronal sulcas (outside of) the **shaft or glands of a penis.**
    - In **females swabs** from:
        - The **vulva**; or
        - **Matted pubic hair.**

- In summary – this includes **swabs** taken from **genitals**.

2 - Authority To Take Intimate Samples

(a) Persons In Police Detention - Section 62(1) PACE 1984 & Code D Paragraph 6.2

- An **intimate sample** may be taken from a person **in police detention**;

- If an *Inspector* or above;

- Has **reasonable grounds** to *believe* that the **intimate sample** will tend to either:
    - **Confirm**; or
    - **Disprove**;
    - their **involvement**.

- Provided **both**:
    - The *Inspector* authorises the sample; and
    - The **suspect consents** *in writing*.

(i) - The Inspector's Authorisation

- An **intimate sample cannot** be taken without the authorisation of an **Inspector** or above.

- The **Inspector's authorisation** can be provided *either*:
    - **Orally**; or
    - **In Writing.**

- Any **oral authorisation** must be **confirmed in writing as soon as practicable.**

(ii) - The Suspects Consent - Code D Paragraph 6.2

- An **intimate sample** <u>cannot</u> be taken without the **written** consent of the **suspect**.
- *No force* is permissible for the taking of an intimate sample.
- **Consent** will be provided by:
    - ☐ 17 or over   -   Suspect *only*.
    - ☐ 14 – 16   -   Suspect *and* Parent or Guardian.
    - ☐ Under 14   -   Parent or Guardian *only*.

(iii) - Consequences Of Taking Samples Without The Suspects Consent

- Taking a sample **without consent** may:
    - ☐ Contravene **Article 3 ECHR** (Inhuman & Degrading Treatment);
    - ☐ Amount to a **criminal assault**;
    - ☐ Result in **tortuous liability**.

(b) - Taking Intimate Samples From A Victim?

- If **intimate samples** are to be taken from a *victim:*
    - ☐ The **victim's** *written* **consent** should be obtained; and
    - ☐ The **authorisation** of an *Inspector* or above:
        - Is *not* required;
        - Unless;
        - The **victim** was *in police detention* at the time of the request.

(c) - Taking Intimate Samples From Persons Not In Police Detention – Section 62(1)(A) PACE 1984

- An **intimate sample** may be taken from a person *not* in police detention if:
    - ☐ The person has **already given 2 or more** *non* **intimate samples;**
    - ☐ In the course of the investigation of the offence;
    - ☐ Which have proved **insufficient** for the same means of **analysis;** and
    - ☐ An *Inspector* or above **authorises;** and
    - ☐ The **suspect consents** *in writing.*

(d) – Intimate Samples Taken For Elimination Purposes From Persons Not In Police Detention - Code D Note 6C

- An **intimate** sample person may be taken from a person **not** in police detention;
- For **elimination purposes**;
- **Only** if the person **consents**.

For example: Asking local male residents in an area where there have been a number of rapes to provide samples.

3 - Warning The Suspect Before Asking The Suspect To Provide An Intimate Sample - Code D Paragraphs 6.3

- **Before** a suspect is **asked** to provide an intimate sample they must be **warned**:
    - ☐ That if they **refuse without good cause it may harm their case at trial** (adverse inferences);
    - ☐ If they are **in police detention** and are **not legally represented**:
        - ☐ They must be **reminded** of their **entitlement** to free and independent **legal advice**; and
        - ☐ The **reminder** and **response** must be **noted** in the custody record.

Exam Tip Up

- The **reminder** of the **right to legal advice** must also be provided to **volunteers** if they are asked to provide the intimate sample **at the police station**

4 - Further Information To Be Provided To The Suspect Who Consents To The Taking Of An Intimate Sample – Code D Paragraph 6.8

- **Prior to taking the sample** the person must be **informed** of:
    - ☐ The **reason** for taking the sample;
    - ☐ The **grounds** on which any relevant **authority** has been given; and
    - ☐ That the sample or information derived from the sample may be retained and be subjected to a **speculative search unless** its **destruction is required** under *Annex F Part A*.

5 - Who May Take An Intimate Sample - Code Paragraph 6.4

- Dental Impressions   -   Registered Dentist
- Other samples except urine   -   Registered Medical Practitioner
                                -    Registered Nurse
                                -    Registered Paramedic
- Urine   -   *Officer*
                                -    Registered Medical Practitioner
                                -    Registered Nurse
                                -    Registered Paramedic

Police Pass OSPRE Part 1 Revision Crammer Textbook ©

Memory Tip

- Remember that the **only** thing **officers** can do is **"take the piss"**.
- For **all other forms** of intimate samples – **leave it to the professionals**.

6 - Recording Obligations Following The Taking Of An Intimate Sample - Code D Paragraphs 6.10 - 6.12

- The following must be **recorded**:
    - The **reasons** for taking a sample;
    - That **written consent** was provided by the **suspect**;
    - That a **warning** was issued explaining that a refusal without good cause may attract **adverse inferences** at trial;
    - If the suspect did not have legal advice - the **reminder** of their right to **free legal advice**;
    - That the suspect was **reminded** that the sample may be subjected to a **speculative search unless destruction is required** under *Code D Annex F Part A*.

C - Non Intimate Samples - Code D Paragraph 6.1

1 – Definition Of Non Intimate Samples – "HMS BIN"

- Non intimate samples include samples of:

Hair (non pubic);	**H**
Mouth swabs (not other orifices);	**M**
Saliva;	**S**
Body swabs;	**B**
Impressions taken from the body (not including fingerprints).	**I**
Nail or under nails;	**N**

Memory Aid

- Just think of a **"BIN"** sitting on the deck of a Royal Navy ship – **"HMS"**.

2 - Authority To Take Non Intimate Samples

(i) - The General Rule - Code D Paragraph 6.5

- As a **general rule** a person's **written** consent is required before the police can take a **non intimate sample**.

For example:

- An officer **cannot** just walk up to a *law abiding citizen* in the street who is not suspected of having committed a crime and **demand a sample without their consent**.
- The officer could only obtain a non intimate sample from such a person if they provide their **written** consent.
- If they **refuse**, it will *not* be possible to obtain a non intimate sample against their will by **force**.

Blue Light Publishing Limited – 4th Edition 2008

(ii) - Exceptions To The General Rule Where The Suspect's Consent Is Not Required To Take A Non Intimate Sample - Code D Paragraph 6.6

- A **non intimate sample** may be taken from a person **without their consent** in the following circumstances.

Memory Aid

- All of the circumstances outlined below relate to situations where the *person has had involvement with the legal process.*

- If they have **had involvement with the legal process**:
    - *No* **consent** is required; and
    - **Reasonable force** *can* be used in the event of a refusal.

(a) – Pursuant To Sections 63(2A) & (3A) PACE 1984 & Code D Paragraph 6.6:

- *No* **consent** is required from a person:
    - Either:
        - **Arrested** and **in police detention**;
        - **Charged** (**whether or not** they are in **police detention**);
        - **Informed** that they will be **reported** (**whether or not** they are in **police detention**);
    - For a **recordable offence** who either:
        - Has **not previously** given a sample of the type required; or
        - Has **previously** given such a sample – but it was **insufficient**.

- NB – The authorisation of an **Inspector** or above is *not* **required**.

Exam Trip Up

- Watch out for questions where:
    - A sample **has** been **taken**;
    - From a person:
        - **Arrested;**
        - **Charged;** or
        - **Reported;**
    - For a **recordable offence**;
    - Which **was sufficient** for analysis;
    - But has been **lost**.

- In such circumstances it will **not** be possible to obtain a further **replacement sample** as the person:
    - **Has** already **given a sample previously**; and
    - That sample **was sufficient** for analysis.

(b) – Pursuant To Section 63(3B) PACE 1984 & Code D Paragraph 6.6:

- **No consent** is required from a person **convicted** for a **recordable offence** (**whether or not** they are in **police detention**).

- The authorisation of an **Inspector** or above is *not* **required.**

(c) – Persons Acquitted Due To Insanity Or Unfit To Plead

- **No consent** is required from a person **detained** following and *acquittal* on the grounds of:
    - *Insanity;* or
    - *Unfitness to plead.*

(d) – Pursuant To Section 63(3)(a) PACE 1984 & Code D Paragraph 6.6:

- **No consent** is required from a person **detained in police custody** on the *authorisation of a court.*

- The **authorisation** of an **Inspector** or above *is* **required** in such circumstances.

- Authorisation may be given **orally** – if so must be **confirmed in writing ASAP** thereafter.

3 - Information To Be Provided To The Suspect Prior Taking Of A Non Intimate Sample Whether The Suspect Consents Or Not – Code D Paragraph 6.8

- **Prior** to **taking** the **sample** the person must be **informed** of:
    - The **reason** for taking the sample;
    - The **grounds** on which any relevant **authority** has been given; and
    - That the sample or information derived from the sample may be retained and be subjected to a **speculative search unless** its **destruction is required** under *Annex F Part A.*

4 - Can Reasonable Force Be Used To Take A Non Intimate Sample? - Code D Paragraph 6.7

- If **no consent is required** to take a non intimate sample – then **reasonable force is permitted.**

- Where **force is used** – a **record** should be made of:
    - The **circumstances** of the force;
    - Those **present** when force was used.

5 - Recording Obligations Following The Taking Of A Non Intimate Sample - Code D Paragraphs 6.10-6.12

- The following *must* be **recorded:**
    - The **reasons** for taking a sample;
    - That **written consent** was provided by the **suspect** (if applicable);

- [ ] If the suspect did not have legal advice - the **reminder** of their right to **free legal advice**;
- [ ] That the suspect was **reminded** that the sample may be subjected to a **speculative search unless destruction is required** under *Code D Annex F Part A*.

C - Notice Requiring The Attendance Of Persons Charged Or Convicted To Provide A Sample – Section 63A PACE 1984

1 – Time Limit For Issuing A Requirement

- A **requirement** can be issued to a person **within 1 month** of the **triggering events** of:
  - [ ] Either:
    - **Charge** for a recordable offence;
    - **Reporting** for a recordable offence;
  - [ ] **Conviction** for a recordable offence; or
  - [ ] The **Appropriate Officer** being *informed* that the sample is either:
    - **Not suitable** for analysis; or
    - Has proved to be *insufficient* for analysis;
- To **attend a police station** to provide a sample;
  - [ ] If the person either:
    - Has *not* **previously had a sample taken** during the course of the investigation; or
    - *Has* **previously had a sample taken** but it proved either:
      - [ ] *Unsuitable* for the same means of analysis; or
      - [ ] The sample was **insufficient**.

2 - Time Limit To Attend The Police Station To Provide The Sample

- In making the **requirement** the officer shall:
  - [ ] Give the person *at least* **7 days** within which they must attend to provide the sample; and
  - [ ] *May* **(discretion)** direct the person to attend either:
    - *At* a **specified time of day**; or
    - *Between* **specified times of day**.

Exam Trip Up

- The request to supply the sample must provide *at least* **7 days notice.**
- **7 days** in an absolute **minimum** period of notice.
- The notice period **may be longer than 7 days.**

Exam Trip Up

- The **7 or more days** period must fall *within* the one month time limit.
- For example:

  If an officer discovers that the sample is insufficient on 15th May, he must have given the accused a period of at least 7 days prior to 15th June.

- Note how this **differs** to the provisions concerning **fingerprints** where the **7 or more days can fall outside the month long period** for issuing a requirement.

Exam Trip Up

- Questions may involve **several different triggering events which arise on differing dates** that might permit a requirement to be issued.
- In such circumstances the **month long period** will be **calculated from** the date of the *last* triggering event.

Who Will Be The Appropriate Officer

- The **Appropriate Officer depends** on the nature of the **triggering event**:

Charged	Reported	Convicted
Investigating officer	Investigating officer	**Officer in charge** of the police station where the offence was investigated.

2 - Consequences Of Failing To Comply With A Request

- If the person fails to comply with the request they may be **arrested by a constable without a warrant**.

D - Who Will Be Present When An Intimate Or Non Intimate Sample Is Taken And Clothing Must Be Removed? - Code D Paragraph 6.9

- Where **clothing needs to be removed**;
- In circumstances likely to cause **embarrassment** to the suspect;
- The following are **not permitted** to be **present**:
    - Any person whose presence is **unnecessary**;
    - No person of the **opposite sex** - **unless** they are a:
        - A **Registered Medical Practitioner**; or
        - A **Registered Health Care Professional**;
        - An **Appropriate Adult** who has been specifically **requested** and is **readily available**.

E - Taking Intimate Or Non Intimate Samples From *Juveniles* In The Absence Of An Appropriate Adult - Code D Paragraph 6.9

- The **removal of clothing** of a **juvenile** may only take place in the **absence** of an **appropriate adult** where:
    - ☐ The **juvenile signifies** in the **appropriate adults presence** that they do not wish them to observe; and
    - ☐ The **appropriate adult agrees.**

Exam Trip Up

- Note that this provision *only* relates to **juveniles** and *not* **mentally disordered** or **mentally vulnerable** suspects.

Summary Table - Intimate And Non Intimate Samples

Type Of Sample	Form	Authorising Officer	Is The Suspect's Written Consent Required?	Is Force Allowed?	Inference For Refusal?	Who May Take The Sample
Intimate	Blood Urine Dental Swab Semen Tissue Fluids Orifice Swab – not mouth Pubic Hair & Genital swabs	Inspector **Always** required	Yes Always required	No Never allowed	Yes	Dentist – Impression *Officer – Urine* GP, Paramedic, or Nurse - Rest
Non Intimate	Hair Mouth Swab Saliva Body swab Impression from body Nails	Inspector Only if s63(3)(a) PACE 1984 applies i.e. held in custody under the authorisation of a court.	General rule – yes Exceptions – no if: ■ Arrested ■ Charged ■ Convicted ■ Reported ■ Court custody ■ Insanity ■ Unfitness to plead	General rule - no Exceptions - yes – if: ■ Arrested ■ Charged ■ Convicted ■ Reported ■ Court custody ■ Insanity ■ Unfitness to plead	NA	*Officer for all*

F - Fingerprints

1 - The Definition Of A Fingerprint - Code D Paragraph 4.1 & Section 65(1) PACE 1984

- A **fingerprint** is defined as:

    *"Any **record** produced by any method, of the **skin pattern** and other **physical characteristics** or **features** of a person's **fingers** or **palms**"*

2 - Authority To Take Fingerprints

(i) - The General Rule - Code D Paragraph 4.2 & Section 61(2) PACE 1984

- As a **general rule** a person's **consent** is required before the police can take **fingerprints**.
- If the person is at a **police station** the **consent** must be **in writing**.

For example:

An officer cannot just walk up to a law abiding citizen in the street who is not suspected of having committed a crime and demand their fingerprints without their consent.

The officer could only obtain fingerprints from such a person if they provide their **consent**.

If they **refuse**, it will *not* be possible to obtain their fingerprints against their will by **force**.

(ii) - Exceptions To The General Rule Where The Suspect's Consent Is Not Required To Take Fingerprints - Code D Paragraph 4.3 & Section 61 PACE 1984

- **Fingerprints** of a person **aged 10 years or over** may be taken **without their consent** in the following circumstances:

Memory Aid

- All of the circumstances outlined below relate to situations where the ***person has had involvement with the legal process.***
- If they ***have had involvement with the legal process:***
    - *No* **consent** is required; and
    - **Reasonable force** *can* be used in the event of a refusal.

(a) - Taking Fingerprints Without Consent Prior To Arrest - Section 61(6)A&B PACE 1984 As Introduced By s118(3) SOCPA 2005

- A **constable** may take a persons **fingerprints** without their consent, *away* from a **police station** where:
    - They reasonably *suspect* that the person is either:
        - **Committing** an offence;
        - **Attempting** to commit an offence;
        - **Has committed** an offence; and

- ☐ **Either** of the following apply:
    - ■ The **name** of the person is **unknown** and **cannot be readily ascertained** by the constable; or
    - ■ The constable has **reasonable grounds for doubting** whether the **name** they have **provided is their real name.**

NB – The **authorisation** of an **Inspector** or above is *not* **required.**

(b) - Taking Fingerprints Without Consent Following An Arrest – Code D Paragraph 4.3 & Section 61 (3),(4)&(6) PACE 1984

- ■ *No* **consent** is **required** from a person **aged 10 years or over** who is:
    - ☐ Either:
        - ■ **Arrested** and in police **detention;**
        - ■ **Charged** and in police **detention;**
        - ■ **Informed** that they will be **reported** and in police **detention;**
    - ☐ For a **recordable offence** who either:
        - ■ Has **not previously** provided fingerprints; or
        - ■ **Has previously** provided fingerprints – but they were **not a complete set** or they were **insufficient** for analysis, comparison, or matching.

NB – The **authorisation** of an **Inspector** or above is *not* **required.**

(c) Taking Fingerprints Without Consent Following A Conviction Charge Reprimand Or Caution

- ■ **No consent** is required from a person **aged 10 years or over** who is:
    - ☐ Either:
        - ■ **Convicted;**
        - ■ **Cautioned;**
        - ■ **Warned;** or
        - ■ **Reprimanded;**
    - ☐ For a **recordable offence.**

(c) - Taking Fingerprints Without Consent Following An Arrest In Bail Situations - Section 61 (4A) PACE 1984

- **No consent** is **required** from a person **aged 10 years or over** who is:
    - **Bailed** to appear either at:
        - **Court**; or
        - A **police station**;
    - If they have either:
        - Answered to bail for a person whose fingerprints were taken previously and there are **reasonable grounds for** *believing* **they are not the same person**; or
        - They **claim to be a different person** from a person whose fingerprints were previously taken; and
    - **Authorisation** is provided by either:
        - An **Inspector** or above; or
        - The **court.**

3 - Can Reasonable Force Be Used To Take Fingerprints? - Code D Paragraph 4.6

- If **no consent is required** to take fingerprints – then **reasonable force is permitted.**

4 - Recording Obligations Following The Use Of Force – Code D Paragraph 4.8

- Where **force is used** – a **record** should be made of:
    - The **circumstances** of the force;
    - Those **present** when force was used.

5 - Notification Provided To Persons Whose Fingerprints Are Taken Either With Or Without Consent - Code D Paragraph 4.7

- The person must be **notified** of:
    - The **reason for taking** their fingerprints;
    - That the fingerprints may be **retained** and be subjected to a **speculative search unless destruction is required** under *Code D Annex F Part A*;
    - That if the fingerprints are required to be **destroyed,** they may **witness their destruction**; and
    - If the **Inspector (or Court's) authorisation** was required in **bail back situations**:
        - That **authorisation** has been **provided**;
        - The **grounds** for the authorisation.

6 - Recording Obligations Following The Taking Of Fingerprints - Code D Para's 4.8 & 4.9

- A **record** shall be made of:
    - ☐ The **reasons** for taking fingerprints **without the persons consent**;
    - ☐ If **force** is used – the **circumstances** and **those present**; and
    - ☐ The **warning** provided to the person in relation to **subjecting the fingerprints to a speculative search unless destruction is required** under *Code D Annex F Part A*.

7 - Notice Requiring The Attendance Of Persons Convicted, Cautioned, Warned, Or Reprimanded To Provide Fingerprints – Section 27 PACE 1984 & Code D Paragraph 4.4

- A **notice** can be issued **within 1 month** of any:
    - ☐ **Conviction**;
    - ☐ **Caution**;
    - ☐ **Reprimand**; or
    - ☐ **Warning**;
- Requiring the person to **attend a police station at the very least within 7 days of the issue of the notice** to provide fingerprints;
- If either:
    - ☐ The person has:
        - **Not been in police detention** for the offence; and
        - **Not previously had their fingerprints taken** during the investigation; or
    - ☐ Their **fingerprints were taken** during the investigation but they were either:
        - An **incomplete set**; or
        - Were **unsatisfactory** for analysis, comparison, or matching.

8 - Consequences Of Failing To Comply With A Request

- If the person fails to comply with the request they may be **arrested by a constable without a warrant.**

Exam Trip Up

- The request to provide fingerprints must afford *at least* **7 days notice.**
- **7 days** in an absolute **minimum** period of notice.
- The notice period **may be longer than 7 days**.

Exam Trip Up

- The **7 day or longer notice period to** *attend* **the police station to provide the fingerprints need** *not* **fall during the month long period** allowed for *issuing the requirement* to provide the fingerprints after the:
    - ☐ **Conviction;**
    - ☐ **Caution;**
    - ☐ **Warning;** or
    - ☐ **Reprimand.**
- Therefore up to the last day of the month long period following the conviction, caution, warning or reprimanding, the requirement may be issued to attend the police station to provide fingerprints within the 7 day or longer period specified thereafter.

G - Subjecting DNA Or Fingerprints To A Speculative Search Without The Persons Consent - Code D Note 4B & Note 6E

- **Fingerprints** or **DNA samples** taken from a person;
- Either:
    - ☐ **Arrested;**
    - ☐ **Charged;** or
    - ☐ **Informed** that they will be **reported;**
- For a **recordable offence;**
- **May** be subjected to a **speculative search;**
- **Without** the persons **consent.**

H - Subjecting DNA Or Fingerprints To A Speculative Search Where The Persons Consent Is Necessary - Code D Note 4B & Note 6E

- **Fingerprints** or a **DNA sample;**
- Taken from a person **suspected** of committing a **recordable offence;**
- But who is **not:**
    - ☐ **Arrested;**
    - ☐ **Charged;** or
    - ☐ Informed that they will be **reported;**
- May only be subjected to a **speculative search;**
- When the person **consents in writing.**

I - Impressions Of Footwear – Section 61A PACE 1984

1 - Authority To Take Impressions Of Footwear

(i) - The General Rule

- As a **general rule** a person's **consent** is required before the police can take an **impression of their footwear**.

- If the person is at a **police station** the **consent** must be **in writing**.

For example:

An officer cannot just walk up to a law abiding citizen in the street who is not suspected of having committed a crime and demand a footwear impression without their consent.

The officer could only obtain a footwear impression from such a person if they provide their **consent**.

If they **refuse**, it will *not* be possible to obtain the impression against their will by **force**.

(ii) - Exception Where Consent Is Not Required To Take A Footwear Impression

- **No consent** is **required** to take a footwear impression from a person **over the age of 10** who is:

  - Either:
    - **Arrested** and in police **detention**;
    - **Charged** and in police **detention**; or
    - **Informed** that they will be **reported**;

  - For a **recordable offence** who either:
    - Has **not previously** provided a footwear impression during the course of the investigation; or
    - Has **previously** provided a footwear impression – but it was either:
      - **Incomplete**; or
      - **Insufficient** for analysis.

Memory Aid

- All of the circumstances outlined above relate to situations where the *person has had involvement with the legal process.*

- If they *have had involvement with the legal process:*
  - *No* **consent** is required; and
  - **Reasonable force** *can* be used in the event of a refusal.

2 - Notification Provided To Persons Whose Footwear Impressions Are Taken Either With Or Without Consent

- The person must be **notified** of:
    - [ ] The **reason for taking** the footwear impression; and
    - [ ] That the footwear impression may be retained and be subjected to a **speculative search**.

3 - Recording Obligations Following The Taking Of A Footwear Impression

- A **record** shall be made of:
    - [ ] The **warning** provided to the person in relation to **subjecting the footwear impression to a speculative search;**
    - [ ] The **reasons for taking any footwear impression without the suspects consent.**

4 - Can Reasonable Force Be Used To Take Footwear Impressions? - Code D Paragraph 4.6

- If **no consent is required** to take footwear impressions – then **reasonable force is permitted.**

J - Terrorism Offences

1 - Fingerprints & Non Intimate Samples – Schedule 8 Paragraph 10(1)-(4) Terrorism Act 2000

- Either:
    - [ ] **Fingerprints**; or
    - [ ] **Non Intimate Samples;**
- May be taken from a *detainee* in relation to a *terrorism offence;*
- If either:
    - [ ] The **detainee consents** *in writing;*
    - [ ] If the detainee does **not** provide their **written consent**:
        - A *Superintendent* or above provides **authorisation;** or
        - The detainee has been **convicted** of a **recordable offence** (and for **non intimate samples** the **conviction** was on or after the **10th April 1995**).

2 - Intimate Samples – Schedule 8 Paragraph 10(5) Terrorism Act 2000

- An **intimate sample** may only be taken from a person if:
    - They are **detained** at a police station;
    - They provide their *written* **consent;** and
    - A **Superintendent** or above authorises the sample to be taken.

The Grounds For The Authorisation To Take Fingerprints Or Intimate Samples From A Suspected Terrorist - Schedule 8 Paragraph 10(6) Terrorism Act 2000

- The **Superintendent** or above may **authorise** the taking of fingerprints or an intimate sample where either:
    - They reasonably **suspect** that:
        - The person has been **involved** in an **offence** specified in **section 40(1)(a) Terrorism Act 2000**; and
        - That the fingerprints or sample will tend to **confirm** or **disprove** the suspects **involvement** in the offence; or
    - They are satisfied that the taking of fingerprints or a sample is necessary in order to **assist** in the **determination** of whether they have been **concerned** in the:
        - **Commission;**
        - **Preparation**; or
        - **Instigation;**

        - of acts of terrorism.
    - Either:
        - The person has **refused** to **identify themselves**; or
        - The officer has reasonable grounds for **suspecting** that the **person is not who they claim to be**; and
        - They are satisfied that the taking of **fingerprints** of the detained person will **facilitate the ascertainment of that persons identity.**

Evidence & Procedure
Unit 12: Police Station Procedure (11)
Photographs

A - Circumstances In Which An Officer May Take Photographs - Section 64A PACE 1984

- An **officer** may **photograph**:
    - Any person whilst they are **detained at a police station**; and
    - Any person who is **elsewhere than at a police station** and who has been:
        - **Arrested** by a **constable** for an **offence**;
        - **Taken into custody** by a **constable** after being **arrested** for an offence by a **person other than a constable**;
        - Made subject to a **requirement** to **wait** with a **community support officer**;
        - Given a **penalty notice** by a constable **in uniform** under Chapter 1 of Part 1 of the Criminal Justice and Police Act 2001;
        - Given a **penalty notice** by a **constable** under section 444A of the Education Act 1996;
        - Given a **fixed penalty notice** by a **constable in uniform** under section 54 of the Road Traffic Offenders Act 1988;
        - Given a **notice** in relation to a relevant **fixed penalty offence** by a **community support officer**; or
        - (vi) given a **notice** in relation to a relevant **fixed penalty** offence by an **accredited person.**

B - Requesting The Removing Head Or Face Coverings When Taking Photographs – Code D Paragraph 5.13

- The officer may **require** the person to:
    - **Remove;**
    - Any:
        - **Item;** or
        - **Substance;**
    - **Worn** either:
        - **On;** or
        - **Over;**
    - Either:
        - **All;** or
        - **Any part** of;

- Their:
  - Head; or
  - Face.

C - What Action Can Be Taken If The Person Refuses To Remove The Item Or Substance?

- If the person **refuses**;
- The **officer** may **remove** the:
  - **Item**; or
  - **Substance**.

D - Is Consent Required To Take Photographs? – Code D Paragraph 5.12A

(i) - The General Rule

- Photographs can only be taken from a person specified in section 64A with the person's **consent**.

(ii) - The Exception To The General Rule

- Photographs **can** be taken from a person specified in section 64A **without** the person's **consent** if either:
  - Consent is **withheld**; or
  - It is *not practicable* to obtain their consent.

E - How May Images Be Taken Without A Persons Consent – Code D Paragraph 5.15

- A photograph may be obtained **without** the person's **consent** by:
  - Making a **copy** of an **image** of them;
  - Taken **at any time**;
  - On a **camera system** installed anywhere in the police station.

F - Can Force Be Used To Take Images Without A Person's Consent – Code D Paragraph 5.14

(i) Detainees

- If it is established that:
  - The **detainee** is **unwilling to co-operate** sufficiently to enable a suitable photograph to be taken; and
  - It is **not reasonably practicable** to take the photograph covertly;
- An **officer** may use **reasonable force** to:
  - To take their **photograph without** their **consent**; and

- For the **purpose of taking the photograph**:
  - **Remove** any:
    - **Item**; or
    - **Substance**;
  - **Worn**:
    - **On**; or
    - **Over**;
  - Either:
    - **All**; or
    - **Any part**;
  - Of the person's:
    - **Head**; or
    - **Face**;
  - Which they have **failed to remove** when asked.

(ii) Volunteers – Code D Paragraph 5.21

- When there are **reasonable grounds** for *suspecting;*
- The **involvement** in a **criminal offence**;
- Of a **volunteer**;
- Who is **at a police station**;
- Force *cannot* be used to take a photograph of the person.

G - What Purposes May The Photographs Be Used For Once Taken? – Code D Paragraph 5.12A

- The **photographs** may be **used** or **disclosed** only for purposes related to:
  - The **prevention** or **detection** of **crime**;
  - The **investigation** of offences; or
  - The conduct of **prosecutions** by or on behalf of:
    - **Police**; or
    - Other **law enforcement** and **prosecuting authorities**;
    - Either:
      - **Inside the UK**; or
      - **Outside the UK**; or
  - The **enforcement** of any **sentence** or **order** made by a court when dealing with an offence.

- **After** the photographs are either:
    - ☐ **Used;** or
    - ☐ **Disclosed;**
- They may be **retained;** and
- Can only be **used or disclosed again** for the **same purposes.**

H - Procedures To Be Followed When Taking A Photograph – Code D Paragraph 5.16

- The person photographed must be **informed** of the:
    - ☐ **Purpose** of taking the **photograph;** and
    - ☐ **Purposes** for which the **photograph may be used, disclosed or retained.**
- **Before** the photograph is **taken;**
- **Unless;**
- The **photograph** is:
    - ☐ To be taken **covertly;**
    - ☐ **Without** the persons **consent.**

- If so, the person must be **informed as soon as practicable after the photograph is taken or obtained.**

I - Recording Obligations Following The Taking Of A Photograph – Code D Paragraph 5.17

- A **record** *must* be made when a detainee is **photographed.**
- The **record** *must* include the:
    - ☐ **Identity** of the **officer** carrying out the taking of the photograph;
    - ☐ The **purpose** of the photograph and the **outcome;**
    - ☐ Either:
        - The **detainee's consent** to be photographed; or
        - The **reason** the person was photographed **without consent.**

J - Further Recording Obligations Where Force Is Used To Take The Photograph – Code D Paragraph 5.18

- If **force** is used when taking a photograph a **record** shall be made of:
    - ☐ The **circumstances;** and
    - ☐ Those **present.**

Evidence & Procedure
Unit 13 – Police Station Procedure (12) Adverse Inferences From Silence, Cautions, Interviews & Excluding Solicitors From Interviews

Adverse Inferences From Silence

A – The General Rule

- At **common law** a suspect is under **no obligation** to **answer any questions** at interview.

- The **right to silence** is **preserved** by the **Criminal Justice Public Order Act (CJPOA) 1994**.

- However **consequences** may arise in the form of the drawing of **adverse inferences at trial** if the right to silence is exercised.

B - Exceptions To The General Rule Permitting The Drawing Of Adverse Inferences

- The legislation has generated the possibility of **adverse inferences** being drawn at trial where the suspect either:

    - **Fails to mention facts** which they **later rely upon at trial (s34)**;

    - **Without good cause** either:

        - **Fails to take the stand** at trial; or

        - **Selectively answers questions** whilst on the stand **(s35)**;

    - **Fails to account** for the presence of **objects, substances or marks (s36)**;

    - **Fails to account** for their **presence** at a **place (s37)**.

C - Opportunity To Consult A Solicitor

- In the case of **Murray v UK [1996] 22 EHRR 29** the European Court of Human Rights established that:

    - It will *not* be possible to draw an **inference**;

    - **Until** the suspect in police **detention**;

    - Who has **requested legal advice**;

    - Has been afforded the **opportunity to consult a solicitor**.

Exam Trip Up

- Watch out for questions involving the drawing of adverse inferences in relation to **questions posed** *prior* **to the suspect's arrival at the police station.**
    - ☐ As the suspect will **not have been afforded the opportunity to consult a solicitor** at this juncture;
    - ☐ **No adverse inferences** may be drawn at trial in relation to any silence exercised by the suspect at this point.

Exam Trip Up

- Watch out for situations where the **detainee's rights to legal advice have been withheld against their wishes** pursuant to either:
    - ☐ **Code C Annex B**; or
    - ☐ **Code C Paragraph 6.6(b).**
- Again **no adverse inferences** can be drawn in such circumstances.

D - The Section 34 Adverse Inference

1 – When Will A Section 34 Adverse Inference Be Drawn?

- If when a **suspect** is questioned under **caution** either:
    - ☐ **Before** they are charged; or
    - ☐ **Upon** being charged;
- By a **constable** or other person charged with a **duty to investigate**; and
- **Fails to mention a fact;**
- Which in the **circumstances existing at the time**;
- They should **reasonably have been expected to have mentioned**; and
- **They later rely on that fact in their defence at trial;**
- The court may **draw such inferences as appear proper** when determining:
    - ☐ Whether to dismiss proceedings;
    - ☐ Whether there is a case to answer; or
    - ☐ Guilt.

2 - Reasonably Mentioning Facts

- In the case of *R v Argent* [1997] 2 Cr App R 27:

    It was established that *personal factors* would be relevant in determining whether the suspect could **reasonably have been expected to have mentioned a fact** whilst questioned.

- Factors to consider include the suspects:
    - Age;
    - Mental capacity;
    - State of health;
    - Sobriety;
    - Tiredness;
    - Personality;
    - Experience of interrogation;
    - The legal advice they have obtained.

3 - Inadequate Disclosure To A Solicitor

- Only the:
    - **Custody record;** and
    - Any **first description** of an identification witness;
    - **Must** *(where practicable)* **be disclosed** to a solicitor upon request.

- The case of *R v Argent* [1997] 2 Cr App R 27:

    Established that in the event of **partial disclosure** - provided the **information is adequate enough to enable the suspect to put forward their basic defence** – **inferences may be drawn.**

- The case of *R v Roble* [1997] Crim LR 449:
    - Established that **no inferences** may be drawn where:
        - There is **so little disclosure;**
        - That the **solicitor is unable to advise** the suspect;
        - Because they **do not understand the basis of the police case** against them.

4 - Remaining Silent At Interview And Instead Handing Over A Pre-Prepared Written Statement At Interview

- The case of *R v Knight* [2004] 1 WLR 340 established that:
    - Where a suspect **refuses to answer questions** under **caution;** and
    - Instead **discloses** the *full facts* of their **defence** in a **pre-prepared written statement;**
    - That is *wholly consistent* with the **defence** that they subsequently **run at trial;**
    - Then **no adverse inferences** may be drawn under section 34 CJPOA 1994.

- The submission of a pre-prepared statement does **not however provide total immunity** from the drawing of **adverse inferences.**
    - **Inferences may still be drawn** at trial where the pre-prepared written statement is either:
        - *Incomplete* in comparison to the defence run at trial (i.e. leaves out any details that are subsequently relied upon at trial; or
        - Is in any way *inconsistent* with the defence run a trial.

5 - The Nature Of The Section 34 Adverse Inference

- A court may **draw such inferences as appear proper**.
- The most common inferences are that the suspect failed to mention the fact because either:
  - [ ] **They knew their story would not stand up to questioning**; or
  - [ ] **They had not thought up their story at that point** – i.e. subsequent fabrication.

E - The Section 36 Adverse Inference

1 – When Will The Section 36 Adverse Inference Be Drawn?

- Such **inferences as appear proper** may be drawn where:
  - [ ] A **constable**;
  - [ ] **Arrests** a person;
  - [ ] Who has an:
    - **Object**; (e.g. Screwdriver for going equipped)
    - **Substance**; or (e.g. Drugs for the offence of possession)
    - **Mark**; (e.g. Bruises to their body in an assault offence)
  - [ ] Either:
    - On their **person**;
    - **In** or **on** their **clothing** or **footwear**;
    - In their **possession**;
    - In any **place where they are** at the **time of arrest**; and
- The **constable** reasonably **believes** that:
  - [ ] The **presence** of the **object, substance, or mark**;
  - [ ] May be **attributable** to the **suspect's participation in a crime**; and
- The **constable**:
  - [ ] **Informs** the **suspect** of their **belief**;
  - [ ] **Asks** the **suspect to account** for the presence of the object, substance, or mark;
  - [ ] **Provides** the **suspect** with a **special warning** under Code C Paragraph 10.11; and
  - [ ] The **suspect fails to account** for the presence of the object, substance, or mark.

2 - Definition Of Objects

- A **person held against their will** has been deemed to be an **object in offences of:**
    - ☐ Kidnap;
    - ☐ False imprisonment;
    - ☐ Child abduction;
    - ☐ Murder.

3 - Definition Of Possession

- **Possession** is a **wide concept** that includes:
    - ☐ Items **physically in a person's possession** at the time of their arrest; or
    - ☐ Anything under their **custody** or **control** at the time of their arrest.

Exam Trip Up

- Watch out for questions involving:
    - ☐ A kidnapper, etc;
    - ☐ Who is arrested away from their home; and
    - ☐ **At the time of their arrest;**
    - ☐ Their victim is locked in their home.

- A **section 36 special warning can be administered** in such circumstances as:
    - ☐ The **victim** is an **object**; and
    - ☐ The victim is **at the time of the arrest**;
    - ☐ **Located** at **premises** under the suspect's **custody** and **control.**

- In cases of **murder**:
    - ☐ A section 36 special warning can be administered in relation to:
        - Any **dead body**;
        - That **at the time of the arrest:**
        - Was located in either:
            - ☐ A **vehicle;** or
            - ☐ **Premises;**
        - Under the arrested person's **custody** or **control.**

Exam Trip Up

- Watch out for questions involving the provision of special warnings to persons questioned at a police station who are attending the station **voluntarily.**

- As they are **not under arrest - no adverse inferences** will be drawn from their silence.

F - The Section 37 Adverse Inference

1 – When Will The Section 37 Adverse Inference Be Drawn?

- Such **inferences as appear proper** may be drawn where:
    - An **person** is **found** by a **constable**;
    - **At a place**;
    - **At or about the time the offence** for which they have been arrested **was committed**; and
    - The **constable** who **found** them has **arrested** them; and
    - The **constable** reasonably **believes** that:
        - The **presence** of the person at the place at that time;
        - May be **attributable to the suspect's participation in a crime**; and
    - The **arresting constable** or **any other investigating constable:**
        - **Informs** the **suspect** of their **belief;**
        - **Asks** the **suspect** to **account** for their **presence:**
            - **At that place;**
            - **At or about the time of the commission of the offence;**
        - **Provides** the **suspect** with a **special warning** under Code C Para 10.11, and
        - The **suspect fails to account** for their **presence** at that place at or about the time of the commission of the offence.

Exam Trip Up – Who Must Be The Arresting Officer To Enable A Section 37 Inference To Be Drawn?

- A **section 37 special warning** may only be administered in such circumstances if the suspect is **subsequently** *arrested* by the *same officer* who *saw them* at the place at or about the time of the commission of the offence.

- NB – The actual **interviewing officer** can be **any other officer.**

Exam Trip Up

- Watch out for questions involving the provision of special warnings to persons questioned at a police station who are attending the station **voluntarily.**

- As they are **not under arrest no adverse inferences** will be drawn from their silence.

G - The Nature Of The Special Warning Administered To Suspects – Code C Paragraph 10.11

- The interviewing officer must tell the suspect in **ordinary language:**
    - The **offence** that is being investigated;
    - The **fact** that the suspect is being asked to account for;
    - That the interviewing officer **believes** that this **fact may be due to the suspect's participation in the offence;**
    - That the **court may draw a proper inference** if the suspect **fails** or **refuses** to **account** for the **fact** in question;
    - That a **record** is being made of the interview which may be **given in evidence at a subsequent trial.**

An Example Of A Section 36 Inference In Operation

- The police are conducting patrols in an area where there have been a spate of recent car crimes. At 5am they approach a lone male behaving suspiciously.

- He is apprehended and following a search of his person a screwdriver, gloves and a hammer **(objects)** are found **in his possession.** He is arrested for going equipped.

- During questioning under **caution** at the police station, after the suspect has been afforded the **opportunity to seek legal advice,** the investigating officer could administer a **section 36 special warning explaining** to the **suspect:**
    - That he is being **investigated** for the offence of going equipped;
    - That they reasonably *believe* that the **objects in his possession indicate** that he has **committed the offence;**
    - That they wish him to **explain** why he had the objects in his possession;
    - That the **court may draw a proper inference** if he **fails or refuses to account** for the presence of the objects;
    - That a **record** is being made of the interview which may be **given in evidence at any subsequent trial.**

- If he **cannot provide an explanation** then **inferences will be drawn** from his silence.

- If however he **explains** that he has just left his house and that he is a builder on his way to work then **no inferences** may be drawn at trial.

An Example Of A Section 37 Inference In Operation

- The police are called to investigate a burglary at a warehouse on a remote industrial estate at 3am. They arrive within minutes of the incident and are provided with a description by the security guard.

- Within 5 minutes a man matching the description is observed by an officer walking on foot 100 meters away from the warehouse. The officer arrests him.

- During questioning under **caution** at the police station, after the suspect has been afforded the **opportunity to seek legal advice,** the investigating officer could administer a **section 37 special warning** explaining to the **suspect**:

    - ☐ That he is being **investigated** for the alleged the **burglary** of the warehouse;

    - ☐ That his **presence** in the **vicinity** of the warehouse **shortly after** the offence was committed leads them to reasonably **believe** that he **committed** the offence;

    - ☐ That they wish him to **explain** his **presence** at the scene at that time;

    - ☐ That the **court may draw a proper inference** if he **fails or refuses to account** for their presence;

    - ☐ That a **record** is being made of the interview which may be **given in evidence at a subsequent trial.**

H - Inferences Alone Cannot Prove Guilt – Section 38(3) CJOPA 1994

- The judge must **direct** the jury at trial that:

    - ☐ The **burden of proof** remains on the **prosecution;**

    - ☐ An **inference cannot prove guilt** in itself; and

    - ☐ There **must be a prima facie prosecution case** to answer before any inference can be drawn.

Summary Table

Adverse Inferences From Silence

Inference	Caution Required?	Special Warning Required?	Pre or Post Arrest	Opportunity To Consult Solicitor A Required?	Failure	Reasonably Have Been Expected To Mention?
Section 34	Yes	No	Pre & Post Arrest	Yes	To mention a fact that they later rely on at trial	Yes
Section 36	Yes	Yes	Post Arrest Only	Yes	To account for an object substance or mark	N/A
Section 37	Yes	Yes	Post Arrest Only	Yes	To account for their presence at a place	N/A

I - Definition Of An Interview - Code C Paragraph 11.1A

- An **interview** is defined as:
    - The **questioning** of a person regarding their:
        - **Involvement**;
        - **Suspected involvement**;
    - In a **criminal offence(s)**;
    - That **must** be carried out under **caution**.

- Whenever a person is interviewed they must be **informed of the nature** of:
    - The **offence**; or
    - Any **further offences** that come to light during questioning.

J – Cautions

1 - When Must A Caution Be Administered? - Code C Paragraph 10.1

- A **caution must** be **administered** where there are **grounds** to **suspect** that a person has **committed an offence**.
- The case of *Batley v DPP* [1998] The Times 5th March, established that:
    - There must be **real grounds** to suspect that the person has committed the offence.
    - A **mere hunch** that the person has committed the offence is **insufficient** to activate the Code.
- The cautioning **must** take place **before** any **questions** are put to the suspect in respect of the offence.

2 - When Is It Not Necessary To Administer A Caution?

- If a person is **not suspected** of an offence at the time a question is asked there is **no need for a caution**.
- The case of *R v McGuinness* [1999] Crim LR 318, established that if a person is asked questions for **reasons other than obtaining evidence** about their **involvement or suspected involvement** in an offence, then:
    - This is **not an interview**; and
    - A **caution need not be provided.**
- Code C Paragraph 10.1 also states that a person **need not be cautioned** where:
    - The **questions are necessary for** *other purposes* including (but not limited to):
        - To solely **establish** their:
            - **Identity**;
            - **Ownership of any vehicle**;

- In furtherance of the **proper and effective conduct of a search:**
  - ☐ To determine the **need** to **search;**
  - ☐ To seek **cooperation** in carrying out the **search;**
- ☐ To seek **verification of a written record;** or
- ☐ When examining a person in accordance with the **Terrorism Act 2000.**

Exam Trip Up – Routine Checks Of Vehicles

- Watch out for questions involving a traffic officer routinely stopping a vehicle for speeding, who then searches the vehicle, directing questions towards the driver in relation to a package found in the boot of the car.

- As at the time of conducting the search the **officer does not suspect the contents of the package to be related to the commission of an offence,** then in accordance with *R v McGuinness* [1999] Crim LR 318, there is **no need** to administer a **caution.**

- Also there is **no need to caution** in such circumstances pursuant to Code C Paragraph 10.1(c), as the questions posed are **in furtherance of the proper and effective conduct of a search.**

Exam Trip Up - The Nature Of The Question Posed

- Provided in such circumstances a **generic question** is posed, **no caution** need be administered.

  An example of such a question would be "What's in the package?"

- However if the question in relation to the package is of a **leading nature** to which a **positive answer would result in implication in an offence** then a **caution must be administered.**

  An example of such a question would be "Are there amphetamine tablets in the package?"

3 - Additional Notification Requirements When Cautioning Persons Who Are Not Under Arrest – Code C Paragraph 10.2

- When a person **not under arrest** is:
  - ☐ First **cautioned;** or
  - ☐ **Reminded** that they are **under caution;**
- They must at the same time be **told:**
  - ☐ They are **not under arrest**; and
  - ☐ Are **free to leave** if they wish.

4 - Caution Upon Arrest – Code C Paragraphs 10.3 & 10.4

- A person **arrested** must be **informed** either:
  - ☐ **At the time;** or
  - ☐ **As soon as practicable thereafter;**

(cont...)

- Both:
    - They are under **arrest;** and
    - The **grounds** for their arrest.
- They must also be **cautioned** unless:
    - They have **already** been **cautioned prior to their arrest**; or
    - It is **impracticable** to do so because of their:
        - **Condition;** or
        - **Behaviour.**

5 - The Terms Of The Caution

- There are **2 forms** of caution:
    - The **standard caution**; and
    - The **modified caution**.

(i) - The Standard Caution – Code C Annex C Paragraph 1

- The **standard caution** will **always apply;**
- **Unless;**
- A situation has arisen where it is **not possible to draw adverse inferences** from the suspect's silence.

The Terms Of The Standard Caution - Code C, Paragraph 10.5

"You do not have to say anything. But it will harm your defence if you do not mention when questioned something which you later rely on in Court. Anything you do say may be given in evidence."

(ii) - The Modified Caution – Code C Annex C, Paragraph 1

- **Code C Annex C** outlined the circumstances in which the **modified caution applies.**
- The courts are **unable to draw adverse inferences from silence** in such circumstances.
- The restriction applies where:
    - A detainee's **right to legal advice has been delayed** by a **Superintendent** or above (**Code C Annex B**);
    - A **Superintendent** or above has **authorised an interview to proceed without waiting for a solicitor requested** (Code C Para 6.6(b)(ii)).
    - **Interviews** in relation to the contents of a **statement by another** which **takes place after:**
        - **Charge;** or
        - The detainee being informed that they will be **reported** for an offence.

The Terms Of The Modified Caution – Code C Annex C, Paragraph 2

Code C, Annex C, Paragraph 2 defines the modified caution:

"You do not have to say anything, but anything you do say may be given in evidence."

6 - Action To Be Taken Following A Break In Interviewing – Code C Paragraphs 10.8 & 11.4

- After any **break** in **questioning** under **caution** the **interviewing officer** *must* when the **interview resumes**:
- Either:
    - **Remind** the **suspect** that they **remain under caution**; or
    - If in **doubt** – **re-administer** the **caution in full**;
- And:
    - **Summarise** the **reason** for the break;
    - **Confirm** the **reason** with the **suspect**;
    - **Remind** the **suspect** of their **right to legal advice**.

7 - Cautioning Juveniles Or Mentally Disordered Or Mentally Vulnerable Persons – Code C Paragraph 10.12

- If the **cautioning** of a:
    - **Juvenile**;
    - **Mentally disordered person**; or
    - **Mentally vulnerable person**;
- Takes place in the **absence** of their **appropriate adult**;
- The **caution** must subsequently be *repeated* in the **presence** of the **appropriate adult** once they are in attendance.

8 - Recording The Caution – Code C Paragraph 10.13

- A **record** must be made of any **caution** administered in either:
    - The **interview record**; or
    - The interviewers **pocket book**.

9 - Consequences Of Failing To Administer A Caution

- When a person is questioned **without being cautioned**; and
- A **caution should have been administered**;
- **Any admissions** made are likely to be ruled as **inadmissible** evidence at trial pursuant to the courts **discretionary** powers under **section 78 PACE 1984**.

K - Unsolicited Comments Prior To Caution

- A person may make an **unsolicited comment** of their **own fee will,** without prompting that **implicates** them, at a **point before** they are **suspected and cautioned.**

- Such comments will be **admissible** provided the procedural measures in **Code C Paragraph's 11.13 and 11.14** are complied with.

1 - Recording The Unsolicited Comments - Code C Paragraph 11.13

- A **written record** shall be made:
    - Of any:
        - **Comments;** or
        - **Unsolicited comments;**
    - Made **outside** the context of an **interview** by a suspect;
    - That may be **relevant** to an offence.

2 - Endorsing The Record Of Any Comments Made – Code C Paragraph 11.13 & 11.14

- The **record** must be:
    - **Timed;**
    - **Signed;**
- By the officer.
- Where **practicable**, the **suspect** must be **given the opportunity** to:
    - **Read** the record; and
    - Either:
        - **Sign** the record as **correct;** or
        - **Indicate** how they consider the record to be **inaccurate** and **sign.**
- If the **suspect refuses to sign** the record the **officer** must **record** this fact.

3 - When Must An Endorsement Take Place?

- It is **good practice** to **endorse** any comments made by a suspect **immediately** or at the **earliest opportunity** thereafter.

- However, in *Bately v DPP* **[1998] The Times, 5th March**, it was established that:
    - The code does **not require** an **immediate endorsement.**
    - **No time limit** is proscribed by the legislation.
    - The police were therefore entitled in this case to return the **next day** to obtain their endorsement of comments made.

L - Interviews Of Persons Who Are Not Under Arrest

1 – Information To Be Provided To Persons Upon Interview Prior To Arrest

- **Prior to the interview,** the person must be:
    - **Cautioned;**
    - **Informed** that they are:
        - **Not** under arrest;
        - **Free to leave** if they wish. (Code C, Paragraph 10.2)
        - If the **interview** takes place **at a police station:**
            - That they are **entitled** to free an independent **legal advice.**
            - If they **ask for legal advice**, they must be given a copy of the **notice** explaining how to obtain such advice. (Code C, Paragraphs 3.21 & 3.22)

2 - The Location Of Interviews Of Persons Who Are Not Under Arrest - Code C Paragraph 11.16

(i) Adults

- **Adults not under arrest** can be interviewed **anywhere**.

(ii) Juveniles

- **Juveniles** may only be interviewed in **places of education** in **exceptional circumstances**.
    - The **principal** must **agree** to the arrangement.
    - The **parent, guardian** and **appropriate adult** must be:
        - **Notified**; and
        - Given **time to attend.**
    - Where **waiting** for the **appropriate adult** would cause an **unreasonable delay**:
        - The **principal** can act as the **appropriate adult**;
        - **Unless**
        - The **offence is committed against the educational establishment.**

An Example Of A Situation Justifying The Interviewing Of A Juvenile At Their Place Of Education

- A juvenile has committed an offence of criminal damage against school property.
- The police have been called and wish to conduct the interview on school premises as the child has to sit a GCSE exam in a couple of hours time.
- The police have contacted their parents but they are both some distance away and cannot attend to act as an appropriate adult for several hours.

- Due to the **exceptional circumstances** of the **exam** and the **urgency** it has generated the principal would ordinarily be able to act as the appropriate adult in the light of the **unreasonable delay** that would be caused by waiting for either of the parents to arrive.

- However, as the offence was **committed against school property** the principal will be **unable to act** as the appropriate adult in this instance.

- If the facts differed in that the offence involved criminal damage to a bus stop **located on non school property** the principal would have been **able to step in and act** as the appropriate adult.

M - Interviews Of Persons Under Arrest

1 - Location Of Interviews Of Persons Who Are Under Arrest - Code C Paragraph 11.1

- **Following arrest** the suspect must be taken for **interview** to:
    - A **police station**; or
    - **Other authorised place of detention**;

- **Unless** the consequent **delay** would be **likely to lead to:**
    - Interference with, or physical harm to other **people**;
    - **Alerting** others suspected of committing the offence but not yet arrested;
    - Serious loss of, or damage to **property**;
    - Interference with, or harm to **evidence**; or
    - Hindering **the recovery** of property obtained during the offence.

Memory Aid

Remember:

- P - People
- A - Alert
- P - Property
- E - Evidence
- R - Recovery

2 - Permitted Duration Of Questioning Away From The Police Station - Code C Paragraph 11.1

- If any of the aforementioned risks exist permitting questioning to take place away from the police station;

- Any questioning away from the police station **must cease as soon as:**
    - The relevant **risk has been averted**; or
    - The **necessary questions have been put to the suspect in an attempt to avert the risk.**

An Example Of A Situation Justifying The Interviewing Of A Suspect Away From A Police Station

- Following surveillance police apprehend one member of a gang of armed robbers who are planning to commit an armed robbery.

- The surveillance has revealed that the heist will be taking place later that day but the police are unaware of the location or identity of the specific bank targeted.

- The police can **interview the gang member immediately away from the station** to **find out the location of the heist** to ensure:

    □ They **avert the danger** to:

        - **Persons;** and
        - **Property.**

- Once the police have **ascertained the whereabouts of the hest**, thereby **averting the danger** they must:

    □ **Stop questioning**; and

    □ **Take the suspect to the police station ASAP** to **continue interviewing them** there.

N - Urgent Interviews Of Juveniles Mentally Disordered Or Vulnerable Suspects In The Absence Of An Appropriate Adult - Code C Paragraph 11.15 & 11.18

- If an **appropriate adult** is required, arrangements should be made for their presence.

- An **appropriate adult** must be present when the suspect is:

    □ **Interviewed**; or

    □ Asked to provide a **written statement**;

    □ And is either:

        - A **juvenile;** or
        - A **mentally disordered** person; or
        - A **mentally vulnerable** person;

    □ **Unless**;

    □ An officer of the rank of **Superintendent** or above;

    □ Considers that any **delay** in **interviewing** caused by **waiting** for the **appropriate adult** to attend would result any of the following **consequences:**

        - Interference with, or physical harm to other **people;**
        - **Alert** others suspected of committing the offence but **not yet arrested**;
        - Serious loss of, or damage to **property;**
        - Interference with, or harm to **evidence;** or
        - Hinder the **recovery** of property obtained during the offence; and

☐ **Interviewing** the suspect in the **absence** of the **appropriate adult** will **not significantly harm** the person's:

- **Mental** state; or
- **Physical** state.

Remember:

- P   -   People
- A   -   Alert
- P   -   Property
- E   -   Evidence
- R   -   Recovery

Permitted Duration Of Urgent Interviews In The Absence Of An Appropriate Adult – Code C Paragraph 11.19

- If any of the aforementioned **risks** exist permitting **interview** to **proceed** in the **absence** of an **appropriate adult**;

- The questioning in the **appropriate adult's** absence **must cease as soon as:**

    ☐ **Sufficient information** has been **obtained** to **avert** the relevant **risk**; or

    ☐ The **necessary questions** have been put to the suspect in an attempt to avert the **risk.**

O - Urgent Interviews Of Persons Who Have A Hearing Disability Or Are Unable To Understand English In The Absence Of An Interpreter – Code C Paragraph 11.18

- Any person who **at the time of interview:**

    ☐ Either:
    - Has **difficulty** in **understanding English**; or
    - Has a **hearing difficulty;**

    ☐ May **not** be **interviewed** in the **absence** of an **interpreter;**

    ☐ **Unless;**

    ☐ An officer of the rank of **Superintendent** or above;

    ☐ Considers that any **delay** in **interviewing** caused by **waiting** for the **interpreter** to **attend** would result any of the following **consequences:**

    - Interference with, or physical harm to other **people;**
    - **Alert** others suspected of committing the offence but **not yet arrested;**
    - Serious loss of, or damage to **property;**
    - Interference with, or harm to **evidence;** or
    - Hinder the **recovery** of property obtained during the offence; and

    ☐ **Interviewing** the suspect in the **absence** of the **interpreter** will **not significantly harm** the person's:

    - **Mental** state; or
    - **Physical** state.

Remember:

- P - People
- A - Alert
- P - Property
- E - Evidence
- R - Recovery

Permitted Duration Of Urgent Interviews In The Absence Of An Interpreter – Code C Paragraph 11.19

- If any of the aforementioned **risks** exist permitting **interview** to **proceed** in the **absence** of an **interpreter**;

- The questioning in the **interpreter's** absence **must cease as soon as:**

    - **Sufficient information** has been **obtained** to **avert** the relevant **risk**; or

    - The **necessary questions have been put to the suspect in an attempt to avert the risk.**

P - Urgent Interviews Of Other Vulnerable Suspects – Code C Paragraph 11.18

- Any person who **at the time of interview** appears **unable** to either:

    - **Appreciate** the significance of:

        - **Questions**;

        - Their **answers;** or

    - **Understand what is happening** due to the **effect** of:

        - **Drink**;

        - **Drugs**;

        - Any **Illness, ailment** or **condition**;

    - May **not** be **interviewed**;

    - **Unless**;

    - An officer of the rank of **Superintendent** or above;

    - Considers that any **delay** in **interviewing** caused by **waiting** for the **suspect to recover** sufficiently to appreciate the significance of the questions and their answers and understand what is happening would result any of the following **consequences:**

        - Interference with, or physical harm to other **people**;

        - **Alert** others suspected of committing the offence but **not yet arrested**;

        - Serious loss of, or damage to **property**;

        - Interference with, or harm to **evidence;** or

        - Hinder the **recovery** of property obtained during the offence; and

    - **Interviewing** the will **not significantly harm** the person's:

        - **Mental** state; or

        - **Physical** state.

Remember:

- P - People
- A - Alert
- P - Property
- E - Evidence
- R - Recovery

Permitted Duration Of Urgent Interviews Of Vulnerable Suspects – Code C Paragraph 11.19

- If any of the aforementioned **risks** exist;

- Permitting **interview** to **proceed prior** to their **recovery**;

- The questioning **must cease as soon as:**

    ☐ **Sufficient information** has been **obtained** to **avert** the relevant **risk**; or

    ☐ The **necessary questions have been put to the suspect in an attempt to avert the risk.**

Q - Recording Obligations – Code C Paragraph 11.20

- If an urgent interview is permitted to proceed under any of the aforementioned circumstances then a **record** must be made of the **reasons** for doing so.

Incommunicado Delays	Urgent Interviews Of Suspects Away From A Police Station	Urgent Interviews Of Juveniles Or Mentally Disordered Or Vulnerable Persons In The Absence Of An Appropriate Adult	Urgent Interviews Of Persons Deaf Or Unable To Understand English In The Absence Of An Interpreter	Urgent Interviews Of Persons Unfit Through Drink, Drugs Or Illness	Urgent Interviews In The Absence Of A Solicitor
Recovery Alert People Evidence R A P E	People Alert **Property** Evidence Recovery P A P E R	People Alert **Property** Evidence Recovery P A P E R	People Alert **Property** Evidence Recovery P A P E R	People Alert **Property** Evidence Recovery P A P E R	**Delay** Alert **Property** Persons Evidence Recovery D A P P E R
Supt's Authorisation Is Required	Supt's Authorisation Is **Not** Required	Supt's Authorisation Is Required	Supt's Authorisation Is Required	Supt's Authorisation Is Required	Supt's Authorisation Is Required

R - Pre Interview Formalities

1 - Transferring Responsibility For The Suspect - Section 39 PACE 1984

- The **Interviewing Officer** must have obtained the **permission** of the **Custody Officer** to interview the detainee; (Code D Paragraph 12.1)

- An **entry** must be made in the **custody record** that the **detainee** has been **delivered** into the **custody** of the **Interviewing Officer**.

NB – The **responsibility** to ensure compliance with PACE 1984 and the Codes rests with the **Interviewing Officer** from this point **until the suspect is returned to the custody of the Custody Officer**.

2 – Risk Assessments

(i) - Custody Officers Obligation To Conducting A Risk Assessment - Code C Annex G Paragraphs 1-2

- The **Custody Officer** must conduct a **risk assessment before releasing the detainee** to the Interviewing Officer to ensure:

    - The interview will **not significantly harm** the detainees **mental or physical state**; or

    - The detainee's **physical or mental state** might result in them **saying something at interview** that is **unreliable**.

- When conducting the assessment the **Custody Officer** should **consult** with:

    - The **officer in charge** of the investigation; and

    - Any appropriate **health care professionals**.

(ii) - Factors To Consider When Conducting A Risk Assessment - Code C Annex G Paragraph 3

- The following factors are taken into account during a **risk assessment:**

    - How the **detainee's physical or mental condition** may affect their **ability to understand** the:

        - **Nature and purpose** of the interview;

        - Any **questions** posed;

        - Significance of any **answers** provided.

    - The extent to which **replies are affected** by their condition;

    - How the **interviewing process** might affect the detainees condition.

(iii) - The Role Of Any Health Care Professional Consulted - Code C Annex G Paragraphs 4 - 6

- Any **health care professional** consulted must **not just diagnose** their condition.
- They should **quantify any risks**, informing the **Custody Officer**:
  - Whether any **treatment is necessary**;
  - Whether their condition is **likely to improve**;
  - **How long it will take** to improve.
- They must focus on whether in the light of their condition the **detainee is fit** for interview.
- They must also **advise** on:
  - Whether an **appropriate adult** need be present;
  - Whether a **further specialised opinion** is necessary;
  - Whether a **further review** of the person's fitness will be necessary after a specified period of interviewing.
- Any **recommendations** of a **health care professional** must be:
  - Made **in writing**;
  - **Recorded** in the custody record.

(iv) - Action Taken By The Custody Officer Following The Recommendation Of Any Health Care Professional Consulted - Code C Annex G Paragraphs 7-8.

- Once the **recommendation** of a **health care professional** has been **obtained**, the **Custody Officer** must **decide**:
  - Whether or not to allow the interview to **proceed**;
  - Whether any **safeguards** are required to minimise any risks.

3 - Preparing For Interview

- The **Interviewing Officer** should ensure:
  - An interview room is **available**;
  - The interview room:
    - Has a **seat**; (Code C Paragraph 12.6)
    - Is adequately **lit, heated and ventilated**; (Code C Paragraph 12.4)
  - The detainee is **clothed** to a reasonable standard of comfort and cleanliness; (Code C Paragraph 8.5)
  - That there are **sufficient tapes or forms** to record;

- That the **notice** in Code E Paragraph 4.19 is available to be handed to the suspect at the end of the interview. This notice specifies:
    - **How** the tape recording shall be used;
    - The arrangements for **accessing** the tape;
    - That if the suspect is **charged**, they will be **provided with a copy as soon as is practicable.**

4 - Rest Periods - Code C Paragraph 12.2

- Regard should be had for the detainees **rest periods** under Code C Paragraph 12.2 when deciding the time that the interview takes place.
    - The detainee in any **24 hour period**;
    - Must be allowed **at least 8 hours rest**;
    - **Free** from **questioning, travel, or interruption.**
    - The period should normally be **at night** or **other appropriate time** that takes into account of when the suspect last slept or rested.
    - If the person is **arrested after** attending the police station **voluntarily** the **24 hour rest period begins** from **the time of arrest** and not the time of arrival.
    - The **rest period** can only be **interrupted** when:
        - There are **reasonable grounds** for **believing** that interrupting the period would:
            - Involve a risk of **harm to people** or **serious loss or damage to property**;
            - **Delay unnecessarily** the persons **release** from custody;
            - Otherwise **prejudice the outcome** of the investigation.
        - At the **request of the detainee**;
        - When a **delay is necessary** to:
            - Comply with the **review** duties;
            - Take action in accordance with **medical advice**.

5 - Legal Advice

- If **legal advice** is requested, arrangements must be made for the legal representative to be present, unless either Code C Paragraph 6.6 or Code C Annex B apply.

6 - Interpreters - Code C Paragraph 13.2

- If an **interpreter** is required, arrangements should be made for their presence.
- An interpreter will be required where:
    - The suspect has difficulty understanding English;
    - The interviewing officer cannot speak the suspects own language; and
    - The suspect wishes an interpreter to be present.

7 – Appropriate Adult

- If an **appropriate adult** is required, arrangements should be made for their presence.

S - Visually Recording Interviews

1 - Circumstances Where Visual Interviews May Be Appropriate – Code F Paragraph 3.1

- A visual recording of an interview **might be appropriate** in the following circumstances:
    - Interviews with a suspect in respect of an **indictable** or **either way** offence;
    - Interviews which take place as a result of an interviewer exceptionally putting further **questions** to a suspect who has been **charged** or **informed** they will be **prosecuted** about an **indictable** or **either way** offence;
    - Interviews after a suspect has been **charged** with, or **informed** they may be **prosecuted** for an **indictable** or **either way** offence where an interviewer wishes to bring to the **notice** of a person either:
        - Any **written statement** made by **another person**; or
        - The **content** of an **interview** with **another person**.
    - Interviews with, or in the presence of a:
        - **Deaf**;
        - **Deaf/blind**;
        - **Speech impaired** person who uses sign language to communicate;
    - Interviews with, or in the presence of anyone who requires an **"appropriate adult"**; or
    - In any case where the **suspect** or their **representative requests** that the interview be recorded visually.

Exam Trip Up

- However, there is **nothing to stop summary offences** from being **visually recorded**. (Code F Note 3A).

2 - Circumstances In Which The Custody Officer May Authorise The Interviewing Officer Not To Visually Record The Interview – Code F Paragraph 3.3

- The **Custody Officer** may authorise the **Interviewing Officer** not to record the interview **visually**:
- Where:
    - It is **not reasonably practicable** to do so because of either:
        - A **failure** of the **equipment**;
        - The **non-availability** of a:
            - **Suitable interview room**; or
            - **Recorder**; and

(cont....)

- - The authorising officer considers on **reasonable grounds** that the interview should **not be delayed until**:
    - The **failure** has been **rectified**; or
    - A **suitable room** becomes **available**; or
    - A **recorder** becomes **available**.
  - In such cases the **Custody Officer** may **authorise** the **Interviewing Officer** to *audio record* the interview.
- Where it is **clear** from the **outset** that **no prosecution** will ensue; or
- Where:
  - It is **not practicable** to do so;
  - Because **at the time** either:
    - The person **resists** being taken to a suitable interview room or other location which would enable the interview to be recorded; or
    - Otherwise **fails** or **refuses to go** into such a room or location; and
  - The authorising officer considers on reasonable grounds that the interview **should not be delayed until these conditions cease to apply.**

3 - Action To Be Taken When It Is Decided Not To Proceed With A Video Identification – Code F Paragraph 3.3 & Note 3F

- In all cases the **Custody Officer** shall make a **note** in the **custody record** of the **reasons** for not taking a visual record.
- A **decision** not to record an interview visually for any reason may be the **subject of comment in court.**
- The authorising officer should therefore be **prepared to justify their decision.**

T - Tape Recording Interviews

(i) - Interviews That Must Be Tape Recorded - Code E Paragraph 3.1

- The following interviews in police stations *must* be tape recorded:
  - When a person has been **cautioned,** in respect of an **indictable or either way offence;**
  - When **further questions** are put to a suspect **after** they have been **charged** with an **indictable or either way offence;**
  - Where **after charge** the officer wishes to draw the suspects attention to:
    - Written statements made by another; or
    - The contents of an interview with another.
- The **mandatory obligation does not apply** in respect of **summary offences.**
- However, there is **nothing to stop** summary offences from being tape recorded. (Code E Note 3A).
- The **whole** of each interview must be recorded including the taking and reading back of any statement. (Code E Paragraph 3.5).

(ii) - Objections By Suspects - Code E Paragraph 4.8

- If the **suspect objects to the interview being tape recorded** the **Interviewing Officer** *must*:
    - ☐ **Explain** the interview is being **recorded;**
    - ☐ Explain that their **objections must be recorded on tape;**

- Once the **objections** or **refusal** to object has been **recorded** on **tape** the **Interviewing Officer** *may* then either:
    - ☐ **Turn off** the tape **explaining their reasons** on tape and make a **written record** of the interview; or
    - ☐ **Continue with the interview on tape** provided they believe it is **reasonable** to do so **in the circumstances.**

(iii) - Custody Officer's Authority Not To Tape Record An Interview - Code E Paragraph 3.3 & Note 3B

- Authorisation may be provided by the **Custody Officer not to tape record** an interview where either:
    - ☐ It is **not reasonably practicable** because:
        - ■ Of **equipment failure**; or
        - ■ The unavailability of a **suitable interview room**; <u>and</u>
        - ■ The **custody officer** decides on **reasonable grounds** that the interview **should not be delayed.**
    - ☐ It is **clear from the outset** that there will be **no prosecution.**

- If the **custody officer authorises** the interview to proceed on this basis:
    - ☐ The interview must be **recorded in writing;** and
    - ☐ The **custody officer** must **record** the specific **reason** for their decision and be prepared to **justify** their decision to a court.

U - Conducting The Interview - Code E Paragraph 4.3 - 4.5

- The **Interviewing Officer** must:
    - ☐ **Break open** the tape seals in the presence of the suspect;
    - ☐ **Load the tapes** in the presence of the suspect and **press record;**
    - ☐ **Inform the suspect** about the tape recording;
    - ☐ **Verbally identify all parties present;**
    - ☐ Administer the relevant **caution;**
    - ☐ Provide any **special warnings** where appropriate;
    - ☐ Remind the suspect of their **right to legal advice,** ensuring their **response is recorded.**

V - Putting Significant Statements To The Suspect At The Commencement Of Interviews – Code C Paragraph 11.4

- **After** the suspect has been **cautioned;**
- The **interviewer** shall **put** to the **suspect** any:
    - Significant **statement;**
    - Significant **silence;**
- That **occurred** in the presence or **hearing** of:
    - A **police officer;** or
    - Other **police staff;**
- **Before** the start of the **interview;** and
- Have **not** been **put** to the **suspect** in the course of the **previous interview.**
- The **interviewing officer** will ask the **suspect:**
    - To **confirm** or **deny** their statement or silence; and
    - **Add** anything they wish.

(i) - Definition Of A Significant Statement – Code C Paragraph 11.4A

- A **statement** will be **significant** if it will be **capable** of being **used in evidence** against the suspect.

(ii) - Definition Of A Significant Silence – Code C Paragraph 11.4A

- A **significant silence** will arise when a suspect under **caution fails to answer a question** that may give rise to an **adverse inference** at trial.

W - Breaks During Interviews - Code C Paragraph 12.8 & Note 12B

- Breaks of **45 minutes** shall be provided at **recognised meal times.**
- **Short breaks** of **15 minutes** for refreshments shall be provided at **2 hour intervals.**
- The **Interviewing Officer** may exercise their **discretion** to **delay** the break if they have **reasonable grounds** to **believe** that taking the break at that point would involve:
    - A risk of harm to people;
    - Serious loss of, or damage to property;
    - An unnecessary delay to the suspects release; or
    - Otherwise prejudice the outcome of the investigation.

X - Recording Breaks During Interviews - Code C, Paragraph 12.12

- Any **decision to delay a break** during an interview must be **recorded,** with **grounds,** in the interview record either:
    - On the **written record;** or
    - On **tape.**
- It would be a good idea to note the delay in the **custody record** as well, as it is more accessible than the tape for all practical purposes.

Y - Tapes Running Out - Code E Paragraph 4.11

- If the **tape runs out** the interviewer shall:
    - **Tell the suspect** the tape is coming to an end;
    - **Round up** the point discussed;
    - **Remove the full tapes** from the recorder;
    - **Unwrap** the new tapes in the **suspects presence;**
    - **Number all tapes;**
    - **Place the new tapes in the recorder** and **press record;**
    - **Continue** to question.

Z - When Must An Interview Be Concluded - Code C Paragraph 11.6

- An **interview must cease** when the **Investigating Officer** considers that:
    - **All relevant questions** have been **posed;**
    - The suspect has been given the **opportunity to provide an innocent explanation;**
    - Any **explanation provided** has been **tested** to ascertain its reliability;
    - There is **sufficient evidence** to provide a **realistic prospect of a conviction.**

AA - Action To Be taken At The Conclusion Of The Interview

- The **suspect** must be offered the **opportunity to:**
    - **Clarify** anything they have said;
    - **Add** anything they wish. (Code E Paragraph 4.17)
- The **Interviewing Officer** must:
    - **Turn off** the tape and **seal it** with the master tape label; (Code E Paragraph 4.18)
    - **Sign** the label themselves and ask **all others present to sign.**
        - If the **suspect** or a **third party refuses to sign:**
            - An **Inspector;** or
            - If the **Inspector** is **unavailable** – a **Custody Officer;**
        - Must **sign** the tape. (Code E Paragraph 4.19)

- Hand the suspect a **notice** explaining how:
    - The tape will be **used**; and
    - To **gain access** to the tape. (Code E Paragraph 4.19)
- Make a **personal pocket book entry** of the interview outlining:
    - That the interview has **taken place**;
    - That it was **tape recorded**;
    - The **date** and **time** it took place;
    - The **master tape identification number**. (Code E Paragraph 5.1)
- Follow **force standing orders** in relation to **tape security**. (Code E Paragraphs 6.1 & 5.2)

BB - Failing Recording Equipment - Code E Paragraph 4.15

- If the **recording equipment fails** either:
    - **Rectify** the fault as soon as possible;
    - Look for an **alternative recorder**;
    - Look for an **alternative interview room**;
    - If none are available - seek the **authority** of the **Custody Officer** to continue without the interview being tape recorded.

CC - Tape Breaks - Code E Note 4H

- If the **tape breaks**:
    - The **broken tape should be sealed** as the master copy in the suspects presence;
    - The interview should be **resumed where it left off**;
    - The **unbroken tape should be copied**; and
    - The **original unbroken tape** should be **sealed** in the **suspect's presence**.

DD - Excluding Legal Representatives From An Interview

1 - The Role of Legal Representatives - Code C Note 6D

- The **solicitor's** only **role** is to **protect and advance the legal rights of their client.**
- The solicitor **may intervene** to:
    - Seek **clarification**;
    - Challenge **improper questions** to their client;
    - Challenge an **improper manner** towards their client;
    - **Advise the client not to answer** particular questions;
    - **Request a break** to be provided for **further legal advice**.

2 – Grounds For Excluding A Legal Representative From An Interview - Code C Paragraph 6.9

- A **solicitor** may only be **excluded** from an interview where their **unreasonable conduct** is such that either:
    - [ ] The interviewing officer is **unable properly to put questions to the suspect;** or
    - [ ] **The responses to questions cannot be recorded properly.**
- Examples of **unreasonable conduct** include:
    - [ ] **Answering questions on a suspects behalf;** or
    - [ ] **Providing written answers for the suspect to read.**

3 - Action To Be Taken If A Legal Representative Is Being Unreasonably Obstructive - Code C Paragraph 6.10 & Code C Note 6E

- If the **interviewer** considers the solicitor is acting in an **unreasonable manner** they must:
    - [ ] **Stop** the interview;
    - [ ] **Consult** a **Superintendent;** or
    - [ ] If a **Superintendent is unavailable** they must consult:
        - An **Inspector;**
        - Who is **unconnected** with the investigation.
- After speaking to the solicitor the **officer consulted must decide** whether the interview should continue in the presence of the solicitor.
- The officer making the decision must be in a position to satisfy the court that the decision was **properly made**.
- In order to do so they *may* need to **observe** what is happening **(discretion)**.
- If they **decide to exclude** the solicitor:
    - [ ] The **suspect** must be given the **opportunity to consult another solicitor;**
    - [ ] That solicitor should be allowed to be present at the interview;
    - [ ] The **interview cannot proceed until any further solicitor requested is in attendance.**

Evidence & Procedure
Unit 14: Police Station Procedure (12) Bail

Introduction – New Developments

Schedule 6 Part 2 Police and Justice Act 2006 has recently introduced some **minor amendments** in relation to the ability to attach **conditions** to bail.

- In essence, whereas in the **past** it was only possible to attach bail conditions from **police custody** where either:

    - There was **sufficient evidence to charge** and the **file has been sent to the CPS for a charging decision**; or

    - **Post charge.**

- **Now,** in **addition** to the aforementioned powers, it is possible to attach bail conditions either:

    - When issuing **street bail;** or

    - From **police custody pre charge** where either:

        - There is **insufficient evidence to charge** and **further enquiries are necessary;** or

        - **There is sufficient evidence to charge.**

- If conditions are attached under the **new powers,** the **full range of conditions** may be imposed **except** for:

    - Sureties;
    - Securities;
    - Residence at a bail hostel.

A - Police Bail

- There are **2 varieties** of police bail:

    - **Street Bail** (CJA 2003);

    - **Bail from Custody** (PACE 1984):

        - Prior to charge; or

        - Following charge.

B - Street Bail – Section 30A – D PACE 1984

- Section 4 CJA 2003 amended the old section 30 PACE 1984.

- **Formerly** the arresting officer **had to take the person arrested to the police station as soon as was reasonably practicable.**

- **Now** the new s30A-D PACE 1984 provides the *discretionary* opportunity for the **arresting officer** to grant **street bail.**

Revision Tip

- When dealing with questions on street bail focus on the **key words** of:
    - *May;*
    - *Must;*
    - *Any;* and
    - *Cannot.*

1 - Issuing Street Bail – Section 30A PACE 1984

- The **arresting officer:**
    - *May* (discretionary power);
    - Following an **arrest**;
    - For *any* **offence**;
    - At *any* time prior to the suspects arrival at the police station;
    - **Release** the suspect on **street bail**;
    - To **attend** *any* **police station** specified at a **later date.**

2 - When Is It Appropriate To Grant Street Bail? – Section 30A PACE 1984

- Street bail can be issued for *any* **offence**.
- It is *not* generally **appropriate** for use in **indictable offences.**
- The officer *must* be satisfied that the suspects **name** and **address** are **correct**.
- The officer should also consider the following:
    - The **nature** and **severity** of the offence;
    - The need to **preserve vital evidence;**
    - The persons **fitness** to be released back onto the street;
    - The persons **ability to understand** what is happening;
    - The likelihood of the suspect being able to **continue to commit the offence or other offences** if they were released.

3 - Which Police Station Must The Person Arrested Be Street Bailed Back To? – Section 30A(5) PACE 1984

- The police station which the person is required to attend may be *any* police station.

Exam Trip Up

- The police station **need** *not* be:
    - The **arresting officer's station;**
    - A **station within the force** in which the suspect was arrested.

4 - Attaching Conditions To Street Bail - Schedule 6 Part 2 Police and Justice Act 2006 inserting a new Section 30A(3)(A)&(B) Bail Act 1976

- **Now** an officer granting street bail *may* impose **conditions**.

5 – Mandatory Obligation To Provide A Written Notice And Verbal Explanation To The Suspect On Issuing Street Bail – Section 30B PACE 1984

- The **officer** *must* issue at the time of granting street bail:
    - ☐ A **written notice** to the suspect; and
    - ☐ A **verbal explanation** of the procedure.

(i) – Mandatory Contents Of The Notice – Section 30B(2) & (3) PACE 1984

- The notice *must* always **specify**:
    - ☐ The **nature** of the offence;
    - ☐ The **grounds** for the arrest; and
    - ☐ That they will be **required to attend** *a* police station.

Additional Mandatory Contents Of The Notice When Conditions Are Attached To Street Bail - Schedule 6 Part 2 Police and Justice Act 2006 inserting a new Section 30B(4A)

- If **conditions** are **attached** to the street bail, the **street bail notice** *must* (in addition to pre existing requirements specified in your textbook which continue to apply) also:
    - ☐ **Specify** the **conditions** imposed;
    - ☐ Explain the **opportunities to seek variation** of those conditions; and
    - ☐ If the street bail notice does **not specify** the **police station** at which the person is **required to attend** – the street bail notice *must* specify a **police station** at which the person may make a **request for variation** of the bail conditions.

(ii) – Discretionary Contents Of The Notice – Section 30B(4) PACE 1984

- The notice *may* also **specify**:
    - ☐ The **police station** the suspect is **required to attend**;
    - ☐ The **date** and **time** they are **required to attend**.
- If the **notice does not specify the last 2 points** at the time of issuing – then a **subsequent written notice** must be issued detailing these points.

6 - Variations Of Street Bail – Section 30B(7) & 30C(1) PACE 1984

- A **notice in writing** *must* be sent to the suspect if:
    - ☐ The officer wishes to **vary** the attendance at the station in terms of the:
        - **Date**;
        - **Time**;
        - **Location**; or
    - ☐ The suspect is **no longer required** to attend the station.

Exam Trip Up - Can The Terms Of The Street Bail Be Varied By Written Notice On More Than One Occasion? Section 30B(7) PACE 1984

- *Yes* – any number of written notices may be served varying the terms of the street bail.

7 - Applications To Vary Street Bail Conditions - Schedule 6 Police & Justice Act 2006 inserting a new Section 30CA(1) Bail Act 1976

- The person to whom an application to **vary street bail conditions** may be made **depends on the contents of the street bail notice.**

  - Where the **street bail notice specifies** the **police station** the person is required to **attend** - the **application to vary conditions** will be made to a **Relevant Officer** at the **police station** at which the person is **required to attend.**

  - Where the **street bail notice** does **not specify** the police station the person is **required to attend** - the **application to vary conditions** will be made to a **Relevant Officer** at the **police station specified** in the **street bail notice** to which the person may make a **request for variation of the bail conditions.**

Options Available To The Relevant Officer - Section 30CA(4) Bail Act 1976

- The **Relevant Officer** can either make the conditions:

  - **More** onerous;
  - **Less** onerous;
  - **Leave** them the **same.**

Action To Be Taken By The Relevant Officer Following A Variation - Section 30CA(3) Bail Act 1976

- The **Relevant Officer** who **varies the conditions must** give the person subject to the street bail a **notice in writing** of the **variation.**

8 – Power of Arrest For Non Attendance At The Return Date – Section 30D PACE 1984

Power 1

- A **constable** may **arrest without a warrant** a suspect subject to **street bail** if they have:

  - **Failed** to attend the specified police station;
  - At the **date** and **time** indicated in their notice.

Exam Trip Up

- Note that this is a **reactive power.**

- The power of arrest without warrant will **not arise until** the person subject to street bail has:

  - **Failed** to attend the specified police station;
  - At the **date** and **time** indicated in their notice.

- Note how this contrasts with the **pre-emptive powers** of arrest without warrant in relation to breaches of **court bail** (see later).

Exam Trip Up

- Note that there is **no scope for conjecture** by the arresting officer.

- The legislation makes **no mention** of either:

    ☐ *Suspecting;* or

    ☐ *Believing;*

    - That the person has *failed* to answer their street bail.

- The arresting officer must *know* that they have *failed* to **attend** at the **date**, **time** and **location** specified in their street bail.

Power 2 (New Power For Breach Of Conditions)

- A **constable** may **arrest without a warrant** a suspect subject to **street bail** if they have reasonable grounds for *suspecting* that the person has **broken** any of the street bail **conditions**.

9 - Which Police Station May The Person Arrested Without Warrant Be Taken To? – Section 30D(2) Bail Act 1976

- The person **arrested without warrant** for failure to attend street bail can be taken to *any* police station.

- They **need not be taken to**:

    ☐ **The police station specified in the notice** when street bail was issued; or

    ☐ **The police station of the arresting officer**.

C - Bailing The Suspect Prior To Charge – Section 37(1A) PACE 1984

- **Prior to charge** it is possible for the **Custody Officer** to bail a suspect where either:

    ☐ There is **insufficient evidence to charge** and **further enquiries are necessary**;

    ☐ When there is sufficient evidence to charge and the file has been sent to the DPP for determination of whether to charge.

D - Bailing The Suspect After Charge – Section 38(1) PACE 1984

1 – Options Available To The Custody Officer Following Charge

- **Following charge** the **Custody Officer** must decide whether to:

    ☐ **Refuse bail** and keep the person in custody until they can be brought before the Magistrates Court; or

    ☐ **Release the person on bail** pending their first appearance before the Magistrates Court on a specified date and time either:

    - **Unconditionally**; or

    - **Subject to bail conditions**.

2 - Listening to Representations Prior To Exercising A Decision In Respect Of Bail - Code C, Paragraphs 15.1-15.7 PACE 1984

- **Prior to making a decision** in respect of whether to grant bail;
- The **Custody Officer** must consider any **representations** made by any one or more of the following individuals:
    - The **detainee**;
    - Any available **legal representative**;
    - Any available **appropriate adult** (if applicable).

E - Bail From Police Custody

Summary Table

Starting Point	Displacing The Presumption In Favour Of Bail	Attaching Conditions To Negate The Risk Of The Section 38 Consequence Arising
General Rule **Presumption** that bail will be granted.	**Custody Officer** has *reasonable grounds* to *believe* that a **section 38 consequence** will arise.	**Bail Before Charge** - Insufficient evidence to charge – **can** attach conditions. - Sufficient evidence to charge – **can** attach conditions. - Sufficient evidence to charge & file sent to the CPS – **can** attach conditions. **Bail After Charge** - **Can** attach conditions.
Exception **Presumption** that bail will be **refused** – Section 25 CJPOA 1994.		

1 - Presumption in Favour of Bail – Section 38 PACE 1984

- There is a **presumption in favour of granting bail**.
- As a **general rule:**
    - The defendant **must be released on unconditional bail**;
    - **Unless;**
    - The **Custody Officer** has **reasonable grounds** to *believe*;
    - That if they were released one of a number of undesirable **consequences** would arise.
- Exception – Where the provisions of **section 25 CJPOA 1994** apply.

2 - Displacing The Presumption In Favour Of Police Bail

- The **grounds displacing the presumption in favour of police bail** differ for:
    - **Imprisonable offences**; and
    - **Non – imprisonable offences**.

(i) - Grounds For Refusing Police Bail: Imprisonable Offences – Section 38(1) PACE 1984

- The **presumption in favour of bail will be displaced** where the **Custody Officer** has **reasonable grounds** to **believe** that either:

    - The defendant would:
        - Fail to appear (abscond);
        - Interfere with the administration of justice;
        - Commit further offences;

    - The defendant's **name** and **address** cannot be ascertained;

    - Detention would be necessary for the defendants **own protection**; (e.g. paedophile with an angry mob outside);

    - For **juveniles** only – Detention would be necessary for their **own welfare**.

Factors To Consider

- In determining the likelihood of the defendant **absconding; interfering with witnesses; or committing further offences** the **Custody Officer** must consider:

    - The **nature and seriousness** of the offence;

    - The **strength of the evidence**;

    - The accused:
        - Character (previous convictions);
        - Antecedents; (education, employment, background, etc)
        - Associations;
        - Community ties;

        - Previous record whilst on bail:
            - Absconded in the past?
            - Interfered with witnesses in the past?
            - Committed offences in the past - (need <u>not</u> be same offence as charged with)?

(ii) - Grounds For Refusing Police Bail: Non - Imprisonable Offences – Section 38 PACE 1984

- The **Custody Officer** must have **reasonable grounds** to **believe** that either:

    - The defendant would be **likely to cause injury** to another;

    - The defendant's **name and address** cannot be ascertained;

    - Detention would be necessary to **prevent loss or damage to property**;

    - For **juveniles** only – Detention would be necessary for their **own welfare**.

3 - Attaching Bail Conditions – Section s3A(5) Bail Act 1976

- If the prima facie **presumption in favour of bail has been displaced**:
    - [ ] **Bail must be refused**;
    - [ ] **Unless**;
    - [ ] **Conditions** can be imposed by the **Custody Officer**;
    - [ ] To **reduce the likelihood of the relevant section 38 consequence from arising**;
    - [ ] Where either:
        - There is **insufficient evidence to charge** and **further enquiries are necessary** (new);
        - There is **sufficient evidence to charge** (new);
        - As well as **the pre existing** powers to attach conditions where either:
            - [ ] There is **sufficient evidence to charge** and the **file has been sent to the CPS for a charging decision** (pre – existing); or
            - [ ] **Post charge** (pre – existing).

4 - The Function Of Conditions

- **Conditions cannot** be attached **indiscriminately.**
- They must be:
    - [ ] **Tailored**;
    - [ ] To **negate the risk** of the **section 38 consequence**;
    - [ ] That **displaced the presumption in favour of bail**;
    - [ ] From **arising** if the suspect is released on bail.

5 - The Range of Conditions – Sections 3A(5)(a)-(c) Bail Act 1976

- Appropriate **conditions** for each consequence include:

Absconding

- [ ] Residency at a specified address – (NB – Cannot impose residence at a bail hostel or a probation hostel);
- [ ] Notification of changes of address;
- [ ] Reporting to the police station periodically;
- [ ] Surety or Security;
- [ ] Surrendering passport.

Committing Further Offences / Interfering With Witnesses

- [ ] Curfew;
- [ ] Exclusion from specified buildings or addresses;
- [ ] Preventing the defendant from contacting specified persons.

6 - Exam Trip Up – Considerations By A Custody Officer When Determining Whether To Attach Or Vary Bail Conditions

- The case of *R v Mansfield Justices – Ex Parte Sharkey* [1985] QB 613 stablished that in determining whether to impose or vary conditions there must be a **"real and not fanciful risk"** of a specified section 38 consequence arising.

7 - Sureties

(i) - Function Of A Surety – Section 3(4) Bail Act 1976

- A **surety's function** is to ensure a **suspect surrenders to custody** at the specified:
    - **Date;**
    - **Time;** and
    - **Location.**

(ii) - Suitability Of Sureties – Section 8 Bail Act 1976

- A **Custody Officer** will consider the following factors in determining whether a **potential surety is suitable**:
    - Their **financial resources;**
    - Their **character;**
    - Their **previous convictions;** and
    - The **relationship** to the accused.

(iii) - Can More Than On Person Act As A Surety?

- Yes – **one or more** individuals can act s a surety.

8 - What Is A Security?

- A **security** may be:
    - A sum of **money;** or
    - A **valuable item;**
- Which is given by:
    - The **defendant;** or
    - **Another person** on the **defendant's behalf;**
- Which will be **forfeited** if the defendant **fails to answer their bail** without a reasonable cause.

Exam Trip Up

- **Foreign currency** would form an **acceptable** security as it is money and it has a **value.**
- However a **debit card** or **credit card** will **not** be an **acceptable** security as it has **no tangible value.**

9 - Forfeiture Of Recognisance By Sureties Or Sureties

(i) - The General Rule

- If an accused fails without a reasonable cause to **answer their bail at the date, time and location specified** in their bail – **i.e. abscond;**

- The surety or security will be required to **forfeit their entire recognisance.**

- The case of *R v Warwick Crown Court – Ex Parte Smailey* [1987] 1 WLR 237 established that this will be the case even if the surety or security **had no involvement in the reasons for their non attendance.**

(ii) - The Exception To The General Rule

- The case of *R v Stipendiary Magistrate for Leicester ex parte Kaur* [2000] 164 JP 127 established that a surety or security will **not forfeit** their recognisance in the event of a breach of bail if they **took *all reasonable steps*** to secure the defendant's attendance.

What Will Amount To Reasonable Steps? - Section 7(3)(c) Bail Act 1976

- *Reasonable steps* will include:
    - The **surety** or **security;**
    - **Notifying** a **constable;**
    - *In writing;*
    - That:
        - The accused is **unlikely to surrender to custody; and**
        - For that reason the **surety wishes to be relieved of their obligations.**

Exam Trip Up

- Watch out for questions involving **oral notification** – this will **not suffice.**

Exam Trip Up

- Note that the **surety** or **security** relates only to **securing the accused attendance at:**
    - **A police station;** or
    - **Court.**
    - i.e. to **prevent** the accused from **absconding.**

- The surety or security will **not have any responsibility** and will therefore **not forfeit their recognisance** if the accused whilst on bail either:
    - **Commits further offences;** or
    - **Interferes with the administration of justice.**

Exam Tip Up - Is It Necessary To Inform A Third Party Who Has Provided A Security That Their Security Has Been Forfeited?

- The case of *R v Stevens v Truro Magistrates Court* [2002] 1 WLR 144, established that it will **not be necessary** to **inform a third party** who has put up a security that it has been **forfeited** in the event of a defendant failing to answer their bail without reasonable cause.

10 - Varying Bail Conditions – Section 5A(2) Bail Act 1976

(i) – To Whom Must The Application To Vary Conditions Be Lodged?

- An accused may make an application to either:
    - ☐ The **Custody Officer who imposed the conditions**; or
    - ☐ **Another Custody Officer serving at the <u>same</u> police station**;
- To have their bail conditions either:
    - ☐ **Varied**; or
    - ☐ **Removed**.
- The application should be considered upon its **merits** based upon the **facts available at the time.**

(ii) - The Options Available To The Custody Officer

- The **Custody Officer** can either make the conditions:
    - ☐ **More onerous**;
    - ☐ **Less onerous**;
    - ☐ **Leave them the same.**

(iii) - Recording Decisions In Relation To Applications To Vary Bail Conditions – Section 5A(4) Bail Act 1976

- The **Custody Officer** must:
    - ☐ Make a **note** of the **reasons for their decision** in the custody record, outlining details of any relevant **risk involved - The risk must be "real"** – *R v Mansfield Justices, ex parte Sharky* [1985] QB 613.
    - ☐ Provide the defendant with a **copy of the note.**

11 - The Reversal Of The Presumption In Favour Of Bail – Section 25 CJPOA 1994

- Bail <u>must</u> be refused (**presumption of refusal**) to a defendant who has been **charged** with either:
    - ☐ **Murder**;
    - ☐ **Attempted murder**;
    - ☐ **Manslaughter**;
    - ☐ **Rape or attempted rape**;
    - ☐ **Assault by penetration**;
    - ☐ **Causing a person to engage in sexual activity without their consent by penetration**;
    - ☐ **Rape of a child under 13**;
    - ☐ **Assault of a child under 13 by penetration**;
    - ☐ **Causing or inciting a child under 13 to engage in sexual activity by penetration**;
    - ☐ **Sexual activity with a person with a mental disorder by penetration**;
    - ☐ **Attempts to commit any of the above offences**;
- If they already have **any prior conviction** for **any** such offence;
- **Unless**;
- The circumstances are **exceptional**.

Memory Aid

- The section 25 list of offences include:

    - ☐ **Homicide** offences   -   **H**

    - ☐ **Penetration** offences   -   **P**

- Just think of a **bottle of "HP sauce"**.

Study Tip

- If a bail question scenario mentions:

    - ☐ The **offence** for which the accused has been **charged**; and

    - ☐ Their **previous conviction**;

- **Alarm bells** should be going off in your head.

- You will need to consider the criteria of **Section 25 CJPOA 1994** to determine whether:

    - ☐ The **offence** for which they have been **charged** and are **seeking bail**; and

    - ☐ Their **previous conviction**;

    - ☐ Are *both* "HP offences".

- It is **not necessary** for **both offences** to be the **same**.

- Provided they are **both "HP offences"**:

    - ☐ The **presumption** in favour of bail will be **reversed**; and

    - ☐ Bail **must** be **refused**;

    - ☐ Unless;

    - ☐ There are **exceptional circumstances**.

Exam Trip Up - Additional Check In Relation To Previous Convictions For Manslaughter Or Culpable Homicide – Section 25(3) CJPOA 1994

- If the **previous conviction** relates to the offence of either:

    - ☐ **Manslaughter**; or

    - ☐ **Culpable homicide**;

- Then double alarm bells should be going off in your head.

- You must carry out an additional step and **check the sentence** the person received for that offence.

- If they received a **custodial penalty** then the **section 25 CJPOA 1994 reversal** of the presumption in favour of bail *applies.*

- If they received a **non custodial penalty** then:
    - The **section 25 CJPOA 1994 reversal** of the presumption in favour of bail will *not* apply;
    - The **presumption in favour of bail** will **remain**; and
    - **Bail** may only be **refused** where:
        - A **section 38 ground** is made out;
        - Which **displaces** the **presumption in favour of bail**.

F - Reviewing The Detention Of Adults Refused Police Bail – Section 40 PACE 1984

- The **Custody Officer** must:
    - Continue to comply with the **Codes of Practice** whilst the defendant is detained pending their appearance in the Magistrates Court.
    - **Review** the detention within **9 hours** of the **last decision to refuse bail**.
- Note that the **refusal of bail upon charge** by the Custody Officer **doubles up as a review** – hence subsequent reviews post charge must take place within 9 hours thereafter.

G - Juveniles Refused Police Bail – Section 38(6) PACE 1984

1 - The General Rule

- The **Custody Officer** must try to make arrangements for the **juvenile** to be taken into the **care of the local authority** pending their appearance in the Magistrates Court.

2 - Exception To The General Rule

- Where it is **impracticable to do so**; or
- Only in relation to those **aged 12 and over**:
    - Where there is **no *secure* accommodation available**; and
    - There is a **risk of *serious* harm to the public** from the juvenile if they were placed in unsecured local authority accommodation.

Revision Tip

- When answering a question on this point firstly **check the age** of the child.
- If the are **under 12** then via a process of elimination there is only one word to look for – *impractability.*
- If they are **12 or over** – the **second ground** can **also be considered**.

H - Appointment At The Magistrates Court For Those Refused Bail – Section 46 PACE 1984

- The defendant must be brought before the court at the **next available sitting**.
- It is for the **Clerk of the Court** to decide when the next available sitting will take place.

- If **no court is sitting the day after charging**:
    - ☐ The **Custody Officer** must **inform** the **Clerk of the Court**;
    - ☐ **Unless** the next day is:
        - A Sunday;
        - Christmas Day; or
        - Good Friday.

I - Appointment At The Magistrates Court For Those Granted Bail – Section 47 PACE 1984

- The **Custody Officer** must specify the **date** the defendant must appear before the Magistrates.
- This date must be:
    - ☐ **No later** than the **first sitting** of the court after the person is charged; or
    - ☐ Any other **later date specified by the designated officer** of the relevant local justice area.

J - Court Bail

Summary Table

Starting Point	Displacing The Presumption In Favour Of Bail	Attaching Conditions To Negate The Risk Of The Part 1 Schedule 1 Bail Act 1976 Consequence Arising
General Rule Presumption that bail will be **granted**. --- **Exception** Presumption that bail will be **refused** under: - Section 25 CJPOA 1994; - Section 2A Pt 1 Schedule 1 Bail Act 1976; - Section 6 A – C Pt 1 Schedule 1 Bail Act 1976.	**Magistrates** have *substantial* grounds to believe that a **Part 1 Schedule 1 Bail Act 1976 consequence** will arise.	- **Can** attach all conditions.

1 - The Presumption In Favour Of Granting Court Bail – Section 4(1) Bail Act 1976

- **Section 4(1) Bail Act 1976** provides a **presumption in favour of granting bail** from court where the person appears before the court in relation to:
    - Proceedings for an **offence**;
    - **Adjournments** for **pre sentence reports**;
    - **Alleged breaches** of a **requirement** in relation to a:
        - **Community rehabilitation order**;
        - **Community punishment order**;
        - **Combined** community rehabilitation and community punishment **order**; or
        - **Curfew order**.

2 - Displacing The Presumption In Favour Of Court Bail

- The **grounds displacing the presumption in favour of court bail** differ for:
    - **Imprisonable offences**; and
    - **Non – imprisonable offences**.
- The **grounds are similar** to those in respect of **police bail**.
- Remember whilst:
    - The **Custody Officer** must have *reasonable* **grounds** to **believe** a consequence will arise;
    - The **court** must have *substantial* **grounds** to **believe** a consequence will arise.

(i) - Displacing The Presumption In Favour Of Court Bail For Imprisonable Offences– Schedule 1 Part 1 Bail Act 1976

- The **presumption in favour of bail** will be **displaced** and **bail** will be **refused** where either:

Paragraph 2

- The court has *substantial* **grounds to believe** that **if** the defendant were **released** on bail they would either:
    - **Fail to surrender to custody (abscond)**;
    - **Commit an offence whilst on bail**; or
    - **Interfere with witnesses or otherwise obstruct the course of justice**.

Paragraph 3

- The defendant should be kept in custody for their **own protection**;
- **Juveniles -** should be kept in custody only for their **own welfare**.

Paragraph 4

- The defendant is **already serving a custodial sentence**.

Paragraph 5

- The court has had **insufficient time to obtain adequate information** upon which to make a bail decision.

Paragraph 6

- The defendant has **already absconded whilst on bail for the current offence**.

The Paragraph 9 Factors Which Assist The Court In Substantiating A Paragraph 2 Ground

- In determining the likelihood of the defendant **absconding; interfering with witnesses; or committing further offences** the **Court** must consider:
    - The **nature and seriousness** of the offence and **probable method of dealing with the offender;**
    - The **strength of the evidence**;
    - The accused's:
        - **Character (previous convictions);**
        - **Antecedents; (education, employment, background, etc)**
        - **Associations;**
        - **Community ties;**
        - **Previous record whilst on bail:**
            - Absconded in the past?
            - Interfered with witnesses in the past?
            - Committed offences in the past (need <u>not</u> be same offence as charged with)?

(ii) - Displacing The Presumption In Favour Of Court Bail For Non Imprisonable Offences – Schedule 1 Part 1 Bail Act 1976

- The **presumption in favour of bail** will be **displaced** where either:
    - The court **believes** that in the light of a **previous failure to surrender** to custody, the defendant will **again fail to surrender** to custody if released on bail;
    - The court is **satisfied** that the defendant should be kept in custody for their **own protection;**
    - The court is **satisfied** that a **juvenile** defendant should be kept in custody for their **own welfare;**
    - The defendant is **already serving a custodial sentence**.

3 - Situations In Which The Presumption In Favour Of Court Bail Does Not Apply

- The **presumption in favour of bail does not apply** to persons **convicted** who are either:
    - Seeking bail pending an **appeal**; or
    - Have been **committed to the Crown Court for sentencing (unless the matter has been adjourned for pre sentence reports)**.
- Bail can still be granted in such circumstances but it is at the *discretion* of the court.

4 - The Reversal Of The Presumption In Favour Of Bail

- The **presumption in favour of granting bail** will be **reversed** to a **presumption in favour of refusing bail** where:
    - *Section 25 CJPOA 1994* applies (as discussed earlier);
    - *Paragraph 2A Schedule 1 Part 1 Bail Act 1976* applies; or
    - *Paragraph 6A - C Schedule 1 Part 1 Bail Act 1976* applies.

(i) - Paragraph 2A Schedule 1 Part 1 Bail Act 1976

- The court *must* **refuse bail (presumption** in favour of **refusing bail)** where the defendant is:
    - An **adult (18 or over)**;
    - Who at the time of committing an indictable offence;
    - Is **already on bail for a prior offence**;
    - **Unless**;
    - The **defendant can satisfy** the court **(burden rests on the defendant)**;
    - There is **no** *significant* **risk** of them **committing further offences if they are released on bail**.

(ii) - Paragraphs 6A – C Schedule 1 Part 1 Bail Act 1976

- The court *must* **refuse bail (presumption** in favour of **refusing bail)** where the defendant is:
    - A **drug user**;
    - Aged **18 or over**; and
    - A **class A drug** is present **in their body**; and
    - They are either:
        - **Charged** with an **offence** which **relates to a class A drug**; or
        - The **misuse of a class A drug caused** or **contributed** to the **commission of the offence** for which they are charged; and
    - They **refuse to undergo assessment** as to their dependence or propensity to use a class A drug;
    - **Unless**;
    - The court is satisfied that there is **no** *significant* **risk of them committing an offence whilst on bail**.

K - The Offence of Absconding

1 – The Definition Of Absconding – Section 6(1) Bail Act 1976

- It is an **offence** for any person;
- Released on bail;
- To **fail to surrender** to custody;
- **Without reasonable cause**.

2 - The Burden Of Showing A Reasonable Cause – Section 6(3) Bail Act 1976

- The **burden** of showing a **reasonable cause** rests upon the **defendant** which they must discharge on the **balance of probability.**
- A **failure to provide** a defendant with a **copy** of the record of the **decision to grant bail** is **not a reasonable cause** for the defendant's failure to surrender to custody. (Section 6(4) Bail Act 1976)

3 - Surrendering To Custody Following A Reasonable Cause – Section 6(2) Bail Act 1976

- Even if the defendant **has a reasonable cause** for failing to surrender at the appointed time;
- They **must still surrender as soon as is practicable** after the appointed time.
- **Failure** to do so will be an **offence.**

An Example Of The Reasonable Cause Exception In Operation

- John is due to attend Southville Magistrates Court in 1 hour's time.
- He travels to the court via a motorway. Before he reaches his exit there is a 20 car pile up in front of him. He is stuck in a traffic jam for 4 hours until the accident is cleared and the motorway reopens.
- If he surrendered to the court as soon as was reasonably practicable after the road was cleared he would not commit the offence of absconding as:
    - He had a **reasonable cause** for failing to attend at the allocated time – the pile up; and
    - He **surrendered as soon as was reasonably practicable** thereafter.
- If however, after the road was cleared he went to the pub for the rest of the day he would commit an offence of absconding as whilst he did initially have a reasonable cause to fail to surrender, he **did not surrender as soon as was reasonably practicable after the reasonable cause ceased to exist.**

Exam Trip Up

- Remember the **section 6 Bail Act 1976** offence relates specifically to **absconding.**
- **No section 6 Bail Act 1976 offence** will be committed if a person merely **breaches** the terms of their bail **conditions.**
- Although a **breach of bail conditions** will give rise to a **power of arrest without a warrant.**

L – Power Of Arrest Without Warrant Of Those Breaching Bail

- There are **differing provisions** which provide a **power of arrest without warrant:**
    - Breaches of **police bail** – Section 46A PACE 1984.
    - Breaches of **court bail** - Section 7 Bail Act 1976

1 - Breaches Of Police Bail – Reactive Powers - Section 46(A) PACE 1984

- A **constable** may **arrest without a warrant** where either:

Power 1

- A person released on bail under a **duty to return to a police station** at a later date and time has *failed* to do so. (s46A(1)); or

Power 2

- A **constable** has **reasonable grounds** for *suspecting* that the person has *broken* any of their **bail conditions.** (s46A(1A)).

Exam Trip Up

- Note that these are **reactive powers.**

- The power of arrest without warrant will **not arise until** the person subject to police bail has:
    - *Failed* to attend the specified police station at the **date** and **time** indicated in their notice; or
    - Has *broken* their bail conditions.

- Note how this contrasts with the **pre-emptive powers** of arrest without warrant in relation to breaches of **court bail** (see later)**.**

Learning Point

- Note that in relation **Power 1** - the failure to answer the bail at the date, time and location specified there is **no scope for conjecture** by the arresting officer.

- The legislation makes **no mention** of either:
    - *Suspecting;* or
    - *Believing;*

    - That the person has *failed* to answer their police bail.

- The arresting officer must *know* that they have *failed* to attend at the **date, time** and **location** specified.

- Note how this contrasts to the mental element in relation to the breach of the bail condition – as the power is **reactive** in nature the constable will be permitted to arrest without warrant where they merely *suspect* that the person has *broken* the terms of their **bail conditions.**

2 - Breaches Of Court Bail – Reactive & Pre-emptive Powers - Section 7 Bail Act 1976

- A **constable** may **arrest without a warrant** if they either:

    Powers 1 & 2

    - Have **reasonable grounds** for *believing* that the defendant:
        - Is *not likely* to **surrender** to custody;
        - *Is likely* to break any of their **bail conditions**;

    Power 3

    - Have **reasonable grounds** to *suspect* that a person has *broken* any of their **bail conditions.**

    Power 4

    - Has been **notified by a surety in writing** that:
        - The person is *unlikely* to **surrender** to custody; and
        - For that reason the surety **wishes to be relieved** of their obligations.

Learning Point

- Note that the powers of arrest without warrant for breaches of court bail are wider and include not only *reactive* powers but also *pre-emptive* powers.

- Note that when a constable uses *pre-emptive* powers they need to be more sure of themselves and therefore the mental element shifts up to *belief.*

- Whereas when the constable uses *reactive* powers they need only *suspect.*

M - Warrant For Arrest Issued By The Court For A Failure To Surrender To Custody

- A **court may issue a warrant** for a defendants arrest when the defendant has *failed* to **surrender** to custody at the time appointed.

Exam Trip Up - Passport Surrender

- If a **condition** is attached to bail for a person to **surrender their passport**; and
- The person **fails to surrender** their passport; and
- Uses the passport to **travel abroad**; and
- The person **returns** and **answers their bail** at the date and time specified;
- Then the case of *R v Ashley 1 WLR 2057* established that the person:
    - Will **not** have committed the offence of **absconding**; and
    - Will **not** be in **contempt of court.**

- In such a situation, if an officer saw the person in the departure lounge of the airport they could merely **arrest them without warrant** on the basis that either they:
    - ☐ Reasonably *believed* that the person was *likely* to **abscond**; or
    - ☐ Reasonably *suspected* that the person had *broken* their bail condition by **failing to surrender their passport**.

N - Bringing A Person Arrested Without A Warrant Before A Magistrate – Section 7(4)(a) Bail Act 1976

- Where a person is arrested under section 7 Bail Act 1976 they must:
- Be **brought before** a **Magistrate** (**not just into the building** of the **Magistrates Court**):
    - ☐ **As soon as practicable**; and
    - ☐ In any event **within 24 hours** of being **arrested**.

Exam Trip Up

- **No account** is to be taken of **Sundays, Christmas Day,** or **Good Friday**.

Exam Trip Up

- The case of *R v Governor of Glen Prava Young Offenders Institution, ex parte G (a minor)* [1998] QB 887 established that:

    A detainee brought before a **Magistrate out of time cannot be remanded in custody** by the **Magistrate**.

O - Which Court Must The Person In Breach Be Brought Before Following An Arrest Without Warrant For A Breach Of Bail? – Section 7(4)(b) Bail Act 1976

(i) - The General Rule

- The person **may** be brought before **any** **Magistrates Court** (even if a **Crown Court** issued the terms of the bail).

(ii) - The Exception To The General Rule

- Where a person is **arrested within 24 hours** of the **time that they were due to surrender to court custody**;
- They must be **brought before the court at which they were due to surrender**.

Evidence & Procedure
Unit 15: Police Station Procedure (14) Cautions, Reprimands & Warnings

Alternatives To Charging Offenders

- There are differing alternatives to charging available depending on whether the offender is:

- Under 18   -   Reprimands
                -    Warnings
- 18 or over –   Simple Cautions

A - Simple Cautions

- The provisions in relation to the issuing of formal cautions are contained in the *Home Office Circular 30/2005: Cautioning Adult Offenders*.

1 - The Aims Of Cautioning – Paragraph 6

- The purpose of formal cautions are:
    - ☐ To deal with less serious offences **quickly** and **cheaply**;
    - ☐ To **divert offenders** from unnecessary court appearances; and
    - ☐ To **reduce** the probability of **re-offending**.

2 - Who Will Make The Decision Whether To Administer A Simple Caution? – Paragraph 32

(i) - The General Rule

- As a **general rule** – the **police** will **decide** whether to administer a simple caution.
- The CPS *may (discretion)* be **asked** for their **advice** on the suitability of issuing a simple caution **at any time**.

(ii) - The Exceptions To The General Rule

- There are **3 exceptional circumstances** where the **CPS** *alone* will make the **decision**:
    - ☐ **Indictable offences**;
    - ☐ **Domestic violence**; and
    - ☐ When reviewing a case where the police have **charged the suspect during the roll out of the statutory charging scheme**.

3 - Factors That Must Be Satisfied Before A Caution May Be Administered – Paragraph 7

- The following criteria *must* (no discretion) be satisfied before a simple caution will be administered:
    - There *must* be **sufficient evidence** of the suspect's guilt to **give a realistic prospect of a conviction** in accordance with the Threshold Test;
    - The suspect *must* make a **clear** and **reliable admission** of the offence either:
        - **Orally**; or
        - In **writing**;
    - It *must* be in the **public interest** to administer a simple caution;
    - The suspect *must* be **aged 18 or over** – If they are **under 18** a **reprimand** or **final warning** would be the equivalent disposal; and
    - The **seriousness** of the **offence** *must* be considered.

Recording The Admission – Paragraph 10

- The **admission** *may* be **recorded** via either:
    - A **tape recorded interview**;
    - An **entry** in an **officers notebook** that is **signed** by the **suspect** as an **accurate** record; or
    - An **entry** in the **custody record** that is **signed** by the **suspect** as an **accurate** record.

4 - Additional Mandatory Considerations – Previous Cautions, Reprimands or Warnings – Paragraph 17

(i) - The General Rule

- If the suspect has **previously received** a:
    - **Caution**;
    - **Reprimand**; or
    - **Final warning**;
- A **further simple caution** should *not* be considered.

(ii) - The Exceptions To The General Rule

- If the suspect has **previously received** a:
    - **Caution**,
    - **Reprimand**; or
    - **Final warning**;

- A **further caution** *can* still be administered where:
    - ☐ There has been a **lapse of 2 years or more** since the **last caution** suggesting that the previous caution had a **significant deterrent effect**; or
    - ☐ The **subsequent offence** is:
        - Trivial;
        - Unrelated; or
        - Part of a **mixed disposal**.

5 - Further Considerations Prior To Exercising The Decision To Administer A Simple Caution – Paragraphs 11 & 12

- If the aforementioned criteria are satisfied it is *desirable* (not mandatory) that the **victim** should be **consulted** before exercising the decision to administer a simple caution to determine:
    - ☐ Their **views** about the offence;
    - ☐ The **nature** and **extent** of any **harm** or **loss** that they have suffered;
    - ☐ The **significance** of their **loss** relative to their circumstances; and
    - ☐ Whether the **offender** has made any form of **reparation** or **compensation**.

- If it is **decided**:
    - ☐ Not to proceed with the prosecution; and
    - ☐ That the matter is instead suitable for a **simple caution**;

- The **victim** *may* be **asked** to:
    - ☐ **Affirm** their **support** for a **simple caution** as a suitable method of disposal;
    - ☐ Provide a **statement** confirming:
        - The **facts** of the case;
        - That they would *not* be prepared to **support** a **prosecution** through the courts;
        - That they would **support** the matter to be dealt with by a **simple caution**.

6 - The Victims Views Are Not Conclusive – Paragraph 15

- *If* (discretion) the **victims views are sought** - they *must* be **informed** that:
    - ☐ Their **views** will be **taken into account**;
    - ☐ But:
        - Their views are *not* **conclusive**; and
        - The **final decision** is left to:
            - ☐ The **police**; and / or
            - ☐ The **CPS**.

7 - Follow Up Information To Be Provided To The Victim – Paragraph 16

- The **victim** *must* be kept **informed** of the **outcome**.

8 - Explaining The Implications Of A Simple Caution To The Suspect – Paragraphs 18, 27 & 28

- The **full implications** of a **simple caution** *must* be **explained** to the suspect:
    - [ ] It is **not** a criminal **conviction**;
    - [ ] It **is** an **admission of guilt**;
    - [ ] It **will** form part of the suspects **criminal record**;
    - [ ] It may **affect** how they are **dealt with** in the event of **further offences**;
    - [ ] It can be **cited** in any future **criminal proceedings**;
    - [ ] If the simple caution relates to a **recordable offence** it will be placed on the **PNC**;
    - [ ] If the offence is a **sexual offence** they will be placed on the **sex offenders register**.

Exam Trip Up

- If the person is *not* **warned** of the **ramifications** of a **simple caution** being issued in relation to a **sexual offence** – the person may **later apply** for the **simple caution** to be **removed**.

9 - The Administration Of A Caution – Paragraph 26

- **Cautions** should be **administered** by:
    - [ ] A **police officer**;
    - [ ] Who has been **suitably trained**.
- Wherever *practical* the cautioning should be conducted at a **police station**.
- In **exceptional circumstances** they may be administered at **another suitable place**.
- The suspect should *not* **be pressed** to make a decision whether to accept a caution.
- They *may* take **independent advice** before exercising their decision.

10 - Procedural Steps To Be Followed Following The Administration Of A Simple Caution – Paragraph 26

- Once a simple **caution** has been **administered**:
    - [ ] The **offender** should **sign** a form accepting the terms of the caution explaining:
        - Their **personal details**;
        - The **consequences** of accepting a caution;
        - **Warning** that the offender's **details** can be **passed to** the **victim** should they wish to pursue civil remedies.
    - [ ] The **person administering** the caution should also **sign** the form.
    - [ ] A **copy** of the form *must* be **given** to the offender.

11 - Recording Obligations Following The Issuing Of A Caution – Paragraphs 30 & 31

- **Records** should be kept of formal **cautions** on the **PNC**.

B - Reprimands Of Young Offenders – Section 65(1)&(2) CDA 1998

1 - Factors That Must Be Satisfied Before A Reprimand May Be Administered

- A **constable** has the power to **reprimand** a **child** or **young person** where:
    - ☐ The constable has **evidence** that they committed an offence;
    - ☐ The constable considers that the **evidence would provide a realistic prospect of a conviction** if the matter were prosecuted;
    - ☐ The offender **admits** that they committed the offence;
    - ☐ The offender has **no previous convictions** for any offence;
    - ☐ The offender has **not previously** been **reprimanded** or **warned** for any offence.
    - ☐ The constable is satisfied that it would **not be in the public interest for the offender to be prosecuted.**

2 - Procedural Matters When Issuing A Reprimand – Section 65(5) CDA 1998

- Where the offender is *under* the age of **17**, the constable *must:*
    - ☐ **Issue the reprimand** in the **presence** of both the **offender** and their **appropriate adult**;
    - ☐ **Explain** to the **offender** and the **appropriate adult** in **ordinary language** that a **reprimand may be cited in subsequent criminal proceedings** in the same way as a conviction.

C - Warnings Of Young Offenders – Section 65(3) CDA 1998

1 - Factors That Must Be Satisfied Before A Warning May Be Administered

- A **constable** has the power to **warn** a **child** or **young person** where either:
    - ☐ The offender has **not been previously reprimanded**, but the constable considers the **offence to be so serious as to require a warning**;
    - ☐ The offender has been reprimanded but has **not previously been warned**; or
    - ☐ The offender **has previously been warned**, but:
        - The offence was committed **more than 2 years after the previous warning**; and
        - The constable considers the offence to be not **so serious as to require a charge to be brought.**

    (NB – The second provision can only be used once).

2 - Procedural Matters When Issuing A Warning – Section 65(5) CDA 1998

- Where the offender is *under* the age of **17**, the constable **must**:

    - **Issue the reprimand** in the **presence** of both the **offender** and their **appropriate adult**;

    - **Explain** to the **offender** and the **appropriate adult** in **ordinary language**:

        - That the **warning may be cited in criminal proceedings** in the same way as a conviction;

        - That they will be **referred ASAP** to a **Youth Offending Team**;

        - That the Youth Offending Team will require them to **participate in a rehabilitation programme unless they consider it inappropriate for them to do so**; and

        - If they are **subsequently convicted** of an offence **within 2 years of the warning** the court will be **prevented from imposing a conditional discharge unless the circumstances are exceptional**.

Evidence & Procedure
Unit 16: Evidence (1)
Facts In Issue, Sources Of Evidence, Presumptions & Burden Of Proof

A - Definition Of Facts In Issue

- **Facts in issue** include those facts which:
    - The **prosecution** must **prove** if it is to succeed in securing a **conviction** - i.e. **each element** of the:
        - **Actus reus**; and
        - **Mens rea**.
    - The **defence** must **prove** if it is to succeed in raising a **positive defence** (e.g. alibi, self defence).

B - Admissibility Of Evidence In Relation To A Fact In Issue

- **Subject** to the **exclusionary rules**:
    - All **evidence** that is *relevant* to a **fact in issue** is *admissible;* and
    - All **evidence** that is *not* relevant to a **fact in issue** is *not* admissible.

C - Proving Facts In Issue

- **Facts in issue** can be **proven** by:
    - **Original evidence;**
    - **Real evidence;**
    - **Secondary evidence;** and
    - **Documentary evidence.**

1 - Original Evidence

- **Original evidence** involves:
    - **Live oral testimony** of a witness **in court;**
    - To **prove:**
        - The **truth;**
        - Of **facts;**
        - That they **perceived** directly **themselves.**
- Such evidence will **not contravene** the **hearsay rules**.

2 - Real Evidence

- **Real evidence** takes the form of **material objects** that are presented before the court as **exhibits.**

- The presentation of the **exhibit** is usually **supported** by the **testimony** of a witness who explains the **relevance** of the **exhibit** in relation to a **fact in issue**.

3 - Secondary Evidence

- **Secondary evidence** involves the presentation before the court of a **copy of a document** as opposed to the original document.

- **Secondary evidence** will be **admissible** in the following circumstances:

  - Where a **party served** with a notice to **produce the original document** to the court has **failed to do so**;

  - Where the original document has been **lost** or **destroyed**;

  - Where production of the original document is **impossible**;

  - Where the original document is **privileged**;

  - Where the production of the original of a **public document** would be either **illegal** or **inconvenient**.

4 - Documentary Evidence

- **Documentary evidence** includes:

  - Maps;
  - Plans;
  - Drawings;
  - Graphs;
  - Photographs;
  - Discs;
  - Video tapes and films (including CCTV);
  - Police tape recorded interviews.

Exam Trip Up – Computer Records

- **Computer records** generated **without any human input** (e.g. an intoximeter reading) are **admissible** as **real evidence**.

- **Computer records** requiring human input to be generated are *not* **prima facie admissible** as they contravene the rule against documentary hearsay.

- Watch out for an exam question involving the admissibility of a till receipt to prove the purchase of an item on the shop where:

  - The items purchased on the receipt are **manually inputted** by the **till operator – non admissible hearsay**; and

  - The items purchased on the receipt are **computer generated** by a till **scanner – admissible real evidence.**

5 - Presumptions

(i) Definition Of A Presumption

- A **presumption** is:
    - A **conclusion**;
    - In relation to a **fact in issue**;
    - That a court will **automatically draw**;
    - **Without** the need to adduce **evidence**;
    - **Unless**;
    - The **contrary** is **proven**.

(ii) - Proving Facts In Issue

The General Rule In Relation To Proving Facts In Issue

- **Facts in issue** must be proved by **adducing evidence** before the court.

The Exception To The General Rule In Relation To Proving Facts In Issue – Presumptions

- There are instances where:
    - The **proof of a fact**;
    - Will **lead** to the **presumption** of the existence of a **further fact**;
    - **Without** the need to **adduce evidence** to **prove** that **further fact**.

(iii) - The Range Of Presumptions

- There are **3 types** of **presumptions**:
    - Presumptions of **law**:
        - **Rebuttable**;
        - **Irrebuttable (conclusive)**; and
    - Presumptions of **fact**.

(a) Irrebuttable Presumptions Of Law – Conclusive Presumptions

- Where the court **accepts** the existence of a **basic fact**;
- The court **must** also **automatically accept** the existence of an **additional fact**; and
- **No evidence** can be presented to **rebut** the existence of this further **irrebuttable fact**.

An Example Of An Irrebuttable Presumption Of Law

- Section 50 C&YPA 1933 states *"It shall be presumed that no child under the age of 10 can be guilty of an offence"*.

- The production of the child's birth certificate will:

    - **Prove** the **fact** that the child is **under 10**; and

    - The court **must automatically presume** the further **fact** that the child is **not guilty** of the offence; and

    - **No** evidence can be produced to **rebut** the **presumption of law**.

(b) - Rebuttable Presumptions Of Law

- A **rebuttable presumption of law** will exist where:

    - **Evidence** is **adduced** to **prove** the existence of a **basic fact**;

    - From which the **existence** of **another fact** *must* also be **presumed** to exist.

- If so - the other party is permitted to **adduce evidence** to **rebut** the existence of the **presumed fact**.

An Example Of A Rebuttable Presumption Of Law

- Section 129(2) CJA 2003 preserves the common law **presumption of law** that **mechanical devices** have been **properly set or calibrated**.

- If **evidence** is **adduced** of the **fact** that an **automated speed camera** caught a motorist driving **over the speed limit** - the court:

    - *Must* **presume** that the automated speed camera was **in working order**;

    - **Unless**;

    - **Factual evidence** is **adduced** by the defence **to the contrary to rebut** the presumption.

(c) – Rebuttable Presumptions Of Fact

- A **rebuttable presumption of fact** will exist where:

    - **Evidence** is **adduced** to **prove** the existence of a **basic fact (circumstantial evidence)**;

    - From which the **existence** of **another fact** *may* also be **presumed** to exist.

- If so - the other party is permitted to **adduce evidence** to **rebut** the existence of the **presumed fact**.

An Example Of A Rebuttable Presumption Of Fact

- The case of *MacDarmaid v Attorney General* [1950] P 218; *Re Peete* [1952] 2 All ER 599 defined the principles of the **presumption of life:**

    ☐ Where **evidence** is **adduced** to **prove** the **fact** that a person was **alive** on a certain date;

    ☐ The court *may* **presume** that the **fact** that the person was **still alive** at a **subsequent date;**

    ☐ **Unless;**

    ☐ **Evidence** is **adduced** to **prove the contrary.**

D - The Burden Of Proof

- There are **2 burdens** that must be discharged:

    ☐ The *legal* burden – the obligation resting upon a **party** to **prove a fact in issue;** and

    ☐ The *evidentiary* burden - the obligation to **adduce sufficient evidence** to **prove a fact in issue.**

1 - Who Bears The Legal Burden Of Proof? – The General Rule

- The House of Lords in the case of *Woolmington v DPP* [1935] AC 462, established that as a **general rule** the **prosecution** bears the **legal burden** to prove **all elements** of the offence in the form of the:

    ☐ **Actus reus;** and

    ☐ **Mens rea.**

"Throughout the web of English criminal law one golden thread is always to be seen; that is the duty of the prosecution to prove the prisoner's guilt."

2 - Who Bears The Evidentiary Burden Of Proof? – The General Rule

- Where there **prosecution** bears the **legal burden** of proof;

- The **prosecution** will also bear the **evidentiary burden** of proof.

- In order to discharge the **evidentiary burden** and secure a conviction the **prosecution** must prove **each element** of the offence **beyond reasonable doubt.**

3 - The Obligations Of The Defence – The General Rule

- The **defence** are under **no obligation to adduce evidence** and can merely **put the prosecution to proof** if they wish.

- As the **legal and evidentiary burdens rest upon the prosecution** they will then be obliged to sufficient adduce evidence to **prove their facts in issue (actus reus** and **mens rea) beyond reasonable doubt.**

- If the **prosecution** is **unable to discharge the burdens of proof** by the close of their case, the **defence** is permitted to enter a plea of **no case to answer.**

- If the **prosecution** are able to discharge the **legal and evidentiary burdens** by adducing sufficient evidence to **prove the actus reus and mens rea beyond reasonable doubt** then the onus will fall upon the **defence** to raise a **new fact in issue** in the form of a **general defence**, such as an **alibi**. If so:

    - The **legal burden** of proof **remains** on the **prosecution**;

    - The **evidentiary burden** will shift onto the **defence** to adduce sufficient evidence to **raise a reasonable doubt** that the defence can be substantiated.

    - If the **defence** are able to do so – the **evidentiary burden** will then shift back onto the **prosecution** to **disprove the defence raised beyond reasonable doubt.**

4 - Exceptional Circumstances Where The Defence Bear The Legal Burden Of Proof

- The **legal burden** of proof is **reversed** onto the **defence** in the following limited circumstances:

    - **Insanity** (Mc'Naughtens Case 1843);

    - **Diminished Responsibility** (Section 2(2) Homicide Act 1957);

    - **Section 101 Magistrates Court Act 1980** (e.g. For the offence of driving without a licence, the legal burden rests upon the defendant to prove that they did have a licence).

- Where the defence bears the **legal burden,** they also bear the **evidentiary burden** which they must discharge on the **balance of probabilities.**

Evidence & Procedure
Unit 17: Evidence (2)
Hearsay, Character, Opinion, Corroboration & Judicial Notice

A – Hearsay
1 - The Rationale Of The Hearsay Rule

- The court always wishes to be presented with the **most reliable forms of evidence.**

- Therefore the court will as a general rule, **only permit those witnesses who have directly perceived the fact upon which they wish to adduce evidence to give live oral evidence in relation to that fact.**

- They are the **most reliable** source as:

    - They **perceived the fact with their own eyes**; and

    - By giving live testimony **the reliability of their testimony can be tested in cross examination.**

- In simplistic terms the court wants to hear the fact *straight from the horse's mouth* and have the opportunity to cross examine the witness.

- There are however **exceptions to this rule that permits prima facie hearsay evidence to be admitted.**

2 - The Definition Of Hearsay

- **Hearsay** was defined in the case of *R v Kearley [1992] 2AC 228* as:

    "Any **statement other than one made by a person while giving oral evidence in the proceedings** is inadmissible to **prove the truth of any fact** stated in it."

- There are **3 key elements**:

    - A **statement**;

    - **Made out of court** by the witness (i.e. other than while giving evidence in the proceedings); and

    - The **purpose** of putting the statement before the court is **to prove the truth of a fact.**

3 - The Definition Of A Statement

- A **statement** will encompass **all forms of communication** including:

    - Written statements;

    - Documents compiled by businesses;

    - Documents compiled by public authorities;

    - Oral evidence;

    - A statement saved electronically;

    - A gesture – nodding head etc.

4 - Made Out Of Court

- The communication must be **made on any occasion** *other than* **while the witness was giving evidence to the court** in the present proceedings.

5 - To Prove The Truth Of A Fact

- The statement must be put in evidence to **prove** the **truth** of a **fact** contained in the statement.

- If the purpose of adducing the statement was for **some other reason** then it will **not** be **hearsay** and will be **admissible** in the circumstances.

6 - The Most Common Forms Of Hearsay

- Hearsay takes 2 common forms:
    - **Oral** hearsay; and
    - **Documentary** hearsay.

(i) - Oral Hearsay

- **Oral hearsay** will arise where:
    - A **witness** seeks to **adduce evidence in court** (a statement);
    - Of **facts** which they **did** *not* **perceive directly themselves**;
    - Because the **fact was passed onto them by a person who is not in court** to give evidence in relation to that fact.

For example:

- Tom is an eyewitness to an assault. Shortly after the assault Tom tells his friend Dick that the perpetrator of the attack was Harry. As Tom was a direct eyewitness he could:
    - Give live testimony (a statement);
    - In court;
    - To prove the truth of the fact that Harry was the attacker.

- Dick would be unable to give evidence that Harry was the attacker as:
    - He would be seeking to adduce evidence of Tom's statement;
    - Which was made out of court; and
    - Dick would be seeking to adduce that statement to prove the truth that Harry was the attacker.

- Such a statement by Dick would contravene the hearsay rule.

(ii) - Documentary Hearsay

- **Documentary hearsay** will arise where:
    - A **witness who has directly perceived a fact** makes a **written statement out of court** in relation to the **fact;** and
    - Instead of attending court to give live oral testimony of that fact;
    - They **seek to submit their written statement as evidence of the fact to the court.**
- The rationale of the rule is that the court wants the person who perceived the fact to take the stand to be cross examined to determine the reliability of their evidence.
- It is not possible to cross examine a document.

For example:

- Tom has made a **written statement** to the police confirming that Harry carried out the attack.
- Tom would be unable to tender his written statement as evidence to prove the truth of the fact that Harry was the attacker as:
    - The **statement** was **made out of court;**
    - The statement would be **seeking to prove the truth of the fact** that Harry was the attacker.
- This is clearly hearsay.
- Instead the court would require Tom to give live oral testimony of the fact that Harry was the attacker, thereby enabling the reliability of his evidence to be tested in cross examination.

7 - The Admissibility Of Hearsay Evidence - The General Rule – Inadmissible Hearsay

- As a **general rule hearsay evidence is** *inadmissible* in court.

8 - The Admissibility Of Hearsay Evidence - The Exceptions To The General Rule – Admissible Hearsay

- Prima facie inadmissible hearsay evidence will become *admissible* where an **exception** applies under **section 114 Criminal Justice Act 2003.**
- The **exceptions to the hearsay rule** under **section 114 Criminal Justice Act 2003** include:
    - Section 114(1)(a) - **statutory exceptions**:
        - Section 9 Criminal Justice Act 1967;
        - Section 116 CJA 2003;
        - Section 117 CJA 2003.
    - Section 114(1)(b) – **common law rules;**
    - Section 114(1)(c) – the **parties agree** to admitting the evidence;
    - Section 114(1)(d) – court deems it to be **in the interests of justice** to admit the evidence.

9 - The Section 114(1)(a) Statutory Exceptions

(i) - Section 9 CJA 1967 Statements

- **Section 9 CJA 1967** permits:
    - A **written statement**;
    - **Made out of court** by a witness;
    - To be presented **to the court** as **proof of facts** contained in the statement;
    - **Without the witness giving live oral testimony in respect of those facts** where all of the following characteristics are present:
        - The statement is **signed** by the maker;
        - The statement contains a **declaration** by the maker that:
            - The **statement is true to the best of their knowledge and belief**; and
            - That they made the statement **knowing that if it were tendered in evidence, they would be liable to prosecution if they wilfully stated anything** that they either:
                - **Knew to be false**; or
                - **Did not believe to be true;**
        - The **statement** has been **served on all other parties** in the proceedings; and
        - Having been **sent** the statement:
            - **None** of the other **parties** or their **solicitors**;
            - Have **within 7 days of service**;
            - **Served a notice** on the party seeking to admit the statement – **objecting** to the statement being tendered in evidence.

Exam Trip Up

- The **opposing side must not object** to the statement being admitted as hearsay.
- **If an objection is raised the court has no power to overrule the objection** and admit the statement in evidence.
- NB – The section 9 provisions are used to save court time by admitting **uncontroversial evidence** which is not in dispute between the parties.

(ii) - Section 116 CJA 2003 Statements

- An **oral** or **written statement will be admissible** under **section 116(1) CJA 2003** where the witness who made the statement out of court containing the relevant facts:
    - **Could have given oral evidence (non hearsay) if they had attended court;**
    - Can be **identified** to the court's satisfaction as the maker of the statement;
    - **At the time of giving the statement** possessed the requisite **capability** - (They could understand questions put to them and give answers that could be understood); and

- Is **unable to attend court** for one of the reasons specified in **sections 116(2)(a) – (e)**.
    - The witness is **dead** or **unfit** because of their **bodily** or **mental condition** - (s116(2)(a)&(b));
    - The witness is **outside the UK** and it is **not reasonably practicable for them to attend** - (s116(2)(c));
    - The witness **cannot be found** although such **steps as are reasonably practicable to take to find them have been taken** - (s116(2)(d));
    - That through **fear** the witness does not give evidence (or does not continue to give evidence) – (s116(2)(e)).

For example:

- Arthur is aged 70. He is the victim of a domestic burglary. He is able to provide a description of the assailant to his neighbour Mick.
- A couple of hours later the shock of the incident causes him to suffer massive stroke.
- Arthur has since been unable to communicate a written statement to the police and is also incapable of providing live testimony at the trial.
- In the circumstances Mick could be called to give evidence in court of the statement made to him by Arthur out of court to prove the truth of the facts relating to the identity of the burglar.
- This hearsay evidence would be admissible because:
    - Arthur could have given live oral testimony of the burglars identity as he had perceived the fact directly himself;
    - At the time of making the statement to Mick, Arthur was capable;
    - Arthur's identity as the maker of the statement is not in dispute; and
    - Arthur is unable to attend due to his bodily condition.

(a) - Where The Witness Is Outside The UK And It Is Not Reasonably Practicable For Them To Attend - Section 116(2)(c) CJA 2003

- In *R v Castillo [1996] 1 Cr App R 438*, the Court of Appeal provided guidance in respect of factors to consider in determining whether it would be *practicable* to secure the attendance of a witness, including:
    - The **importance** of the witnesses evidence;
    - The **expense** and **inconvenience** of securing the witnesses attendance;
    - The **seriousness** of the offence;
    - Whether the witnesses evidence could be provided via a **live link**; and
    - The **prejudice** likely to be caused to the defendant due to their **inability to cross examine** the witness.

For example:

- Jack, a botanist, is one of several eyewitnesses to an offence of common assault. He has provided a written statement of the police of his account.
- Since giving his statement Jack has been researching rare plant species in an extremely remote area of the Amazon rain forest where there is no means of electronic communication and it takes a weeks hiking just to get to the nearest mud track.

- He:
  - ☐ **Could have given oral evidence (non hearsay) if they had attended court;**
  - ☐ Can be **identified** to the court's satisfaction as the maker of the statement;
  - ☐ **At the time of giving the statement** possessed the requisite **capability to make the statement; and**
  - ☐ Is **unable to attend court** because:
    - He is **outside** the **UK**; and
    - In the circumstances it will **not** be **practicable** to secure his attendance at court because:
      - ☐ **He is only one of several witnesses and is not therefore of critical importance;**
      - ☐ The **expense** and **inconvenience** of securing his attendance would be prohibitive;
      - ☐ The offence is of **low seriousness** and dragging him back to give evidence would not be proportionate in the circumstances;
      - ☐ He is **unable** to give evidence via a **live link**;
      - ☐ Little **prejudice** is likely to be caused to the defendant due to their **inability to cross examine** them.

(b) - Where Through Fear The Witness Does Not Give Evidence (Or Does Not Continue To Give Evidence – Section 116(2)(e) CJA 2003

- **Fear** is defined in section 116(3) as:
  - ☐ A **fear** of either:
    - Death;
    - Injury; or
    - Financial loss;
  - ☐ To:
    - Themselves; or
    - Another.

Leave Of The Court – Fear

- Section 116(4) states that **leave of the court will be required** before a statement will be admitted under the head of **fear.**
- **Leave will only be granted if** the court deems that it would be in the **interests of justice to admit the statement** having regards to:
  - ☐ The **contents of the statement**;
  - ☐ Any **risk of the admission or exclusion of the statement resulting in unfairness to any party** (due to the difficulty in challenging the contents of a document);
  - ☐ The fact that a **special measures direction** could be made in relation to the witness in fear;
  - ☐ **Any other relevant circumstance.**

For example:

- Mary is a veterinarian who works in a laboratory that tests cosmetic products upon animals.
- She has been assaulted by an animal rights protestor. She has provided the police with a written statement describing her attacker.
- Mary has since received death threats from animal protestors warning her against giving evidence at the trial and she is no longer prepared to risk taking the stand. She
    - ☐ **Could have given oral evidence (non hearsay) if she had attended court;**
    - ☐ Can be **identified** to the court's satisfaction as the maker of the statement;
    - ☐ **At the time of giving the statement** she did possess the requisite **capability** to make the statement; and
    - ☐ She is **unable to attend court** because she is in **fear**.
- Her statement will only be admitted if the court grants **leave** which will depend on whether the court deems it in the **interests of justice** to do so.
- Given that Mary is the **sole witness** and the case revolves around her evidence there is a **significant risk of unfairness to the defence if they are unable to test her evidence in cross examination.**
- It is likely that her statement will not be admitted and that instead her evidence will be tendered via a special measures direction such as a live link.

(iii) - Section 117(2) CJA 2003 – Business Documents

(a) - The General Rule – Inadmissible

- A **business document** (statement) made out of court which is produced in court to prove the truth of a fact will **prima facie be inadmissible hearsay.**

(b) - The Exception To The General Rule – Admissible Business Documents

- A **business document** will be ruled **admissible** where the following **conditions** are satisfied:
    - ☐ The **document** was either:
        - Created; or
        - Received;
    - ☐ In the **course** of a:
        - Trade;
        - Business;
        - Profession;
        - Occupation;
        - As a **holder of paid or unpaid office**; and
    - ☐ The **person who supplied the information** contained in the document **(the relevant person);**

□ Either:

- **Had**; or
- **Might reasonably be expected to have had**;

- **Personal knowledge** of the matters dealt with in the statement; and

□ **Each person (if any) through whom the information was supplied** from the **relevant person**;

□ **Received the information in the course** of a:

- Trade;
- Business;
- Profession;
- Occupation;
- As a **holder of a paid or unpaid office**.

(c) - Additional Safeguards - Documents Prepared For The Purpose Of A Criminal Investigation Or Proceedings – Section 117(4)&(5) CJA 2003

- Section 117(4) provides **additional safeguards** where the **written documents** that a party seeks to admit have been **prepared for the purpose of pending or contemplated criminal proceedings.**

- The additional safeguards are necessary due to the possibility that in such circumstances the **documents may have been doctored with the pending proceedings in mind.**

- The additional safeguards are contained in:

    □ **Section 117(5)**; and
    □ **Section 117(7).**

Safeguard 1 – Section 117(5) CJA 2003

- Where the **written documents** that a party seeks to admit have been **prepared for the purpose of pending or contemplated criminal proceedings:**

    □ **As well as satisfying the criteria of section 117(2);**
    □ It is also necessary to prove that either:

    - The **relevant person** is **unable to attend court** for one of the reasons specified in **sections 116(2)(a) – (e):**

        □ The witness is **dead** or **unfit** because of their **bodily** or **mental condition** - (s116(2)(a)&(b));

        □ The witness is **outside the UK** and it is **not reasonably practicable for them to attend** - (s116(2)(c));

        □ The witness **cannot be found** although such **steps as are reasonably practicable to take to find them have been taken** - (s116(2)(d));

        □ That through **fear** the witness does not give evidence (or does not continue to give evidence) – (s116(2)(e)); or

- The **relevant person cannot be reasonably expected to have any recollection of the matters dealt with in the statement** having regard to:
    - [ ] The **length of time since they supplied the information**; and
    - [ ] All other circumstances.

Safeguard 2 – Section 117(7) CJA 2003

- Even if the business document satisfies the provisions of sections 117(2) and 117(5) the court may still exercise its **direction to exclude** a document **if its reliability is doubtful** in view of:
    - [ ] The **document's contents**;
    - [ ] The **source of the information** contained in the document;
    - [ ] The **way in which** or the **circumstances in which** the information was **supplied** or **received**;
    - [ ] The **way in which** or the **circumstances in which** the document was **created** or **received**.

10 - The Section 114(1)(b) Statutory Exceptions – Preserved Common Law Exceptions

- The CJA 2003 has **preserved** many of the **common law exceptions** to the hearsay rule including:
    - [ ] **Res Gestae;**
    - [ ] **Statements made in public documents;**
    - [ ] **Reputation or family tradition;**
    - [ ] **Admissions by agents;**
    - [ ] **Confessions;**
    - [ ] **Expert opinion drawn on published works.**

(i) - Res Gestae – Section 118(4) CJA 2003

- Section 118(4) CJA 2003:
    - [ ] Permits an earlier out of court statement to be adduced in evidence providing the statement was:
        - Either:
            - [ ] Made by a person so **emotionally overpowered**;
            - [ ] By an **event**;
            - [ ] That the **possibility** of either:
                - **Concoction;** or
                - **Distortion;**
            - [ ] Can be **disregarded**; or
        - The **statement accompanied an act** which can be properly evaluated as **evidence only if considered in conjunction with the statement**; or
        - The statement relates to either:
            - [ ] A **physical sensation**; or
            - [ ] A **mental state** (such a **intention** or **emotion**).

(ii) - Public Information

- The case of *Sturla v Freccia [1880] 5 App Cas 623* established that **public information** is **admissible provided:**
    - The **statements** and **entries in records** have been made:
        - By **authorised agents** of the public;
        - **In the course** of their **official duties**; and
    - The **facts recorded** are either:
        - Of **public interest** or **notoriety**; or
        - Required to be **recorded for the benefit of the public**.

- Examples of **public information** include:
    - Registers of births, marriages and deaths;
    - University records;
    - Surveys of Crown Lands; etc.

- Documents admissible under this common law exception will invariably **also be admissible under the section 117 CJA 2003 exception** in relation to documentary hearsay produced in the course of a business trade or profession.

(iii) - Reputation Or Family Tradition

- **Evidence of reputation or family tradition** is **admissible** in criminal proceedings for the **purpose of proving** either:
    - **Pedigree;**
    - The existence of a **marriage;**
    - The existence of a **public or general right;**
    - The **identity** of any:
        - **Person;** or
        - **Thing.**

(iv) - Admissions By Agents

- An **admission by an agent** on behalf of an accused will be **admissible** as evidence against the accused.
- The agent will usually be the accused's **solicitor** or **barrister.**
- The case of *R v Tuner [1975] 61 Cr App R 67,* established that:
    - If a legal representative;
    - Makes an admission in court on behalf of the accused;
    - In the accused's presence;
    - It will be inferred that they were authorised to make the admission.

(v) - Confession Evidence – Section 118(5) CJA 2003

- **Confession evidence** has always been **admissible** as a common law exception to the hearsay rule.

11 – Hearsay Will Be Admissible Where The Parties Agree To The Evidence Being Admitted – Section 114(1)(c) CJA 2003

- The **parties** must **agree** to the admission of a hearsay statement in the circumstances.

12 – The Court Deems It To Be In The Interests Of Justice To Admit The Hearsay Evidence – Section 114(1)(d) CJA 2003

- The court retains the *discretion* to **admit** any **hearsay evidence that does not fall within any of the aforementioned exceptions** to the hearsay rule.

- The court will only admit such hearsay evidence where it is in the *interests of justice* to do so.

- In determining whether it is in the **interests of justice** to do so the court will take into consideration the factors contained in section 142(a)-(i) CJA 2003:

    a) How much **probative value** the statement has (assuming it to be true) in relation to a matter in issue in the proceedings; **How valuable** is the statement for the **understanding of other evidence in the case**;

    b) **What other evidence** has been, or can be given on the matter, or evidence mentioned in part (a)

    c) **How important** is the matter or evidence mentioned in paragraph (a) **in the context of the case as a whole**;

    d) The **circumstances** in which the **statement was made**;

    e) **How reliable the maker** of the statement appears to be;

    f) **How reliable the evidence of the making of the statement** appears to be;

    g) **Whether oral evidence** of the matter stated **can be given**, and if not – why it cannot;

    h) The **amount of difficulty involved in challenging the statement**; and

    i) The **extent** to which the **difficulty** would be likely to prejudice the party facing it.

13 - Multiple Hearsay – Section 121 CJA 2003

- **Multiple hearsay** arises when **information is passed though more than one intermediary** - i.e. there are several links in the chain.

- The question arises – can evidence be provided by the last link in the chain to whom the information was passed to prove the truth of facts contained in their statement?

- Multiple hearsay will not be admissible in court unless either:

    ☐ The evidence is **admissible under section 117** as a **business document**;

    ☐ The **parties agree** to the statement being admitted under section 141(1)(c) CJA 2003;

    ☐ The court is satisfied that the value of the evidence, taking into account how reliable the statement appears to be, is so high, that the **interests of justice** require it to be allowed under section 141(1)(d).

14 – Excluding Hearsay Evidence That Falls Within Any Of The Aforementioned Exceptions

(i) - The Overriding Discretion Of The Court To Exclude Hearsay Evidence – Section 126 CJA 2003

- Section 126(2) CJA 2003 preserves the courts **discretion to exclude hearsay evidence** even when the evidence falls within one of the aforementioned exceptions to the hearsay rules where either:
    - The admission of the hearsay evidence would have an **adverse effect on the fairness of the proceedings** under **section 78 of PACE 1984**; or
    - The **prejudicial effect of admitting the hearsay evidence would outweigh its probative value** under **section 82(3) PACE 1984**.

(ii) - Excluding Unnecessary Hearsay Due To An Undue Waste Of Time – Section 126 CJA 2003

- Section 126 CJA 2003 provides the court with a **discretion** to **exclude superfluous out of court statements** where the court is satisfied that:
    - The **value** of the evidence;
    - Is **substantially outweighed**;
    - By the **undue waste of time** that its admission would cause.

15 - Stopping The Case Where The Evidence Is Unconvincing – Section 125 CJA 2003

- A court *must:*
    - **Stop** a case; and
    - **Acquit** the defendant;
- Where the **case** against the defendant is **based** either:
    - **Wholly**; or
    - **Partly**;
- On an **out of court statement**;
- Which is **so unconvincing**;
- That considering the **statement's importance** to the case;
- A **conviction** would be **unsafe** in the circumstances.

16 - Admitting Section 10 CJA 1967 Statements

- **Formal admissions fact** that will be **conclusive evidence** of the fact where:
    - They are made either:
        - **Before** the proceedings; or
        - **At** the proceedings;
    - If they are made **otherwise than at court** – they *must* be **in writing**;
    - If they are made **in writing** – they shall be **signed** by the **maker**;
    - If they are made **on behalf** of a defendant – they shall be made by their **counsel** or **solicitor**;
    - If made **before the trial** by the **defendant** – they shall be **approved** by their **counsel** or **solicitor**.
- Any admission made under section 10 may only be **withdrawn** with the **leave of the court**.

B - Character Evidence

1 - The Definition Of Bad Character – Section 98 Criminal Justice Act 2003

- **Bad character** is defined as:
    - Either:
        - **Evidence** of; or
        - A **disposition** towards;
    - **Misconduct** on a person's part;
    - **Other than evidence**:
        - That has to do with the alleged **facts** of the **offence for which the person is charged**; or
        - **Evidence** of **misconduct** in connection with the investigation or prosecution of the **offence for which the person is charged**.

2 – The Definition Of Misconduct - Section 112 Criminal Justice Act 2003

- **Misconduct** is defined as either:
    - The commission of an **offence** including:
        - Previous **convictions**;
        - **Concurrent charges**;
        - Previous **charges** that were **not prosecuted**;
        - Previous **charges** that resulted in an **acquittal**; or
    - Other **reprehensible behaviour**.

3 - Gateways To Admitting Evidence Of A Non Defendant's Bad Character – Section 100 Criminal Justice Act 2003

- Evidence of the previous **bad character** of a **person other than the defendant** can be admitted via one of **3 gateways.**

- They include that the previous **misconduct** either:
  - Is **important explanatory evidence;**
  - Has **substantial probative value** in relation to:
    - A **matter in issue** in the proceedings; and
    - Is of **substantial importance** in the **context** of the **case as a whole**; or
  - **All parties agree** to the evidence being admitted.

(i) - Definition Of Important Explanatory Evidence - Section 100(1)(a) Criminal Justice Act 2003

- **Important explanatory evidence** is:
  - Evidence **without which** the court or jury would find **impossible** or **difficult** to **understand other evidence** in the case; and
  - Its **value** for **understanding** the **case as a whole** is **substantial.**

(ii) - Factors The Court Will Consider In Determining The Probative Value Of The Evidence Is Substantial - Section 100 (3) Criminal Justice Act 2003

- The court will consider:
  - The **nature** and **number** of **events** to which the evidence relates;
  - **When** those events or things were alleged to have **occurred;**
  - The **nature** and **extent** of the **similarities** and **dissimilarities** between alleged **instances** of misconduct;
  - The **extent** to which the **evidence** shows or tends to show that the **same person was responsible** each time.

(iii) - Procedural Considerations

- A party seeking to adduce evidence of a non defendant's bad character under one of the aforementioned permitted grounds must **seek the leave (permission) of the court** to do so.

4 - Admitting Evidence Of The Previous Convictions Of Non Defendant Witnesses – Section 6 Criminal Procedure Act 1865

- Evidence of a **witnesses previous convictions** will be **admissible by the cross examining party** where:
  - The witness in **response** to **questions** about their **previous convictions** either:
    - **Denies** the existence of their previous convictions;
    - **Does not admit** their previous convictions; or
    - **Refuses to answer** the questions posed.

5 - The Approach Of The Criminal Justice Act 2003 To Admitting Evidence Of The Defendants Bad Character

- The provisions of the Criminal Justice Act 2003 have adopted an **inclusive approach** to admitting evidence of the defendants:
    - **Previous convictions;**
    - **Disposition for reprehensible behaviour.**

6 - Gateways To Admitting Evidence Of The Defendant's Bad Character - Section 101(1) Criminal Justice Act 2003

- Evidence of the **defendant's bad character** will be admissible through one of the following **7 gateways** - either:

Gateway A
- **All** of the **parties agree** to the evidence being admitted;

Gateway B
- The evidence is either:
    - **Adduced by the defendant** themselves; or
    - Is given in **answer to a question in cross examination**;

Gateway C
- It is **important explanatory evidence;**

Gateway D
- It is relevant to an **important matter in issue** between the **defendant** and **prosecution;**

Gateway E
- It has **substantial probative value** in relation to an **important mater in issue** between the **defendant** and the **co defendant**;

Gateway F
- It is evidence to **correct a false impression given by the defendant;**

Gateway G
- The **defendant** has **attacked another person's character.**

7 - Courts Discretion To Exclude Evidence Of A Defendant's Bad Character Even Where Either Of Gateways D or G Are Satisfied – Section 101(3) & (4) CJA 2003

- The court **must not admit** evidence of the **defendants bad character** where either:
    - It is relevant to an **important matter in issue** between the **defendant** and **prosecution;** or
    - The **defendant** has **attacked another person's character.**

- If on the **application** of the **defendant**;
- It appears to the court that:
  - The **admission** of evidence;
  - Would have such an **adverse effect** on the **fairness** of the **proceedings** that the court **ought not** to admit it.
- The court must have regard to the **length of time between:**
  - The **matters** to which the **evidence of bad character** relates; and
  - The **matters** which form the **subject of the offence charged**.

8 - Excluding Evidence Under The Remaining Gateways

- The legislation does **not expressly preclude** the operation of either:
  - **Section 78 PACE 1984**; or
  - The **common law discretion** to exclude evidence.
- The Court of Appeal obiter dicta in the case of *R v Highton; R v Van Nguyen; R v Carp* [2005] 1 WLR 3472, confirmed that both section 78 PACE 1984 and the common law judicial discretion could be adopted to exclude evidence under the remaining gateways.

Gateway C - Important Explanatory Evidence – Section 101(c) Criminal Justice Act 2003

- The provision is **identical** to that in relation to admitting evidence of the **bad character of non defendants**.
- **Important explanatory evidence** is:
  - Evidence **without which** the court or jury would find **impossible** or **difficult** to **understand other evidence** in the case; and
  - Its **value** for **understanding** the **case as a whole** is **substantial**.

Gateway D - Important Matters In Issue Between The Defendant And The Prosecution - Section 101(c) Criminal Justice Act 2003

- **Important matters in issue** may include whether the **defendant** has a **propensity** to either:
  - **Commit similar offences** to the kind with which they are charged **except** where their **propensity** makes it **no more likely that they committed the offence**.

    These may include either:
    - Offences of the **same description**; or
    - Offences of the **same category**;
    - Offences **not of the same description** or category if they are of the **same generic nature** as the current charge (**e.g. violence offences etc**);
      - Proof of **prior conduct** that was **not criminal** (e.g. previous unusual sexual behaviour that was consented to in the prior instance which has been repeated without consent in relation to the offence charged);
  - Be **untruthful, except** where it is **not suggested** that the **defendant's case is untruthful**.

(i) - Definition Of Offences Of The Same Description

- An offence will be of the **same description** if the **statement of offence is the same.**

(ii) - Definition Of Offences Of The Same Category

- An offence will be of the **same category** if they fall within the categories **specified** by the **Secretary of State**, which currently include:
    - [ ] All **theft offences**; and
    - [ ] All **child sex offences.**

(iii) - The Courts Discretion Not To Admit Evidence Of Similar Offences

- If the defendant does have similar previous convictions the court can exercise its **discretion not to admit the convictions** if the court considers it **unjust to do so** by virtue of either:
    - [ ] The **length of time since the conviction**; or
    - [ ] **Any other reason.**

Gateway E - Matters In Issue Between The Defendant And The Co-Defendant – Section 101(e) Criminal Justice Act 2003

- **Important matters in issue** may include whether the **defendant** has a **propensity** to either:
    - [ ] **Commit similar offences** to the kind with which they are charged **except** where their **propensity** makes it **no more likely that they committed the offence.**

    These may include either:
    - Offences of the **same description**; or
    - Offences of the **same category**;
    - Offences **not** of the **same description** or **category** if they are of the **same generic nature** as the current charge **(e.g. violence offences etc)**;
    - Proof of **prior conduct** that was **not criminal** (e.g. previous unusual sexual behaviour that was consented to in the prior instance which has been repeated without consent in relation to the offence charged);

    - [ ] Be **untruthful, except** where it is **not suggested** that the **defendant's case is untruthful.**

Exam Trip Up

- The **defendants propensity to be untruthful** is only admissible where:
    - [ ] Either the:
        - **Nature**; or
        - **Conduct**;
    - [ ] Of the **defendant's defence**;
    - [ ] **Undermines** the **defence** of their **co-defendant.**

Gateway F - Evidence To Correct A False Impression – Section 101(e) Criminal Justice Act 2003

(i) - Definition Of Creating A False Impression

- A defendant **creates a false impression** if they are:
    - **Responsible;**
    - For making an **assertion** that is either:
        - **Express;** or
        - **Implied;**
    - That may give a **false impression** about themselves.

(ii) - Definition Of Correcting A False Impression

- Evidence which **corrects** a **false impression** is evidence which:
    - Has **probative value;**
    - In **correcting** the **false impression.**

(iii) - Responsibility For The Assertion – Section 105(2) CJA 2000

- The **defendant will be responsible for the assertion** where it is **made** either:
    - By the **defendant** in the **proceedings;**
    - By the **defendant:**
        - On being **questioned** under **caution** either:
            - **Before** charge;
            - **On** being charged;
            - On being **officially informed** that they might be prosecuted for the offence; and
        - **Evidence of the assertion is given in the proceedings;**
    - Is made by a **witness called by the defendant;**
    - Is made by **any witness** in **cross examination** in response to **questions asked by the defence** that were either:
        - **Intended** to elicit it; or
        - Is **likely** to do so; or
- Was made by a **person out of court** and the **defendant adduces** evidence of it **in the proceedings.**

(iv) - Avoiding Responsibility For The Assertion – Section 105(3) Criminal Justice Act 2003

- The defendant will **not be responsible for an assertion** if they either:
    - [ ] **Withdraw** the assertion; or
    - [ ] **Disassociate** themselves from the assertion.

(v) - Asserting Good Character Without Taking The Stand – Section 105 Criminal Justice Act 2003

- If it appears to the court that the defendant;
- **Other than** by means of **giving evidence**;
- Is giving a **false** or **misleading impression** of themselves;
- By their:
    - [ ] **Conduct**;
    - [ ] **Appearance**; or
    - [ ] **Dress**;
- The court may **admit evidence to correct the impression**.

Gateway G - Attacking Another Person's Character - Section 101(g) Criminal Justice Act 2003

- An **attack on another person's character** can be achieved by:
    - [ ] **Adducing evidence** attacking the other person's character;
    - [ ] The **defendant** or their **legal representative** asking in **cross examination questions** that are either:
        - **Intended** to elicit such information;
        - **Likely** to elicit such information; or
    - [ ] **Evidence is given** of an **imputation** about the other person when the defendant was **questioned under caution** either:
        - [ ] **Before** charge;
        - [ ] **On** being charged;
        - [ ] On being **officially informed** that they might be prosecuted for the offence.

The Courts Discretion Not To Admit Evidence

- The court can exercise its **discretion not to admit the convictions** if the court considers it **unjust to do so** by virtue of either:
    - [ ] The **length of time since the conviction**; or
    - [ ] **Any other reason**.

9 - Admissibility Of Evidence Of The Defendant's Good Character

- The Court of Appeal in the case of *R v Vye and Others* [1993] 97 Cr App R 134 outlined the rules governing good character directions:
    - A **defendant** with **no previous convictions** is:
        - **Always entitled** to a **good character direction** as to their **propensity irrespective** of whether they **take the stand** to give evidence.
        - **Entitled** to a **good character direction** as to their **credibility provided** either:
            - They **asserted** their **innocence** at the **police station**; or
            - They **took the stand** to give evidence at their trial.

C - Opinion Evidence

- Evidence of **opinion** may be given by either:
    - **Non-expert** witnesses; or
    - **Expert** witnesses.

1 - Non Expert Evidence

- **Non experts** are permitted to give evidence in relation to **matters of accepted knowledge** that any member of the public would be able to understand and could comment on.
- For example:
    - The lighting at the time of an incident;
    - Whether a person looked upset;
    - Whether a person was drunk etc.

2 - Expert Evidence

- Only the opinion of an **expert** is admissible in relation to a **matter requiring subject specific expertise,** that the average person would not possess such as:
    - Medical diagnosis;
    - Matters of science; etc.

D - Judicial Notice

- The courts may take **judicial notice** of facts that are **common knowledge** and **require no further proof**.
- For example:
    - The human gestation period is 9 months;
    - There are 7 days in a week; etc.

E – Corroboration

1 – Definition Of Corroboration

- In the case of *R v Baskerville* [1916] 2KB 658, Lord Reid defined corroboration as follows:

    "Evidence in corroboration **must** be **independent testimony** which affects the accused by **connecting him with the crime**. In other words, it must be evidence which **implicates him**, that is, which **confirms** in some material particular not only the evidence that the **crime has been committed**, but also that the **prisoner committed it**".

- The **corroborating evidence** *must:*
    - Be **admissible**;
    - Be derived from an **independent source** to the evidence requiring corroboration;
    - **Confirm** that:
        - The offence was **committed**; and
        - The offence was committed **by the accused.**

2 - When Is Corroboration Required To Secure A Conviction

(i) - The General Rule

- As a **general rule:**
    - **No corroboration** is required; and
    - A **conviction** can be secured from the **evidence of a single uncorroborated witness.**

(ii) - The Exceptions To The General Rule Requiring Corroboration

- **Corroboration will be required** in the following circumstances:
    - As a **matter of law;**
    - **Obligatory** care warnings;
    - **Discretionary** care warnings; and
    - **Identification** evidence.

(a) - Corroboration Required As A Matter Of Law

- It will only be possible to secure a conviction for the following offences if the evidence in the case is **corroborated:**
    - **Treason;**
    - **Perjury**; and
    - **Speeding.**

(b) - Obligatory Care Warnings – Section 77 PACE 1984

- Section 77 PACE 1984 states that:
    - If the **case** against a **mentally handicapped defendant**;
    - **Depends** either:
        - **Wholly**; or
        - **Substantially**;
    - Upon a **confession**;
    - Which was **not made** in the **presence** of an **independent person**;
    - Then there is a **special need for caution** before convicting the defendant in reliance upon the confession alone.

(c) - Discretionary Care Warnings

- The Court of Appeal in the case of *R v Makanjuola* [1995] 1 WLR 1348 confirmed that courts retain a *discretion* to:
    - **Warn** a jury about:
        - **Convicting** a defendant **solely** on the basis of the **evidence** of an **unreliable witness**; and
        - **Why** the witnesses evidence should be **treated with caution** (i.e. explain **why** they are **unreliable**);
    - **Point out** to the jury any **evidence** that potentially **corroborate**s the evidence of the unreliable witnesses.

(d) - Identification Evidence – Turnbull Warnings

- In the Court of Appeal case of *R v Turnbull* [1977] QB 224, Lord Widgery set **guidelines** on the judicial approach towards identification evidence:

1 - When Will It Be Necessary To Issue A Turnbull Warning?

- Whenever the **prosecution case**:
    - **Depends** either:
        - **Wholly**; or
        - **Substantially**;
    - Upon the **correctness** of **identification evidence**; and
- The **defence alleges** that the identification witness is **mistaken**;
- The judge *must* **warn** the jury of the **special need for caution** before convicting the accused in reliance upon the identification evidence.

2 - The Contents Of The Turnbull Warning

- The judge *must:*
    - ☐ **Warn** the jury of the **special need for caution** when dealing with **disputed identification evidence**;
    - ☐ **Explain** why a warning is necessary:
        - **Honest** witnesses can make **mistakes**;
        - **Mistaken** witnesses can be **convincing**;
        - A **number** of witnesses may be **mistaken**; and
        - **Miscarriages of justice** have occurred **in the past** due to **mistaken identification**.
    - ☐ **Direct** the jury on the **circumstances of the identification** highlighting its **strengths** and **weaknesses**, including:

        - **A** – **A**mount of time under observation;
        - **D** – **D**istance between suspect and witness;
        - **V** – **V**isibility;
        - **O** – **O**bstructions;
        - **K** – **K**nown personally to the witness or seen them before;
        - **A** – **A**ny reason to remember them;
        - **T** - **T**ime lapse between incident and subsequent identification;
        - **E** - **E**rror or material discrepancy.

3 - When Is It Necessary To Corroborate The Disputed Identification Evidence?

- The determination on whether it is necessary to corroborate the disputed identification evidence **depends** on the **quality** of the **identification evidence**.

Good Quality Identification

- If the identification evidence is of a *good* **quality**:
    - ☐ Once the **Turnbull warning** has been **issued**;
    - ☐ The jury can be **left to assess the value** of the identification;
    - ☐ There is **no need to corroborate** the identification; and
    - ☐ A **conviction** can be **based** upon the **good quality identification evidence alone**.

Poor Quality Identification Evidence

- If the identification evidence is of a *poor* quality:
    - Once the **Turnbull warning** has been **issued**;
    - The judge *must:*
        - **Withdraw the case; and**
        - **Direct an acquittal;**
    - **Unless;**
    - There is **corroborating evidence** that supports the poor quality identification evidence.
    - If so – they *must* **identify** to the jury what **evidence** would be **capable** of **corroborating** the identification evidence.

Evidence & Procedure
Unit 18: Evidence (3) - Disclosure Rules

A - Personnel Involved In Disclosure Procedures

- A variety of **personnel** will be involved in a disclosure procedure:

1 - Officer In Charge Of The Case

- The **Officer In Charge Of The Investigation coordinates** the **investigation.**
- They must ensure that **procedures** are in place for:
    - **Recording;** and
    - **Retaining;**

    - all **relevant material** gathered during the investigation.

2 - Disclosure Officer

- The **Disclosure Officer** acts as the **link** between the:
    - **Investigation team;** and
    - **Prosecutor.**
- In **small investigations**:
    - The **disclosure officer;**
    - Can be the **same person;**
    - As the **officer in charge of the investigation.**

Who May Perform The Role Of Disclosure Officer?

- The role of **Disclosure Officer** may be **performed by** either:
    - A **police officer;** or
    - **Support staff.**

Duties Of The Disclosure Officer

- The **Disclosure Officer's** duties include:
    - **Examining** material retained by the **investigation team;**
    - **Revealing** to the **prosecutor:**
        - Schedules of:
            - Sensitive material;
            - Non sensitive material;

- Any **unused material** that might either:
  - **Undermine** the **prosecution** case; or
  - **Assist** the case for the **defence**.

3 - Prosecutor

- This includes any **individual** or **body** acting as **prosecutor**.

B - Disclosure Obligations

1 – When Will Disclosure Obligations Arise

- Disclosure obligations arise whenever a suspect pleads **not guilty** to a charge.

2 – The Rationale For Disclosure Obligations

- The ECHR in the case of *Rowe & Davis v United Kingdom* [2000] 30 EHRR 1 established that:
  - The right to a fair trial requires the prosecution to **disclose**:
    - All **material evidence** both:
      - **For**; and
      - **Against**;
    - The **accused**;
  - That is **in their possession**.

3 - Classes Of Material Subject To Disclosure Obligations

- There are different disclosure obligations in respect of **2 classes of material**:
  - Material that the **prosecution intends to use at trial** – *used material*; or
  - Material that the **prosecution** does **not intend to use at trial** – *unused material*.

(i) - Disclosure of Used Material

(a) - Either Way and Indictable Offences

- The **prosecution** is required;
- **On request**;
- To **supply** the **defence** with:
  - A **summary** of the **prosecution case**; and / or
  - Copies of the **statements** of the proposed **prosecution witnesses**.
- The rules state that advance disclosure is only necessary when it has been **requested** by the **defence**.
- However, **in practice** advance disclosure should where possible, be made available **prior to the first hearing**.

(b) - Summary Offences

- The case of *R v Stratford Justices, ex parte Imbert* [1999] 2 Cr App R 276 established in relation to **advance disclosure** in **summary offences:**
    - ☐ **Article 6 HRA does not give an absolute right to pre trial advance disclosure;** and
    - ☐ It will be a **question of fact** whether the presence or absence of advance disclosure has afforded the defendant the opportunity of a **fair trial.**
- It will be easier to satisfy this test when advance disclosure has been provided.

Exam Trip Up

- Where a person has given **several statements;**
- But all of the **information the prosecution seeks to rely upon** is **contained in just one of the statements;**
- **Only that individual statement need be supplied** in advance disclosure.

Time Limits For Disclosure Of Used Material - Attorney Generals Guidelines On Disclosure Paragraph 57

- **Indictable offences** — Within 50 days of sending if the suspect is on remand.
  — Within 70 days of sending if the suspect is on bail.
- **Either way offences** — Prior to the mode of trial hearing.
- **Summary offences** — In sufficient time to enable the defence to consider the evidence.

2 - Disclosure Of Unused Material – CPIA 1996

- A large volume of material may be generated during an investigation which the **prosecution will not seek to rely upon.**
- The rules governing the disclosure of unused material are governed by the provisions of the **Criminal Procedure and Investigations Act 1996.**

Examples Of Unused Material

- Examples of **unused material** include:
    - ☐ Details of witnesses who will not be called;
    - ☐ Police officers notebook entries;
    - ☐ Non incriminating CCTV footage;
    - ☐ Crime reports etc.

C - The Criminal Procedure and Investigations Act 1996 Disclosure Regime

- There are **6 stages** to the **disclosure regime:**
    - The **investigators record** and **retain** all **relevant material** gathered during the course of their **investigation;**
    - The **disclosure officer** compiles a **disclosure schedule** of all **sensitive** and **non-sensitive unused material.**
    - **Primary disclosure** by the **prosecutor.**
    - **Defence disclosure** of their **defence statement.**
    - **Secondary disclosure** by the **prosecutor.**
    - **The disclosure officer's ongoing duty to review the unused materials** in the light of the content of any **defence statement** served.

Stage 1
The Investigators Record And Retain All Relevant Material Gathered During The Course Of The Investigation

- The **investigators** must:
    - **Record;** and
    - **Retain;**

- all **relevant material** gathered during the course of their **investigation.**

When Will An Investigation Commence – CPIA 1996 Code Of Practice Paragraph 2.1

- A **criminal investigation** is:
    - An **investigation** conducted by police officers with a view to it being **ascertained** whether:
        - **A person should be charged** with an offence; or
        - **A person charged** with an offence **is guilty** of it.
- This includes investigations:
    - Into crimes that *have* been committed - (reactive in the knowledge there has been a crime);
    - To *ascertain* whether crimes have been committed - (determining whether there has been a crime);
    - In the belief that a crime *may* be committed - (in the future) – e.g. where the police keep premises or individuals under surveillance.

- In the case of *R v Uxbridge Magistrates Court, ex parte Patel* [2000] 164 JP 209:
    - It was confirmed that:
        - A **criminal investigation;**
        - *Could* begin *before* an offence is committed;
        - Where there was **advance surveillance in operation.**

What Is Relevant Material - CPIA 1996 Code Of Practice Paragraph 3.4

- In conducting the investigation the **investigator** should:
    - Pursue all **reasonable lines of enquiry**;
    - Whether these point **towards** or **away** from the suspect.

Stage 2
The Disclosure Officer Compiles A Disclosure Schedule Of All Sensitive And Non-Sensitive Unused Material

- The **disclosure officer** must compile **disclosure schedules** of all:
    - **Sensitive**; and
    - **Non-sensitive**
    - unused material.

- The **disclosure officer** must also:
    - **Draw to the prosecutor's attention** any **unused material** that might either:
        - **Undermine** the **prosecution** case; or
        - **Assist** the case for the **defence**.

- The **disclosure officer** will then forward:
    - The **schedules**; and
    - Any **unused material** that might either:
        - **Undermine** the **prosecution** case; or
        - **Assist** the case for the **defence**.
    - To the **prosecutor** who will **decide** what **unused material** will be **disclosed**.

Definition Of Sensitive Material

- **Sensitive material** involves information that it is **not in the public interest to disclose**.
- It can include material:
    - From **informants**;
    - Detailing **observation posts**;
    - **Police communications**.

Stage 3
Primary Disclosure By The Prosecutor

- The **prosecutor:**
    - **Considers the schedules;** and
    - **Discloses** to the **defence** any:
        - **Unused material** that might either:
            - **Undermine** the **prosecution** case; or
            - **Assist** the case for the **defence.**

Time Limit For Primary Prosecution Disclosure

- There is **no prescribed time limit.**
- **Primary prosecution disclosure** must take place **"as soon as practicable after the duty arises".**
- In reality the obligation kicks in upon:
    - **Committal** to the **Crown Court;** or
    - **Proceeding to trial** in the:
        - **Magistrates Court;** or
        - **Youth Court.**

Stage 4
Defence Disclosure Of A Defence Statement – Sections 5 & 6 CPIA 1996

- The **defence:**
    - Either:
        - *Must* in the **Crown Court;**
        - *May (discretion)* in the **Magistrates Court;**
    - Within **14 days** of **prosecution disclosure;**
    - **Serve** a **defence statement** upon:
        - The **court;** and
        - The **prosecution.**

Contents Of The Defence Statement – Section 6A CIPA 1996

- The **defence statement** must:
    - Set out the **nature** of the **accused's defence** that they will rely upon. **(e.g. "I did not assault the victim");**
    - Indicate the **matters of fact** that they **take issue** with the prosecution. **(e.g. "I disagree with the victims statement comment that I assaulted him");**
    - Explain why they take issue with the prosecution (e.g. "I was not present at the scene");
    - Indicate:
        - Points of law which they wish to take; and
        - Any authority they wish to rely upon for that purpose (e.g. exclusion of a confession pursuant to s76(2)(b) PACE 1984).
    - If the defence wish to rely upon an **alibi** – **details** of the **alibi** and any **supporting alibi witnesses** must be provided.
    - A **request for disclosure** of any material from the schedule of non sensitive **unused material** that either:
        - **Undermines** the **case** for the **prosecution**; or
        - **Assists** the **case** for the **accused**.

Inferences And Defence Statements

- **Once a defence is raised** in a defence statement the defendant is **stuck with it.**

- If a **different defence is run at trial from that contained in the defence statement** the court may draw **adverse inferences.**

- It was established in the case of *R v Lowe* [2003] EWCA Crim 3182 that the court may exercise its *discretion* to admit the defence statement:
    - In **cross examination** - when it is alleged that the defendant has **changed their defence**; or
    - In **re-examination** to **rebut** a suggestion of **recent fabrication** of the facts of their defence at the trial.

Circumstances In Which The Discretion To Serve A Defence Statement In A Summary Matter Is Likely To Be Exercised

- The **discretion** to serve a defence statement in a **summary offence** is likely to be exercised where the defence either:
    - Is **not satisfied** with the **material disclosed** by the **primary disclosure**; or
    - Wishes to **examine items** listed on the **schedule of non-sensitive material** (MG 6(c)); or
    - Wishes to **show the strength of their case** in order to **persuade the prosecution not to proceed.**

Stage 5
Secondary Prosecution Disclosure – Section 6E CPIA 1996

- Once a **defence statement** has been **provided**, the **disclosure officer** must:
    - **Review** the **schedules** of **unused materials;**
    - **Inform** the **prosecutor** of any **unused material** in the light of the defence raised in the defence statement that **assists** the **defence** raised by the accused.

Duties Of The Prosecutor Following Notification By The Disclosure Officer – Section 6E CPIA 1996

- The **prosecutor** must then either:
    - **Disclose** to the **defence** any such material; or
    - **Provide** the **defence** with a **written statement** that there is **no such material.**

Stage 6
The Disclosure Officer's Ongoing Duty To Review Unused Materials In the Light of The Contents Of Any Defence Statement Served – Section 7A CPIA 1996

- Both the:
    - **Disclosure officer;** and
    - **Prosecutor;**
- Have a **continuing duty** to keep the issue of **disclosure** under **review** at all times **until the case is completed** by virtue of:
    - **Acquittal;**
    - **Conviction;** or
    - **Discontinuance.**
- The **duty** is **not dependant** upon the **service of a defence statement** (which is **discretionary** in the **Magistrates Court**).
- However:
    - The **more comprehensive** the contents of a **defence statement;**
    - The **more likely** that it will **trigger** the **disclosure of unused material that supports any defence raised.**
- If any **unused material** is **subsequently revealed** that either:
    - **Undermine** the **case** for the **prosecution;** or
    - **Assist** the **defence** raised by the accused.
    - The material must be **disclosed** to the **defence** as soon as is reasonably practicable.

D - Retention Of Material As Outlined By CPIA 1996

- Paragraphs 5.6 – 5.10 of the Code of Practice outlines that:
    - **Following** a **conviction**;
    - **All relevant material** must be **retained** at least until:
    - Either:
        - The time the defendant is **released** from **custody** following a **custodial sentence**;
        - The time the defendant is **discharged** from **hospital** following the imposition of a **hospital order**;
    - In **all cases** - for **6 months after conviction**.

Exam Trip Up

- If the defendant is:
    - **Released** from:
        - **Custody**; or
        - **Hospital**;
    - **Prior to the 6 month watershed**;
    - Then the **relevant material must still be retained for at least 6 months from the time of the conviction**.

For example:

- A defendant is sentenced to a 12 month custodial sentence, although is released after 4 months.
- In these circumstances the material should be retained for an additional 2 months after release.

Evidence & Procedure
Unit 19 – Evidence (4)
Excluding Confessions & Other Evidence

Confessions

A - Admissibility Of Confessions – Section 76(1) PACE 1984

- **Section 76(1) PACE 1984** provides that:
    - ☐ Whilst confessions are prima facie **hearsay** in nature;
    - ☐ They are **admissible** in evidence as an **exception** to the **rule against hearsay**.

B - Definition Of A Confession – Section 82 PACE 1984

- Section 82 PACE 1984 defines a **confession** as:
- Any **statement**;
- Which is either:
    - ☐ **Wholly** or
    - ☐ **Partly**;
- **Adverse** to the **maker**;
- Whether made to a person:
    - ☐ **In authority**; or
    - ☐ **Not in authority**;
- Whether:
    - ☐ **In words**; or
    - ☐ **Otherwise**.

C - Definition Of A Statement

- The **statement** may take the form of either:
    - ☐ **Words**;
    - ☐ **Writing**;
    - ☐ **A video taped re-enactment;** *Li Shu-Ling v The Queen* [1989] AC 270; or
    - ☐ **Conduct** – e.g. - The defendant nodding head in acknowledgement to a question posed implicating themselves.

Exam Trip Up

- **Silence** in response to a question posed will **not** amount to a **statement**.

Summary Table

Overview Of The Courts Exclusionary Powers

	Section 76(2)(a)	Section 76(2)(b)	Section 78	Section 82(3)
Key Word	Oppression	Said or Done Unreliable	Unfairness	Probative value Prejudicial effect
Relates To Excluding What?	Confessions only	Confessions only	All evidence including confessions	All evidence including confessions
Must or May Exclude	Must	Must	May (discretion)	May (discretion)

D - Excluding Improperly Obtained Confessions

1 – Oppression

(i) Criteria Of Oppression - Section 76(2)(a) PACE 1984

- **Section 76(2) PACE 1984** stipulates that a court:
    - ☐ **Must** exclude (**no discretion**);
    - ☐ A **confession**;
    - ☐ If it was obtained by **oppression** of the accused.

(ii) – Definition Of Oppressive Behaviour

- **Section 76(8) PACE 1984** defines **oppression** as:
    - ☐ **Torture**;
    - ☐ **Inhuman treatment**;
    - ☐ **Degrading treatment**;
    - ☐ **Use of violence**; or
    - ☐ **Threats of violence**.

- The Court of Appeal in the case of *R v Fulling* [1987] QB 426, further defined **oppression** as:

    "The exercise of authority or power in a burdensome, harsh, or wrongful manner; unjust or cruel treatment of subjects, inferiors etc, the imposition of unreasonable or unjust burdens."

- Think of oppressive behaviour as a **sliding scale** - At one extreme there is torture and at the other extreme are unjust burdens which pressurise the suspect into confessing.

(iii) - Examples Of Oppressive Behaviour

- In *R v Paris* [1993] 97 Cr App R 99, a mentally vulnerable person was bullied into confessing by being repeatedly asked over 300 times if he had committed the offence.

- In *R v Heron* [1993], unreported a suspect confessed because they were falsely informed that they had been identified.

- In *R v Howden-Simpson* [1991] Crim LR 49, a choirmaster was threatened that if he did not confess members of his choir would have to be interviewed.

- In *Barbera v Spain* [1988] 11 EHRR 360, a person was unjustifiably denied access to a solicitor.

- In *R v Silcott* [1991] The Times, 9 December, a person was interviewed in the absence of an appropriate adult.

(iv) - Who Does The Burden Of Proof Rest Upon To Substantiate Oppression?

- The **defence** must **raise a reasonable doubt** that the confession was induced by oppressive behaviour.

- If the **defence** are able to do so – the burden then shifts upon the **prosecution** to **prove beyond all reasonable doubt** that the confession was not obtained by oppression.

(v) - Proving The Causal Connection Between The Oppressive Act And The Confession

- There must be a **direct causal connection** between:
    - The **oppressive act**; and
    - The **consequent** making of the **confession.**

Exam Trip Up

- Watch out for questions where the detainee:
    - **Confesses;**
    - **Before;**
    - **The oppressive act.**

- As:
    - The **confession** comes **before** the **oppressive act;**
    - The **confession** will **not** have **caused** by the **oppression**; and
    - The confession will **not be excluded.**

Exam Trip Up

- Watch out for questions where a suspect:
    - During an **initial interview**:
        - Is **oppressed;** but
        - Remains **silent**; and
        - **Does not confess**; and
    - During a **subsequent interview** conducted by **different interview team:**
        - Is **not oppressed**; and
        - **Confesses.**

- In such circumstances:
    - The **initial oppression**;
    - Will **not** have **caused** the **subsequent confession**; and
    - The confession will therefore remain **admissible.**

Exam Trip Up

- The **truth or otherwise** of the confession is **irrelevant.**
- All that maters is whether the oppressive act caused the confession.

(vi) – What Effect Will An Excluded Confession Obtained Via Oppression In An Initial Interview Have Upon The Admissibility Of A Subsequent Confession Obtained During A Properly Conducted Interview

- The case of *R v Ismail* [1990] Crim LR 109 established that:
    - Where an **initial confession** has been obtained as a consequence of **oppressive** behaviour;
    - That **initial oppressive confession must** be **excluded**; and
    - Any **subsequent confession** obtained fairly **may** also be **excluded.**

2 - Unreliability

(i) – Criteria Of Unreliability - Section 76(2)(b) PACE 1984

- **Section 76(2)(b) PACE 1984** stipulates that:
    - A court **must** exclude **(no discretion)** a **confession** if it was obtained:
        - In **consequence** of anything:
            - **Said**; or
            - **Done**;
        - That was likely in the **circumstances existing at the time** to render the confession **unreliable.**

(ii) Definition Of Unreliability

- There is **no statutory definition** of **unreliability.**

(iii) - Examples Of Something Said

- Things **said** usually involve a **positive act** or **inducement.**
- Examples of things said include:
    - **Offering bail** as an inducement to confessing;
    - **Telling** the suspect that they will be **kept in custody indefinitely** until they confess.

(iv) - Examples Of Something Done

- Things **done** usually involve a **failure** to **comply** with the detainee's **rights.**
- Examples of things **done** include:
    - **Failing** to caution;
    - **Failing** to offer the right to legal advice and intimation where the rights cannot be justifiably withheld under Code C;
    - **Breaching** the PACE Codes of Practice.

(v) – Establishing A Causal Connection

- There must be a **direct causal connection** between:
    - The **thing said** or **done** by the police; and
    - The **consequent** making of the **confession.**

(vi) - Who Does The Burden Of Proof Rest Upon To Substantiate Unreliability?

- The **defence** must **raise a reasonable doubt** that the confession was unreliable.
- If the **defence** are able to do so – the burden then shifts upon the **prosecution** to **prove beyond all reasonable doubt** that the confession was not unreliable.

3 - The Fruit Of The Poisoned Tree – Section 76(4) PACE 1984

- If a confession is excluded under section 76(2) PACE 1984 any **additional evidence gained after the confession**:
    - **Will remain admissible**;
    - But the prosecution will be **prevented from linking the evidence to the confession.**
- This may **affect the probative value** of the evidence.

    For example:

- If following the making of a confession that was later excluded, a person identified the whereabouts of drugs:
    - The prosecution would be **allowed** to adduce **evidence** that **drugs** were **recovered;**
    - The prosecution would **not** be able to adduce **evidence** of **how** they became **aware** of the **drug's whereabouts**.
- Therefore unless there was other evidence linking the drugs to the defendant such as:
    - DNA evidence; or
    - The drugs being recovered from the defendant's property;
- The recovery of the drugs would be of little probative value.

E - Excluding Evidence In General (Including Confessions)

1 – Unfairness

(i) – Criteria For Unfairness – Section 78 PACE 1984

- **Section 78 PACE 1984** provides that:
- A court *may* **(discretion)** exclude *any* evidence if:
    - Having regard to **all the circumstances;**
    - Including the **circumstances** in which the **evidence was obtained;**
    - The admission of the evidence would have an **adverse effect** on the **fairness** of the proceedings.

(ii) - Examples of Improper Circumstances Which Caused Unfairness

- Fabricating evidence causing a suspect to confess due to a misleading impression of the strength of the evidence against hem.
- Failure by a Custody Officer to inform a detainee of their rights.
- Failure to secure the attendance of a:
    - Solicitor;
    - Appropriate Adult; or
    - Interpreter.

2 - Retention Of The Common Law Discretion To Exclude Evidence - Section 82(3) PACE 1984

- Section 82(3) PACE 1984 retains the courts **common law discretion** to **exclude any evidence**.

- The court will consider the **effect** of admitting the evidence on the trial and will conduct a **balancing exercise**.

- If the **probative value** of the evidence **outweighs** the **prejudicial effect** caused to the defendant then the evidence will be **admitted** at trial.

- If the **prejudicial effect** caused to the defendant **outweighs** the **probative value** of the evidence then the court will **exclude** the evidence at trial.

Evidence & Procedure
Unit 20: Criminal Justice System (2) Court Procedure

A - Categories of Offences

- There are **3 categories** of offences:
    - **Summary offences** – which can *only* be tried in the **Magistrates Court**;
    - **Indictable offences** - which can *only* be tried in the **Crown Court**;
    - **Either way offences** – which can be tried in *either* the **Magistrates Court** or the **Crown Court**.

1 - Definition Of Summary Offences

- An offence will be **summary** where a **statute**:
    - **Only** provides a maximum penalty imposable on **summary conviction**; and
    - Does *not* provide a penalty for a conviction on **indictment**.

Maximum Penalty For A Summary Offence – Section 78 Powers of Criminal Courts Sentencing) Act 2000

- The **maximum custodial sentence** for a summary offence is:
    - **6 months** imprisonment; or
    - Any **lesser period specified** in legislation in relation to the offence.
- The **maximum fine** for a summary offence is:
    - **£5000.00**; or
    - Any **lesser amount specified** in legislation in relation to the offence.

2 - Definition Of An Indictable Offence

- An offence will be **indictable** where either:
    - It is a **common law** offence; or
    - A **statute** which:
        - **Only** provides a maximum penalty imposable on **indictment**; and
        - **Does not** provide a penalty for a **summary** conviction.

Maximum Penalty For Indictable Offences

- The **maximum penalty** for an **indictable offence** is **that specified** in relation to each offence.

3 - Definition Of An Either Way Offence

- An offence will be **either way** where a **statute** provides a **maximum penalty** for:
    - A **summary** conviction; and
    - A conviction on **indictment**.

Maximum Penalty For Either Way Offences

- If an either way offence is dealt with in the **Magistrates Court:**
    - The **maximum custodial sentence** is:
        - **6 months** imprisonment; or
        - Any **lesser period specified** in legislation in relation to the offence.
    - The **maximum fine** is:
        - **£5000.00**; or
        - Any **lesser amount specified** in legislation in relation to the offence.
- If an either way offence is dealt with in the **Crown Court:**
    - The **maximum penalty** is **that specified** in relation to each offence.

B - Mode Of Trial Hearing For Either Way Offences

- The **Magistrates** will initially decide whether they wish to **accept** or **decline** jurisdiction in the matter.

- The Magistrates will listen to **representations** from the **prosecutor** and the **defence** in a **mode of trial hearing** prior to exercising their decision.

- If the Magistrates *decline* jurisdiction:
    - The matter will be **sent** to the **Crown Court** for trial; and
    - The **defendant** will have *no choice* in the matter.

- If the Magistrates *accept* jurisdiction the **defendant** will have the *choice* of being tried either:
    - In the **Magistrates Court**; or
    - In the **Crown Court**.

1 - Factors The Magistrates Will Consider In Determining Whether To Accept Jurisdiction – Section 19 Magistrates Court Act 1980

- In determining whether the matter is most suitable for trial in the Magistrates Court or the Crown Court, the Magistrates will consider the following factors:
    - The **nature** of the case;
    - Whether the **circumstances** of the offence make it of a **serious character;**

        (With reference to the **aggravating** and **mitigating factors** outlined in the *National Mode of Trial Guidelines);*

    - Whether the **Magistrates Court's sentencing powers** are **adequate** if the defendant was found guilty;

- **Any other circumstances** which appear to the court to make it more suitable for the offence to be tried either in the Magistrates Court summarily or in the Crown Court on indictment.

2 - The National Mode of Trial Guidelines

- The *National Mode of Trial Guidelines* assist Magistrates in determining mode of trial issues. They state that:
    - The court should **never** make its **decision** on the grounds of:
        - **Convenience**; or
        - **Expedition;**
    - The court should assume for mode of trial purposes that the **prosecution version of events is true**;
    - Cases should be **referred** to the **Crown Court** if they **involve complex:**
        - Questions of **law;** or
        - Questions of **fact;**
    - Where **two or more** persons are **jointly charged** – **each person** has the **right to elect** their mode of trial;
    - There is a **presumption** that:
        - **Either way offences** should be **tried summarily**;
        - **Unless;**
        - There is **one** or **more seriousness indicator present**; and
        - The **Magistrates Court's sentencing powers** are **inadequate.**
    - The Magistrates must consider its power to **commit** an offender to the **Crown Court** for **sentence** under section 3 PCC(S)A 2000 if:
        - **Information emerges during the trial;**
        - That leads them to **believe** that their **sentencing powers** are **inadequate** because of:
            - The **seriousness** of the offence; or
            - The **offender** posing such a **risk to the public.**

3 - Are The Defendant's Previous Convictions Relevant In Determining Mode Of Trial

(i) - The General Rule

- The case of *R v Colchester Justices, ex parte North East Essex Building Company* [1977] 1 WLR 1109, established that *no account* should be taken of the defendant's previous convictions when determining mode of trial.

(ii) - The Exception To The General Rule – Section 111 PCC(S)A 2000

- If a defendant:
    - ☐ Has **2 previous convictions** for **domestic burglary**;
    - ☐ Is **charged** with a **3rd offence** of **domestic burglary**; and
    - ☐ **All 3 offences** were committed **after 30th November 1999**;

- In the **event** of the person being **convicted** for the **3rd domestic burglary** - the court will be **obliged** to:
    - ☐ Impose a custodial sentence of **3 years**;
    - ☐ **Unless**;
    - ☐ The **circumstances to not justify** imposing such a sentence.

- As this **penalty exceeds the maximum sentencing powers of the Magistrates Court** – the Magistrates *must:*
    - ☐ **Automatically** treat the offence as **indictable** in nature;
    - ☐ **Decline** jurisdiction; and
    - ☐ **Refer** the matter to the **Crown Court** for **trial.**

C - Summary Offence Procedure

Investigation.

Charge.	Summons.

1st appearance in the Magistrates Court.	
Guilty Plea.	Not guilty plea.
Sentence immediately or adjourn for a pre sentence report then sentence.	Bail, legal aid and adjourn for disclosure.

Summary trial in the Magistrates Court.

D - Either Way Offence Procedure

| Investigation. |

| Charge. | Summons. |

| 1st appearance in the Magistrates Court. |
| Guilty Plea. | Not guilty plea. |
| Sentence immediately or adjourn for pre sentence report then sentence. | Bail, legal aid & adjourn for disclosure. |

Mode of trial hearing in the Magistrates Court.

- If the Magistrates accept jurisdiction – choice for the defendant.

- If the defendant chooses trial in the Magistrates Court – the matter is adjourned and a date is set for the trial in the Magistrates Court.

- If the defendant chooses trial in the Crown Court - the matter is adjourned for a committal hearing.

- If the Magistrates decline jurisdiction – the matter is adjourned for a committal hearing.

Committal hearing.

- If there is a case to answer the matter is committed to the Crown Court and a date will be set for a Plea and Case Management Hearing.

Plea and Case Management Hearing In The Crown Court

- Defendant enters their plea.

- If a guilty plea is entered – sentence there and then or adjourn for a pre sentence report and then sentence.

- If not guilty plea is entered – a date is set for the Crown Court Trial and the matter is adjourned.

Trial in the Crown Court.

E - Indictable Offence Procedure

Investigation.

Charge.

1st appearance in the Magistrates Court.

- Bail addressed.
- Legal aid addressed.
- Matter is referred to the Crown Court.

1st appearance in the Crown Court.

- Timetable set for disclosure.
- Bail reconsidered.
- Matter adjourned for a Plea and Case Management Hearing.

- Disclosure takes place.
- Defence may apply to have the charges dismissed where appropriate.

Plea and Case Management Hearing In The Crown Court.

- Defendant enters their plea.
- If a guilty plea is entered – sentence there and then or adjourn for a pre sentence report and then sentence.
- If not guilty plea is entered – a date is set for the Crown Court Trial and the matter is adjourned.

Trial in the Crown Court.

F - Offences Committed By Juveniles

1 - The General Rule – Trial And Sentence In The Youth Court

- Persons **under** the age of **18**;
- *Must* be:
    - ☐ **Tried**; and
    - ☐ **Sentenced**;
- In the **Youth Court**;
- For both:
    - ☐ **Summary** offences; and
    - ☐ **Indictable** offences.

2 - Exception – Trial Of Juveniles In The Crown Court – Section 24 Magistrates Court Act 1980

- A **juvenile** may be **tried** in the **Crown Court** in relation to:
    - ☐ Offences relating to:
        - **Homicide**;
        - **Firearms**;
        - **Serious sexual offences**;
    - ☐ Offences carrying a sentence of **14 years or more imprisonment** for an adult;
    - ☐ Circumstances where:
        - The **juvenile**:
            - ☐ Has been **jointly charged** with an **adult**;
            - ☐ Who has been **sent for trial** in the **Crown Court** for:
                - The **same** offence; or
                - **Related** offences.

3 - Exception – Sentencing Of Juveniles In The Crown Court – Section 91 PCC(S)A 2000

- A juvenile **tried** in the **Youth Court** can be referred for **sentence** in the **Crown Court** where:
    - ☐ The **Youth Court** considers its **sentencing powers** to be **insufficient**; or
    - ☐ The **juvenile** has:
        - **Pleaded guilty** to an **offence** in the **Youth Court**; and
        - Has been **committed** to the **Crown Court** for the **trial** of other **related offences**.

4 - Exception - Trial Of Juveniles In The Magistrates Court

- A **juvenile** may be **tried** in the **adult Magistrates Court** where:
    - ☐ The **juvenile** is **jointly charged** with an **adult** - Section 46(1) Children and Young Persons Act 1933; and
    - ☐ The **juvenile** is **charged**:
        - With:
            - ☐ **Aiding;**
            - ☐ **Abetting;**
            - ☐ **Causing;**
            - ☐ **Procuring;**
            - ☐ **Allowing;** or
            - ☐ **Permitting;**
        - An **adult** to **commit** an offence – Section 18 Children and Young Persons Act 1963.

Evidence & Procedure
Unit 21 – Criminal Justice System (1)
Summonses & Warrants

A - Securing A Defendant's Attendance Before A Magistrates Court

- The defendant's attendance can be secured via a variety of means:
    - **Arresting** the defendant **without warrant, charging** them and then either:
        - **Bailing** them to attend **court**;
        - **Refusing them bail** and **bringing them before the court in police custody**;
    - The **prosecutor laying an information before a Magistrate or a Magistrate's Clerk** resulting in the Magistrate (Clerk) issuing either:
        - A **summons** requiring them to attend court on a specified date or time;
        - A **warrant** for them to be arrested. Following arrest they are then either:
            - Brought immediately before the court; or
            - Bailed to attend court at a later date and time.

B – Laying An Information

1 - The Meaning Of Laying An Information – Rule 4 MCR 1981 & Section 1 MCA 1980

- **Laying an information** means:
    - Either a:
        - A Prosecutor;
        - A barrister or solicitor on the Prosecutor's behalf;
        - Any other authorised person (e.g. a Probation Officer);
    - May provide a:
        - **Written allegation**; or
        - **Verbal allegation**;
    - To a **Magistrate** that a person has either:
        - **Committed an offence**; or
        - **Is suspected of having committed an offence.**
- An information *must* be presented before a summons or warrant can be issued.

2 - When Is An Information Laid?

- The case of *R v Manchester Stipendiary Magistrate, ex parte Hill* [1983] 1 AC 328 established that:
    - ☐ A *written* information is **laid** when it is **received in the office of the Clerk of the Justices.**
    - ☐ An *oral* information is **laid** by:
        - The **informant going before** either:
            - ☐ A **Magistrate;** or
            - ☐ A **Clerk;**
        - To make their allegation for the issue of a **summons.**

3 - Exam Trip Up – Informations Laid To Obtain A Warrant For Arrest – Section 1(3) Magistrates Court Act 1980

- If the information is laid *orally:*
    - ☐ It can **only** be used to obtain a **summons;**
    - ☐ It *cannot* be used to obtain a **warrant for arrest.**
- If a **warrant for arrest** is sought it *must* be laid in **writing.**

4 - Exam Trip Up - Establishing The Identity Of The Individual laying An Information

- The information *must:*
    - ☐ Be **laid** by an actual **named person;** and
    - ☐ **Disclose** their **identity.**
- The case of *Rubin v DPP* [1990] 2 QB 80 established that:
    - ☐ A **police force** itself *cannot* **lay an information** – e.g. an information laid in the name of Greater Manchester Police;
    - ☐ But the information *can* be laid on the **forces behalf** by the **named** Chief Constable of that force.

4 - Options Available To A Magistrate Following The Laying Of An Information – Section 1 MCA 1980

- When an information is laid;
- A **Magistrate** *may* issue either:
    - ☐ A *summons* requiring the person to **(voluntarily) attend** the Magistrates Court; or
    - ☐ A *warrant to arrest* that person and **bring them** before the Magistrates Court.
- A **Magistrate's Clerk** *may* only issue a *summons* requiring the person to **(voluntarily) attend** the Magistrates Court.

Exam Trip Up

- A **Magistrate's Clerk** cannot issue a *warrant to arrest* that person and **bring them** before the Magistrates Court.

C – Summons

1 - The Meaning Of A Summons

- A **summons** is:
    - A **written order** issued either by:
        - A **Magistrate;** or
        - A **Magistrates Clerk** on the Magistrates behalf;
    - Ordering the person to:
        - **Attend** a named court;
        - At a specified **date and time;**
    - To either:
        - **Answer the offence** set out in the summons; or
        - **Attend to give evidence or produce exhibits** (witness summons).

2 – The Criteria For Issuing A Summons

- The **Magistrate** or their **Clerk** must be satisfied:
    - The information relates to an **offence known to law;**
    - The information was laid within any **relevant time limits** for the offence in question;
    - Any **consents necessary** for bringing the prosecution have been **obtained;**
    - That there is **jurisdiction** to issue a summons.

3 - The Contents Of A Summons – Criminal Procedure Rules 2005 – Rule 7.7(2)

- The **summons** should state:
    - The **substance** of the **allegations** contained in the information laid against them;
    - The **location, date,** and **time** they are required to **attend** to answer the charge.

4 - Who Signs A Summons? – Criminal Procedure Rules 2005 – Rule 7.7(1)

- The summons *must* either:
    - Be **signed** by the:
        - **Justice** issuing it;
        - **Clerk** issuing it; or
    - In the case of a summons **issued** by a **Justice:**
        - Contain the **name** of the **Justice** issuing it;
        - Be **authenticated** by the **signature** of the **Clerk.**

5 - Service Of A Summons

(i) - Standard Procedure - Criminal Procedure Rules 2005 – Rule 4.1(1)

- The summons may be **served** on the **defendant** by either:
    - **Personal delivery**; or
    - Determining the defendant's **last known** or **usual place of abode** and either:
        - **Posting** the summons there; or
        - **Leaving** the summons there with **another person**.

(ii) - Service Upon A Corporation - Criminal Procedure Rules 2005 – Rule 4.1(2)

- Service of the summons upon a **corporation** may be achieved by either:
    - **Delivering** it to its **registered office** in the UK;
    - **Posting** it to its **registered office** in the UK; or
    - If the corporation is **not registered in the UK** either:
        - **Delivering** it to its **place of trade or business**; or
        - **Posting** it to its **place of trade or business**.

(iii) Service Upon Members Of The Armed Services - Criminal Procedure Rules 2005 – Rule 4.1

- **Service** upon a member of the **armed services** is effected by serving the summons upon **both**:
    - The **defendant** themselves; and
    - Their **Commanding Officer** (Army & RAF); or
    - The **Commanding Officer** of their ship or other establishment (Navy & Marines).

7 - Proceeding In The Defendant's Absence Following Service

- A court can **proceed in the absence of the accused** where a **signed certificate of service** is produced from person delivering the summons.

D – Warrants

1 – The Range Of Warrants

- There are several **different forms of warrant**:
    - Warrant to **arrest an offender**;
    - Warrant to **arrest a witness**;
    - Warrant to **arrest in default**;
    - Warrant to **commit to prison**;
    - Warrant to **distrain property**.

2 - Magistrates Power To Issue Warrants – Section 1(1)(b) MCA 1980

- When a **Magistrate receives** an **information**; and
- Has the **power to issue a summons**;
- The **Magistrate** *only* (not a Clerk);
- May choose instead to issue a **warrant for arrest** provided:
    - ☐ The information is **in writing**; and
    - ☐ Either:
        - The offence *must* be **indictable or punishable with imprisonment**; or
        - The defendant's **address** *must* be **insufficiently established** for a summons to be served.

Exam Trip Up

- A **Magistrate's Clerk** <u>cannot</u> issue a *warrant* – **only the Magistrate** can issue a warrant.

3 - Execution Of A Warrant

(i) Who May Execute The Warrant? – Criminal Procedure Rules 2005 – Rule 18.3(3)

- A **warrant** for:
    - ☐ **Arrest**;
    - ☐ **Commitment**; or
    - ☐ **Detention**;
- May be **executed** by either:
    - ☐ The persons to whom it is **directed**; or
    - ☐ **Irrespective** of whether they were **directed**:
        - A **constable** from **any police area** in **England & Wales** – providing they are *acting in their own police area;* or
        - Any **authorised**:
            - ☐ **Civilian Enforcement Officers**; or
            - ☐ **Enforcement Agencies.**

(ii) - Warrants That Need Not In The Constables Possession At The Point Of Execution – Section 125D Magistrates Court Act 1980

- The following warrants may be **executed** by a **constable** even when they are *not* in the constables possession at the time:
    - ☐ Warrants to arrest a person in connection to an offence;
    - ☐ Warrants of commitment;
    - ☐ Warrants of distress;
    - ☐ Warrants to arrest a witness;

- Warrants in relation to:
  - The armed forces;
  - Insufficiency of distress;
  - Failure to comply with an occupation order or non molestation order;
  - Unwilling witnesses;
  - Offenders referred to court by a young offender panel;
  - Non appearance of a defendant.

(iii) - Defining "In Possession"

- In *R v Purdy* [1974] 3 All ER 465, a warrant in a police car **60 yards away** from the scene of the arrest **was** deemed to be **in possession.**

- In *De Costa Small v Kirkpatrick* [1979] Crim LR 41, a warrant in a police station **half a mile** away was deemed **not** to be **in possession.**

(iv) - Procedural Steps To Be Followed By A Constable When Executing A Warrant – Criminal Procedure Rules 2005 – Rule 18.3(4)

- Where a **constable** executes a **warrant** of:
  - **Arrest;**
  - **Commitment;** or
  - **Detention;**
- They *must* when arresting:
  - Either:
    - **Show** the **warrant** – *only if* they **have it with them**; or
    - **Explain:**
      - **Where** the warrant is; and
      - The **arrangements** that can be made to **inspect** the warrant;
  - **Explain** in **ordinary language:**
    - The **charge;** and
    - The **reason** for their **arrest;**
  - **Show documentary proof** of their **identity** – *unless* they are **in uniform.**

(v) – Additional Procedural Steps To Be Followed By A Civilian Enforcement Officer Or Approved Agencies When Executing A Warrant – Criminal Procedure Rules 2005 – Rule 18.3(4)

- **In addition** to the aforementioned steps;
- The:
    - ☐ Civilian Enforcement Officer; or
    - ☐ Officer of the Approved Agencies;
- *Must* show a **written statement** specifying:
    - ☐ The officer's **name;**
    - ☐ The **authority** by which they are employed;
    - ☐ That they are **authorised** to execute warrants.

(vi) - Powers Of Entry & Search When Executing A Warrant – Sections 17(1)(a) & 117 PACE 1984

- When executing a warrant for:
    - ☐ **Arrest** in criminal proceedings; or
    - ☐ **Commitment;**
- A **constable** may:
    - ☐ **Enter;** and
    - ☐ **Search;**
- Any *part* of a **premises** where they **reasonably** *believe* the **person sought is located**; and
- **Reasonable force** may be used where necessary.

Exam Trip Up

- The search is only permitted to extend to any *part* of a **premises** where they **reasonably** *believe* the **person sought is located** and cannot extend to areas where the constable does not believe the person may be located.

Evidence & Procedure
Unit 22: Criminal Justice System (3) Witnesses

A - Witness Competence & Compellability

1 - Definition Of Competence

- A witness is **competent** if they can be **called** by a party to **give evidence**.

2 - Definition Of Compellability

- A witness is **compellable** if they can be **compelled (forced)** by the court to give evidence.

3 - The General Rule – Section 53(1) YJCEA 1999

- **All** witnesses are **competent**.
- **All** competent witnesses are **compellable**.
- As a **general rule** - if a witness receives a witness summons and does not attend court to give evidence, they will be:
    - In **contempt of court**; and
    - Liable to **imprisonment**.

4 - The Exceptions To The General Rule

(a) - The Accused As A Witness For The Prosecution

(i) - The Accused As A Witness For The Prosecution Against Themselves - Section 53(4) YJCEA 1999

- An accused is **not** a **competent** witness for the prosecution against themselves.
- As they are **not competent** to give evidence against themselves they **cannot be compelled** to do so.

(ii) – The Accused As A Witness For The Prosecution Against Their Co-Accused

The General Rule – Section 53(4) YJCEA 1999

- An accused is **not** a **competent** witness **for the prosecution against their co-accused**.

The Exception To The General Rule – Section 53(5) YJCEA 1999

- If an accused **ceases to be a co-accused**, then they **will be competent and compellable by the prosecution against their former co-accused**.

- The accused will **cease to be a co-accused** in the following ways:
    - ☐ The accused **pleads guilty**;
    - ☐ The accused **acquitted**;
    - ☐ The accused is **tried separately** from the co-accused;
    - ☐ Proceedings are **discontinued** against the accused.

(b) - The Accused As A Witness For The Defence

(i) – The Accused As A Witness For Their Own Defence - Section 1 CEA 1898.

- An accused is **competent** but **not compellable** to give evidence in their **own defence**.

(ii) – The Accused As A Witness For The Defence Of Their Co-Accused

The General Rule

- An accused **is competent** to give evidence for the **defence** of a **co-accused**.
- But the accused is **not compellable** to give evidence for the **defence** of a **co-accused**.

The Exception To The General Rule

- If the **accused ceases to be a co-accused** then the former accused becomes both **competent** and **compellable** as a witness for the **defence of their former co-accused**.

(c) - The Competence And Compellability Of Spouses And Civil Partners

The Definition Of A Spouse – Section 80(5) PACE 1984

- A **spouse** is a person **married** to the accused *at the time of the trial.*
- A *former spouse* is **treated as if they were never married** to the accused for the purposes of the legislation.

The Definition Of A Civil Partnership

- A **civil partner** is a person **in an ongoing civil partnership** with the accused *at the time of the trial.*
- A *former civil partner* is **treated as if they never entered into a civil partnership** with the accused for the purposes of the legislation.

Exam Trip Up

- Watch out for questions where the parties were **married or in a civil partnership** at the time of the commission of the **offence** or their **arrest** for the offence but have **subsequently divorced or had their civil partnership dissolved prior to the trial.**
- In such circumstances they will be **treated as if they have never been married or had never entered into a civil partnership.**

(i) - Spouses Or Civil Partners As Witnesses For The Prosecution Against Either The Accused Or The Co-Accused – Section 80(1)(a) PACE 1984

Competence

- The **spouse** is **competent** to give evidence **for the prosecution** against the:
    - ☐ **Accused**; or
    - ☐ **Co-accused**.

Compellability - The General Rule

- The **spouse** or **civil partner cannot** generally be **compelled** to give evidence against either the:
    - ☐ **Accused**; or
    - ☐ **Co-accused**.

Compellability – The Exception To The General Rule – Section 80(3) PACE 1984

- The only **exception** is where the offence involves falls within the **circumstances** specified in section 80(3) PACE 1984:
    - ☐ **Assault, injury**, or **threat of injury** to the **spouse**;
    - ☐ **Assault, injury**, or **threat of injury** to a child **under** the age of **16**;
    - ☐ A **sexual offence** committed in respect of a child **under** the age of **16**;
    - ☐ **Attempting, conspiring, aiding, abetting, counselling, procuring** or **inciting** any of the above.

Negating The Exception To The General Rule – Spouses Or Civil Partners As Co-Accused – Section 80(4) PACE 1984

- This **exception** does **not apply** in circumstances where the **husband** and **wife** or **civil partners** are **jointly charged**.
- In such circumstances it is necessary to **revert to the rules governing the competence and compellability of co-accused for the prosecution**.

(ii) - Spouses Or Civil Partners As Witnesses For The Defence

Spouses Or Civil Partners As Witnesses For The Defence On Behalf Of The Accused

Competence – Section 80(1)(b) PACE 1984

- The accused's **spouse** or **civil partner** is **competent** to give evidence **on behalf of the accused**.

Compellability – Section 80(2) PACE 1984

- The accused's **spouse** or **civil partner** is **compellable** to give evidence on **behalf of the accused**.

Exception – Section 80(4) PACE 1984

- The only **exception** is where the **husband** and **wife** or **civil partners** are **jointly charged**.
- In such circumstances it is necessary to **revert to the rules governing the competence and compellability of co-accused for the prosecution**.

Spouses Or Civil Partners As Witnesses For The Defence On Behalf Of The Co-accused

Competence – Section 80(1)(b) PACE 1984

- The **accused's spouse** or **civil partner** is **competent** to give evidence **on behalf of the co-accused**.

Compellability - The General Rule

- The **accused's spouse** or **civil partner cannot** generally be **compelled** to give evidence on **behalf of co-accused**.

Compellability - The Exception To The General Rule

- The only **exception** is where the offence involves falls within the **circumstances** specified in section 80(3) PACE 1984:
    - **Assault, injury**, or **threat of injury** to the **spouse**;
    - **Assault, injury**, or **threat of injury** to a child **under** the age of **16**;
    - A **sexual offence** committed in respect of a child **under** the age of **16**;
    - **Attempting, conspiring, aiding, abetting, counselling, procuring** or **inciting** any of the above.

Negating The Exception To The General Rule – Spouses Or Civil Partners As Co-accused – Section 80(4) PACE 1984

- This **exception** does **not apply** in circumstances where the **husband** and **wife** or **civil partners** are **jointly charged**.
- In such circumstances it is necessary to **revert to the rules governing the competence and compellability of co-accused for the prosecution**.

5 - The Capacity Of Witnesses To Give Evidence – Section 53(3) YJCEA 1999

- **All** witnesses;
- **Irrespective** of their **age**;
- Will have the **capacity** to give evidence;
- **Unless**;
- They are **unable to give intelligible testimony** because they **cannot** either:
    - **Understand questions** put to them as a witness; or
    - **Give answers** which can be **understood**.

- If the witness does **not possess** the requisite **capacity** – they will **not be permitted to give evidence** even if they are a compellable witness.

6 - Sworn Testimony – Section 55(2) YJCEA 1999

- Witnesses aged **14 or over**;
- Possessing the requisite **capacity (capable of giving intelligible testimony)**;
- Will give their evidence via **sworn testimony**;
- Provided they have **sufficient appreciation** of:
    - The **solemnity of the occasion**; and
    - The particular **responsibility to tell the truth** whilst under oath.

7 - Unsworn Testimony

- If the witness possessing the requisite **capacity** either:
    - Is **under 14**; or
    - Does **not have** a **sufficient appreciation** of:
        - The **solemnity of the occasion**; and
        - The particular **responsibility to tell the truth** whilst under oath.
- Then they will give **unsworn testimony**.

B - Witness Testimony

1 – Swearing By Taking An Oath Or Affirmation

(i) - The General Rule – Sworn Testimony

- As a **general rule** every witness who gives evidence must be **sworn** by either:
    - Taking an **oath**; or
    - Making an **affirmation**.

Which Method Of Swearing Is Appropriate? – Section 1 Oaths Act 1978

- The following will swear an **oath**:
    - Christians – On the New Testament;
    - Jews – On the Old Testament;
    - Muslims – On the Koran;
    - Hindus – On the Vedas.

- An **affirmation** will be sworn where either:
    - The **witness objects** to swearing on an **oath**; or
    - Their **request** for an **alternative form of oath** is **not reasonably practicable** and would **delay** or **inconvenience** the proceedings.

Consequences Of Refusing To Be Sworn

- A **refusal to be sworn** will be **contempt of court** and can result:
    - In the **Magistrates Court** – up to **1 months imprisonment** and / or a **fine** of up to **£2,500.00** – Section 97(4) Magistrates Court Act 1980.
    - In the **Crown Court** – **imprisonment** (indeterminate sentence) – Section 45(4) Supreme Courts Act 1981.

(ii) - Exceptions To The General Rule - Witnesses Permitted To Give Unsworn Testimony?

- The following are **not required to be sworn** when giving evidence:
    - **Children under 14** – Section 55 YJCEA 1999; and
    - Witnesses who **only produce documents** – *Perry v Gibson* [1834] 1 A & E 48.

2 - Examination Of Witnesses

(a) - Examination In Chief

- **Examination in chief** involves questions posed to the witness by the advocate who called the witness.

Leading Questions And Examination In Chief

General Rule

- As a **general rule** - it is **not permissible** to pose **leading questions** during **examination in chief**. (i.e. "was the car blue?" as opposed to "what colour was the car?")

Exception To The General Rule

- **Leading questions are allowed** during **examination in chief** in the following circumstances:
    - Where **uncontroversial issues** are **accepted** by **all parties**;
    - **Hostile witnesses**;
    - To **refresh** a witnesses **memory**;
    - For the purpose of **identification**.

(b) - Cross Examination

- **Cross examination** involves one party **asking questions of another party's witness**.

Leading Questions And Cross Examination

- It is **permissible** to **lead** a witness in **cross examination.**

Can A Defendant Personally Cross Examine A Witness?

The General Rule

- As a **general rule** the **defendant is permitted** to conduct their own defence and **examine witnesses in person** without the assistance of an advocate.

The Exceptions To The General Rule

- The **defendant** will *not* be permitted to cross examine prosecution witnesses in person under the following provisions:
    - ☐ Section 34 YJCEA 1999;
    - ☐ Section 35 YJCEA 1999; or
    - ☐ Section 36 YJCEA 1999.
- If any of these provisions apply either:
    - ☐ The **defendant** *must* appoint an advocate to conduct the **cross examination on their behalf;** or
    - ☐ If the **defendant refuses** to do so – the **court** *must* appoint an **advocate** to conduct the **cross examination on their behalf.**

Sections 34 & 35 YJCEA 1999

- **No person charged** with:
    - ☐ A sexual offence;
    - ☐ Kidnapping;
    - ☐ False imprisonment;
    - ☐ Child abduction;
    - ☐ An offence under section 1 Children & Young Persons Act 1933;
    - ☐ Any offence involving either:
        - Assault;
        - Injury; or
        - Threat of injury;
- May **cross examine in person** during criminal proceedings;
- Either:
    - ☐ The **complainant;**
    - ☐ A **witness** to the offence; or
    - ☐ A person aged **under 17.**

Sections 36 YJCEA 1999

- If neither sections 34 or 35 YJCEA 1999 apply;
- Then either:
    - Upon an **application** of the **prosecution**; or
    - The courts **own motion**;
- The **defendant** will be **prohibited from cross examining a witness** if it appears to the court that both:
    - The **quality** of the witnesses evidence on cross examination would be likely to be:
        - **Diminished** if the **defendant conducted** the cross examination; and
        - **Improved** if the **defendant** were **prohibited** from conducting the cross examination; and
    - That it would **not be contrary to the interests of justice** to prohibit the defendant to do so.

Cross Examination Of A Complainant About Their Previous Sexual Behaviour – Section 41(1) YJCEA 1999

The General Rule

- If a person is charged with a **sexual offence** then:
    - Both:
        - **No** evidence may be **adduced**; and
        - **No questions** can be asked in **cross examination**;
    - Either:
        - By the **defendant**; or
        - **On behalf** of the **defendant**;
    - About any **sexual behaviour** of the **complainant**;
    - **Unless**;
    - The court grants **leave** (permission) to do so.

The Exceptions To The General Rule – Sections 41(3)&(5) YJCEA 1999

- The court will grant **leave to adduce evidence of the complainants sexual behaviour** where:
    - It is necessary to **rebut prosecution evidence**; or
    - It is **relevant to an issue** in the case; and
    - Either:
        - It does **not relate** to the issue of **consent**; or
        - It **relates** to the issue of **consent**; and either:

- It relates to **sexual behaviour** alleged to have **taken place at or about the same time as the event** which is the subject matter of the charge;

- The **sexual behaviour** of the complainant is **so similar** that it **cannot** be described as a **coincidence** in relation to either:
  - Any **sexual behaviour** that **took place as part of the event** which is the subject matter of the charge; or
  - Any **sexual behaviour** that took place at or about the time of the event which is the subject matter of the charge.

(c) - Re-Examination

- **Re-examination** takes place after cross examination and involves the **party who called the witness** posing further questions in relation to the **matters raised during cross examination.**

Leading And Re-Examination

- **Leading** is **not permitted** during **re-examination**.

C - Special Measures Directions

1 - Eligible Witnesses – Sections 16 & 17 YJCEA 1999

- The following groups of witnesses (excluding defendants) are **eligible** for **special measures** when giving evidence:
  - Witnesses **under 17** at the **time of the hearing;**
  - Witnesses where the **quality** of their testimony will be **diminished** by either a:
    - **Mental disorder;**
    - **Significant impairment** of **intelligence** and **social functioning;**
    - **Physical disability;**
    - **Physical disorder;**
    - **Fear** or **distress** in connection with testifying.

2 - Who May Initiate An Application For A Special Measures Direction – Section 19(1) YJCEA 1999

- The **application for a special measures direction** in relation to a witness *may* be made by:
  - The **prosecution;**
  - The **defence;**
  - The **court** of is **own motion.**

3 - When Must The Court Make A Special Measures Direction? – Section 21 YJCEA 1999

- The witness will be **in need of special protection** and the court *must* make a **special measures direction** for **video recorded evidence in chief, cross examination** and **re-examination** if the witness is:
    - **Under 17;** and
    - Their **testimony** relates to any **offence** under:
        - Sexual Offences Act 1956;
        - Indecency with Children Act 1960;
        - Sexual Offences Act 1967;
        - Section 54 Criminal Law Act 1977;
        - Protection of Children Act 1978;
        - Kidnapping;
        - False Imprisonment;
        - Section 1 or 2 Child Abduction Act 1984;
        - Section 1 Children and Young Persons Act 1933;
        - Any offence which involves an assault on, or injury, or a threat of injury to any person.
    - **Unless:**
        - **Video** recording is **unavailable** - If so, the testimony in chief must be via **live link**; or
        - In the case of **cross examination** and **re-examination** via video – the **witness has informed the court that they do not wish** for their cross examination and re-examination to be conducted by video.
- The remaining special measures *may* be made in relation to a child under 17 in accordance with the provisions of section 19(2) YJCEA 1999.

4 - When May The Court Make A Special Measures Direction In Relation To An Eligible Witness? – Section 19(2) YJCEA 1999

- If a witness is **eligible** the court *must* determine:
    - **Whether** any **special measure(s)** would **improve** and **maximise** the **quality** of the **evidence** given by the witness; and
    - **If so** – make a **direction** for such special measures.

5 - The Range Of Special Measures

- There are a variety of special measures available:
    - **Screening Witnesses** – Section 23;
    - Evidence given via **live link** – Section 24;
    - Evidence given **in private** – Section 25;

- ☐ **Removal** of **wigs** and **gowns** – Section 26;
- ☐ **Video recording** evidence in **chief** – Section 27;
- ☐ **Video recording cross examination** and **re-examination** – Section 28;
- ☐ **Intermediaries** – Section 29;
- ☐ **Communication aids** – Section 30.

D - Live Links For Defendants – Section 57 Crime and Disorder Act 1998

- **Live television links** can be used for **preliminary court hearings prior to the start of the trial** where the defendant is already **in custody**:
    - ☐ In **prison;** or
    - ☐ Any **other institution**.
- Provided:
    - ☐ The **Secretary Of State** has **notified** the court that it has **adequate facilities** for the use of live television links;
    - ☐ The **accused** can be **seen** and **heard** by the court and the accused can see and hear the **court.**

Exam Trip Up

- The use of live links is entirely at the **court's** *discretion*.
- *No consent* **is required** from either the **defendant** or their **legal representatives.**

E - Witnesses Refreshing Their Memory – Section 139 Criminal Justice Act 2003

- A person whilst **in the course of giving evidence** in criminal proceedings about any matter;
- May **at any stage**;
- **Refresh their memory;**
- From either:
    - ☐ A **document;** or
    - ☐ A **transcript** of a **sound recording**;
- Either:
    - ☐ **Made**; or
    - ☐ **Verified**;
- At an **earlier time;**
- If:
    - ☐ They **state** in their oral evidence that the **document** or **transcript records their recollection** of the matter at that earlier time; and
    - ☐ Their **recollection** of that matter is **likely to have been significantly better at that time** than it is at the time of giving evidence.

Exam Trip Up

- The fact that a witness has **already refreshed their memory** from the document **before entering the witness box** will **not prevent** them from requesting to **refresh their memory** from the document whist **subsequently giving their testimony.**

F - Evidence Of Oral Statements Made Through An Interpreter

- The case of *R v Attard* [1958] 43 Cr App R 90, established that a **police officer cannot** give testimony of the **contents of a conversation held through the use of an interpreter.**

- Only the **interpreter** themselves **can** give evidence of the **contents of the conversation.**

Exam Trip Up

- Section 140 Criminal Justice Act 2003 defines a **document** as **anything in which information of any description is recorded.**

- Section 140 Criminal Justice Act 2003 expressly **excludes** from the definition of a **document** any **recordings of sounds** or **moving images.**

- However the **common law** decision in *R v Bailey* [2001] All ER (D) 185 (Mar), established that a **document** will **include** a **tape recording.**

G - Witnesses Who Fail To Come Up To Proof

- It is expected that a witness called by a party will provide **testimony** that is **consistent** with the contents of their **earlier witness statement** and **supports the case** for the party that called the witness.

- However a witness may **fail to come up to proof** by giving **testimony** that is **inconsistent** with their **prior witness statement.**

- The appropriate **action** that can be taken by the advocate that called them will **depend** upon whether the witness is either:

    - **Unfavourable**; or
    - **Hostile.**

(i) - Unfavourable Witnesses

- If the witness simply provides **inconsistent testimony** then the party calling the witness **cannot:**

    - **Impeach their credit** by **cross examining** them on their previous inconsistent statements; or
    - Pose **leading questions** to do so.

(ii) - Hostile Witnesses

- If the witness has *deliberately* **changed their story** since giving their witness statement and is **deliberately lying** then an **application** can be made to the court to **declare the witness as hostile.**

- If the witness is **declared as hostile**:
    - The party who called them will be permitted to:
        - **Impeach their credit** by **cross examining** them on their previous inconsistent statements; and
        - Pose **leading questions** to do so.
    - The **judge** should **remind** the **jury** that the contents of the previous inconsistent statements do *not prove the truth* of those statements, but instead go to *undermine the credibility of the witness.*

H - Restrictions On Witnesses Permitted To Be Present In Court

1 - The General Rule

- As a **general rule all witnesses** are **not permitted** to be **present** in court **until** they have **given** their **evidence**.
- If a witness attends court prior to giving their evidence, having **refused** a judges **request** to **withdraw** until they have given their evidence, the judge *may* not admit their **evidence**.

2 - Exception To The General Rule

- **Experts** are **permitted** to **attend** the **entire trial** both before and after they give evidence.

I - Reporting Restrictions In Relation To Adults – Section 46 YJCEA 1999

1 - The Nature Of A Reporting Restriction

- **Any party** to the proceedings may **apply** to the **Attorney General** for a **reporting restriction** in relation to:
    - Any **adult (18 or over) witness**;
    - **Except** for the **accused**.
- Which will **prevent** the **publication** during the **witnesses' lifetime** of **any matter** which would be **likely to lead to members of the public identifying them.**

2 - The Criteria Governing Issuing Reporting Restrictions

- A **reporting restriction** will be granted where the **Attorney General** is satisfied that:
    - Either:
        - The **quality** of the witnesses **evidence**; or
        - The **level of co-operation** given by the **witness;**
    - Is **likely** to be **diminished**;
    - By reason of either:
        - **Fear**; or
        - **Distress;**
    - **At being identified** by members of the public.

J - Reporting Restrictions In Relation To Juveniles – Section 49 Children And Young Persons Act 1933

- It is **not permissible** to **report** either:
    - A **juvenile defendant**: or
    - A **juvenile witnesses**;
- **Name**;
- **Address**; or
- **Any other detail** which might lead to **revealing the identity of the juvenile concerned.**

Exam Trip Up

- The provisions of section 49 Children And Young Persons Act 1933 **no longer apply** once the juvenile reaches the **age of 18.**
- Watch out for questions where the **juvenile attains 18 mid trial.**

K - Contempt Of Court – Section 12 Contempt of Court Act 1981

- A person will be in **contempt of court** if they either:
    - **Wilfully interrupt** proceedings in court;
    - **Misbehave** in court;
    - **Wilfully insult**:
        - The **justice** or **justices**;
        - Any **witnesses** before an officer of the court; or
        - Any **solicitor** or **barrister** having business in the court;
    - During:
        - Their **sitting** in court;
        - Their **attendance** in court;
        - Their **going to** court; or
        - Their **returning from** court.

Sanctions For Contempt Of Court

- The court **may** order either:
    - Any **officer of the court**; or
    - A **constable**;
- To **detain** the offender in **custody until** the **rising of the court;** and
- **May** if it thinks fit:
    - **Commit** the offender in **custody** for up to **1 month**; and / or
    - Impose a **fine** not exceeding **£2,500.**

Evidence & Procedure
Unit 23: Criminal Justice System (4) Sentencing

A – Licences

(i) - Release Of Short Term Prisoners On Licence – Section 246 Criminal Justice Act 2003

- The **Secretary of State** *may* **release** a prisoner **on licence** when they have served the *requisite period* of their sentence.

- Prisoners **under 18 are also entitled** to this right.

  Release of Short Term Prisoners on Licence (Repeal of Age Restriction) Order 2003 (SI 2003/1691)

(ii) - The Duration Of A Licence

- The **period** of a **licence** depend upon the **duration** of the prisoners sentence:

  - Those imprisoned for **4 months or more but less than 18 months** = ¼ of their term.

  - Those imprisoned for **18 months or more** = **135 days less than ½ of their term.**

(iii) - Attaching Conditions To A Licence

- A number of **conditions** may be attached to a **licence** including:

  - Electronic tagging (home detention curfew scheme);
  - Residence;
  - Exclusion from areas;
  - Exclusions from contacting persons;
  - Not to consume intoxicating substances.

(iv) - Prisoners Not Eligible For Release On Licence – Section 65 Criminal Justice and Court Services Act 2000

- Prisoners covered by the **notification requirements** of the **Sex Offenders Act 1997** are **not eligible** for release on licence.

B – Home Detention Curfews

(i) - Release Of Short Term Prisoners On Home Detention Curfew Schemes – Section 253 Criminal Justice Act 2003

- Prisoners may be permitted to **complete part of their sentence** under the **home curfew scheme**.

(ii) - Conditions Attached To Home Detention Curfew Schemes

- **Conditions** may be **attached** to home curfew as determine by the **Prison Governor.**
- The **prisoner must agree** to the terms of the home curfew **conditions**.

(iii) - Total Periods Of Home Detention Curfews

- **Home curfew schemes** may last for a **minimum** of **14 days** and a **maximum** of **60 days**.

(iv) - Maximum Daily Duration Of Home Detention Curfews

- They generally have a **minimum daily duration of 9 hours**.
- They have **no maximum daily duration**.

(v) - Monitoring Home Detention Curfews (Electronic Tagging)

- **HM Prison Service Parole Unit** is **responsible** for the **management** and **monitoring** of home detention curfews.
- The curfew electronic tagging is **operated** and **monitored** by an **approved private contractor** that:
    - **Tags** the **prisoner**;
    - Fits a **home monitoring unit** at their **designated place of residence**.

(vi) - Notifying The Police Prior To The Release Of A Prisoner On Curfew

- The **police** must be **notified** of all prisoners subject to a home detention curfew **14 days prior to their release**.

(vii) - Requests For Information By The Police

- A **Superintendent** or above;
- *May* request information from the **monitoring contractor**;
- As to the **offenders compliance** or otherwise with the curfew.

(viii) - Monitoring Contractors Responses To Requests For Information

- The **monitoring contractor** *must* reply to requests within **24 hours**.

(ix) - Recall Of Prisoners Released Early On Licence Or Subject To A Curfew – Section 255 Criminal Justice Act 2003

- Where a person released on licence either:
    - **Fails to comply** with any **conditions of the licence**; or
    - Their **whereabouts cannot be electronically monitored** at the place specified in the curfew condition;

- The **Secretary of State** *may:*
    - ☐ **Revoke the licence**; and
    - ☐ **Recall the person to prison.**

(x) - Police Arrests Of Persons Subject To A Curfew

- The guidance provided to police forces in relation to persons who are subject of a detention curfew is as follows:

1 - When The Person Subject To The Curfew Is Arrested

- The **Custody Officer** *must* **notify** the **monitoring contractor immediately** of:
    - ☐ Details of the **prisoner;**
    - ☐ Details of the **offence;**
    - ☐ Whether the prisoner is to be **bailed or remanded;** and
    - ☐ **Whether** the prisoner continues to **wear the electronic tag.**

- The **Custody Officer** *must* also **notify** the **monitoring contractor** when the prisoner is subsequently **released.**

2 - When The Person Subject To The Curfew Is Charged

- Where a prisoner has been **charged** with an offence:
    - ☐ The **Custody Officer** *must* **immediately inform:**
        - **HM Prison Service Parole Unit** at the Home Office;
        - The **monitoring contractor** to **remove and collect the monitoring unit** - if the prisoner is to be returned to prison.
    - ☐ The provisions of **Code C of PACE 1984** in relation to detention following charge **continues to apply** in such circumstances.
    - ☐ The **decision whether to revoke the prisoner's licence** is a matter for the **HM Prison Service Parole Unit** and *not* the **Police.**

(xi) - Police Requests For Revocation Of Home Detention Curfews

- A **Superintendent** *may* make a **request** that a home detention curfew be **revoked** where they consider that a prisoner subject to the curfew represents a **serious risk to the public.**

- The request must be made to the **HM Prison Service Parole Unit of the Home Office.**

C - Custody Of Young Offenders

- The following sentences are available in respect of young offenders:

    - **Detention at Her Majesty's Pleasure - Section 90 PCC(S)A 2000**
      For the offence of **murder** by a person who was **under 18** at the time of committing the offence.

    - **Custody For Life - Sections 93-94 PCC(S)A 2000**
      For the offence of **murder** by a person aged **18-21** at the time of the offence.

    - **Detention For Life – Section 91 PCC(S)A 2000**
      Certain serious offences where the court may sentence a person under 18 to detention for a term not exceeding the maximum available when it is of the opinion that there is **no other way of dealing with the matter.**

    - **Detention In A Young Offenders Institution – Section 96 PCC(S)A 2000**
      For **imprisonable offences** by a person aged **18-21**.

    - **Detention And Training Orders - Section 91 PCC(S)A 2000**
      For **imprisonable offences** by a person aged **18-21**.

D - Community Order Requirements – Section 177 Criminal Justice Act 2003

- A court *may* impose:

    - Any **one or more**;
    - Of the following **community requirement orders**;
    - In respect of a person **aged 16 or over**;
    - Who has been **convicted** for an offence.

- **Unpaid Work Requirement**
  Between **40 – 300 hours** to be completed within a **12 month** period.

- **Activity Requirement**
  To complete up to **60 days** of activities as specified within the order.

- **Programme Requirement**
  To participate in an **accredited programme** as specified within the order. Programmes are designed to address offending behaviour – e.g. anger management; sex offending; substance abuse; etc.

- **Prohibited Activity Requirement**
  To **refrain from specified activities** during specified days or periods.

- **Curfew Requirement**
  To **remain in a specified place** for between **2 – 12 hours** for a specified periods of time.

- **Exclusion Requirement**
  Not to enter a specified place for a **specified period** of up to **2 years**.

- **Residence Requirement**
  To **reside at a specified place** for a **specified period**.

- **Mental Health Treatment Requirement**
  To submit to **treatment** by a **registered medical practitioner** or **chartered psychologist** for a specified period(s).

- **Drug Rehabilitation Requirement**
  To submit **(consent)** to **treatment** and **testing** by a **qualified person** for **at least 6 months**.

- **Alcohol Treatment Requirement**
  To submit **(agree)** to **treatment** by a **qualified person** for **at least 6 months**.

- **Supervision Requirement**
  To **attend appointments with a responsible officer (Probation Service)** for the promotion of rehabilitation for **between 6 months and 3 years**.

- **Attendance Centre Requirement**
  To **attend an attendance centre** for **between 12 - 36 hours**. This requirement may only be imposed upon those **aged 18 - 25**.

Evidence & Procedure
Unit 24 – Criminal Justice System (5) Youth Justice & Youth Crime & Disorder

Youth Justice

A - Youth Justice Schemes

1 - Aims Of Youth Justice Schemes – Section 37(1) CDA 1998

- The principal **aim** of the **Youth Justice Scheme** is to **prevent offending** by:
    - **Children**; and
    - **Young persons.**
- All **bodies** including:
    - **Local Authorities**;
    - **Health Authorities**;
    - The **Probation Service**;
    - The **Courts**;
    - The **Police**; and
    - **Voluntary Agencies**;
- Must have **regard to this aim**;
- When conducting functions in relation to the youth justice system.

2 - Youth Offending Teams – Section 39 CDA 1998

(i) – Multi Disciplinary Approach

- The **multi disciplinary** nature of the **Youth Offending Teams (YOT's)** requires:
    - Each **Local Authority**;
    - To **establish** for their area;
    - One or more **Youth Offending Team**;
    - In **co-operation** with their local:
        - The **Chief Officer Of Police**;
        - **Probation board**;
        - **Strategic Health Authority**;
        - **Health Authority** or **Primary Care Trust**.

(ii) - Functions Of A Youth Offender Team

- The **functions** of a **Youth Offender Team** include engaging in:
    - ☐ An appropriate adult service;
    - ☐ Bail information and support;
    - ☐ Youth Offender Panels;
    - ☐ Court work;
    - ☐ Preparing court reports;
    - ☐ Placement of young offenders;
    - ☐ Assessment and intervention work;
    - ☐ Supervision of community sentences;
    - ☐ Acting as the Responsible Officer in relation to:
        - Parenting Orders;
        - Child Safety Orders.

3 - Youth Offender Panels – Section 21 Powers Of Criminal Courts (Sentencing) Act 2000

- **Youth Offender Panels** will consist of:
    - ☐ **One** member of the **Youth Offender Team (YOT);** and
    - ☐ **Two volunteer** members from the **local community.**
- The **first meeting** with the **Youth Offender Panel** will involve:
    - ☐ The **Panel devising** a **programme** to prevent re-offending;
    - ☐ Which will be **agreed** with the **offender.**
- Examples of programmes include:
    - ☐ Reparation to the victim;
    - ☐ Attending:
        - Mediation;
        - Education;
        - Drug or alcohol rehabilitation.
    - ☐ Unpaid work;
    - ☐ Curfews.
- The **Youth Offender Team** will **oversee** the **programme** devised by the **Youth Offender Panel** by:
    - ☐ Providing **administrative support**;
    - ☐ Providing **accommodation** and **facilities**; and
    - ☐ **Supervising** and **recording** the offender's compliance with the programme.

4 - Youth Justice Plans – Section 40 CDA 1998

- **Youth Justice Plans** are **strategic plans** devised **annually** by each **local authority** in **consultation** with all **relevant persons** and **bodies** outlining:

    - How **youth justice services** in their area are **provided** and **funded**; and

    - How the **Youth Offender Teams** in their area are:
        - **Composed**;
        - **Funded**;
        - **Operate**; and
        - **Function**.

5 - Youth Justice Board – Section 41 CDA 1998

- The **Youth Justice Board** is comprised of between **10 – 12 members** who are **appointed** by the **Secretary of State** to:

    - **Monitor** the youth justice system;

    - **Report** their findings;

    - **Promote** good practice;

    - **Fund** projects; and

    - **Advise** the Secretary of State.

B - Youth Crime & Disorder

The Range Of Orders Available

- A variety of provisions are available:

    - Parenting Orders;

    - Binding Over Parents Or Guardians;

    - Child Safety Orders;

    - Child Curfew Schemes;

    - Removal Of Truants To Designated Premises.

1 - Parenting Orders

(i) – Function Of Parenting Orders

- **Parenting Orders** are designed to **prevent** "latch key kids" by providing:

    - **Support**;

    - To **parents** or **guardians**;

    - Of **young offenders**;

    - To **help** the **parent** or **guardian**;

    - **Change** the criminal or anti-social **behaviour of their children**.

(ii) - Definition Of A Guardian - Section 117(1) CDA 1998

- **Section 117(1) CDA 1998 defines a guardian as:**

    "A person who in the opinion of the court has, for the time being, care of a child or young person."

    It is **not** a matter of **legal guardianship**.

(iii) - When Will The Court Impose A Parenting Order? – Section 8 CDA 1998

- A **court** must consider whether it would be **desirable** to make a **Parenting Order** in respect of either:
    - One or both **biological parents**; or
    - Any **guardian**;
- Of a:
    - Child (under 14); or
    - Young person (under 18);
- Following any:
    - A Child Safety Order;
    - An ASBO;
    - A Sex Offence Order;
    - A Failure To Comply With School Attendance Order; or
    - Conviction of a child or young person for an offence.

(iv) - The Desirability Of Imposing A Parenting Order – Section 9(1) CDA 1998

- The **court must** make a **Parenting Order** where the child is:
    - Under 16;
    - **Convicted** of an offence; and
    - The making of an order would be **desirable** in the interests of **preventing the commission of further offences** by the **child** or **young person**.
- The court may choose **not to impose** an order if it **believes** that an order would be **unlikely to prevent the commission of further offences.**
- If so the basis of the decision must be **stated in open court.**

(v) - Information The Court Must Obtain Prior To Reaching A Decision Whether To Impose A Parenting Order – Section 9(2) CDA 1998

- **Before** making a **parenting order** the court **must** obtain and **consider information** as provided by a **report** by the **Young Offenders Team (YOT)** about the:
    - Person's **family circumstances;** and
    - The **likely effect of an order** in those circumstances.

(vi) - The Nature Of Parenting Orders – Sections 8(4) & (5) CDA 1998

- A **parenting order** may require a **parent** or **guardian** to:
    - ☐ **Comply** with any **requirements** specified in an order for a period of up to **12 months**.

        Examples include:
        - Escorting the child to school;
        - The child being supervised by a responsible adult during the evenings.
    - ☐ Attend once **weekly counselling and guidance sessions** as specified by the **Responsible Officer** for a period of up to **3 months**.

(vii) - The Responsible Officer – Section 8(8) CDA 1998

- The **Responsible Officer** will be specified by the terms of the order and will comprise a member of a **multi disciplinary Young Offender Team** comprised of:
    - ☐ **Probation officers**;
    - ☐ **Social workers**;
    - ☐ **Persons nominated by the Chief Education Officer**.

(viii) - Information To Be Provided By The Court To The Parent Following The Imposition Of A Parenting Order

- Once an order is made the **court** must **explain** to the parent:
    - ☐ The **effect** of the order;
    - ☐ The **consequences** of failing to comply.

(ix) - Varying The Terms Of A Parenting Order – Section 9(3) CDA 1998

- The court may **review and vary** an order upon the **application** of either:
    - ☐ The **parent**; or
    - ☐ The **Responsible Officer**.

(x) - Consequences Of A Breach Of A Parenting Order – Section 9(7) CDA 1998

- If a **parent** or **guardian**;
- **Without reasonable excuse**;
- **Fails to comply** with:
    - ☐ A **requirement** imposed by an order; or
    - ☐ Any **directions** given by the **responsible officer**;
- They will have committed an **offence**.

2 - Binding Over A Parent Or Guardian – Section 150 PCC(S)A 2000

(i) – Criteria For Binding Over A Parent Or Guardian

- A **court** must make an **order binding over**:
    - ☐ A **parent** or **guardian**;
    - ☐ Of a child **under 16**;
    - ☐ For **up to 3 years** where:
        - The **child** or **young person** is **convicted** of an offence; and
        - The making of an order would be **desirable** in the interests of **preventing the commission of further offences** by the **child** or **young person**.
- If the court **does not bind over** the parent because it is of the opinion that binding over the parent will not prevent the commission of further offences, the **reasons must be stated in open court**.

(ii) - Consent Is Required From The Parent Or Guardian – Section 150 PCC(S)A 2000

- The **parent** or **guardian** are required to provide their **consent** to the making of a recognizance to ensure they:
    - ☐ Take **proper care** of the child (protection and guidance);
    - ☐ Exercise **proper control** (discipline) over the child.
    - ☐ Also if the child is subject to a **community penalty** – to ensure they **comply with its terms**.
- If the **parent** or **guardian unreasonably refuses to consent** - the court may order them to pay a **fine of up to £1,000**.

3 - Child Safety Orders

(i) – Function Of A Child Safety Order

- The **Child Safety Orders** are intended to **stop children under 10 from turning to crime**.
- Child Safety Orders impose **obligations upon the child themselves**.
- They will commonly be made **in conjunction** with **Parenting Orders** which impose obligations upon the parent or guardian of the child.

(ii) - When May A Child Safety Order Be Imposed? – Section 11 CDA 1998

- A Magistrates Family Proceedings Court;
- On the **application** of a **local authority**;
- May impose a **Child Safety Order** upon a **child under 10** if it is satisfied that either:
    - ☐ The **child** has **committed** an **act** which, **had they been 10 or over**, would have **constituted an offence**;
    - ☐ That a child safety order is **necessary to prevent** the commission of an **act** which **had they been 10 or over**, would have **constituted an offence**;

☐ That the **child** has **breached a curfew notice**; or

☐ That the child has **acted in a manner likely to cause**:

- **Harassment;** H
- **Alarm;** or A
- **Distress.** D

(iii) - Obligations Imposed By A Child Safety Order – Section 11 CDA 1998

- A **Child Safety Order** can:

    ☐ Place the child under the **supervision** of a **Responsible Officer** for between **3 to 12 months;**

    ☐ Oblige the child to **comply** with any **requirements** specified.

    NB - There is **no minimum age** to which a child may be made subject to an order.

(iv) - Consequences Of A Breach Of A Child Safety Order – Section 12 CDA 1998

- If the **child fails to comply** with the terms of an order;
- The court may:

    ☐ **Vary** the order;

    ☐ Insert any **provision** in an order;

    ☐ **Discharge** the order and **substitute** a **Care Order.**

4 - Child Curfew Schemes

(i) – Function Of A Child Curfew Scheme

- The **Child Curfew Schemes** are designed to prevent:

    ☐ **Unsupervised groups;**

    ☐ Of children **under 16;**

    ☐ From **committing:**

    - **Crimes;** and
    - Other acts of **anti social behaviour;**

(ii) - The Effect Of A Child Curfew Scheme – Section 14 CDA 1998

- A **Child Curfew Scheme** may be introduced by either:

    ☐ A **Local Authority;** or

    ☐ **Chief Officer of Police;**

- If they consider it necessary to do so for the purposes of **maintaining order;**
- **Banning children** of an **age specified** in the order who must be under **16;**
- From being in a **specified area** of a **public place;**

- For a **specified period** not exceeding **90 days**;
- During **specified hours** (9pm-6am);
- **Unless** they are in the **effective supervision** of:
    - A **parent**; or
    - A **responsible person aged over 18**.

(iii) - Consultation Requirements – Sections 14(3)&(5) CDA 1998

- **Consultation** must take place between:
    - The **Local Authority**;
    - **Chief Officer of Police**;
    - Such other **individuals or bodies** as they consider **appropriate**.
- If appropriate **community groups** are **not consulted** the Home Secretary may decide **not to confirm the scheme**.
- The **extent** of consultation is **discretionary**.
- Schemes will **come into effect 1 month** after **confirmation** by the **Home Secretary**.

(iv) - The Consequences Of A Breach Of A Curfew Orders – Section 15 CDA 1998

- If a **constable** has **reasonable cause** to **believe** that a child has **breached** the terms of an order;
- The constable must **inform** the **local authority** as soon as is practicable;
- The constable **may**:
    - **Remove** the child to their place of **residence**;
    - **Unless**;
    - They have reasonable cause to **believe** that the child would be likely to suffer **significant harm**.

(v) - The Duty Of The Local Authority Once Notification Has Been Received – Section 15(4) CDA 1998

- Once the **constable** has **notified** the **Local Authority** of the breach;
- The **Local Authority** must:
    - Within **48 hours**;
    - **Enquire** into the **circumstances of the child**.

(vi) - Omissions In The Legislation

- The legislation is silent on the following points:
    - What the constable should do with the child if it is not practicable to take them home?

        The child should be removed to suitable accommodation:
        - The care of Social Services;
        - A police station;   Section 46 Children Act 1989

    - Whether the constable can use force to remove the child?
        - Applying common law principles the officer can use reasonable force in exercising a lawful power.

5 - Removal Of Truants To Designated Premises – Section 16(1) CDA 1998

(i) - What Are Designated Premises?

- A Local Authority **may**:
    - **Designate premises** in a **police area** as premises to which truant children and young persons of compulsory school age **may be removed**; and
    - **Notify** the **Chief Officer of Police** for that area of the designation.
- The legislation does not define the meaning of **"designated premises"**.
- The Local Authority are therefore **free to determine the nature of the premises** the child **may** be returned to.

(ii) - Action Required From A Superintendent Following Notification – Section 16(2) CDA 1998

- Once **notified**, a **Superintendent** or above;
- **May** direct that the **constables** power to remove truants will be exercisable:
    - Within **any part of the police area specified** in the notification;
    - For any **period specified** in the notification.

(iii) - Removal Of Truants By Constables To Designated Premises – Section 16(3) CDA 1998

- If a **constable** has **reasonable cause** to **believe** that:
    - A **child** or **young person**;
    - Found in a **specified area** of a **public place**;
    - During a **specified period**;
    - Is of **compulsory school age**; and
    - Is **absent** from school **without a lawful authority**;
- The **constable** may **remove** the child either to:
    - **The designated premises** specified; or
    - The **school** from which they are absent.

(iv) - Defining A Lawful Authority – Section 16(4) CDA 1998

- A child may be absent from school **with** a lawful authority:
    - **During school holidays**;
    - **Religious observation**;
    - **When they are sick**;
    - **When there is an unavoidable cause** e.g. visit to dentist.

Crime
Unit 1: Actus Reus & Mens Rea

A – The Meaning Of Actus Reus & Mens Rea

1 - Actus Reus

- The physical **act** or **omission** of a crime.

2 - Mens Rea

- The guilty **state of mind** of a crime.

B - Coincidence Of The Actus Reus And Mens Rea

1 - The General Rule – Coincidence Is Necessary

- As a general rule an act or omission *(actus reus)* **alone cannot constitute a crime**.

- The *actus reus* must be **accompanied** by the guilty mind *(mens rea)*.

- There must be a **coincidence** of the *actus reus* and *mens rea* **at the time** of committing the offence.

(i) - Need The Coincidence Of Actus Reus And Mens Rea Be Continuing?

- There is **no need for the mens rea to remain unchanged** throughout the entire offence.

- Provided at some point during the commission of the offence the **two factors coincide** the offence will be complete.

- If after committing the actus reus with the necessary mens rea the person changes their mind they will still be guilty even if they take steps to remedy their actions.

    For example in the case of R v Jakeman [1983] Cr App R 23:

    A poisoned B and at the time of administering the poison (actus reus) intended to kill B – thereby possessing the necessary mens rea. A was guilty in this case despite having changed their mind about wishing to kill B and taken all the steps they could to halt the effects of the poison.

(ii) - Coincidence Of Actus Reus And Mens Rea And Continuing Acts

- There may be instances where the *actus reus* is **continuing**.

- At the point of **commencing** the act a person may **not possess** the necessary *mens rea*, but due to a **change in the factual circumstances whilst carrying out the act**, the *mens rea* may subsequently be formed.

- Classic examples include **consent based situations** where:
    - ☐ A gives B **consent** to carry out an act.
    - ☐ B starts to carry on the act *(actus reus)* and due to the presence of consent, **lacks the necessary *mens rea*.**
    - ☐ Whilst B is carrying out the act A **withdraws their consent**.

- ☐ If B **continues their actions despite the withdrawal of consent** - at this point the *mens rea* is **formed** and there will be a **coincidence** of the *actus reus* and *mens rea*.

- For example in the case of *Kaitamaki v The Queen* [1985] AC 147:

    A initially had B's **consent** (**no *mens rea***) at the commencement of sexual intercourse (***actus reus***).

    During the intercourse B **withdrew her consent**. A **ignored the withdrawal of consent** by B and **continued to have sex** with B (***mens rea* formed**).

    At this point there was a **coincidence** of the *actus reus* and *mens rea* of rape and A was found guilty of the offence.

2 - Exception To The General Rule – Strict Liability Offences

- In instances of **strict liability** offences there is **no *mens rea*** requirement to accompany the *actus reus*.

- **All that is required** is the *actus reus*.

- The **state of mind** of the defendant at the time of committing the *actus reus* is **irrelevant**.

- There is a **presumption** that a *mens rea* is **required** for all offences **unless legislation indicates otherwise**.

- Strict liability offences are therefore **rare** and are usually used to enforce statutory regulations (e.g. road traffic offences).

C - Mens Rea

- There are differing levels of *mens rea* that apply to different offences. These include acting with:
    - ☐ **Intent;**
    - ☐ **Recklessness.**

D – Intent

1 - The Differing Forms Of Intent

- There are various different forms of intent including:
    - ☐ Specific intent;
    - ☐ Ulterior intent; and
    - ☐ Basic intent.

(i) - Specific Intent

- Offences of **specific intent** are only committed when:
    - ☐ **At the time** of committing the *actus reus;*
    - ☐ The defendant has the **specific intention** to bring about a **specific result**.

- For example: In relation to the offence of murder - the intention to either kill or cause GBH.

(ii) - Ulterior Intent

- An offence of **ulterior intent** involves:
    - ☐ As well as an **intention** to carry out the *actus reus* of the offence;
    - ☐ A further **intention** to cause a **consequence** prohibited by the offence.
- For example: For section 9(1)(a) Theft Act 1968 burglary it is necessary to show the **intention** to **both:**
    - ☐ Enter the building as a trespasser **(actus reus);**
    - ☐ With the **intent (offence complete)** to either:
        - Inflict GBH;
        - Cause damage; or
        - Steal.

(iii) - Basic Intent

- An offence of **basic intent** requires **no further proof of anything other than the basic intention to bring about a set of circumstances.**
- Whilst:
    - ☐ It is **necessary** to prove an **intention** to carry out the *actus reus* of the offence;
    - ☐ It is **not necessary** to prove that the person **also intended any further prohibited consequence.**
    - ☐ Merely carrying out the further prohibited consequence will suffice.
- For example: For section 9(1)(b) Theft Act 1968 burglary it is only necessary to show that:
    - ☐ A person entered a building or part of a building as a trespasser; and
    - ☐ They went on to commit one of the prohibited consequences of either:
        - Steal, or attempt to steal; or
        - Inflict or attempt to inflict GBH.

2 - Proving Intent

- Section 8 Criminal Justice Act 1967 states that a court or jury in determining whether a person possessed the requisite **intent:**
    - ☐ Shall **not be bound** in law to **infer** that they **intended** or **foresaw a result** of their actions by reason of it being a **natural and probable consequence of their actions**; but
    - ☐ **Shall decide whether they did intend or foresee the result** by **reference to all the evidence** drawing such inferences from the evidence as appear proper in the circumstances.

- The House of Lords cases of *R v Moloney* [1985] AC 905 and *R v Hancock* [1986] AC 455 also established:
  - That **foresight** of the probability of a consequence:
    - Does **not amount in itself to the intention** to bring about the consequence; but
    - May be used as **evidence** to prove the intention to bring about the consequence.

- The combined effect of the legislation and the case law is that:
  - Just because a **consequence** is **highly probable** or **virtually certain** to occur it does **not necessary mean that a person intended the consequence to arise**.
  - **Evidence** of the defendant's **foresight** can be put before the court and the court may then **infer** the presence of the defendants **intention** from it.

- The prosecution will:
  - Indicate the **probability** of the **consequence** arising from an act;
  - Argue that the **higher the probability** of the consequence the **more likely the defendant foresaw** the consequence; and
  - If they **foresaw** the consequence it is **likely** that they **intended** it to happen.

3 - Transferred Malice

- The **mens rea** for an offence can be **transferred** from an original intended victim to another person who instead inadvertently suffers harm as a result of the commission of the actus reus.

- In the case of *R v Latimer* [1886] 17 QBD 359:
  - Latimer swung his belt intending to injure a person but missed them and inadvertently hit another person instead.
  - The **intent** formed towards the **intended victim** was **transferred** to the eventual **unintended victim** forming the mens rea for the offence of wounding.

- For example:
  - A intends to punch B and cause them really serious harm.
  - A throws the punch and B ducks.
  - A's punch lands in C who was standing behind B – breaking C's jaw.

- In such circumstances A's **intention** to cause B to suffer really serious harm at the time of throwing the punch will be **transferred** to C resulting in a guilty GBH verdict.

Exam Trip Up

- The principles of transferred malice do **not apply** if the **nature of the offence committed against the unintended victim differs from that which was directed towards the intended victim.**

- For example:
    - A intends to punch B and cause them really serious harm.
    - A throws the punch and B ducks.
    - A's punch smashes a glass window behind B.
- A **intended (mens rea)** to cause the offence of **GBH** but his **actions (actus reus)** relate to the offence of **criminal damage.**
- Therefore there is a **lack of coincidence of actus reus and mens rea** in the circumstances.

Exam Trip Up – Incitement And Transferred Malice

- If the **intentions** of a **principle** are to be **extended** to an **accessory** - it must be established that the accessories **intention** was either:
    - **Contemplated and accepted** by the principle; or
    - **Transferred.**

  For example:

- A incites B to assault C.
- If following the incitement – B were to decide to attack another person (D) then A will not be guilty because D was not the victim contemplated or accepted by A that B would attack.
- If however, following the incitement - B swings for C who ducks and D is inadvertently hurt by the blow then A the inciter will be guilty by virtue of the principles of transferred malice.

E - Recklessness

- **Recklessness** is an important concept in many offences within our criminal justice system.
- Unfortunately for revision purposes there are **2 different forms of recklessness** that we must consider:
    - **Subjective** recklessness; and
    - **Objective** recklessness.

1 - Subjective Recklessness

- The test for **subjective recklessness** is derived from the case of *R v Cunningham* [1957] 2 QB 396.
- **Subjective recklessness** will be proven when:
    - A person **foresees the risk** of a **consequence** from their **actions;** and
    - They go on to **take the risk**; and
    - In all the **circumstances** it was **unreasonable** for them to have taken the risk.
- It is **not adequate** to merely show that the **defendant** *ought* **to have foreseen the consequences** of their actions.

An Example Of Subjective Recklessness

- **Subjective recklessness** is the relevant mens rea in **criminal damage.**

- It is **inadequate** to display that a person throwing a stone at a window **ought** to have foreseen the consequence of the window being broken as a result.

- It must be proven that:
    - The person **foresaw** the **risk** of the window being damaged; and
    - Still went on to **take** the **risk** by throwing the stone.

- In the case of *R v G & R* [2003] 3 WLR 1060, two children set light to some papers under a bin and left the paper burning, expecting the fire to burn out. The fire went on to cause £1,000,000 worth of damage.

- The House of Lords quashed their convictions for criminal damage, accepting that the **children did not see foresee the risk that was posed by leaving the fire to burn itself out.**

- The decision reaffirmed the subjective nature of the mens rea in instances of criminal damage.

2 - Objective Recklessness

- The test for **objective recklessness** is derived from the case of *Metropolitan Police Commissioner v Caldwell* [1982] AC 341.

- Objective recklessness relates to a defendant who:
    - **Takes** a **risk;**
    - That would be **obvious** to a hypothetical **reasonable man;**
    - **Irrespective** of **whether** *they* **foresaw** the **obvious risk.**

- It cannot be emphasised enough that this type of recklessness has now been abandoned in favour of subjective recklessness in cases of criminal damage.

Which Recklessness Test Do You Apply?

- The different types of recklessness are applied to different offences.

- The Blackstone's guide states that **'generally'** the **subjective** form of recklessness will apply.

- To aid your revision - **apply the test for subjective recklessness unless told otherwise in this textbook.**

F - Actus Reus

- The *actus reus* is the physical **act** or **omission** of a crime.

- As a **general rule** the *actus reus* will only be commissioned by a **voluntary act.**

- However in limited **exceptional circumstances** an **omission to act** may instead suffice.

1 - Voluntary Acts

- The *actus reus* must be committed **voluntarily** – the actions must be under a persons own free will.

2 – Involuntary Acts

- **Involuntary actions** will include situations where the defendant is either:
  - ☐ **Physically compelled** to act; or
  - ☐ Has **suddenly lost control** of their actions.

(i) - Physical Compulsion To Act

- A is pushed by B and B accidentally clashes heads with C, breaking C's nose.
- B will not be guilty of GBH as B's actions were involuntary.
- B was physically compelled by the force of A.

(ii) - A Sudden Loss Of Control

- The loss of self control must be both:
  - ☐ **Sudden;** and
  - ☐ **Unexpected.**
- For example:
  - ☐ A sudden cramp;
  - ☐ A sudden blackout;
  - ☐ Sleepwalking.

Exam Trip Up – Foreseeable Involuntary Acts

- If the onset of the impairment could reasonably be **foreseen** or **anticipated** due to a **pattern of previous similar incidents** then the actions will still be deemed to be **voluntary** despite the inability to control the impairment the defendants actions
- For example: A narcoleptic should foresee that they might fall asleep at the wheel of a car and should therefore avoid driving.

G - Omissions

- Liability for **omissions** will arise where a person is under a **duty to act** and has **failed to do so.**
- A defendant's duty to act can arise in the following circumstances:
  - ☐ Duties arising under:

■ **Statute;**	S
■ Public **office;** or	O
■ **Contract;**	C

  - ☐ **Parental relationships** with a child or young person; P
  - ☐ **Assumption** of a duty of care; A
  - ☐ **Dangerous situations** created by the defendant. D

H - The Chain Of Causation

- It is necessary to prove a **causal link** between:
  - The ***actus reus***; and
  - The relevant **consequence**.

- You must ask yourself:

  "**But for** (or if it wasn't for) the defendant's **act** or **omission** would the **consequence** have **arisen**?"

- If the **act** or **omission** was **not an operating and substantial cause** of the consequence then the defendant will **not be guilty** of the offence.

Breaking The Chain Of Causation – Intervening Acts

- The **chain of causation can be broken** by a **new intervening act** provided that new act:
  - Is **free, deliberate and informed** – *R V Latif* [1996] 1 WLR 104; and
  - Becomes the **operating** and **substantial cause** of the consequence.

Exam Trip Up – Medical Treatment As An Intervening Act

- **Intervening medical treatment** may be given to a victim and ultimately cause their death.
- If the intervening medical treatment was:
  - **Accepted practice** for dealing with the relevant injuries, the actions of the doctors will **not break the chain of causation** – *R v Smith* [1959] 2 QB 35.
  - **Wholly inconsistent with accepted medical practice,** the actions of the doctors **will break the chain of causation** – *R v Jordan* [1956] 40 Cr App R 152.

Exam Trip Up - The Actions Of The Victim As An Intervening Act

- If the intervening acts of a victim are those that which might **reasonably be anticipated from a victim placed in such a situation** – then their actions will **not break the chain of causation.**
- If the intervening actions of the victim were either:
  - **Voluntary** (not a forced response to the situating they were placed in);
  - **Daft** – Stuart Smith LJ in *R v Williams* [1992] 1 WLR 380;
- They **will break the chain of causation.**

Exam Trip Up - The Eggshell Skull Rule

- The defendant **must take their victim as they find them.**
- If the victim has a particular **characteristic** that makes the **consequence** of an action against them **more acute** than against the average person then it is the defendant's bad luck.

  For example: If a victim with an incredibly thin skull is struck by a blow which fractures their skull and kills them then the defendant will still be guilty of causing their death.

  The fact that the blow would have not caused the same injuries to a person with a skull of average resilience would be irrelevant.

Crime
Unit 2: Incomplete Offences

A - Incitement
Triable As Per The Offence Incited
Penalty In The Crown Court – Unlimited Penalty
Penalty In The Magistrates Court – As Per The Offence Incited

1 - Definition Of Incitement – Common Law Offence

- It is a common law offence to:
    - **Unlawfully**;
    - **Incite** by:
        - **Encouraging**; or
        - **Pressuring**;
    - **Somebody to commit an offence**.

    For Example: It would be an offence to advertise a radar detection system and encourage motorists to break the speed limit.

Exam Trip Up

- It is **not necessary** for the **person to go on to commit the offence**.

- It is the actual **incitement itself** that constitutes the **offence** by the inciter.

- If the **person goes on to commit the offence** that they were encouraged to carry out – the **inciter becomes an accessory** to that crime.

- However - A defendant (15 year old girl) **cannot incite** another (30 year old man) to **commit an offence which exists to protect her**.

B - Conspiracy
Triable As Per The Completed Offence
Penalty In The Crown Court – As Per The Completed Offence
Penalty In The Magistrates Court – As Per The Completed Offence

1 - Definition Of A Conspiracy – Sections 1 & 2 Criminal Law Act 1977

- A **conspiracy** is:
    - An **agreement**;
    - Between **2 or more persons**;
    - To **pursue a course of conduct**;
    - Which **if carried out** would:
        - Amount to an **offence**;
        - Amount to an **offence - if it were not impossible to commit**.

        (For example, conspiring to smash a window without knowing that it is re-enforced glass).

2 - Exceptions To Conspiracy - Sections 2(2) Criminal Law Act 1977

- It is **not possible to conspire** with:
    - A **child under 10**;
    - The **intended victim**;

    - Your **spouse**:
        - Unless;
        - The **husband** and **wife conspire together** with another **3rd party**.

Exam Trip Up

- You **cannot incite** another to commit a **conspiracy**.

C – Conspiracy To Defraud
Indictable Only Offence
Penalty In The Crown Court – 10 Years Imprisonment

1 - Definition Of Conspiracy To Defraud – Common Law Offence

- It is a **common law** offence when:
    - **2 or more** persons;
    - **Dishonestly**;
    - **Agree** to either:
        - **Deprive** a person of something; or
        - **Injure** the **proprietary rights** of the victim.

2 – An Example Of Conspiracy To Defraud

- In the case of R v Cooke [1986] AC 909, two or more buffet car staff sold their own home made sandwiches on British Rail trains, depriving the company of selling their own sandwiches.

D - Definition Of Criminal Attempts – Section 1(1) Criminal Attempts Act 1981
Triable As Per The Completed Offence
Penalty In The Crown Court – As Per The Completed Offence
Penalty In The Magistrates Court – As Per The Completed Offence

- A person will be guilty of a **criminal attempt** if:
    - With **intent** to **commit an offence**;
    - They do an **act which is more than merely preparatory** to the commission of an offence.
- It is for the Magistrates or jury to decide if an act is more than merely preparatory.

Exam Trip Up

- A criminal attempt **can** be committed even if the offence would be impossible.

E - Interfering With Vehicles
Summary Only Offence
Penalty In The Magistrates Court – 3 Months Imprisonment And / Or A Fine

1 - Definition Of Interfering With Vehicles – Section 9 Criminal Attempts Act 1981

- A person commits an offence of **vehicle interference** if they:
    - **Interfere** with a:
        - Motor vehicle;
        - Trailer; or
        - Anything **carried in** or **on** the **trailer** or **motor vehicle**;
    - **Intending (offence complete)** for either:
        - Them; or
        - Another;
    - To **commit** an **offence** of either:
        - **Stealing** the **vehicle, trailer** or **parts**;
        - **Stealing** anything **in** or **on** the **vehicle** or **trailer**;
        - **TWOC'ing** the vehicle.

2 - Which Of The Three Do You Charge With?

- There is **no need to prove which one of the three the person was intending to do**, so long as they were intending to commit one of them.

Crime
Unit 3: General Defences

A - Automatism

- An **involuntary reflex action**.
- Where a person **loses control of their voluntary actions** they cannot be held liable.
- For example in the case of *Hill v Baxter*:
  - A swarm of bees flew into a man's car causing him to involuntarily thrash around and lose control of his vehicle, resulting in an accident.
  - The driver successfully relied upon the defence of automatism.

B - Intoxication

- There are **2 forms of intoxication**:
  - **Voluntary** – **No defence** if the intoxication was **voluntary** but you **still have to prove specific intent**.
  - **Involuntary** – If a **drink was spiked** with something resulting in a person **not being able to form the mens rea** it is a **defence**.

C - Insanity – *The McNaughten Rules*

- Where a person claims to be insane they are judged by the *McNaughten Rules (1843)*:
  - **At the time** of committing the **act**;
  - The person was labouring under a **defect of reason**;
  - From a **disease of the mind**;
  - As to either:
    - **Not know** the **nature** and **quality** of the **act** that they were doing; or
    - If they **did know** the **nature** and **quality** of the **act** that they were doing; - they **did not know that the act was wrong**.

D - Mistake

- **Mistake** is only a **defence** if the **mistake negates the mens rea** needed to prove the offence.

  For example: Leaving a shop in the honestly held belief that your partner had paid for an item in your possession.

E - Infancy

- A **child under 10 cannot commit a criminal offence**. (Doli incapax).

F - Duress By Threats

- The defence of **duress by threats** may be raised by a person who has been:
    - **Threatened** with either:
        - **Death**; or
        - **Serious injury**;
    - Of either:
        - **Themselves**; or
        - **Another**;
    - **Unless** they **do some criminal act.**
- It must be established that:
    - The threat **caused** the defendant to commit the crime;
    - A **reasonable person** would also have **acted in the same manner** in the circumstances;
    - The **threat** must be **capable of being carried out more or less immediately**;
    - They must **not have voluntarily exposed themselves** to an otherwise avoidable risk of duress **(e.g. joining a gang).**

Exam Trip Up

- NB – Duress by threats is **not a defence** to:
    - **Murder**; or
    - **Manslaughter.**

G - Duress Of Circumstances

- **Duress of circumstances** will be established where a person commits an offence **to avoid serious consequences** because they have **no real alternative.**
- The court will determine the **reasonableness** of the defendant's actions in the circumstances.

    For example: A disqualified driver driving a person who urgently requires life saving medical treatment to a hospital would have this defence.

H - Martial Coercion

- There is a defence available to *married* women to prove that:
    - They **committed an offence**:
    - Both:
        - In the **presence** of; and
        - Under the **coercion** of;
        - Their **husband.**

Upon Whom Does The Burden Of Proving Marital Coercion Lie?

- The **burden** of proving the marital coercion rests upon the **defence** on the **balance of probability**.

Exam Trip Up

- The defence is available even when the **threat** from the husband relates to something **less** than:
    - **Death;** or
    - **Serious bodily harm.**

Exam Trip Up

- This defence is **not available** for the crimes of:
    - **Murder;** or
    - **Treason.**

I - Defence Of Either Oneself, Another Or Property

- A person **may use such force as is reasonable in the circumstances** in:
    - The **prevention of crime;**
    - In **effecting or assisting in a lawful arrest** of either:
        - **Offenders;**
        - **Suspected offenders;**
        - **Persons unlawfully at large.**
- A **pre-emptive strike** may be **justified** in the circumstances and there is no need to be attacked first in such circumstances.

Crime
Unit 4: Homicide

A - Murder
Indictable Only Offence
Penalty In The Crown Court – Life Imprisonment

1 - Definition Of Murder

- The **common law** offence of **murder** is committed where a person:
    - ☐ **Unlawfully;**
    - ☐ **Kills;**
    - ☐ Another **human being;**
    - ☐ Under the **Queens peace;**
    - ☐ With **malice** aforethought.

2 – Definition Of An Unlawful Killing

- An **unlawful killing** involves **actively causing** the **death** of **another** without **justification**.

    Exam Trip Up – Can An Omission To Act Cause A Killing?

- An **omission can cause a killing** where somebody:
    - ☐ Under a **duty to act;**
    - ☐ Has **failed** to **act.**

    For example: In the case of *R v Stone* [1977] QB 722 the defendant was guilty of unlawfully killing a mentally ill person whom they had accepted a duty to care for when their neglect resulted in their death.

3 – Definition Of A Reasonable Person In Being

- The **person in being** must have an **independent existence**.

Exam Trip Up

- A baby can only be murdered when it is maintaining an **independent existence of its mother**.
- This in essence means the baby must have **completely emerged into the world**.
- It is *not* necessary for the **umbilical cord** to have been **cut** but it must have **breathed**.

4 – Definition Of Under The Queen's Peace

- This **excludes deaths** that occur **during** *legitimate* **warfare**.

Exam Trip Up

- If a **prisoner of war** was **killed** whilst **in captivity** this would **not** be an **act of legitimate warfare** and the killer would be guilty of **murder**.

5 – Definition Of Malice Aforethought

- **Malice aforethought** involves an **intention** to:
    - ☐ **Kill**; or
    - ☐ **Cause GBH**.

Exam Trip Up

- There is **no need** for **premeditation** as the word 'aforethought' may suggest.

6 - Murders Committed Abroad – Section 9 OAPA 1861

- British subjects who **murder** people **abroad** can be **tried in this country** for murder.
- They **do not have to be tried in the country where the act was committed**.
- Previous exam questions have mentioned that the murder happened outside of the *commonwealth*. This is **immaterial** and is a **red herring**.
- An offence committed **anywhere** in the **world** can be tried in this country.

7 - Accessory To Murder

- If A tells B that they would like to purchase a gun from B to go and murder C; and
- B sells A the gun; and
- A goes on to commit the murder C;
- B will be an accessory to the murder of C;
- As B knew what use the gun will be put to by A.

8 - Is Consent Required To Prosecute For Murder?

(i) - General Rule

- **No consent** is required to prosecute for murder.

(ii) - Exception To The General Rule

- **Consent** to prosecute for murder **is required** from either the:
    - ☐ **Attorney General**; or
    - ☐ **Solicitor General**;
- Where either:
    - ☐ The victim dies more than 3 years after sustaining their injuries; or
    - ☐ The defendant has already been convicted for an offence connected with the death (e.g. ABH or GBH).

B - Special Defences To Murder

- There are **3 special defences** to murder:
    - ☐ **Diminished Responsibility**;
    - ☐ **Provocation**; and
    - ☐ **Suicide Pact**.

- The 3 special defences have developed because a straightforward **conviction** for **murder** leaves the judge with **no discretion** in **sentencing.**

- If one of the 3 special defences are established the murderer will **not** be **acquitted**.

- They are instead convicted of **voluntary manslaughter**.

1 - Diminished Responsibility - Section 2 Homicide Act 1957

(i) – Definition of Diminished Responsibility

- The special defence of **diminished responsibility** will be established where:
    - ☐ **At the time** of the **killing**;
    - ☐ The defendant was suffering from an **abnormality of the mind**;
    - ☐ That **substantially impaired** their **mental responsibility** for their acts.

(ii) - Definition Of An Abnormality Of The Mind

- An **abnormality of the mind** was defined in the case of *R v Byrne* [1960] 2 QB 396 as:

    '...a state of mind so different from that of ordinary human beings that the reasonable man would deem it abnormal'.

- Examples of accepted **abnormalities of the mind** include:
    - ☐ **Pre-menstrual symptoms** (*R v Reynolds* [1988] Crim LR 679);
    - ☐ **Battered wives syndrome** (*R v Hobson* [1998] 1 Cr App R 31);
    - ☐ Being **overcome** by **grief** (*R v Dietschmann* [2003] 1 AC 1209)

Exam Trip Up

- **Minor lapses of lucidity** will **not suffice**.

Exam Trip Up

- There is **no need** to prove that the **abnormality of the mind** was the **sole cause** of the defendant's act.

(iii) – Definition Of A Substantial Impairment Of Mental Responsibility

- The **mental impairment** must be **'substantial'**.
- This is a **question of fact** for the jury to decide.

2 - Provocation – Section 3 Homicide Act 1957

(i) – Definition Of Provocation

- The special defence of **provocation** will be established where:
    - The defendant was **provoked**;
    - To **lose** their **self control**;
    - By things either:
        - Said; or
        - Done.

(ii) The Reasonable Man Test

- The jury will decide whether the provocation was sufficient to make **a reasonable person** act as the defendant did.
- The jury will consider **two factors**:
    - Was the **defendant** actually **provoked** to act? - **Subjective element**.
    - Would a **reasonable person** have **acted** in the **same way** as the defendant if they had been placed in the same circumstances? - **Objective element**.

(iii) – Examples Of Provocation

- Examples of **provocative acts** accepted by the courts include:
    - **Words** - *R v Camplin* [1978] AC 705;
    - Sounds of a **baby crying** - *R v Doughty* [1986] 83 Cr App R 319;
    - **Battered Wives Syndrome** over a prolonged period - *R v Ahluwalia* [1992] 4 All ER 889.

Exam Trip Up

- You could be provoked by something X says to you and go on to murder Y.
- It does not therefore have to be the person that provoked you that you kill.

Exam Trip Up

- The defence of provocation will **not** be **available** to a defendant who merely acts out of:
    - **Panic**; or
    - **Fear**.

Exam Trip Up

- If there is **no loss of control** by the defendant the special defence of provocation will not be made out.

  In *R v Cocker* [1989] Crim LR 740, the defendant had endured calls from his chronically ill wife to end her life.

  He mercy killed her and at the time of doing so he did **not lose his self control**.

  He was very much aware and in control of his actions. The judge had to pass a mandatory life sentence for murder.

3 - Suicide Pact - Section 4 Homicide Act 1957

- The defence of **suicide pact** will be established where:
  - The **defendant acts** in pursuance of a **suicide pact**;
  - Between:
    - **Themselves**; and
    - **Another**;
  - To either:
    - **Kill** the **other**; or
    - **Be party** to the **other being killed**; and
  - The **defendant** had the **intention** of **dying at the time of the killing**.

Exam Trip Up

- The suicide pact defence obviously relates to the **survivor** of such an incident.

Exam Trip Up

- It is **not necessary** for there to be a **written agreement** in place between the members of the pact.

C - Manslaughter - Common Law
Indictable Only Offence
Penalty In The Crown Court – Life Imprisonment

- **Manslaughter** can be separated into **two different forms**:
  - **Killing** by an **unlawful act** which was **likely** to **cause bodily harm**;
  - **Killing** by **gross negligence**.

1 - Killing by Unlawful Act Likely To Cause Bodily Harm

- It is necessary to prove:

  - An **unlawful act** by the defendant.

    The act must be inherently unlawful in itself. For example - the act of driving is not inherently unlawful even if done in a way that attracts criminal liability.

  - The **act** involved the **risk** of somebody being **harmed.**

    This will be an **objective test** and it must be **physical harm**.

    Psychological or **emotional harm** is **insufficient.**

  - That the defendant had the relevant **mens rea** for the **unlawful act.**

    In *R v Lamb* [1967] 2 QB 981 the defendant waved a pistol at his friend. The defendant did not believe that the revolver would fire, but the gun fired, killing his friend. As he did not have the mens rea for the assault, his conviction was quashed.

Exam Trip Up

- The case of *R v Goodfellow* [1986] 83 Cr App R 23, established that the **act:**

  - **Does not need to be directed at any person;** and

  - Can include **acts** committed **against property.**

Exam Trip Up

- If the actions of the **victim** or **another break the chain of causation** between the defendant's unlawful act and the cause of death, the defendant's actions will **not be the operating and substantial cause of death** and the **defendant** will **not be responsible** for the death of the victim.

- As a result drug dealers are not usually liable for the death of addicts from an overdose from the drugs they've provided for them - *R v Dalby* [1982] 1 WLR 621.

- However if the victim buys drugs and **immediately** injects them and dies, the supplier may attract liability for the death - *R v Kennedy* [2005] EWCA Crim 685.

- Medical treatment given to the victim following injuries caused by another (e.g. a stabbing) will not be regarded as an intervening act providing the initial injuries remain the operating and substantial cause of death.

- For example if a victim is stabbed numerous times and is taken to hospital and the doctor misses the vital stab wound which results in the death of the victim the chain of causation is not broken and the attacker is still responsible for the death.

2 - Manslaughter By Gross Negligence

- Essentially this offence involves:

  - A **death;**

  - Resulting from a **neglected duty of care** by the defendant;

  - In circumstances that are so bad that they amount to **gross negligence.**

- For example in the case of *R v Dytham* [1979] 2 QB 722, a police officer was guilty of gross negligence manslaughter when he breached his duty of care by failing to intervene in an assault of a man who died from his injuries.

Exam Trip Up

- The task of **defining** the **degree of negligence** that qualifies as **gross** will fall to the **trial judge**. This is therefore a **question of law.**

- The **determination** of whether the **conduct** will amount to **gross negligence** will be a **question of fact** for the **jury** to decide.

D - Causing or Allowing the Death of a Child or Vulnerable Adult - Section 5 Domestic Violence, Crime and Victims Act 2004
Indictable Only Offence
Penalty In The Crown Court – 14 Years Imprisonment

- An offence will be committed where:
    - A **victim** who is either a:
        - **Child**; or
        - **Vulnerable Adult**;
    - Dies as a result of the unlawful act of the defendant who:
        - Was a member of the same household as the victim; **and**
        - Had frequent contact with the victim; and
    - At the time there was **significant risk** of **serious physical harm** being caused to the victim; and
    - The defendant's **act caused** the **victim's death**;
    - The defendant either:
        - Was **aware** of the **risk**; or
        - **Ought** to have been **aware** of the **risk**;
    - The defendant **failed** to take **reasonable steps** to **protect** the **victim** from the **risk**; and
    - The defendant either:
        - **Foresaw** the act; or
        - **Ought** to be **foreseen** the act.

Learning Points

- A **child** means a person aged **under 16.**

- A **vulnerable adult** means a person:
    - Aged **16 or over**;
    - Whose **ability** to **protect themselves** from **violence, abuse** or **neglect** is **significantly impaired** through a:
        - **Physical disability**;
        - **Mental disability**; or
        - **Illness.**

- **Serious physical harm** means **GBH** for the purposes of the Offences Against the Persons Act 1861.

- It is necessary to prove the **victim died** as a result of the **unlawful act** of a **person who fits the criteria**.

Exam Trip Up

- It is not necessary for the person to live with the person to be a member of the same household.

- As long as the person visits the victim often and for long periods it is sufficient.

E - Aiding Another to Commit Suicide – Section 2 Suicide Act 1961
Indictable Only Offence
Penalty In The Crown Court – 14 Years Imprisonment

- An offence will be committed by a person who:
    - Either:
        - **Aides;**
        - **Abets;**
        - **Counsels;** or
        - **Procures;**
    - Either:
        - The **suicide** of **another**; or
        - An **attempt** by **another** to **commit suicide**.

F - Solicitation Of Murder – Section 4 OAPA 1861
Indictable Only Offence
Penalty In The Crown Court – Life Imprisonment

- It is an offence to:
    - **Solicit;**
    - **Encourage;**
    - **Persuade;** or
    - **Endeavour to persuade;**

    - any person to **murder** another person.

- There is **no need** for the **contract to kill to be concluded by** an **actual killing**.

- It is only necessary to prove that a person has made a **positive attempt to arrange with another person to kill on their behalf**.

Crime
Unit 5: Misuse Of Drugs Offences

A - Possession of Drugs - The Basic Offence

Class A
Either Way Offence
Penalty In The Crown Court – 7 Years Imprisonment And / Or A Fine
Penalty In The Magistrates Court – 6 Months Imprisonment And / Or A Prescribed Amount

Class B
Either Way Offence
Penalty In The Crown Court – 5 Years Imprisonment And / Or A Fine
Penalty In The Magistrates Court – 3 Months Imprisonment And / Or A Fine

Class C
Either Way Offence
Penalty In The Crown Court – 2 Years Imprisonment And / Or A Fine
Penalty In The Magistrates Court – 3 Months Imprisonment And / Or A Fine

1 – Definition Of Possession Of Drugs - Section 5 Misuse of Drugs Act 1971

- It is an offence for any person to:
    - **Unlawfully;**
    - Have a **controlled drug;**
    - In their **possession.**

2 - Proving Possession

- To prove **possession** it is necessary to establish either:
    - **Physical** possession of the drug; or
    - A **lack** of **physical possession** but **control** of the drug; and

      For example: If A gives B their drugs for safekeeping both **A (in control)** and **B (in physical possession)** will be guilty of **possession.**

    - **Knowledge** of possession.

      For example: If X slips drugs into Y's pocket **without their knowledge**, then Y will not attract criminal liability.

Exam Trip Up

- In the case of *R v Marriot* [1971] 1 WLR 187, a male was convicted of possession of heroin when he admitted to possessing a knife with a substance which he thought was sand on it. The substance in fact turned out to be heroin.

- He was convicted as he:
    - Was **in possession** of the substance; and
    - **Knew** he was in **possession** of the substance.

- For the purposes of proving possession - it **did not matter that he thought he was in possession of a different substance.**

3 – The 2 Special Defences To Possession Only – Section 5 Misuse Of Drugs Act 1971

- There are **2 defences** to possession specifically:
    - ☐ **To prevent another committing an offence**; and
    - ☐ **Innocent possession.**

- In order to successfully plead the defences it is necessary for the person to establish that they:
    - **As soon as possible;**
    - Took **reasonable steps** to either:
        - ☐ **Destroy the drugs**; or
        - ☐ **Surrender the drugs** to a person lawfully entitled to possess them.

(i) - An Example Of Taking Possession To Prevent Another Committing An Offence

- A parent comes home to find their son smoking cannabis.
- The parent could take possession of the cannabis and would have a **defence** if they **flushed the cannabis down the toilet to destroy it** as soon as possible after taking possession.
- If instead of flushing it down the toilet to destroy it, they **locked the cannabis in their cupboard**, they would have **no defence.**

(ii) - An Example of Innocent Possession With View To Surrender

- A teacher walks down the road and finds a kilo of heroin.
- If they take possession of the heroin:
    - ☐ *Solely* for the **purpose of surrendering it to a person who would be lawfully entitled to possession** (e.g. the police) then **no offence** would be committed;
    - ☐ In order to **take it into the classroom to warn his pupils of the dangers of heroin**, he could **not rely on this defence** as he did **not** take possession of the heroin for the *sole purpose* of surrendering it to a person lawfully entitled to possession.

Exam Trip Up

- As mentioned above, there are **two special defences** to **possession:**
    - ☐ **Preventing another committing an offence**; and
    - ☐ **Innocent possession.**

- If your defence is *innocent possession* your *only* option is to **surrender the drugs to a person lawfully entitled to possess.**

- You *cannot* rely on the defence of **innocent possession** if you *destroy* the drug.

Exam Trip Up – Changes Of Heart By Drug Addicts

- Watch out for questions where an addict finds drugs and takes them into their **possession**, **initially intending to use them personally** and **subsequently** has a **change of heart** and **decides to surrender** the drugs at a police station.

- The addict will **not be able to rely on this defence**, as when they took possession of the drugs, it was **not their** *sole* **intention to surrender** them to a person lawfully entitled to possession.

4 - The 3 General Defences To Possession – Section 28 Misuse of Drugs Act 1971

- There are **3 general defences** which relate to the **following offences**:

    - Cultivation of **cannabis**;   C
    - Offences related to **opium**;   O
    - **Possession**;   P
    - **Supply**;   S
    - Unlawful **production**; and   P
    - Possession with **intent** to supply.   I

Memory Aid

- Just think of "COPS P.I." - (Magnum P.I.)!

Exam Trip Up

- The **3 general defences do not apply to conspiring** to do any of the "**COPS PI**" activities, as conspiracy is not an offence under the Misuse of Drug Act 1971.

The 3 General Defences

- The **3 general defences** are:

    - Lack of knowledge of **fact**;   -   F
    - Belief that they were **entitled** to possess; and   -   E
    - Lack of knowledge of **drug**.   -   D

Memory Aid

- Just think of the "Feds" putting somebody's door in on a drugs raid:

    - F   -   Fact
    - E   -   Entitled
    - D   -   Drug

(i) - Lack Of Knowledge Of Fact - Section 28 (2) Misuse of Drugs Act 1971

- **Lack of knowledge of fact** will be established where:
    - In relation to a fact alleged by the prosecution;
    - The person either:
        - **Did not know** of the existence of a fact alleged;
        - **Did not suspect** the existence of that fact; or
        - **Had no reason to suspect** the existence of that fact.

An Example Of Lack Of Knowledge Of Fact

- A youth is standing in the street and is approached by a person **unknown** to them, who offers them £1 to deliver a package to a house down the road.

- If the youth was stopped and the package contained a controlled drug they could run the defence of lack of knowledge of fact as given the minimal sum offered for the task and the lack of knowledge of the person's background they:
    - **Did not know;**
    - **Did not suspect**; and
    - **Had no reason suspect**;
    - that there would be drugs in the package.

- If however a person who they **knew to be drug dealer** offered them £500 to carry out the same task they would be unable to run the defence of lack of knowledge of fact because even if they were not told that drugs were in the package, the person's reputation as a dealer and the sum offered for the minimal task would generate **reason to suspect** that there may be drugs in the package.

(ii) - Lack Of Knowledge Of Drug - Section 28(3)(a) Misuse of Drugs Act 1971

- **Lack of knowledge of drug** will be relevant where:
    - It is necessary for the prosecution to prove that the drug in question was a **specific drug;** and
    - The prosecution have **proven** that the drug in question **was of that type**.
    - If so a **defence** will be established where the person either **believed the substance:**
        - Was something other than a controlled drug; and
        - Had **no** reason to believe it was a controlled drug.

(iii) - Belief They Were Entitled To Possess - Section 28(3)(b) Misuse of Drugs Act 1971

- A person's **belief** that they were **entitled to possess** will be established where:
    - They believed it was a **controlled drug;**
    - They believed that it had been:
        - **That controlled drug;** or
        - **A particular controlled drug.**

An Example Of A Belief By A Person That They Were Entitled To Possess

- A registered heroin addict is prescribed Methadone by their doctor and is mistakenly given Pethidine by their chemist.
- If they are later stopped by the police, they could run the defence that they believed the drug in their possession was Methadone.

B – Unlawful Production Of Controlled Drugs

Class A
Either Way Offence
Penalty In The Crown Court – Life Imprisonment And / Or A Fine
Penalty In The Magistrates Court – 6 Months Imprisonment And / Or A Prescribed Sum

Class B
Either Way Offence
Penalty In The Crown Court – 14 Years Imprisonment And / Or A Fine
Penalty In The Magistrates Court – 6 Months Imprisonment And / Or A Fine

Class C
Either Way Offence
Penalty In The Crown Court – 5 Years Imprisonment And / Or A Fine
Penalty In The Magistrates Court – 3 Months Imprisonment And / Or A Fine

1 - Definition Of Unlawful Production Of Controlled Drugs – Section 4(2) Misuse of Drugs Act 1971

- It is an offence to:
    - Either:
        - **Produce;** or
        - Be **concerned** in the **production;**
- Of a **controlled drug.**

Exam Trip Up

- In the case of *R v Russell* [1992] 94 Cr App R351, it was established that **converting one type of Class A drug into another type of Class A drug** amounted to the **production of a controlled drug.**

Exam Trip Up

- To establish guilt it is essential to prove that controlled **drugs were** *actually* **produced**.
- However, where a person:
    - *Attempts* to **produce** a **controlled drug**;
    - But fails to do so;
  - They may still be convicted of an *attempt.*

Exam Trip Up

- For the **concerned in the production** of controlled drugs offence it will be sufficient to prove that a person **delivered ingredients to the place of manufacture** as long as they **knew what the ingredients were being used for.**

C - Supplying Controlled Drugs

Class A
Either Way Offence
Penalty In The Crown Court – Life Imprisonment And / Or A Fine
Penalty In The Magistrates Court – 6 Months Imprisonment And / Or A Fine

Class B
Either Way Offence
Penalty In The Crown Court – 14 Years Imprisonment And / Or A Fine
Penalty In The Magistrates Court – 6 Months Imprisonment And / Or A Fine

Class C
Either Way Offence
Penalty In The Crown Court – 5 Years Imprisonment And / Or A Fine
Penalty In The Magistrates Court – 3 Months Imprisonment And / Or A Fine

1 - Definition Of Supplying Controlled Drugs – Section 4(3) Misuse of Drugs Act 191

- It is an offence to:
    - Either:
        - **Supply**;
        - Be **concerned** in the **supply**;
        - **Offer to supply**; or
        - Be **concerned** in making an **offer to supply**;
    - A **controlled drug.**

(i) - Supplying

- The following are examples of acts of **supplying**:
    - **Deriving a benefit from holding onto drugs for another.**
    - **Dividing up joint purchases.**

Exam Trip Up

- Injecting another with their own supply is not an act of supplying.

(ii) - Offering To Supply

- **Once the offer is made**, the offence of **offering to supply** is **complete**.

Exam Trip Up

- It is **not necessary** to have the **means of supplying** - merely **making the offer is enough**.

Exam Trip Up

- Even if a person is **fooled** by an **offer to supply them a controlled drug** which is in fact **talcum powder** - the offence of offering to supply controlled drugs is *still* **complete**.
- This is the case even if the person offered knows that they are been offered talcum powder.

Exam Trip Up

- If the drug is **not actually a drug**, the offence of **offering to supply** is **still complete**.

(iii) - Concerned In Supply

- To establish that a person is **concerned in supplying**, it is necessary to establish:
    - Either an act of:
        - **Supplying**; or
        - **Offering** to supply;
    - **Participation** of the defendant;
    - **Guilty knowledge** of the defendant.

D – Possession With Intent To Supply

Class A
Either Way Offence
Penalty In The Crown Court – Life Imprisonment And / Or A Fine
Penalty In The Magistrates Court – 6 Months Imprisonment And / Or A Proscribed Sum

Class B
Either Way Offence
Penalty In The Crown Court – 14 Years Imprisonment And / Or A Fine
Penalty In The Magistrates Court – 6 Months Imprisonment And / Or A Proscribed Sum

Class C
Either Way Offence
Penalty In The Crown Court – 14 Years Imprisonment And / Or A Fine
Penalty In The Magistrates Court – 3 Months Imprisonment And / Or A Fine

1 - Definition Of Possession With Intent To Supply – Section 5(3) Misuse of Drugs Act 1971

- It is an offence for a person to:
    - Have a **controlled drug**;
    - In their **possession**;
    - Either:
        - **Lawfully (for example a doctor)**; or
        - **Unlawfully**;
    - With the **intent (offence complete)**;
    - To **unlawfully supply** it to **another**.

Exam Trip Up

- The doctor in lawful possession of methadone would commit this offence by giving it to their partner who is not a registered addict in order to get them off the drug.

Exam Trip Up

- The offence is complete **at the time the *intent* is *formed* to supply another**
- The offence is not complete at the time that the drug is ***supplied*** **to another.**

E - Cultivation Of Cannabis

1 – Penalty For Cultivation Of Cannabis

Either Way Offence
Penalty In The Crown Court – 14 Years Imprisonment And / Or A Fine
Penalty In The Magistrates Court – 6 Months Imprisonment And / Or A Prescribed Sum

2 – Definition Of Cultivation Of Cannabis – Section 9 Misuse of Drugs Act 1971

- It is an offence to:
    - **Unlawfully**;
    - **Cultivate**;
    - **Cannabis**.

3 - Points To Prove

- It is only necessary to prove:
    - The plant was **cannabis**; and
    - The plant was **cultivated**.

4 - Definition Of Cultivation

- **Cultivation** requires the defendant to have given **attention** to the plant by either:
    - Watering;
    - Feeding;
    - Artificial lighting etc.

Exam Trip Up

- The case of *R v Champ* [1981] 73 Cr App R 367 established that it is **not necessary to prove that the defendant knew that the plant was cannabis.**

Exam Trip Up

- An officer will not be permitted to keep cannabis plants alive in the police station to enable them to be produced at court – as doing so would result in the commission of the offence.

Exam Trip Up

- The **general defences** are available for this offence as the offence falls under the **COPS PI** definition.

F – Opium Misuse

1 – Penalty For Opium Misuse

Either Way Offence
Penalty In The Crown Court – 14 Years Imprisonment And / Or A Fine
Penalty In The Magistrates Court – 6 Months Imprisonment And / Or A Fine

2 – Definition Of Opium Misuse – Section 9 Misuse Of Drugs Act 1971

Offence A

- It is an offence for a person to:
    - Either:
        - **Smoke;** or
        - Otherwise **use;**
    - **Prepared opium.**

Offence B

- It is an offence for a person to:
    - **Frequent** a **place used** for the purpose of **smoking opium**.

Offence C

- It is an offence for a person to **possess**:
    - Any:
        - **Pipes**; or
        - **Utensils**;
    - That are either:
        - **Made**; or
        - **Adapted**;
    - For **use in connection** with the **smoking of opium**;
    - Which either:
        - Have been **used by them**; or
        - Have been **used by others** with their **knowledge** or **permission**;
        - They **intend** to **use themselves**; or
        - They **intend** to **permit others to use** with their **knowledge** or **permission**.

Offence D

- It is an offence for a person to **possess**:
    - Any **utensils**;
    - Which have either been:
        - **Used by them**; or
        - **Used by others** with their **knowledge** or **permission**;
    - For the **preparation** of **opium** for **smoking**.

G – Controlled Drugs On Premises

Classes A & B
Either Way Offence
Penalty In The Crown Court – 14 Years Imprisonment And / Or A Fine
Penalty In The Magistrates Court – 6 Months Imprisonment And / Or A Proscribed Sum

Class C
Either Way Offence
Penalty In The Crown Court – 14 Years Imprisonment And / Or A Fine
Penalty In The Magistrates Court – 3 Months Imprisonment And / Or A Fine

1 - Definition Of Controlled Drugs On Premises – Section 8 Misuse of Drugs Act 1971

- An offence will be committed by:
  - Either:
    - The **occupier** of **premises**; or
    - A person concerned in the **management** of **premises**;
  - Who either **knowingly**:
    - **Permits**; or
    - **Suffers (includes turning a blind eye)**;
  - Either the:
    - **Production** or attempted production of a controlled drug;   P
    - Smoking **cannabis** or **prepared opium**;   C
    - **Supply** or attempted supply of a controlled drug;   S
    - Preparing **opium** for smoking.   O

Memory Aid

Remember:

- P - Production (attempt)
- C - Cannabis / prepared opium (smoking)
- S - Supply (attempt)
- O - Opium (preparing for smoking)

H – Closure Notices

1 - Circumstances In Which A Closure Notice May Be Issued – Section 1 Anti Social Behaviour Act 2003

- If a **Superintendent** or above;
- Has reasonable grounds to **believe**;
- That **premises** have been **used** in connection with the **unlawful**:
  - **Use**;
  - **Production**; or
  - **Supply**;
- Of a **Class A controlled drug**;
- During the **previous 3 months**; and

- That the use of the premises is associated with the occurrence of:
    - ☐ **Disorder;** or
    - ☐ **Serious nuisance** to members of the public;
- They may **authorise** the **issue** of a **closure notice** in respect of the **premises** if they are satisfied:
    - ☐ That the **local authority** has been **consulted**; and
    - ☐ That **reasonable steps** have been taken to **discover** the **identity** of anyone:
        - **Residing** on the premises;
        - With **control** of the premises;
        - With **responsibility** for the premises; or
        - Who has an **interest** in the premises.

2 - The Nature Of The Superintendent's Authorisation - Section 1(3) Anti Social Behaviour Act 2003

- The **Superintendent** may provide their authorisation either:
    - ☐ **Orally;** or
    - ☐ In **writing.**
- If the authorisation is provided orally – it must be confirmed in writing as soon as practicable thereafter.

3 - Definition Of Premises - Section 11 Anti Social Behaviour Act 2003

- **Premises** includes any:
    - ☐ Enclosed; or
    - ☐ Unenclosed;
    - ☐ Land; or
    - ☐ Other place; and
    - ☐ Outbuildings used as part of the premises.

4 - Service Of A Closure Notice

- The **Closure Notice** must be **served** by a **police officer.**

5 - Contents Of A Closure Notice

- The **Closure Notice** must provide **notice** of the following:
    - ☐ The an application will be made to close the premises;
    - ☐ That access to the premises by any person (other than an habitual resident or owner) is prohibited;
    - ☐ The date and time and place where the application will be heard;
    - ☐ The effect of the closure order;
    - ☐ That failure to comply with the notice is an offence;
    - ☐ Information about housing and legal organisations in the area who may be contacted for advice.

6 – Service of a Closure Notice - Section 1(6) Anti Social Behaviour Act 2003

- The **police officer** must:
    - ☐ **Fix** a copy of the Closure Notice to:
        - **At least one prominent place** on the premises;
        - **Each normal means of access** to the premises;
        - Any **outbuildings** which appear to be the constable to be used with or as part of the premises; and
    - ☐ **Give** a copy of the Closure Notice to:
        - **At least one person** who appears to the constable to have:
            - ☐ **Control** of the premises;
            - ☐ **Responsibility** for the premises;
        - Any person who **lives** on the premises.

7 - Applying To The Magistrates Court For A Closure Order – Section 2 Anti Social Behaviour Act 2003

- Following the **issue** of a **Closure Notice** a **police officer** must **apply** to a **magistrates' court** for a **Closure Order**.
- The **application** must be **heard** not later than **48 hours after** the **notice** has been **served**.
- However, the application may then be **adjourned** for up to **14 days** to **allow persons with an interest in the premises to contest the application.**

8 - Criteria That The Must Be Satisfied For The Magistrates Court To Issue A Closure Order – Section 2(3) Anti Social Behaviour Act 2003

- A **Closure Order** may be made only if the **Magistrates** are satisfied:
    - The **premises** have been **used** in connection with the **unlawful use, production,** or **supply** of a **Class A controlled drug**;
    - The **use** of the **premises** is **associated** during the period of the notice with the occurrence of:
        - **Disorder;** or
        - **Nuisance;** and
    - Making an **order** is **necessary** to **prevent** a **reoccurrence** of such **disorder** or **nuisance** during the period of the notice.

9 - Duration Of A Closure Order - Section 2(3) Anti Social Behaviour Act 2003

- A Closure Order closes a premises (or specified part of it) to all persons for **such period as decided by the court.**
- The **maximum initial period** of a Closure Order is **3 months**.
- An **extension** for a **further 3 months** may be applied for at any time before the initial Closure Order expires.
- A **Superintendent** must provide authority for the further Closure Order following consultation with the **local authority.**
- **No further extensions** may be sought thereafter.

10 - Police Powers of Entry Under a Closure Order - Section 3(4) & (5) Anti Social Behaviour Act 2003

- Either a:
    - **Police officer**; or
    - Other **authorised person**;
- May either:
    - **Enter** the premises; and / or
    - **Secure** the premises against entry;
- Using **reasonable force** if necessary; and
- May **enter** at any time during the period of the order to **carry out maintenance or repairs**.

- If they are **challenged**;
- By either the:
    - **Owner**; or
    - **Occupier**;
- They must produce **evidence** of their:
    - **Identification**; and
    - **Authority** to act.

11 - Breach Of A Closure Order – Section 4 Anti Social Behaviour Act 2003
Summary Only Offence
Penalty In The Magistrates Court – 6 Months Imprisonment And / Or A Fine

- A person commits an offence if:
    - ☐ **Without reasonable excuse**;
    - ☐ They either:
        - **Remain** on the premises; or
        - **Enters** the premises;
    - ☐ In **contravention** of a **closure order**.
- It is also an offence to **obstruct a constable or other authorised person exercising his powers of entry** – **no reasonable excuse** provision applies to this offence.

I - Importation Of Controlled Drugs – Section 3 Misuse Of Drugs Act 1971

- It is an offence for a person to:
    - ☐ Either:
        - **Import**; or
        - **Export**;
    - ☐ **Controlled drugs**;
    - ☐ **Unless**;
    - ☐ They are **authorised** to do so.

J - Definition Of Assisting Or Inciting Offences Outside The UK – Section 20 Misuse of Drugs Act 1971
Either Way Offence
Penalty In The Crown Court – 14 Years Imprisonment And / Or A Fine
Penalty In The Magistrates Court – 6 Months Imprisonment And / Or A Fine

- A person commits an offence if:
    - ☐ **Whilst inside the UK**;
    - ☐ They either:
        - **Assist in**; or
        - **Induce**;
    - ☐ The **commission** of an **offence**;
    - ☐ **In any place outside the UK**;
    - ☐ Which is contrary to the **laws in force in that other place**.

Exam Trip Up

- For the offence to be complete you must show that the offence in the other country actually took place.

Police Pass OSPRE Part 1 Revision Crammer Textbook ©

Exam Trip Up

- In the case of *R v Evans* [1977] 64 Cr App R 237, a male who took a lorry with empty containers from this country to country B to be filled with drugs and shipped to country C was found guilty of this offence.

K – The Power To Search, Enter and Seize - Section 23 Misuse of Drugs Act 1971

- If a **constable**;
- Has **reasonable grounds** to **suspect**;
- That a person is in **possession** of a **controlled drug**;
- They may:
    - **Detain** and **search** any **person**;
    - **Stop, detain** and **search** any:
        - **Vehicle**; or
        - **Vessel**;
    - **Seize** and **detain anything offending** under the act.

Exam Trip Up

- I'm sure you are all well aware of the 1968 Hovercraft Act!
- The legislation in your book makes direct reference to this legislation.
- You are familiar with your power to stop **vehicles**, but remember that you also have powers to stop **vessels** too, including hovercrafts!

L - Grounds For A Warrant – Section 23 Misuse Of Drugs Act 1971

- **Grounds for a warrant** will be established where
    - A **magistrate** is satisfied on **oath**;
    - That there are **reasonable grounds** to **suspect** that either:
        - **Controlled drugs** are **unlawfully** in the **possession** of a **person** on the **premises**; or
        - A **document** is in the **possession** of a **person** at the **premises** that relates to:
            - Either:
                - **An unlawful transaction**; or
                - **Dealing**;
            - Either:
                - **Inside** the **UK**;
                - **Outside** the **UK**.

M - Obstruction - Section 23 (4) Misuse of Drugs Act 1971
Either Way Offence
Penalty In The Crown Court – 2 Years Imprisonment And / Or A Fine
Penalty In The Magistrates Court – 6 Months Imprisonment And / Or A Fine

- A person commits an offence if they either:
    - Intentionally:
        - **Obstruct** a person exercising their powers;
        - **Conceal** from a person exercising their powers any:
            - Books;
            - Documents;
            - Stocks; or
            - Drugs; or
    - Without reasonable excuse (burden of proof rests on the defendant) fail to produce books or documents where their production is demanded.

N - Supplying Articles For Administering Controlled Drugs - Section 9A(1) Misuse of Drugs Act 1971
Summary Only Offence
Penalty In The Magistrates Court – 6 Months Imprisonment And / Or A Fine

- An offence will be committed by:
    - A person who either:
        - **Supplies**; or
        - **Offers to supply**;
    - Any **article** which may be either:
        - **Used**; or
        - **Adapted for use**;
    - In the **unlawful administration** of a **controlled drug** to either:
        - **Themselves**; or
        - **Another**;
- **Believing** that the **article will be so used**.

O - Supplying Articles For Preparing Controlled Drugs - Section 9A(3) Misuse of Drugs Act 1971
Summary Only Offence
Penalty In The Magistrates Court – 6 Months Imprisonment And / Or A Fine

- An offence will be committed by :
    - A person who either:
        - **Supplies**; or
        - **Offers** to **supply**;
    - An **article** which may be **used** to **prepare** a **controlled drug**;
    - For the **unlawful administration** to either:
        - **Themselves**; or
        - **Another**;
    - **Believing** the **article** will be **so used**.

Compare And Contrast The Two Offences

- Section 9A(1) deals with the **administration** of the **controlled drug**.
- Section 9A(3) deals with the **preparation** of the **controlled drug**.

Exam Trip Up

- This offence does **not** encompass **hypodermic needles** or any part of them.

Exam Trip Up

- The **administration** must be *unlawful* for the offence to be made out.

P - Travel Restriction Orders – Section 36 Criminal Justice and Police Act 2001

1 - The Nature Of A Travel Restriction Order

- **Travel Restriction Orders** can be imposed on offenders **convicted** of **drug trafficking** offences.
- They **prohibit** the offender from **leaving the UK:**
    - **From** the time they **leave custody;**
    - **To** the **expiry** of the **order.**
- The **minimum period** of an order is **two years.**
- An offender may also have to **surrender their passport** as part of the order.

2 - When Must The Court Consider Imposing A Travel Restriction Order?

- The court **must consider** whether to impose a **Travel Restriction Order** where:
    - ☐ A person has been **convicted** of a **drug trafficking** offence; and
    - ☐ The person has been **sentenced** to **four years or more**.
- If the court **decides not to impose** a **Travel Restriction Order** they must provide their **reasons** for doing so.

3 - Contravening A Travel Restriction Order - Section 36 Criminal Justice and Police Act 2001

- A person will be guilty of an offence if:
    - ☐ They **leave** the **UK** at a time when they are **prohibited** from doing so; or
    - ☐ They are **not in** the **UK** at the **end** of a **period of restriction** which has been **suspended**.

Exam Trip Up

- This offence relates to **not being in** the **UK**.
- It does **not state England** and **Wales**.
- Therefore the offence will **not** be **committed** if the person subject to the order travelled to:
    - Scotland
    - Northern Ireland;
    - Isle of Man; or
    - Channel Isles.

Exam Trip Up

- There is **no need** for the person subject to the order to have **left the UK voluntarily** to be guilty of the offence.
- Even if they **leave the UK involuntarily** they will commit an **offence**.

    For example: A plane a person subject to an order was travelling in from London to Belfast (which is in the UK) being re-directed due to adverse weather conditions to Dublin (outside the UK).

Exam Trip Up

- If a person subject to an order is **deported** by the **Home Secretary** they do **not commit** the offence.

Q - Supply of Intoxicating Substances
Either Way Offence
Penalty In The Crown Court – 5 Years Imprisonment And / Or A Fine
Penalty In The Magistrates Court – 6 Months Imprisonment And / Or A Proscribed Sum

1 – Definition Of The Supply Of Intoxicating Substances - Section 1 Intoxicating Substances Act 1985

- It is an offence to:
    - Either:
        - **Supply**; or
        - **Offer to supply**;
    - A **substance other than** a **controlled drug**;
    - Either:
        - To a person **under 18** whom they either:
            - **Know** is **under that age**; or
            - Have **reasonable cause** to **believe** to be **under that age**; or
        - To:
            - A **person who is acting on behalf** of a person **under 18**; and
            - Whom they **know** or has **reasonable grounds** for **believing** to be so **acting**;
    - If the either
        - **Know**; or
        - Have **reasonable cause** for **believing**;
    - That the **substance** or its **fumes** are likely to be **inhaled** by a **person under 18** for the **purpose** of causing **intoxication**.

2 - Defence To Supply Of Intoxicating Substances - Section 1(2) Intoxicating Substances Act 1985

- A defence will be established where:
    - The person was **under 18**; and
    - Was **acting other than** in the **course of furtherance of a business**.

R - SOCPA 2005 And Warrants

- A warrant is now valid for **three months**.
- It is permissible to gain entry to **more than one premises controlled by a person**.

Crime
Unit 6: Offences Against The Person

A - Common Assault Or Battery – Section 39 Criminal Justice Act 1988

Basic Offence – Summary Only Offence
Penalty In The Magistrates Court – 6 Months Imprisonment

Racially Or Religiously Aggravated Offence - Either Way Offence
Penalty In The Crown Court – 2 Years Imprisonment And / Or A Fine
Penalty In The Magistrates Court – 6 Months Imprisonment And / Or A Fine

- A person must be charged with **one offence or the other.**
- **Not both!**

1 – Definition Of Common Assault

- An offence of **common assault** will be committed:
    - Where the perpetrator:
        - **Intentionally** or **recklessly;**
        - Causes the victim to **apprehend an immediate assault (unlawful personal violence);**
    - But **force is not actually used.**

Exam Trip Up

- The person must **apprehend** an **immediate assault**.
- For example:
    - If a person swings a punch at a blind person which misses the offence will not be complete as the blind person will **not** have **apprehended** an assault.
    - If a person **apprehends** the immediate application of force from a gun held to their head the offence will be complete even if there was no bullet in the gun.

2 - Definition Of Battery

- **Battery** is the **actual laying of force** against the victim **(assault by beating).**

Exam Trip Up - Conditional Threats

- A **conditional threat** will **not** constitute an **assault.**
- An example of a conditional threat would be a person saying to another *"I'd chin you if there wasn't a copper over there"*.

Exam Trip Up - Is It Possible To Consent To An Assault?

- The case of *R v Brown* [1994] 1 AC 212, established that:

    - You **can consent** to an assault.

    - However, you **cannot consent** to anything **beyond transient harm unless** there is a **good reason** for allowing the plea of consent.

- **Good reason** will be determined in light of the following considerations:

    - The practical **consequences** of the behaviour

    - The **dangerousness** of the behaviour

    - The **vulnerability** of the 'consenting person'.

- The case of *R v Brown* related to a group of sadomasochists who inflicted injuries on each other. Whilst it was acknowledged that they **all consented** to the injuries they inflicted upon each other, it was held that there was an **absence of a good reason** for allowing a consent plea in the circumstances.

- The outcome of this case can be contrasted with that in *R v Wilson* [1997] QB 47, where a husband **consensually branded** his initials on his wife's buttocks with a hot knife.

    The court held that there **was a good reason** for the actions, as the branding was recognised a form of **tattooing** and that **consenting behaviour between husband and wife** was not a matter for criminal investigation.

3 - Certificate Of Dismissal

- If a defendant is found **not guilty** of a **common assault**, the **Magistrates** must issue a **Certificate of Dismissal**.

- **Certificate of Dismissal** means that the defendant **cannot be sued in a civil court** for the same offence.

B - Definition Of Assault With Intent To Resist Arrest – Section 38 OAPA 1861
Either Way Offence
Penalty In The Crown Court – 2 Years Imprisonment
Penalty In The Magistrates Court – 6 Months Imprisonment

- It is an offence to:

    - **Assault**;

    - **Any person**;

    - With the **intent (offence complete)** to:

        - **Resist arrest**; or

        - **Prevent the arrest**;

    - Of either:

        - **Themselves**; or

        - **Another**.

Who Is Covered ?

- Any person **discharging their duties** if they are **acting lawfully**.

C - Definition Of Assaulting A Police Officer – Section 89(1) Police Act 1996
Summary Only Offence
Penalty In The Magistrates Court – 6 Months Imprisonment And / Or A Fine

- An offence is committed by:
    - Any person who **assaults** either:
        - A **constable** in the **execution of their duty**; or
        - A **person assisting a constable** in the **execution of their duty**.

Exam Trip Up

- The **constable** must be **exercising their duty at the time of the assault** upon either:
    - The **constable**; or
    - The **person assisting the constable**.

Exam Trip Up

- There is **no need** for the prosecution to show that the **defendant knew** or **suspected** that:
    - The person was a **police officer**; or
    - They were **acting in the execution of their duty**.
- The fact that they were executing their duties and that the assault took place at the time of doing so will suffice.

D - Definition Of Obstructing A Police Officer – Section 89(2) Police Act 1996
Summary Only Offence
Penalty In The Magistrates Court – 6 Months Imprisonment And / Or A Fine

- An offence is committed by any person who:
    - Either:
        - **Resists**; or
        - **Wilfully obstructs**;
    - Either:
        - A **constable** in the **execution of their duty**; or
        - A **person assisting a constable** in the **execution of their duty**.

Exam Trip Up

- A person **warning other drivers that there is a speed check in operation** will commit this offence.

- NB - The offence will only be committed if the vehicles warned were found to be speeding.

- If the vehicle was not actually speeding, the offence will not be made out.

Exam Trip Up

- A person who **drinks alcohol before a breath test** will commit this offence.

Exam Trip Up

- A person who **tips another off that they are going to be arrested** will commit this offence.

Exam Trip Up

- Simply **not answering the questions** of a police officer will **not** amount to a offence **unless** the person is **under a duty** to provide information.

E - Definition Of Assaulting or Obstructing Accredited Persons – Section 46 Police Reform Act 2002

Assault - Summary Only Offence
Penalty In The Magistrates Court – 6 Months Imprisonment And / Or A Fine

Obstructing - Summary Only Offence
Penalty In The Magistrates Court – 1 Months Imprisonment And / Or A Fine

- An offence is committed by any person who:

    - Either:

        - **Assaults;**
        - **Resists**; or
        - **Wilfully obstructs;**

    - Either:

        - A person in the **execution of their duties** who is:

            - **Designated;**
            - **Accredited**; or

        - A **person assisting those designated** or **accredited in the execution of their duties.**

F - Actual Bodily Harm (ABH)

Basic Offence – Either Way Offence
Penalty In The Crown Court – 5 Years Imprisonment
Penalty In The Magistrates Court – 6 Months Imprisonment And / Or A Fine

Racially Or Religiously Aggravated Offence - Either Way Offence
Penalty In The Crown Court – 7 Years Imprisonment And / Or A Fine
Penalty In The Magistrates Court – 6 Months Imprisonment And / Or A Fine

1 - Definition Of Actual Bodily Harm (ABH) – Section 47 OAPA 1861

- The offence of **ABH** will be committed where the defendant:
    - Commits an **assault**;
    - Occasioning **actual bodily harm.**

    - **Actual Bodily Harm (ABH)** means any:
        - **Hurt;** or
        - **Injury;**
        - **Calculated to interfere with the victim's:**
            - **Health;** or
            - **Comfort.**

Exam Trip Up

- The definition of **harm** includes **shock.**

Examples Of ABH

- Examples of ABH include:
    - Loss or breaking of teeth;
    - Temporary loss of sensory functions;
    - Extensive or multiple bruising;
    - Minor fractures and cuts requiring stitches;
    - Psychiatric harm going beyond fear, distress, or panic.

G – Unlawful Wounding

Basic Offence – Either Way Offence
Penalty In The Crown Court – 5 Years Imprisonment
Penalty In The Magistrates Court – 6 Months Imprisonment And / Or A Fine

Racially Or Religiously Aggravated Offence - Either Way Offence
Penalty In The Crown Court – 7 Years Imprisonment And / Or A Fine
Penalty In The Magistrates Court – 6 Months Imprisonment And / Or A Fine

1 - Definition Of Unlawful Wounding - Section 20 OAPA 1861

- A **section 20 offence** will be committed by any person who:
    - **Unlawfully;** and
    - **Maliciously;**
    - Either:
        - **Wounds;** or
        - **Inflicts GBH;**
    - Upon any person;
    - Either:
        - **With** a **weapon;** or
        - **Without** a **weapon.**

2 - Definition of Wounding

- **Wounding** involves **breaking** the **whole skin**.

3 - Definition of Grievous Bodily Harm

- **GBH** involves either:
    - **Serious harm;** or
    - **Really serious harm.**

4 - Definition of Maliciously

- The defendant behaves **maliciously** if they **realise** that there is a **risk of either:**
    - **Serious harm;** or
    - **Really serious harm.**

H – Grievous Bodily Harm
Indictable Only Offence
Penalty In The Crown Court – Life Imprisonment

1 - Definition Of Grievous Bodily Harm - Section 18 OAPA 1861

- The **section 18 offence** will be committed where a person:
    - ☐ **Unlawfully**; and
    - ☐ **Maliciously**;
    - ☐ **Either**:
        - **Wounds**; or
        - **Causes GBH**;
    - ☐ With the **intent** to either:
        - **Commit GBH**; or
        - **Resist** or **prevent** the **arrest** of **any person**.

- The **section 18 offence**:
    - ☐ Is exactly the **same** as a **section 20 offence**;
    - ☐ With the **added requirement**;
    - ☐ That the assault was committed with the **intent** to either:
        - **Cause GBH**; or
        - **Resist or prevent the arrest of any person**.

Key Similarities And Differences Between Section 20 And Section 18 Offences Against The Persons Act 1861

Factor	Section 18	Section 20
Unlawfully	Yes	Yes
Maliciously	Yes	Yes
Actus Reus	■ Wound; or ■ Causes GBH	■ Wound; or ■ Inflicts GBH
Mens Rea	Intent to: ■ Wound; ■ Cause GBH; ■ Resist the arrest of any person; Prevent the arrest of any person.	Subjective recklessness to: ■ Wound; ■ Inflicts GBH.
With Or Without A Weapon Or Instrument	N/A	Yes

I - Racially And Religiously Aggravated Assaults – Section 29(1)(c) Crime & Disorder Act 1998

1 – Offences That Can Become Racially And Religiously Aggravated

- Any of the following **assaults** can be **aggravated** either:
    - ☐ **Racially**; or
    - ☐ **Religiously**.
- Either:
    - ☐ **Common assault**,
    - ☐ **Section 47 assaults**; and
    - ☐ **Section 20 assaults**.

Exam Trip Up

- NB - **Section 18 assaults can** be racially or religiously aggravated but as this offence already carries life imprisonment there is no practical consequence in terms of sentencing.

2 - How Does An Offence Become Racially Or Religiously Aggravated? – Section 29(1)(c) Crime & Disorder Act 1998

- An offence will become **racially** or **religiously aggravated** where:
    - ☐ Either:
        - **At the time**;
        - **Immediately before**; or
        - **Immediately after**;
    - Committing the offence;
    - ☐ The defendant demonstrates **hostility** towards the **victim**; and
    - ☐ The **hostility** is **based** on the **victims**:
        - **Membership**; or
        - **Presumed membership** of a:
            - ☐ **Racial** group; or
            - ☐ **Religious** group.

3 - Examples Of Racially Or Religiously Aggravated Assaults

- A husband and his wife are walking down the road. They are both Caucasian and are agnostic. The wife is wearing clothing concealing her entire body and the husband is wearing a suit.

- The wife is assaulted and at the time of the assault, a comment is directed towards her stating *"Take that Persian"*. The assault will be **racially aggravated** in nature as:

    - **At the time** of the assault;
    - **Hostility** was directed towards the victim;
    - Based upon her *presumed* membership of a **racial group**.

- The fact that the wife is not Persian is irrelevant.

- Provided the attacker presumed that she was Persian, by virtue of her wearing a burka, the hostility will be directed towards her due to her presumed membership of a racial group.

- The husband is assaulted and immediately after the attack, as he lay on the floor, the attacker comments *"Take that Muslim"*.

- The assault will be **religiously aggravated** in nature as:

    - **Immediately following** the assault;
    - **Hostility** was directed towards the victim;
    - Based upon his *presumed* membership of a **religious group**.

- The fact that the husband is not a Muslim is irrelevant.

- Provided the attacker presumed that he was a Muslim, by virtue of his wife wearing a burka, the hostility will be directed towards him due to his presumed membership of a religious group.

J - Definition Of Torture – Section 134 Criminal Justice Act 1988
Indictable Only Offence
Penalty In The Crown Court – Life Imprisonment

- The offence is committed by:

    - Any:
        - **Public official;** or
        - Person acting in an **official capacity**;
    - **Whatever** their **nationality**;
    - If they are:
        - **In the UK;** or
        - **Elsewhere;** and
    - They **intentionally inflict** on another **(by acts or omissions)**;
    - **Severe (physical or mental)**:
        - **Pain;** or
        - **Suffering**
    - In the **performance** or **purported performance** of their **official duties**.

Exam Trip Up

- The **permission** of the **Attorney General** is required to prosecute an offence of torture.

Exam Tip Up

- The offence of torture can be committed by a **non public official** provided they:
    - Have the:
        - **Consent**; or
        - **Acquiesce**;
    - Of either a:
        - **Public official**; or
        - Person **purporting** to act as such.

Exam Trip Up

- **Police officers** are **public officials.**
- However if a police officer is **off duty**:
    - They will **not be acting** in their capacity as a public official; and
    - The offence will **not** be made out.

Exam Trip Up

- This offence can take place **anywhere in the world**.

Defence To Torture

- It is a **defence**:
    - For a person to prove that they had either:
        - **Lawful authority**;
        - **Justification**; or
        - **Excuse**;
    - To **commit torture.**

Exam Trip Up

- There is an absolute prohibition on torture under the European Convention of Human Rights.
- This is therefore in direct conflict with the defence above.
- The European law supersedes our laws.

K - Definition Of Poisoning - Section 23 OAPA 1861
Indictable Only Offence
Penalty In The Crown Court – 10 Years Imprisonment

- It is an offence to:
    - ☐ **Unlawfully;** and
    - ☐ **Maliciously;**
    - ☐ Either:
        - **Administer;** or
        - **Cause** to be **administered** any:
            - ☐ **Poison;**
            - ☐ **Destructive** thing;
            - ☐ **Noxious** thing;
    - ☐ **Resulting (offence complete)** in either:
        - **Lives being endangered;** or
        - **GBH** being caused.

When Is The Offence Complete?

- There must be a **result** for the offence of **poisoning** to be **complete** in the form of either:
    - ☐ **Lives being endangered;** or
    - ☐ **GBH being caused.**

Exam Trip Up

- Substances that are innocuous in themselves can become **poisonous** by their **volume.**

    For example if you force fed a person several kilograms of salt they could be poisoned as a result.

L - Definition Of Poisoning with Intent - Section 24 OAPA 1861
Indictable Only Offence
Penalty In The Crown Court – 5 Years Imprisonment

- It is an offence to:
    - ☐ **Unlawfully;** and
    - ☐ **Maliciously;** (cont….)

- Either:
  - **Administer**; or
  - **Cause** to be **administered** any:
    - **Poison**;
    - **Destructive** thing;
    - **Noxious** thing;
- With **intent (offence complete)** to:
  - **Aggrieve**;
  - **Injure**; or
  - **Annoy**.

Exam Trip Up

- The offence is complete once the **intent** is formed to aggrieve, injure, or annoy.
- There is **no need** for a **result**.

Similarities And Differences Between Section 23 and Section 24 Offences Against The Persons Act 1861

Factor	Section 23	Section 24
Unlawfully	Yes	Yes
Maliciously	Yes	Yes
Actus Reus	■ Administer; ■ Cause to administer; ■ Cause to take.	■ Administer; ■ Cause to administer; ■ Cause to take.
Thing Administered Or Taken	■ Poison ■ Destructive thing ■ Noxious thing	■ Poison ■ Destructive thing ■ Noxious thing
Result Required?	Yes Thereby: ■ Causing GBH; ■ Endangering Life.	No With intent to: ■ Injure; ■ Aggrieve; ■ Annoy.

M - Definition Of False Imprisonment
Indictable Only Offence
Penalty In The Crown Court – Unlimited Maximum Penalty

- It is an offence at **common law** to **falsely imprison** another.

- All you need is evidence that:
    - **Somebody's freedom of movement has been curtailed**; and
    - The perpetrator either:
        - **Intended** to curtail freedom of movement; or
        - Was **subjectively reckless** that freedom of movement would be curtailed.

N – Kidnapping
Indictable Only Offence
Penalty In The Crown Court – Unlimited Maximum Penalty

1 - Definition Of Kidnapping

- The **common law** offence of **kidnapping** will be established where a person:
    - Either:
        - **Takes**; or
        - **Carries away**;
    - **Another** person;
    - **Without** either:
        - Their **consent**; or
        - **Lawful authority**.

2 - Taking Away

- The **taking away** can be achieved via either:
    - **Force** (physical or psychological pressure); or
    - **Fraud**. (somebody pretending to be a taxi driver would use fraud to gain your consent - this would not be real consent and would therefore constitute an offence - R – v- Cort [2003] 3 WLR 1300).

3 - Withdrawal Of Consent

- If the victim **consents** - but **later withdraws** that **consent**;
- The **offence** will be **complete** once the perpetrator **continues** to:
    - **Take them**; or
    - **Carry them away**.

4 - Authorisation to Prosecute For Kidnapping

(i) - The General Rule

- **No permission is required** to prosecute for kidnapping offences.

(ii) – Exception To The General Rule

- The **permission** of the **DPP** will be required where either:
    - The **victim** is **under 16**; or
    - The **prosecution** is bought against either a:
        - **Parent**; or
        - **Guardian**.

O - Hostage Taking
Indictable Only Offence
Penalty In The Crown Court – Life Imprisonment

1 – Definition Of Hostage Taking – Section 1 Taking of Hostages Act 1982

- It is an offence:
    - For a person **whatever their nationality**;
    - Who is either:
        - **In the UK**; or
        - **Elsewhere**;
    - Who **detains** another person in order to **compel** a:
        - **State**; (e.g. the USA);
        - **International government organisation**; (e.g. the UN, NATO); or
        - **Person**; (e.g. me or you);
    - To either:
        - **Do an act**; (e.g. release prisoners of war); or
        - **Abstain** from doing any **act** (e.g. stop the war in Iraq);
    - By **threatening** to:
        - **Kill**;
        - **Injure**;
        - Continue to **detain**.

2 - Permission To Prosecute For The Offence Of Hostage Taking

- The **permission** is required to bring a prosecution for **hostage taking** from either:
    - ☐ The **Attorney General**; or
    - ☐ The **Solicitor General**.

Summary Table

Offence	Actus Reus	Mens Rea	Consent To Prosecute
False Imprisonment	Detention without lawful excuse	Intention; or Subjective Recklessness	None required.
Kidnapping	Taking or carrying away without: ■ Consent; or ■ Lawful excuse	Intention; or Subjective Recklessness	DPP if: ■ The victim is under 16; or ■ Parent or guardian is the offender.
Hostage Taking	Detention plus threats to: ■ Kill; ■ Injure; ■ Continue detention.	Intention only	■ Attorney General; or ■ Solicitor General.

Crime
Unit 7: Sexual Offences

A – Rape
Indictable Only Offence
Penalty In The Crown Court – Life Imprisonment

1 - The Definition Of Rape – Section 1 Sexual Offences Act 2003

- A person commits an offence by:
    - ☐ **Intentionally**;
    - ☐ **Penetrating** with **his penis** another's:
        - ■ Mouth;
        - ■ Vagina;
        - ■ Anus;
    - ☐ **Without consent**; and
    - ☐ At the time of the act they **do not reasonably believe the person consented.**

Memory Aid

- Remember **V.A.M.P.**
    - ☐ Vagina   -   V
    - ☐ Anus   -   A
    - ☐ Mouth   -   M
    - ☐ With a **penis** -   P

Exam Trip Up

- **Only males** can **commit rape** as you need a **penis** to non-consensually penetrate one of the specified orifices.

- However, person who has undergone **gender reassignment** can also commit rape if they penetrate a person with a **surgically constructed penis.**

- Likewise non consensual penetration of a **victim's surgically constructed vagina** will constitute an offence.

2 - Establishing Consent – Section 74 Sexual Offences Act 2003

- A person **consents** if they:
    - ☐ Agree by **choice**;
    - ☐ Have the **freedom to choose**; and
    - ☐ The **capacity** to choose.

3 - Evidential Presumptions And Consent - Sections 75 Sexual Offences 2003

- It will be **presumed** that the **victim did not consent** to the act in any of the following situations.
- If any of the situations do arise - the defendant will have to produce evidence to displace the presumption that consent was not present.

(i) - Situation A

- **Immediately before** or **at the time** of the act **anybody** was either:
  - **Using violence** against the **complainant**; or
  - Was **causing** the **complainant** to **fear** the use of **violence against them**.

Exam Trip Up

- This provision relates to **any person**.
- Therefore a **second person** within the room could be either:
  - **Using violence** against the **complainant**; or
  - **Causing** the **complainant** to **fear the use of violence against them**.

(i) - Situation B

- **Immediately before** or **at the time** of the act **anybody** was either:
  - **Using violence** against **another person**; or
  - Was **causing** the **complainant** to **fear** that **violence** would be used **against another person**.

Exam Trip Up

- This provision relates to:
  - **Violence** either:
    - Being **used**; or
    - Causing the **victim** of the sexual assault to **fear** that **violence will be used**;
  - Against **somebody else other than the victim** of the sexual act.

(iii) - Situation C

- The complainant was unlawfully detained and the defendant was not so detained at the time of the relevant act;

Exam Trip Up

- This situation will **not apply** if **both** the complainant and the defendant are **unlawfully detained**.

(iv) - Situation D

- The complainant was **asleep** or **unconscious** at the time of the act;

Exam Trip Up

- If a person consented to intercourse prior to falling asleep, and intercourse takes place after they have fallen asleep - consent will be presumed to be absent.

(v) - Situation E

- ☐ Due to physical disabilities the complainant was not able to communicate their consent

(vi) - Situation F

- ☐ Any person administered or caused to be administered without the complainant's consent a substance that would have stupefied or caused the complainant to be overpowered.

4 - Conclusive Presumptions Relating To Consent – Section 76 Sexual Offences Act 2003

- There is a **presumption** that the **victim did not consent** to the act where the defendant:
    - ☐ **Intentionally deceived** the complainant as to the **nature** or **purpose** of the relevant act; or
    - ☐ **Intentionally impersonated somebody** known to the complainant.
- If one of these criteria is satisfied there is a conclusive presumption that the complainant did not consent and that the defendant did not believe that the complainant consented.
- **The defendant cannot argue against the presumption once it is proved.**

An Example Of Intentionally Deceiving The Complainant As To The Nature Or Purpose Of The Relevant Act

- A person goes to the doctor and states that they have a tickly cough. The doctor states that his **semen** would provide the **perfect medicine** and tells the person to perform **oral sex** on him.
- The **presumption** would apply in the circumstances as the doctor had **deceived** the complainant as to the **purpose of the act.**

An Example Of Intentionally Impersonating Somebody Known To The Complainant

- A man walks into a dark bedroom and impersonating a female's husband, has sex with the wife.
- Although the female will have intended to have consensual intercourse with her husband, she will not be presumed to have consented to having intercourse with the impersonator.

5 - Consent and Victims Under 13 – Section 5 Sexual Offences Act 2003

- **Section 5 Sexual Offences Act 2003** established that:
    - ☐ If the victim is **under 13:**
        - **Consent is not an issue – they cannot consent.**
        - It is only necessary to establish:
            - ☐ Penetration;
            - ☐ The child's age.

6 - Reasonable Belief In Consent

- In determining the **reasonableness of the belief in consent**:
    - ☐ The court will have regard to **all the circumstances.**
    - ☐ The test is a **question of fact.**

B – Assault By Penetration
Indictable Only Offence
Penalty In The Crown Court – Life Imprisonment

1 - The Definition Of Assault By Penetration - Section 2 Sexual Offences Act 2003

- It is an offence to:
    - ☐ **Intentionally;**
    - ☐ **Sexually penetrate another's:**
        - **Vagina;** or
        - **Anus;**
    - ☐ With:
        - **Any body part (e.g. finger);** or
        - **Anything else (e.g. bottle);**
    - ☐ **Without their consent;** and
    - ☐ They **do not reasonably believe they have the others consent.**

Exam Trip Up

- Note that in **contrast** to the offence of **rape** – **no reference** is made to the **mouth** in the definition of **this offence.**

Exam Trip Up

- Section 75 and 76 can be used to help you establish that consent was not present during the offence.

2 - Consent and Victims Under 13 - Section 6 Sexual Offences Act 2003

- It is established that:
    - ☐ If the victim is **under 13 consent is not an issue – they cannot provide consent.**
    - ☐ It is only necessary to establish:
        - **Intentional penetration;**
        - **The child's age.**

C – The Definition Of Sexual Assault By Touching – Section 3 Sexual Offences Act 2003

Victim 13 Or Over – Indictable only Offence
Penalty In The Crown Court – 10 Years Imprisonment
Penalty In The Magistrates Court – 6 Months Imprisonment

Victim Under 13 – Either Way Offence
Penalty In The Crown Court – 14 Years Imprisonment

- It is an offence to:
    - Intentionally;
    - **Sexually touch** another;
    - **Without their consent**; and
    - The perpetrator **does not reasonably believe they have the others consent.**

Exam Trip Up

- Whether something is **'sexual'** is a **question of fact** for the jury to decide.
- The **body part touched** does **not have to be:**
    - A sexual organ; or
    - An orifice.
- For example: In the case of *R v H* [2005], The Times, 8th February, a man asked a woman 'do you fancy a shag?' As she walked away, he **grabbed her by the pocket of her tracksuit bottoms**. The court deemed this act of **touching** to be of a **sexual nature**.

D – The Definition Of Causing A Person To Engage In Sexual Activity Without Consent - Section 4 Sexual Offences Act 2003

Penetration – Indictable Only Offence
Penalty In The Crown Court – Life Imprisonment

Non Penetration - Either Way Offence
Penalty In The Crown Court – 10 Years Imprisonment
Penalty In The Magistrates Court – 6 Months Imprisonment

- A person commits an offence if they:
    - Intentionally;
    - **Cause another person** to;
    - **Engage** in a **sexual activity**;
    - **Without** their **consent**.

For example:

- ☐ A woman forcing a man to penetrate her.
- ☐ A man forcing another man to masturbate him or making him masturbate a third person.

E – Sexual Activity With A Victim Under 13 Years Old – Section 8 Sexual Offences Act 2003
Indictable Only Offence
Penalty In The Crown Court – Life Imprisonment

- It is an offence to:
    - ☐ Either:
        - **Cause (result** required); or
        - **Incite (no result** required – only incitement to cause the result);
    - ☐ A child **under 13**;
    - ☐ To **engage in a sexual activity**.
- The issue of **consent** is **irrelevant** in such instances.

F – The Definition Of Sexual Activity With A Child - Section 9 Sexual Offences Act 2003

Penetration – Indictable Only Offence
Penalty In The Crown Court – 14 Years Imprisonment

Non Penetration - Either Way Offence
Penalty In The Crown Court – 14 Years Imprisonment
Penalty In The Magistrates Court – 6 Months Imprisonment

- A person **aged 18 or over** commits an offence if they:
    - ☐ **Intentionally**;
    - ☐ **Touch** in a **sexual manner**;
    - ☐ A person who is:
        - Under 16 (Defence - the perpetrator reasonably believes the victim is 16 or over); or
        - Under 13 (No reasonable belief defence).

NB – If the **perpetrator** is **under 18** they will commit an offence under **s13 Sexual Offences Act 2003**.

G – The Definition Of Causing Or Inciting A Child To Engage In A Sexual Activity – Section 10 Sexual Offences Act 2003
Either Way Offence
Penalty In The Crown Court – 14 Years Imprisonment
Penalty In The Magistrates Court – 6 Months Imprisonment And / Or A Fine

- A person **aged 18 or over** commits an offence if they:
    - ☐ **Intentionally;**
    - ☐ **Either:**
        - **Cause - (result** required); or
        - **Incite - (no result** required – only incitement to cause the result);
    - ☐ **Another** who is:
        - **Under 16;**
        - **Under 13;**
    - ☐ To **engage in a sexual activity.**

H – The Definition Of Engaging In A Sexual Activity In The Presence Of A Child – Section 11 Sexual Offences Act 2003
Either Way Offence
Penalty In The Crown Court – 10 Years Imprisonment
Penalty In The Magistrates Court – 6 Months Imprisonment

- A person **aged 18 or over** commits an offence if they:
    - ☐ **Intentionally;**
    - ☐ **Engage** in a **sexual activity;**
    - ☐ For the **purpose** of **obtaining sexual gratification (to get a sexual kick out of the act);**
    - ☐ When **another person** is either:
        - **Present;** or
        - In a **place** where the **perpetrator can be observed;** and
    - ☐ The perpetrator **knows, believes, or intends** for the **person to be aware** that they are engaging in the activity; and
    - ☐ The other person is:
        - **Under 16 (Defence - the perpetrator reasonably believes the victim is 16 or over);** or
        - **Under 13 (No reasonable belief defence).**

I – The Definition Of Causing A Child To Watch A Sexual Activity - Section 12 Sexual Offences Act 2003
Either Way Offence
Penalty In The Crown Court – 10 Years Imprisonment
Penalty In The Magistrates Court – 6 Months Imprisonment

- A person **aged 18 or over** commits an offence if:
    - For **purpose of sexual gratification**;
    - They **intentionally**;
    - **Cause another person**:
        - **Under 16;** or
        - **Under 13;**
    - To either:
        - **Watch a 3rd person engage in a sexual activity**; or
        - **To look at an image of a sexual activity.**

Exam Trip Up

- If a father shows his 12 year old son a pornographic movie **for the purpose of teaching him about the facts of life**, the father would **not commit this offence** as he was **not showing the image to his son for the purpose of sexual gratification** (i.e. to get a kick out of it)

Exam Trip Up

- Watch out for questions involving:
    - A couple babysitting for a young child;
    - Who knowing the child is watching;
    - Decide to have sex;
    - However, *prior* to starting the sexual activity the child leaves the room.
- The offence is **not complete** as the child is not present during the act even if the babysitters *intended* for the child to watch.

J - Sections 9 – 12 Sexual Offences Act 2003 And Offenders Under 18 Years Old

- The above sections relate to persons **aged 18 or over**.
- What about persons **under 18?**
- The same offence exactly applies with a reduced **maximum sentence of 5 years**.

K - Arranging Or Facilitating Child Sex Offences

1 – Penalty For Arranging Or Facilitating Child Sex Offences
Either Way Offence
Penalty In The Crown Court – 14 Years Imprisonment
Penalty In The Magistrates Court – 6 Months Imprisonment

2 – Definition Of Arranging Or Facilitating Child Sex Offences - Section 14 Sexual Offences Act 2003

- A person commits an offence if they:
    - **Intentionally;**
    - Either:
        - **Arrange;** or
        - **Facilitate;**
    - Something that either:
        - **They intend to do;**
        - **They Intend another person to do;** or
        - **They believe that another person will do;**
    - In *any* part of the world; and
    - Doing it will involve the **commission** of an **offence** under **sections 9 – 13 Sexual Offences Act 2003.**

L - Meeting A Child Following Sexual Grooming

1 – Penalty For Meeting A Child Following Sexual Grooming
Either Way Offence
Penalty In The Crown Court – 10 Years Imprisonment
Penalty In The Magistrates Court – 6 Months Imprisonment

2 – Definition Of Meeting A Child Following Sexual Grooming – Section 15 Sexual Offences Act 2003

- An offence will be committed where:
    - A person **(A)** aged **18 years or over;**
    - Who has either:
        - **Met;** or
        - **Communicated;**
    - With another person **(B);**
    - On **at least two prior occasions;** and

(cont....)

- ☐ **Later** either:
  - ■ **Intentionally meets (B);** or
  - ■ **Travels with the intention of meeting (B)** in *any* part of the world; and
- ☐ At the time of doing so **(A) intends (offence complete)** to do anything to or in respect of (B) either during or after the meeting and in any part of the world, which if done will involve the **commission by (A) of an offence under Part 1 Sexual Offences Act 2003**; and
- ☐ **(B) is under 16;** and
- ☐ **(A) does not reasonably believe that B is 16 or over.**

Exam Trip Up

- The **2 or more initial communications** or **meetings** with the **victim under 16** *can* be **innocuous.**

Exam Trip Up

- The **initial communications** or **meetings** can have taken place **anywhere in the world.**

Exam Trip Up

- The offence will be triggered at the time of the subsequent intentional meeting or travelling with the intention of subsequently meeting provided the perpetrator **intended** to **commit** an **offence under Part 1 Sexual Offences Act 2003.**
- The perpetrator may **intend** to commit the Part 1 Sexual Offences Act 2003 offence either:
  - ☐ **At the time** of the meeting; or
  - ☐ **After** the meeting.

Exam Trip Up

- There is **no need** for the **result** of a Part 1 Sexual Offences Act 2003 offence.
- The offence is **complete** once the **intention** is formed to commit the Part 1 Sexual Offences Act 2003 offence.

Defence

- The perpetrator will have a **defence** even where the victim is under 16 if they **reasonably believe** that the **victim is 16 or over.**

M - Sexual Activity with Child Family Member

1 – Penalty For Sexual Activity with Child Family Member

Where The Offence Involves Penetration And The Defendant Is Aged 18 Or Over – Indictable Only Offence
Penalty In The Crown Court – 14 Years Imprisonment

Otherwise Or Where The Defendant Is Aged Under 18 – Either Way Offence
Penalty In The Crown Court – 14 Years Imprisonment
Penalty In The Magistrates Court – 6 Months Imprisonment And / Or A Fine

2 – Definition Of Sexual Activity with Child Family Member – Sections 25 - 26 Sexual Offences Act 2003

- A person **(A)** commits and offence if they:
    - **Intentionally;**
    - **Touch** another person **(B);** and
    - The **touching** is **sexual;** and
    - The **relationship** between **(A) and (B)** falls within any of the following:
        - Parent;
        - Grandparent;
        - Brother or sister;
        - Half brother or half sister;
        - Aunt or uncle;
        - Is or has been foster parent;
        - Where:
            - (A) and (B) either:
                - Live or lived in the same household; or
                - A is or has been regularly involved in caring for, training, supervising or being in sole charge of B; and
            - Either:
                - One of them is or has been the other's step-parent;
                - They are cousins;
                - One of them is or has been the other's step brother or step sister; or
                - They have the same parent or foster parent; and
    - (A) knows or could reasonably be expected to know that their relationship to (B) is one of the above; and

(cont....)

- Either:
  - (B) is under 18 and (A) does not reasonably believe that (B) is 18 or over; or
  - (B) is under 13.

3 - Defences

- The defendant will have a **defence** where either:
  - The defendant and the victim are **lawfully married** at the time of the offence; or
  - The **sexual relationship pre dates the family relationship**.

    For example - a boyfriend and girlfriend are both aged 17 engaged in a sexual relationship. They introduce their single parents to each other who subsequently marry. They become step brother and step sister and will not commit an offence if they continue with their sexual relationship.

N - Making Indecent Photographs

1 – Penalty For Making Indecent Photographs
Either Way Offence
Penalty In The Crown Court – 10 Years Imprisonment
Penalty In The Magistrates Court – 6 Months Imprisonment And / Or A Fine

2 – Definition Of Making Indecent Photographs – Section 1 Protection of Children Act 1978

Offence A

- It is an offence for a person to:
  - Either:
    - **Take;**
    - **Permit** to be taken; or
    - **Make;**
  - Any **indecent:**
    - **Photographs;** or
    - **Pseudo-photographs;**
  - Of a **child.**

Offence B

- It is an offence for a person to:
    - Either:
        - **Distribute**; or
        - **Show**;
    - Such an **indecent**:
        - **Photograph**; or
        - **Pseudo photograph.**

Offence C

- It is an offence for a person to:
    - Have in their **possession**;
    - Such **indecent**:
        - **Photographs**; or
        - **Pseudo photographs**;
    - With a **view** to them being:
        - **Distributed**; or
        - **Shown.**

Offence D

- It is an offence for a person to:
    - Either:
        - **Publish**; or
        - **Cause** to be **published**;
    - Any **advertisement** likely to be **understood** as **conveying** that the **advertiser** either:
        - **Distributes**;
        - **Shows**; or
        - **Intends** to:
            - **Distribute**; or
            - **Show**;
    - Such **indecent**:
        - **Photographs**; or
        - **Pseudo-photographs.**

3 - Defences – Sections 1, 1A & 1B – Protection of Children Act 1978

- A defence will be established where the person either:
    - ☐ Had a legitimate reason for distributing or showing the photos;
    - ☐ Had not themselves seen the photos and did not know, nor had any cause to suspect, that they were indecent;
    - ☐ Was lawfully married or a partner in an enduring family relationship with a child aged 16 or over.
    - ☐ Made such photos for the purpose of prevention, detection or investigation of a crime or criminal proceedings in any part of the world;
    - ☐ Is a member of the Security Service and the photos were taken in pursuance of the functions of the service; or
    - ☐ Is a member of GCHQ and the photos were taken in pursuance of the functions of GCHQ.

4 – Consent Of The DPP Is Required

- The **Director Of Public Prosecution (DPP)** must provide their consent to secure a prosecution.

O - Possession Of Indecent Photographs

1 – Penalty For Possession Of Indecent Photographs
Either Way Offence
Penalty In The Crown Court – 5 Years Imprisonment
Penalty In The Magistrates Court – 6 Months Imprisonment And / Or A Fine

2 – Definition Of Possession Of Indecent Photographs - Section 160 Criminal Justice Act 1988

- It is an offence for a person to:
    - ☐ Have any **indecent**:
        - **Photographs**; or
        - **Pseudo-photographs**;
    - ☐ Of a **child**;
    - ☐ In their **possession**.

3 - Defences – Section 160 & 160A Criminal Justice Act 1988

- A defence will be established where the person either:
    - ☐ Had a legitimate reason for having the photograph or pseudo-photograph in his possession;
    - ☐ Had not themselves seen the photograph or pseudo-photograph and did not know, nor have any cause to suspect, it to be indecent;

- ☐ Had the photograph or pseudo-photograph sent to themselves without any prior request made by them or on their behalf; and they did not keep it for an unreasonable time; or

- ☐ Was married to the child or lived with them as partners in an enduring family relationship.

P - Harmful Publications

1 – Penalty For Harmful Publications
Summary Only Offence
Penalty In The Magistrates Court – 4 Months Imprisonment And / Or A Fine

2 - Definition Of Harmful Publications – Sections 1 & 2 Children & Young Persons (Harmful Publications) Act 1955

- An offence will be committed by any person who:
    - ☐ Either:
        - **Prints**;
        - **Publishes**;
        - **Sells**; or
        - **Lets on hire**;
    - ☐ A **work**; or
    - ☐ Has a **work** in their **possession** for the **purpose** of:
        - **Selling** it; or
        - **Letting** it on hire.

3 - Definition Of Works – Section 1 Children & Young Persons (Harmful Publications) Act 1955

- **Works** include:
    - ☐ Either:
        - **Books**;
        - **Magazines**; or
        - Other **like works**;
    - ☐ Of a kind that would be **likely to fall in the hands** of **children** or **young person**s;
    - ☐ Which consists **wholly** or **mainly** of **stories** in **pictures**;
    - ☐ Which **portrays** either:
        - The commission of **crimes**;
        - Acts of **violence** or **cruelty**; or
        - Incidents of a **horrible** or **repulsive** nature;
    - ☐ In such way that the work as a whole would be likely to **corrupt** a **child** or **young person**.

4 - Defence - Section 1 Children & Young Persons (Harmful Publications) Act 1955

- A defence will be established where the person:
    - Has not examined the contents of the work; and
    - Had o reason to suspect the contents would result in an offence.

5 - Consent Of The Attorney General Or Solicitor General Is Required

- The Attorney General Or Solicitor General must provide their consent to secure a prosecution.

Q – Position Of Trust Offences

1 - Definition Of An Abuse Of A Position Of Trust – Sections 16-19 Sexual Offences Act 2003

- **All abuse of a position of trust offences:**
    - Are the **same** as the aforementioned **child sex offences**;
    - Except for **two differences:**
        - The **offender** is in a **position of trust with the victim**; and
        - The **offences relate to children:**
            - **Under 13;** or
            - **Under 18.**

2 - Defining A Position Of Trust?

- Your Blackstone's book goes into great detail as to what a position of trust is. On a cost versus reward basis it would be silly to learn them all off pat. If you feel that someone is in a position of trust using your **common sense**, then they will be in such a position.

- Examples of a **position of trust may** include:
    - **Working in a residential home for children;**
    - **Hospital;**
    - **Teachers;**
    - **Local authority social workers etc.**

3 - Determining Whether A Person Knew They Were In A Position Of Trust? – Section 21 Sexual Offences Act 2003

- If a person is in a **position of trust**:
    - They are **taken to know** that they are in such a position;
    - **Unless**;
    - **Evidence is adduced**;
    - To **raise an issue** as to whether:
        - They knew; or
        - Could have been reasonably expected to have known.

Exam Trip Up - Teachers

- A teacher's awareness of whether they are in a position of trust in relation to a child may depend upon the size and set up of the school in which they teach.

    It would be difficult for a teacher to argue that they could not have reasonably have known that they were in a position of trust in relation to a child attending their small school based on just one campus.

    It may be easier for them to prove they could not have reasonably have known that they were in a position of trust in relation to a child that they had met in a nightclub who attended their school, but was taught on a entirely different campus to the campus that teacher worked at.

4 – Defences To Position Of Trust Offences

(i) - The Marriage Exception – Section 23 Sexual Offences Act 2003

- The defendant must prove:
    - They were **married at the time of the offence**; and
    - The child was **16 or over**.

(ii) - Relationships That Pre Date The Position Of Trust – Section 21 Sexual Offences Act 2003

- If the defendant can prove that:
    - **Immediately before the Position of Trust arose**;
    - They were in a **lawful sexual relationship**;
    - **No offence** is committed.

An Example Of A Relationship That Pre Dates The Position Of Trust

- Thomas is a teacher in school A and he has a lawful sexual relationship with a 17 yr old female from school B.
- There is no problem at this point, as they are at different schools and he is not in a position of trust.

- If the girl were to move to school A, the teacher would now be in a position of trust.
- However, there would be no offence as there was a lawful relationship prior to the position of trust situation arising.

R – The Definition Of Exposure – Section 66 Sexual Offences Act 2003
Either Way Offence
Penalty In The Crown Court – 2 Years Imprisonment
Penalty In The Magistrates Court – 6 Months Imprisonment

- A person commits an offence if they:
    - **Intentionally**;
    - **Expose their genitals**; and
    - **Intend** for:
        - Another **to see them**; and
        - They be **caused** either:
            - **Alarm**; or
            - **Distress**.

Exam Trip Up

- The perpetrator must show the **genitals**.
- A person's **backside is not enough.**

Exam Trip Up

- The perpetrator must **intend** to **show their genitals** - accidental exposure is inadequate.

Exam Trip Up

- There is no need for anyone to actually see their genitals.
- It is only necessary that they:
    - **Intended** for somebody to **see them**; and
    - **Intended** somebody to be **alarmed or distressed**.

Exam Trip Up

- It is **not necessary** for the perpetrator to be in a **public place**.

Exam Trip Up

- **Intention** is paramount to the offence.

    Therefore a male exposing his genitals to his wife in the bedroom would not commit the offence as:

    ☐ Although he **exposed** his **genitals;** and

    ☐ **Intended** for **somebody** to **see them** (his wife);

    ☐ He did **not intend** for her to be **caused:**

    - **Alarm;** or
    - **Distress.**

NB - It doesn't mater if she did feel that way! He did **not intend it**!

S - Sexual Offences Against Persons With A Mental Disorder

- The sexual offences against persons with a mental disorder are very **similar** to some of the child sex offences.

- There are some obvious key **differences.**

- It is advisable to know the child sex offences and simply substitute the differences where applicable.

- This will save you valuable time during revision.

1 - Sexual Activity With a Person With a Mental Disorder – Section 30 Sexual Offences Act 2003
Either Way Offence
Penalty In The Crown Court – Life Imprisonment
Penalty In The Magistrates Court – 6 Months Imprisonment And / Or A Fine

- An offence will be committed where:

    ☐ **A intentionally sexually touches** another **(B);**

    ☐ **B** is **unable** to **refuse** due to their **suffering** from a **mental disorder**; and

    ☐ **A** either:

    - **Knows**; or
    - **Should have known**;

    ☐ That:

    - **B** had such a **disorder**; and
    - Due to the **disorder B** was **unable** to **refuse.**

Learning Points

- This offence is the **same** as the simple **sexual touching** offence with the **added caveat** of the **mental disorder**.

- It is necessary to prove that:
    - The **sexual touching** was intentional; and
    - The **victim** was **unable** to **refuse due to** their **mental disorder**.

When Is A Person Unable To Refuse?

- A person will be **unable** to **refuse** when:
    - They **lack** the **capacity** to **choose** due to a **lack of understanding**; or
    - They are **unable** to **communicate** such a **choice**.

2 - Sexual Activity In The Presence Of A Person With A Mental Disorder – Section 32 Sexual Offences Act 2003
Either Way Offence
Penalty In The Crown Court – 10 Years Imprisonment
Penalty In The Magistrates Court – 6 Months Imprisonment And / Or A Fine

- An offence will be committed where:
    - **A engages** in a **sexual activity**;
    - For the **purpose** of **obtaining sexual gratification**; and
    - At the time **A engages** in the **sexual activity**;
    - **B** is either:
        - **Present**; or
        - In a **place** that **A** can be **observed**; and
    - **A** either:
        - **Knows**;
        - **Believes**; or
        - **Intends**;
      - that **B** is **aware**; and
    - **B** is **unable** to **refuse due to** their **suffering** from a **mental disorder**; and
    - **A** either:
        - **Knows**; or
        - **Should have known**;
    - That:
        - **B** had such a **disorder**; and
        - **Due** to the **disorder B** was **unable** to **refuse**.

3 - Causing A Person With A Mental Disorder to Watch a Sexual Act – Section 33 Sexual Offences Act 2003
Either Way Offence
Penalty In The Crown Court – 10 Years Imprisonment
Penalty In The Magistrates Court – 6 Months Imprisonment

- An offence will be committed by **A** where:
    - For the **purpose** of **obtaining sexual gratification**;
    - A **intentionally** causes **B** to:
        - **Watch** a **third person** engaging in a **sexual activity**; or
        - To **look** at an **image** of **sexual activity**; and
    - **B** is **unable** to **refuse** due to their **suffering** from a **mental disorder**; and
    - **A** either:
        - **Knows;** or
        - **Should have known;**
    - That:
        - **B** was **suffering** from a **mental disorder**; and
        - Due to the **disorder B** was **unable** to **refuse**.

T - Voyeurism - Section 67 Sexual Offences Act 2003
Either Way Offence
Penalty In The Crown Court – 2 Years Imprisonment
Penalty In The Magistrates Court – 6 Months Imprisonment

1 – Separate Voyeurism Offences

- There are 3 separate voyeurism offences:
    - **Part 1**;
    - **Part 2**; and
    - **Part 3**.

(i) - Part 1 Offence

- A person commits an offence if:
    - For the **purpose** of **sexual gratification**;
    - They **observe another doing** a **private act**; and
    - They **know** the **other does not consent to being observed** for the **purpose** of **sexual gratification**.

(ii) - Part 2 Offence

- A person commits an offence if:
  - ☐ They **operate equipment**;
  - ☐ With the **intention** of:
    - Enabling **another** to **observe**;
    - For the **purpose** of **sexual gratification**;
    - A **third person** doing a **private act**; and
  - ☐ They **know** the **third person** does **not consent** to being **observed** for the **purpose** of **sexual gratification**.

(iii) - Part 3 Offence

- A person commits an offence if:
  - ☐ They **record** another **person doing** a **private act**; and
  - ☐ They do so with the **intention** that:
    - **They;** or
    - **Somebody else;**
  - ☐ Will for the **purpose** of **sexual gratification**;
  - ☐ **Look** at an **image** of the **person doing the private act**; and
  - ☐ They **know** the **person** does **not consent** to the **recording** of their **private act**.

2 - What Is A Private Act? - Section 68 Sexual Offences Act 2003

- An **act** will be **in private** if:
  - ☐ The person observed is in a **place** which would be expected to provide **privacy**; and
  - ☐ Either:
    - Their **genitals, buttocks** or **breasts** are:
      - ☐ **Exposed;** or
      - ☐ **Covered** only by **underwear;**
    - They are **using** a **lavatory;** or
    - They are doing a **sexual act** which is **not normally done in public**.

Learning Point

- All three offences relate to people who do the act for **sexual gratification**, **not** for **any other purpose**.

Learning Point

- The **first offence** deals with people who observe others doing a private act (this includes looking at an image).

Learning Point

- The **second offence** deals with people such as hoteliers or landlords using **web cams** for the **sexual gratification** of **another**.
- They do not have to have derive sexual gratification themselves.

Learning Point

- The **third offence** relates to the **recording** of such an act.

Learning Point

- It is also an offence to:
    - Either:
        - **Install equipment**; or
        - **Adapt** a **structure** (e.g. drilling peepholes);
    - With the **intention** of either:
        - **Committing** the **Part 1** offence **themselves**; or
        - **Letting others commit the Part 1 offence.**

3 - Definition Of A Structure – Section 67 Sexual Offences Act 2003

- A **structure** can include:
    - **Tents**;
    - **Vehicles**; or
    - **Vessels**.

Exam Trip Up

- The offences under this section do **not** cover the activity of **filming up women's skirts** as they go about their **public acts** such as shopping.

U - Sexual Activity in a Public Lavatory – Section 71 Sexual Offences Act 2003
Summary Only Offence
Penalty In The Magistrates Court – 6 Months Imprisonment And / Or A Fine

1 - Definition Of The Offence

- A person commits an offence if:
    - When they are **in a lavatory**:
        - Which is **accessible** by:
            - The **public**; or
            - A **section** of the **public**;

(cont...)

- Either:
    - On **payment**; or
    - **Otherwise**;
- They **intentionally engage** in a **sexual activity**.

Exam Trip Up

- The **public** must have **access** to the **lavatory** for the offence to be complete.

2 – Definition Of Sexual Activity – Section 78 Sexual Offences Act 2003

- An **activity** will be deemed **sexual** in relation to this specific offence if:
    - A **reasonable person**;
    - Would in all the **circumstances**;
    - **Consider** it **sexual**;
    - **Regardless** of any persons **purpose**.
- This definition is narrower that the meaning used in other sections of this act.

V - Notification Periods For Sexual Offenders – Section 82 Sexual Offences Act 2003

Description Of The Offender	Notification Period
Sentenced to imprisonment for 30 months or more	An indefinite period
Admitted to a hospital on a restriction order	An indefinite period
Sentenced to more than 6 months but less than 30 months	10 years
6 months or less	7 years
Admitted to hospital without a restriction order	7 years
Cautioned	2 years
Conditional discharge	Period of conditional discharge
Any other person	5 years

Learning Point

- All periods begin with the **relevant date** – which is the **date of conviction**.

Learning Point

- **Caution** means either a:
  - ☐ **Caution**; or
  - ☐ **Reprimand**.

Learning Point

- When **notifying** the police the offender must provide the following **information:**
  - ☐ Date of birth;
  - ☐ National insurance number;
  - ☐ Name on relevant date and on the date the notification was made;
  - ☐ Home address on relevant date and on date notification was given.

Exam Trip Up

- The **period** of **notification** in relation to the period of **10, 7, 5 or 2 years** is **halved** for offenders **under 18**.

Exam Trip Up

- An **absolute discharge** does **not count**.

W – Prostitution Offences

1 – Definition Of A Prostitute – Section – Section 51(2) Sexual Offences Act 2003

- A **prostitute** is defined as:
  - ☐ A person who on **at least one occasion**;
  - ☐ **Whether** or **not compelled** to do so;
  - ☐ Either:
    - **Offers**; or
    - **Provides**;
  - ☐ **Sexual services** to another;
  - ☐ In return for either:
    - **Payment**; or
    - A **promise** of **payment**;
  - ☐ To either:
    - **Them**; or
    - A **third person**.

Learning Point

- Both men and women can be prostitutes.

2 - Offence Of Causing, Inciting Or Controlling Prostitution For Gain - Sections 52 & 53 Sexual Offences Act 2003
Either Way Offence
Penalty In The Crown Court – 7 Years Imprisonment
Penalty In The Magistrates Court – 6 Months Imprisonment And / Or A Fine

- There are 2 separate offences:
  - **Part 1 offence**; and
  - **Part 2 offence.**

(i) - Part 1 Offence

- A person commits an offence if:
  - They **intentionally**;
  - Either:
    - **Cause**; or
    - **Incite**;
  - **Another** to become a **prostitute**;
  - **Anywhere** in the world; and
  - Does so for the:
    - **Gain**; or
    - **Expectation** of **gain**;
  - For either:
    - **Themselves**; or
    - **Another.**

(ii) - Part 2 Offence

- A person commits an offence if:
  - They **intentionally**;
  - **Control** any of the **prostitution activities** of another **person**;
  - **Anywhere** in the world; and
  - Does so either:
    - For **gain**; or
    - In the **expectation of gain**;

(cont....)

- For either:
  - **Themselves**; or
  - **Another**.

Exam Trip Up

- The **Part 1** offence **not necessarily** have to produce a **result** of a person becoming a prostitute – as **incitement** will complete the offence.

Exam Trip Up

- The **Part 2** offence deals with **pimps**.
- There is **no need** to show a **financial payment**.
- It is only necessary to prove a **gain**.
- This could include the **remission of a debt already in existence**.
- The definition is so wide it could include the actions of a person who hopes to build up a relationship with someone like a drug dealer who will eventually give them cheaper drugs as a result of their activities.

3 - Keeping a Brothel Used For Prostitution – Section 33A Sexual Offences Act 1956
Either Way Offence
Penalty In The Crown Court – 7 Years Imprisonment
Penalty In The Magistrates Court – 6 Months Imprisonment And / Or A Fine

- Its an offence for:
  - A person to:
    - **Keep**;
    - **Manage**;
    - **Act**; or
    - **Assist**;
- In the **management** of a **brothel** which people resort for practices involving prostitution.

Exam Trip Up

- The **premises do not have to be solely used for prostitution** to commit the offence.

4 - Keeping A Disorderly House – Common Law
Indictable Only Offence
Penalty In The Crown Court – Unlimited Maximum Sentence

- It is an offence at common law to **keep** a **disorderly house**.

Learning Point

- It is necessary to prove that:
    - The **premises** was:
        - **Open to customers;**
        - **Unregulated** by the **constraints of morality.**
        - Run in a way that **violates law and good order** (*R v Tan* [1983] QB 1053)
    - The **defendant knew** that the house was **so used** (*Moores v DPP* [1992] QB 125)
    - There was a degree of **persistence** – the offence does not cover a singe act (see *Moores* above).

5 - Soliciting By Common Prostitutes – Section 1 Street Offences Act 1959
Summary Only Offence
Penalty In The Magistrates Court – Fine Only

- Its an offence for:
    - A **common prostitute**;
    - Who is either:
        - **Male;** or
        - **Female;**
    - To either:
        - **Loiter;** or
        - **Solicit;**
    - In a:
        - **Street;** or
        - **Public place;**
    - For the **purposes** of **prostitution.**

Exam Trip Up

- A **street** includes:
    - Any:
        - **Bridge; road; lane; footway; subway;** etc
        - Which is **open** to the **public;** and
    - Any:
        - **Doors;** or
        - **Entrances**
            - **Abutting** onto the **street.**

6 - Soliciting By Kerb Crawling – Sections 1 and 2 Sexual Offences Act 1985
Summary Only Offence
Penalty In The Magistrates Court – Fine Only

- There are **2 kerb crawling offences** under:
    - **Section 1;** and
    - **Section 2.**

(i) - Section 1 Offence

- A person commits an offence if:
    - They **solicit another person** for the **purposes of prostitution;**
    - Either:
        - **From** a **motor vehicle;**
        - While in the **immediate vicinity** of a **motor vehicle** that they have **just got out of or off;**
    - Whilst in a:
        - **Street;**
        - **Public place;** or
    - Either:
        - **Persistently;** or
        - In such a **manner;**
    - As to be **likely** to **cause** either:
        - **Annoyance** to the **person solicited;** or
        - A **nuisance** to **others** in the **neighbourhood.**

(ii) - Section 2 Offence

- A person commits an offence if:
    - Whilst in a:
        - **Street;** or
        - **Public place;**
    - They **persistently solicit another** for the **purpose** of **prostitution.**

Exam Trip Up

- It is only necessary to prove that there was a *likelihood* of **nuisance** or **annoyance.**
- It is **not necessary** to prove that **nuisance** or **annoyance** was actually *caused.*

Exam Trip Up

- To establish that the prohibited actions were **persistent** it is necessary to prove that they occurred on **more than one occasion.**

Learning Point – Prostitutes Cautions

- For a conviction for this offence it is usual for the prostitute to have been **cautioned at least twice** in the **12 months** prior to committing the offence.

- This is not a normal 'police caution' but is a **specific caution** which relates to offences under this section.

- The details of the persons cautioned are kept in a **register** at the station as a means of allowing the person to **reform** rather than convicting on each time.

- A **prostitutes caution** can **no longer** be given to a **prostitute** who is **under 18**.

- An **appeal** may be lodged at a court within **14 days** of a prostitutes caution for the **caution to be removed.**

7 - Placing An Advertisement Relating To Prostitution
Summary Only Offence
Penalty In The Magistrates Court – 6 Months Imprisonment And / Or A Fine

(i) - Definition Of The Offence - Section 46 Criminal Justice and Police Act 2001

- A person commits an offence if they:

    - **Place** an **advert relating to prostitution;**

    - Either:

        - **On;** or

        - In the **immediate vicinity;**

        - Of a **public pay phone**; and

    - Does so with the **intention (offence complete);**

    - That the **advert** should come to the **attention of others.**

(ii) - Definition Of A Public Phone - Section 46(5) Criminal Justice and Police Act 2001

- A **public phone** will include a:

    - **Phone:**

        - Kiosk;

        - Booth;

        - Acoustic hood;

        - Shelter; or

        - Other housing.

    - Located in a **public place**; and

(cont....)

- Made **available** for use by:
    - The **public**; or
    - A **section** of the **public**.

(iii) - Definition Of A Public Place - Section 46 Criminal Justice and Police Act 2001

- A **public place** is defined as:
    - Any **place** which the **public** has **access** by:
        - **Payment**; or
        - **Otherwise**;
    - Other than:
        - A **place** to which **children under 16 are not permitted** to have **access**; or
        - **Premises** used:
            - **Wholly**; or
            - **Mainly**;
        - as **residential premises**.

Exam Trip Up

- The offence includes placing **adverts** in the **immediate vicinity of the phone**.
- This could include for example lampposts or shop windows in the immediate vicinity of the telephone.
- Determining the **immediate vicinity of the phone** will of course be a **question of fact** for the court to determine.

8 - Trafficking For Sexual Exploitation Either Into, Within, Or Out Of The UK – Section 57-59 Sexual Offences Act 2003
Either Way Offence
Penalty In The Crown Court – 14 Years Imprisonment
Penalty In The Magistrates Court – 6 Months Imprisonment And / Or A Fine

- There are **3 offences** of **trafficking for sexual exploitation**:
    - Section 57;
    - Section 58; and
    - Section 59.

(i) - Section 57 Offence

- A person commits an offence if they:
    - **Intentionally**;
    - Either:
        - **Arrange**; or
        - **Facilitate**;
    - The **arrival** in the **UK** of **another person (B)**; and
    - Either:
        - **They intend** to **do anything** to or in respect of **B after B's arrival**; or
        - They **believe** that **another person** is likely to do something to or in respect of **B after B's arrival**;
    - In **any part of the world**;
    - Which **if done** will involve the **commission** of a **relevant offence**.

(ii) - Section 58 & 59 Offences

- Sections 58 & 59 are exactly the same as section 57 other than the fact they relate to travel:
    - **Within** the **UK**; or
    - **Outwards from** the **UK**.

(iii) - Definition Of A Relevant Offence

- A **relevant offence** includes offences under:
    - Part I of the Sexual Offences Act 2003 (All of the regularly occurring ones);
    - Taking or making indecent photos of children (Section 1 of the Protection of Children Act 1978;
    - Includes **acts committed** either:
        - **Inside** the **UK**; or
        - **Outside**:
            - **England**;
            - **Wales**; and
            - **Northern Ireland**;
    - Which if they **had been done in any of those countries would constitute an offence.**

Exam Trip Up

- Bringing people to the UK temporarily on the way to somewhere else would be caught by this offence.

Exam Trip Up

- The fact the **relevant offence never took place** will **not matter.**
- It is the **intention** or **belief** of the offender that is important.

X - Committing A Criminal Offence With The Intent To Commit A Sexual Offence

1 - Penalty For Committing A Criminal Offence With The Intent To Commit A Sexual Offence

If The Offence Committed Is Kidnapping Or False Imprisonment – Indictable Only Offence
Penalty In The Crown Court – Life Imprisonment

Any Other Offence Committed – Either Way Offence
Penalty In The Crown Court – 10 Years Imprisonment
Penalty In The Magistrates Court – 6 Months Imprisonment And / Or A Fine

2 – Definition Of Committing A Criminal Offence With The Intent To Commit A Sexual Offence – Section 62 Sexual Offences Act 2003

- It is an offence for a person to:
    - **Commit** *any* **offence**;
    - With the **intention (offence complete)**;
    - Of **committing** an **offence** under **Part 1 Sexual Offences Act 2003.**

Exam Trip Up

- The offence does not extend to other sexual offences outside the scope of Part 1 Sexual Offences Act 2003

Exam Trip Up

- It is **not necessary** for the subsequent **sexual offence** to be **committed.**
- It is only necessary to show that the person committed the initial offence and that they did so with the purpose of facilitating the sexual offence thereafter.

Y - Trespassing With The Intent To Commit A Sexual Offence

1 – Penalty For Trespassing With The Intent To Commit A Sexual Offence
Either Way Offence
Penalty In The Crown Court – 10 Years Imprisonment
Penalty In The Magistrates Court – 6 Months Imprisonment And / Or A Fine

2 – Definition Of Trespassing With The Intent To Commit A Sexual Offence – Section 63 Sexual Offences Act 2003

- An offence will be committed by a person who:
    - Is a **trespasser**;
    - On *any* **premises**; and
    - Either:
        - **Knows**; or
        - Is **reckless**;
    - As to whether they are a **trespasser**; and
    - **Intends (offence complete)**;
    - To **commit** an **offence** under **Part 1 Sexual Offences Act 2003**;
    - *On* the **premises**.

3 - Definition Of Premises – Section 63(2) Sexual Offences Act 2003

- **Premises** include a:
    - **Structure**; or
    - **Part** of a structure.

- The structure may be:
    - **Fixed**;
    - **Temporary**; or
    - **Movable**.

Exam Trip Up

- The definition is wider than that of "premises" in relation to Burglary offences and can include tents, vehicles or vessels.

Exam Trip Up

- It is **not necessary** for the subsequent **sexual offence** to be **committed** on the premises.
- It is merely necessary to show that whilst trespassing the person intended to commit the sexual offence.

Z - Administering A Substance With Intent - Section 63 Sexual Offences Act 2003

1 – Penalty For Administering A Substance With Intent
Either Way Offence
Penalty In The Crown Court – 10 Years Imprisonment
Penalty In The Magistrates Court – 6 Months Imprisonment And / Or A Fine

2 – Definition Of Administering A Substance With Intent - Section 63 Sexual Offences Act 2003

- An offence will be committed by a person (x) who:
    - **Intentionally** either:
        - **Administers** a **substance** to **another person** (Y); or
        - **Causes** a **substance** to be **taken** by **another person** (Y);
    - **Knowing** that the **other person (Y)** does **not consent**; and
    - With the **intention (offence complete)** of either:
        - **Stupefy**; or
        - **Overpowering**;
        - The **other person** (Y);
    - So as to **enable** *any* **person** to **engage in a sexual activity** that **involves** the **other person** (Y).

3 - Rationale Of The Offence

- The offence was introduced to combat date rape drugs.

- However the substance administered need not specifically be a date rape drug such as Rohypnol.

- It need only be any substance which the person *intends* to have the effect of either overpowering or stupefying the victim.

- It is not necessary for the substance to be capable of actually overpowering or stupefying the victim or indeed for the victim to be suffer the result of being overpowered or stupefied.

- Provided the person *intended* the substance administered or taken to have such an effect the offence will be complete.

- For example - the offence may include surreptitiously slipping vodka into a person's soft drink, with a view to them being overpowered to facilitate non consensual sexual activity.

Crime
Unit 8: Offences Against Children Or Vulnerable Persons

A – Child Abduction By A Person Connected With A Child
Either Way Offence
Penalty In The Crown Court – 7 Years Imprisonment
Penalty In The Magistrates Court – 6 Months Imprisonment And / Or A Fine

1 – Definition Of The Offence – Section 1 Child Abduction Act 1984

- It is an offence for a person:
    - **Connected**;
    - With a **child** who is aged **under 16**;
    - To either:
        - **Take**; or
        - **Send**;
    - The **child outside the UK**;
    - **Without** obtaining the appropriate **consent**.

2 - Definition Of Persons Connected To The Child – Section 1(2) Child Abduction Act 1984

- **Connected persons** will include:
    - **Parents**;
    - An **unmarried father** who has **reasonable grounds to believe they are the child's father**;
    - **Guardians**;
    - A person with the benefit of a **Residence Order**; or
    - A person with **custody** of the child.

Exam Trip Up

- The offence can only be committed by the above connected persons.

3 - Definition of Appropriate Consent – Section 1(3) Child Abduction Act 1984

- **Consent** will only be **appropriate** when **each** of the following have provided their **consent**:
    - **Mother**;
    - **Father** (if they have **PR**);
    - Any **Guardian**;

- Any person with the benefit of a **Residence Order**;
- Any person with **custody**;
- The **court** that **awarded custody** to a party.

Exam Trip Up

- It is necessary to prove that the person has done the act **without the permission of** *all* **the above persons**.

4 - Permission to Prosecute

- The **consent** of the **DPP** is required to secure a prosecution.

5 - Defence – Section 1(4)-(5) Child Abduction Act 1984

- **No offence** is committed where either:
    - The person has the **benefit** of a **Residence Order** and **removes** the **child from the U.K** for **less than a month** (unless they act in **breach** of a **Prohibited Steps Order**); or
    - Either:
        - They **believe** the other person either **consented** or **would have consented** if they knew the relevant circumstances;
        - They **cannot reasonably communicate with the other person**; or
        - The **other person has unreasonably refused to consent** (unless that person has **custody** or **residence** of the child).

B - Definition Of Child Abduction By Persons Not Connected With The Child
Either Way Offence
Penalty In The Crown Court – 7 Years Imprisonment
Penalty In The Magistrates Court – 6 Months Imprisonment And / Or A Fine

1 - Definition Of The Offence - Section 2 Child Abduction Act 1984

- It is an offence:
    - For a **person not connected** with a child;
    - To either:
        - **Take**; or;
        - **Detain**;
    - A **child under 16** years of age;
    - Without any **lawful authority**;
    - So as to **remove them** or **keep them** from the **lawful control** of a **person entitled to lawful control**.

2 - Defence – Section 2(3) Child Abduction Act 1984

- A person will have a **defence** if they can prove that either:
    - At the time of acting they **believed the child had attained 16 years of age**; or
    - Where the **father and mother are not married at the time of the child's birth**:
        - They are the **father**; or
        - They **believed** on **reasonable grounds** that they are the child's **father**.

C – Child Cruelty
Either Way Offence
Penalty In The Crown Court – 10 Years Imprisonment
Penalty In The Magistrates Court – 6 Months Imprisonment And / Or A Fine

1 - Definition Of Child Cruelty – Section 1 Children & Young Persons Act 1933

- An offence is committed:
    - By a **person aged 16 or over**;
    - Who has **responsibility for a child under 16** years of age;
    - Who **wilfully** either:
        - **Assaults**;
        - **Ill treats**;
        - **Neglects**;
        - **Abandons**;
        - **Exposes**;
    - The **child** in a **manner likely to cause unnecessary suffering or injury to the health of the child**; or
    - **Causes** or **procures** any of the above.

2 - Learning Points

- It is necessary to prove both:
    - The **defendant** was aged **16 or over**; *and*
    - Had **responsibility** for a **child under 16**.
- Any person who has **Parental Responsibility** for a child will be **presumed to have responsibility** even when the child is not under their care.

Exam Trip Up

- Babysitters will have responsibility for a child.

3 - Wilful Acts

- The offence must have been committed **wilfully.**

Exam Trip Up

- If the exam question states that there has been a lack of medical care for the child, the requirement of *wilfulness* can only be satisfied where either:
    - ☐ The accused was aware that the child's health might be at risk if he was not provided with medical care; or
    - ☐ The accused's non-awareness of the risk to the child was due to not caring whether the child's health was at risk or not.

4 - Definition Of Abandonment

- To *abandon* a child means leaving it to its fate.

Exam Trip Up

- It is **not necessary** to prove *actual* unnecessary suffering or injury to health.
- It is only necessary to prove that the person **acted in a manner** *likely* **to cause unnecessary suffering or injury to health.**

Exam Trip Up

- It is possible to consider this offence even where the baby has died (in addition to homicide).

D – Harmful Publications
Summary Only Offence
Penalty In The Magistrates Court – 4 Months Imprisonment And / Or A Fine

1 - Definition Of Harmful Publications – Section 2 Children and Young Persons (Harmful Publications) Act 1955

- An offence will be committed by any person;
    - ☐ Who either:
        - **Prints;**
        - **Publishes;**
        - **Sells;** or
        - **Hires out;**
    - ☐ **Works likely to fall into the hands** of either a **child** or **young person;**
    - ☐ **Portraying** either:
        - The commission of **crimes;**
        - Acts of **violence;**
        - Incidents of a **repulsive** or **horrible** nature;
    - ☐ In such a way that would tend to **corrupt** a **child** or **young person.**

2 - Permission to Prosecute Is Required

- The **consent** of the **Attorney General** (or **Solicitor General**) is required to secure a prosecution.

E - Placing Children In Police Protection

1 – Powers Of A Constable – Section 46 Children Act 1989

- Where a **constable**;
- Has **reasonable cause** to **believe** that a **child** would otherwise be likely to **suffer significant harm**;
- They may either:
    - **Remove** the child to **suitable accommodation**; or
    - **Prevent** the child's **removal** from either:
        - **Hospital**; or
        - Other accommodation.

2 - The Maximum Duration Of Police Protection

- **Police protection** may last for a **maximum** duration of **72 hours**.

3 - Action To Be Taken Once A Child Has Been Taken Into Police Protection – Section 46(3) Children Act 1989

- Tell the Local Authority within whose area the child was found the:
    - The steps that:
        - Have been taken; and
        - Are proposed to be taken; and
    - Why they are to be taken.

- Give details to the Local Authority in the area the child is ordinarily resident of the place they are being kept.

- Tell the child of:
    - The steps that:
        - Have been taken; and
        - Are proposed to be taken; and
    - Why they are to be taken.

- Take steps to discover the feelings of the child.

- Make sure the case is inquired into by a 'designated officer'

- Take such steps as are reasonable practicable to inform:
    - The child's parents;
    - Every other person with parental responsibility; and
    - Any other person the child was living with immediately before being taken into police protection.

- of:
    - ☐ The steps the officer has taken;
    - ☐ The reasons for taking the steps; and
    - ☐ Further steps that may be taken.

F - Removal Of Mentally Disordered People From Public Places

1 – Powers Of A Constable – Section 136 Mental Health Act 1983

- If a **constable** finds in a **public place**:
- A person appearing to suffer from a **mental disorder**; and
- In **immediate need** of:
    - ☐ **Care**; or
    - ☐ **Control**;
- The officer may either:
    - ☐ In acting in the **person's interests**; or
    - ☐ For the **protection of others**;
- **Remove** them to a **place of safety** for either:
    - ☐ **Examination** (up to **72 hours**);
    - ☐ **Interview** by a **social worker**;
    - ☐ **Arranging treatment**.

2 - Definition Of A Place Of Safety – Section 135 Mental Health Act 1983

- A **place of safety** will include any:
    - ☐ Social services accommodation;
    - ☐ Hospital;
    - ☐ Police station;
    - ☐ Mental nursing home;
    - ☐ Anywhere suitable where the occupier is willing to receive them.

3 - Definition Of A Mental Disorder - Section 1 Mental Health Act 1983

- A **mental disorder** will encompass any:
    - ☐ **Mental illness;**
    - ☐ **Arrested or incomplete development of the mind;**
    - ☐ **Psychopathic disorder** (any persistent disorder or disability resulting in abnormally aggressive or seriously irresponsible conduct);
    - ☐ **Any other disorder or disability of the mind.**

Crime
Unit 9: Theft (1) – Basic Theft, Burglary & Robbery

A - Definition Of Theft – Section 1 Theft Act 1968
Either Way Offence
Penalty In The Crown Court – 7 Years Imprisonment
Penalty In The Magistrates Court – 6 Months Imprisonment And / Or A Fine

- A person is guilty of **theft** if they:
    - ☐ **Dishonestly;**
    - ☐ **Appropriate;**
    - ☐ **Property;**
    - ☐ **Belonging** to **another;**
    - ☐ With the **intention** of **permanently depriving** the other of it.

1 – Dishonestly

(i) - Definition Of Dishonesty

- The principles from the case of *R v Ghosh* [1982] QB 1053, established that:
    - ☐ The determination of whether an individual is **dishonest** is a **question of fact** for the jury to decide; and
    - ☐ There are **two hurdles** that the jury must 'jump' to determine whether an individual is **dishonest.**

Hurdle 1

- ☐ The jury must ask whether by the **ordinary standards of reasonable and honest people**, the act was **dishonest.**
- ☐ If the jury decide **no** – the test would **fail** at the first hurdle and the jury must **acquit.**
- ☐ If the jury decide **yes** – the jury progress onto the second hurdle.

Hurdle 2

- ☐ Whether the **defendant** would have **realised by those ordinary standards of reasonable and honest people** that **what they were doing was dishonest.**
- ☐ If the jury decide **no** – the test would **fail** at the second hurdle and the jury must **acquit.**
- ☐ If the answer is **yes -** then the defendant will have behaved dishonestly.

- The **objective** nature of the test ensures that a defendant who has a **subjective belief** that their actions are **not dishonest** can still be **convicted.**

(ii) - What is Not Dishonest? – Section 2 Theft Act 1968

- A person will **not** be regarded as **dishonest** if either:
    - They **believed** they had a **right in law** to the property;
    - They **believed** that **if the owner knew** of the **appropriation** and it's **circumstances** they would have **consented**;
    - They **believe** that the **owner cannot be discovered by taking reasonable steps**.

(iii) - Willingness To Pay?

- It is possible for behaviour to be deemed to be **dishonest despite a willingness to pay.**

    For example: A person who takes a newspaper delivered to your doorstep and leaves money to cover the cost of the paper will still be deemed to be dishonest.

2 – Appropriation

(i) - Definition Of Appropriation – Section 3 Theft Act 1968

- An **appropriation** is:
    - Any **assumption** by the person of the **rights of the owner**.
    - The assumption can be:
        - **Innocent**; or
        - **Otherwise**;
    - By either:
        - **Keeping** the property;
        - **Dealing** with the property as the owner.

Exam Trip Up

- An appropriation can be for a **very short period of time.**
- For example, a thief who takes a purse out of a handbag, is almost immediately disturbed, drops the purse and runs off will have **appropriated** the purse.

(ii) - Appropriation And Consent

- It is possible for an appropriation to take place even when the victim consents to the appropriation.

- In the case of *R v Lawrence [1982] AC 510*:

    A tourist, who had a wallet full of unfamiliar cash, offered his wallet to the taxi driver to remove the correct fare. The driver took more than the fare. He was convicted of theft even though he had the owners consent to remove the cash.

- In the case of *R v Gomez* [1993] AC 442:

    Gomez worked in a shop in London and was asked by a friend to accept two stolen building society cheques in exchange for expensive electrical goods.

    Knowing the cheques were stolen, Gomez asked the manager to authorise the sale assuring him the cheques were as good as cash.

    As a result, the manager consented to release the goods to Gomez's friend. Some time later the cheques returned from the bank without being paid.

    Gomez's counsel argued that the manager had consented to the appropriation and therefore there was no case to answer.

    The House of Lords upheld the conviction on the basis that it was possible to 'appropriate' property despite the presence of consent.

(iii) - Appropriation Exception – Section 3 Theft Act 1968

- The following will **not** amount to an **appropriation**:
    - A **purchase** for **value**;
    - By a person **acting in good faith**;
    - Who **assumes the rights of the owner**.

An Example Of A Purchase For Value In Good Faith

- A person gets a good deal at a **legitimate car auction** and **purchases** a vehicle **worth £5000 for £4000**.

- There is **no problem** as they have:
    - **Purchased**;
    - The vehicle for **value**;
    - Whilst **acting in good faith**; and
    - Have **assumed the rights of the owner** by taking the registration documents and driving away.

- However, a person buying the same **car worth £5000 from a stranger in a pub for £200** will **not** be able to **rely** upon the **appropriation exception**.
    - They **have**:
        - **Purchased**;
        - The vehicle for **value**;
        - Have **assumed the rights of the owner** by taking the vehicle;
        - But they have **not acted in good faith**.

3 – Property

(i) - Definition Of Property - Section 4 Theft Act 1968

- **Property** includes:
  - **Money**;
  - All **other property** including:
    - **Real** – (land and things forming part of the land);
    - **Buildings**;
    - **Personal** – (movable things that can be owned e.g. CD, TV, cars etc);
    - **'Things in action'** (capable of being enforced in a legal action); and
    - **'Other intangible property'** – (e.g. copyrights, trademarks, gas, etc).
  - **Items that cannot be physically stolen** – (e.g. trade secrets and exam questions).

Exam Trip Up

- A teacher was convicted of the theft of exam papers in London. She was convicted of the theft of the **paper** that the exam questions were written on.
- It is **not** possible to be convicted of the theft of the **information** on the examination papers itself.
- If she had simply **memorised** the questions and subsequently **written them down on her own paper** she would not have been convicted.

(ii) - Can Land Be Stolen? - Section 4(2)(a) - (c) Theft Act 1968

(a) – The General Rule

- As a **general rule land cannot be stolen**.

(b) - Exceptions To The General Rule

- There are **3 exceptions**:
  - **Trustees** or **Personal Representatives** can steal land by dealing with it in **breach of a confidence**;

    For example: An executor of an estate selling land for their own benefit.

  - A **person not in possession** of the land can steal by **severing** it.

    For example: A enters B's land and removes a stone statue fixed to the land.

  - A **tenant in possession** can steal **fixtures and structures.**

    For example: A tenant removing a fireplace fixed to the wall from premises that they rent.

(iii) – Can Things Growing Wild Be Stolen? - Section 4(3) Theft Act 1968

- It is **not** an offence of theft to:
  - **Pick** any:
    - **Mushrooms**;
    - **Flowers**;
    - **Fruit**; and
    - **Foliage**;
  - Growing **wild**;
  - On **any** land;
- **Unless** they are picked for:
  - **Sale**;
  - **Reward**;
  - Any other **commercial purpose**.

Exam Trip Up

- It is permissible to pick things growing wild on *any* land.
- Watch out for questions involving the picking of things growing wild in a persons **back garden**.
- It is **permissible** to pick such items provided they are not picked for sale, reward or other commercial purpose.
- For example:

  You walk down the road and strike up a conversation with a man standing in his garden and he tells you that the daffodils in his garden **grow wild**.

  You would **not commit** the offence of theft if you picked those daffodils, as they were **growing wild** on **any land**.

  If the facts were the same, but this time the man tells you that he **planted** the daffodils last year, then as the daffodils were **cultivated** and **not growing wild**, you would **commit an offence** if you picked them.

Exam Trip Up

- It is **permissible** to pick *wild* mushrooms, flowers, fruit and foliage growing wild on any land such as blackberries from a bush.
- It is **not permissible** to dig up the whole bush and take it away.

Exam Trip Up

- It is **permissible** for a person to pick wild mushrooms for their own use.
- It is **not permissible** to pick wild mushrooms on a large scale commercial basis.

(iv) - Can Wild Creatures Be Stolen? – Section 4 Theft Act 1968

- You **cannot** steal a **wild animal**;
- **Unless** it has been:
- Either:
  - ☐ **Tamed;** or
  - ☐ Ordinarily **kept in captivity;**
- Or has been:
  - ☐ **Reduced** into possession; or
  - ☐ Is in the **course** of being reduced into possession; and
- **Possession** has **not** been:
  - ☐ **Lost;** or
  - ☐ **Abandoned.**

Examples Of Wild Animals Tamed Or In Captivity:

- Generally speaking a wild tiger cannot be stolen.
- However it is possible to steal a tiger:
  - ☐ Bred in **captivity** at Longleat Safari Park; or
  - ☐ That was Siegfried and Roy's **pet (tamed).**

Examples Of Reducing Animals Into Possession:

- If a fisherman catches a fish and leaves it by his side in readiness to take it home to eat, they have **reduced the fish into their possession** and **become the owner of the fish.** It is therefore **possible for the fish to be stolen from them.**

- A fisherman **reeling in a fish** will be **in the course of reducing the fish into their possession.** If somebody cut the line and took the fish then the fish would be stolen from them.

- If a fisherman having reduced a fish into their possession either:
  - ☐ **Leaves and forgets to take the fish;** or
  - ☐ **Throws the fish away to feed the birds;**

  - **The fish reverts to its wild state.** If any person subsequently saw the fish and took it home to eat **(reducing the fish into their possession)** they would **not have stolen the fish.**

(v) - Are Corpses Property?

- A **corpse** is **not property** – *(Doodeward v Spence* [1908] 6 CLR 406);
- **Unless;**
- It has been **changed** in some way by:
    - ☐ Amputation;
    - ☐ Dissection;
    - ☐ Preservation.

- In the case of *R v Kelly* [1999] QB 621, an individual was convicted of theft of **dissected body parts** from the Royal College of Surgeons.

- Lenin's **preserved** corpse in its glass mausoleum would be deemed to be property.

4 – Property Belonging To Another

(i) - Defining "Belonging To Another" - Section 5 Theft Act 1968

- Property **belongs** to the person who has **possession** or **control** of it.

    For example:

    A PC being repaired in a computer repair shop can have **three owners:**

- Technician   –   Possession
- Shop manager –   Control
- Owner   –   Proprietary Interest

(ii) - Receiving Property By Mistake – Section 5(4) Theft Act 1968

- Where a person receives property by **mistake;**
- They are **obliged to restore it** to the person who made the mistake.
- **Failure** to do so will form an **intention** to **permanently deprive** the other of that property.
- For example:
    - ☐ Having too much change given to you in a shop; or
    - ☐ An employee being paid for overtime that they did not work.

5 - An Intention To Permanently Deprive – Section 6 Theft Act 1968

- There are **3 circumstances** which may amount to an **intention to permanently deprive:**
    - ☐ A person treating the property as their own;
    - ☐ A person borrowing beyond the scope of the agreed terms;
    - ☐ A person parting with property under a condition for its return.

(i) – A Person Treating The Property As Their Own - Section 6(1) Theft Act 1968

- The intention to permanently deprive will be established where a **person treats property of their own regardless of the rights of the owner.**

(ii) - Borrowing Beyond The Scope Of The Agreed Terms - Section 6(1) Theft Act 1968

- The intention to permanently deprive will be established where a **person borrows or lends property in circumstances that make it an outright taking.**

- For example:
    - Y lends Z their season ticket specifically to watch the first league game of the season.
    - Z does not return the season ticket and instead uses the ticket to watch all of the remaining games that season.
    - In the circumstances Z will have exceeded the scope of the lending and their actions will have amounted to an outright taking.

(iii) - Parting With Property Under A Condition For Its Return – Section 6(2) Theft Act 1968

- The intention to permanently deprive will be established where a **person parts with another's property under a condition for its return that they may not be able to perform.**

- For example:
    - When someone **borrows (condition** being the **return of the item);**
    - A lawnmower **(another's property)** for a week; and
    - **Pawns** the lawnmower **(parts with the property);**
    - Even if they intended to return the lawnmower, the **theft is complete** at the time of **parting.**

    This is due to the fact that they **may not be able to perform the condition of return** of the item borrowed.

B – Burglary

Violence Used In A Dwelling – Indictable Only Offence
Penalty In The Crown Court – 14 Years Imprisonment

Other Offences - Either Way Offence
Penalty In The Crown Court – 10 Years Imprisonment
Penalty In The Magistrates Court – 6 Months Imprisonment And / Or A Fine

1 - Definition Of Burglary - Section 9(i)(a) Theft Act 1968 Offence

- A person commits an offence if they:
  - **Enter** a:
    - **Building**; or
    - **Part** of a building;
  - As a **trespasser**;
  - With the **intent (offence complete)** to:
    - **Steal**;
    - Do **GBH**;
    - Do unlawful **damage**.

2 - Definition Of Burglary - Section 9(i)(b) Theft Act 1968 Offence

- An offence is committed by a person who:
  - Having **entered** a:
    - **Building**; or
    - **Part** of a building;
  - As a **trespasser**;
  - And **either (result)**:
    - **Steals** or **attempts** to do so; or
    - Commits **GBH or attempts** to do so.

Exam Trip Up

- A burglary can take place in an *inhabited* **vehicle**.

Exam Trip Up

- **Rape** is **no longer included** in the definition of the offence.

Exam Trip Up

- The defendant must be a **trespasser at the time of entry** of the building.

Exam Trip Up

- Entering a building to either **TWOC** or **steal electricity** do **not** amount to an **offence**.
- **Stealing gas does** result in an offence.

Exam Trip Up

- Entry simply needs to be **effective.**
- It is **not necessary** for the **whole body** to enter the premises.

Exam Tip – Burglary Under Section 9(i)(a)
Intent Offence

- The offence is **complete** at the **time of entry**.
    - If a person **enters** a building as a trespasser **intending... offence complete.**
    - If they **change their mind once inside** – They still **entered intending….. offence complete.**
    - If they **run off** after being disturbed having **stolen nothing** – They still **entered intending….. offence complete**.

Exam Tip – Burglary Under Section 9(i)(b)
Result Offence

- Look for the **result.**
- At the time of the **result** – the **offence is complete.**

Summary Table – Burglary

Burglary 9(1)(a)	Burglary 9(1)(b)
Enters: - Building; or - Part of a building.	Having **entered**: - Building; or - Part of a building.
As a **trespasser.**	As a **trespasser.**
With **intent to** (**offence complete**):	They produce a **result** of:
- Steal; - Inflict GBH; - Does unlawful damage.	- Stealing; - Inflicting GBH; - Attempting either of the two above. (**Offence complete** upon the **result**)

C – Aggravated Burglary
Indictable Only Offence
Penalty In The Crown Court – Life Imprisonment

1 - Definition Of Aggravated Burglary – Section 10 Theft Act 1968

- **Aggravated burglary** will arise where:
    - ☐ A person commits **burglary**; and
    - ☐ **At the time;**
    - ☐ Has **with them (readily to hand)**;
    - ☐ One of a **"F.E.W."** things:
        - F   -   **Firearm** or **imitation firearm**;
        - E   -   **Explosive**;
        - W   -   **Weapon of offence made** or **adapted** for causing **injury** or **incapacitating** a person.

2 - Definition Of An Explosive

- An **explosive** includes:
    - ☐ Any **article**;
    - ☐ Either:
        - **Manufactured** for the **purpose** of **producing** a practical effect by **explosion**; or
        - **Intended** by a person having it with them for that **purpose**.

Exam Trip Up

- An **empty box** with "BOMB" written on it would be **insufficient** to constitute an explosive.
- However, an empty box with BOMB written on it **will constitute a weapon of offence** if the burglar gave it to a security guard stating, 'if you move the movement activated bomb in this box will explode'.
- In this set of circumstances, it may be **any article made for causing incapacity to a person**.

3 - Definition Of A Weapon Of Offence – Section 10(1) Theft Act 1968

- A **weapon of offence** will include:
    - ☐ Any **article** either:
        - **Made (sole purpose)**;
        - **Adapted (e.g. rolling pin with nail driven through it)**; or
        - **Intended**;
    - ☐ For **causing** either:
        - **Injury**; or (e.g. knife, baseball bat, etc)
        - **Incapacity**; (e.g. rope, gaffer tape, etc)
    - ☐ To a **person**.

Exam Trip Up

- If a weapon of offence is **made** or **adapted** for causing injury or incapacity to a person:
    - You are simply required to **have it with you**; and
    - **No additional mens rea** is required to commit the offence.

- If a person has **anything else** (e.g. a screwdriver which is **not made** or **adapted** for causing injury or incapacity to a person:
    - Simply having a screwdriver to gain entry is not enough.
    - It is also necessary for the person to have the **intention** to **use it** as a **weapon of offence** to **cause injury** or **incapacity** to a person.

4 - At The Time

(i) - For The Aggravated S9(1)(a) Offence:

- It must be shown that they **had one of a FEW things with them** at the **point of entry.**

(ii) - For The Aggravated S9(1)(b) Offence:

- It must be shown that they **had one of a FEW things with them** at the **point of stealing** or **causing GBH.**

D - Definition Of Robbery – Section 8 Theft Act 1968
Indictable Only Offence
Penalty In The Crown Court – Life Imprisonment

- An offence of **robbery** is committed by a person who:
    - **Steals**; and
    - Either:
        - **Immediately before**; or
        - **At the time** of doing so;
    - Either:
        - **Uses force** on any person **in order to steal**; or
        - Puts or seeks to put any person **in fear of being then and there subjected to force.**

Robbery - Memory Aid

- **Robbery** is simply **stealing aggravated** by either:
    - The use of force; or
    - The threat of force.
- Remember: **No theft - no robbery;**

Exam Trip Up

- The **use or threat of force** must be **used at the time of stealing**.
- But a robbery will **not arise** if force is used only **to make good an escape after stealing**.

Exam Trip Up

- **Indirect force = Robbery (e.g. a handbag snatch).**

Exam Trip Up

- The **force** used must be used **'in order to steal'**.
- For example:
    - If A and B got into a fight; and
    - By chance during the fight B's wallet falls out of B's pocket; and
    - A then decides to steal the wallet and runs away;
- The offence of robbery will **not** be **committed** as:
    - The force:
        - Was **used** for the **purposes of fighting**; and
        - Was *not* **used in order to steal.**

Exam Trip Up

- Using **force** to **TWOC** is **not robbery** as this does not amount to an offence of theft.

Exam Trip Up

- Using or threatening force at any **place other than at the scene** is **insufficient**.

Exam Trip Up

- A **future threat** of force is **insufficient**.

Crime
Unit 10: Theft (2) – Fraud & Other Dishonesty Offences

A - Fraud By False Representations
Either Way Offence
Penalty In The Crown Court – 10 Years Imprisonment And / Or A Fine
Penalty In The Magistrates Court – 12 Months Imprisonment And / Or A Fine

1 - Definition Of Fraud By False Representations - Section 2(1) Fraud Act 2006

- It is an offence to:
    - **Dishonestly**;
    - Make a **false representation**; and
    - **Intend** by making the representation to either:
        - To make a **gain** for:
            - **Themselves**;
            - **Another**; or
        - **Cause loss** to **another**; or
        - **Expose another** to a **risk of loss.**

2 - When Is A Representation False - Section 2(2) Fraud Act 2006

- A **representation** is **false** if:
    - It is either:
        - **Untrue**; or
        - **Misleading**; and
    - The person making the representation **knows** that it:
        - **Is**; or
        - **Might be**;
    - Either:
        - **Untrue**; or
        - **Misleading.**

3 - The Definition Of A Representation - Section 2(3) Fraud Act 2006

- A **representation** means:
    - [ ] Any **representation**;
    - [ ] As to either:
        - **Fact**; or
        - **Law**;
    - [ ] Including a **representation** as to the **state of mind** of:
        - The **person making the representation**, or
        - Any **other person**.

4 - How May The Representation Be Made? - Section 2(4) Fraud Act 2006

- The **representation** may be either:
    - [ ] **Express**; or
    - [ ] **Implied**.

5 - When Will A Representation Be Made? - Section 2(4) Fraud Act 2006

- A representation will be made where:
    - [ ] Either:
        - The **representation**; or
        - Anything **implying** to be a **representation**;
    - [ ] Is submitted;
    - [ ] In **any form**;
    - [ ] To **any**:
        - **System**; or
        - **Device**;
    - [ ] **Designed** to:
        - **Receive**;
        - **Convey**; or
        - **Respond**;
    - [ ] **To communications**;
    - [ ] Either **with or without human intervention**.

6 - Definition Of A Gain – Section 5(3) Fraud Act 2006

- A **gain** will include either:
    - [ ] **Keeping** what you already have; or
    - [ ] **Getting** what you don't already have.

7 - Definition Of A Loss – Section 5(4) Fraud Act 2006

- A **loss** includes either:
    - [ ] **Parting** with what you have **already got**; or
    - [ ] **Not getting** what you **haven't already got** but you might get in future.

8 - What Must The Gain Or Loss Relate To? – Section 5(2) Fraud Act 2006

- The:
    - [ ] **Gain;** or
    - [ ] **Loss;**
- Must be in relation to either:
    - [ ] **Money;** or
    - [ ] Other **property** that is:
        - Real;
        - Personal;
        - Things in action;
        - Intangible property.
- Which can be either:
    - [ ] **Permanent;** or
    - [ ] **Temporary.**

Exam Trip Up

- The offence is **complete** as soon as the **intent** is **formed.**
- There is **no need** for the **result** of either:
    - A **gain** for:
        - [ ] Themselves;
        - [ ] Another; or
    - Causing loss to another; or
    - Exposing another to a risk of loss.

- Examples of offences committed under this section include:
  - Sending e-mails to individuals claiming to be from a financial institution.
  - Selling fake designer goods.

B - Fraud By Failing To Disclose Information
Either Way Offence
Penalty In The Crown Court – 10 Years Imprisonment And / Or A Fine
Penalty In The Magistrates Court – 12 Months Imprisonment And / Or A Fine

1 - Definition Of Fraud By Failing To Disclose Information - Section 3 Fraud Act 2006

- Its an offence for a person to:
  - **Dishonestly;**
  - **Fail** to **disclose** to **another person;**
  - **Information** that they are under a **legal duty to disclose**; and
  - **Intends** by **failing** to **disclose** the **information** to either:
    - To make a **gain** for:
      - **Themselves;** or
      - **Another;** or
    - To **cause loss** to **another;** or
    - To **expose another** to a **risk of loss.**

2 – The Basis Of The Legal Duty

- A **'legal duty'** may be derived from:
  - Statute;
  - A transaction in good faith;
  - Express contractual terms;
  - Implied contractual terms;
  - Trade customs;
  - The existence of a relationship.

Exam Trip Up

- The offence is **complete** as soon as the **intent** is **formed.**
- There is **no need** for the **result** of either:
  - A **gain** for:
    - **Themselves;**
    - **Another;** or

- - Causing **loss** to **another**; or
  - Exposing **another** to a **risk of loss**.
- For example the offence would be committed by a person who fails to disclose to an insurance company:
  - ☐ A relevant medical condition when applying for life insurance cover; or
  - ☐ Motoring convictions when applying for motor insurance.

C - Fraud By Abuse Of A Position
Either Way Offence
Penalty In The Crown Court – 10 Years Imprisonment And / Or A Fine
Penalty In The Magistrates Court – 12 Months Imprisonment And / Or A Fine

1 - Definition Of Fraud By Abuse Of A Position - Section 4(1) Fraud Act 2006

- It is an offence:
  - ☐ For a person to **occupy a position** in which they are **expected to** either:
    - **Safeguard**; or
    - **Not act against**;
  - ☐ The **financial interests** of **another person**; and
  - ☐ They **dishonestly abuse** that **position**; and
  - ☐ **Intends** by **means** of that **abuse** of that **position** to either:
  - ☐ Make a **gain** for:
    - **Themselves**; or
    - **Another**; or
  - ☐ **Cause** a **loss** to **another**; or
  - ☐ **Expose another** to a **risk of loss**.

2 - Rationale Of This Offence

- The offence is aimed at:
  - ☐ Those who are in a position to safeguard another's financial interest; and
  - ☐ Have authority to exercise discretion on behalf of the client.

Exam Trip Up

- The dishonest abuse of the position can arise from either:
  - ☐ A positive **act**; or
  - ☐ An **omission**.
- An example of a **dishonest abuse of the position** by an **omission** would include the person **failing to act** to **win a contract** on behalf of another whose interests they are expected to safeguard, in order to enable a competitor to win the contract instead.

Exam Trip Up

- The offence is **complete** as soon as the **intent** is **formed.**
- There is **no need** for the **result** of either:
    - A **gain** for:
        - Themselves;
        - Another; or
    - Causing **loss** to **another**; or
    - Exposing another to a **risk of loss.**

D - Possession Of Articles For Use In Fraud
Either Way Offence
Penalty In The Crown Court – 5 Years Imprisonment And / Or A Fine
Penalty In The Magistrates Court – 12 Months Imprisonment And / Or A Fine

1 - Definition Of Possession Of Articles For Use In Fraud - Section 6 Fraud Act 2006

- A person commits an offence if:
    - They have:
        - In their **possession**; or
        - Under their **control;**
    - Any **article;**
    - For **use** either:
        - In the **course** of any fraud; or
        - In **connection** with any fraud.

2 - Definition Of An Article – Section 8 Fraud Act 2006

- The term **'article'** can include:
    - Any:
        - **Program**; or
        - **Data;**
    - Held in **electronic form.**

3 - Learning Point

- This offence:
    - Is exactly the **same** as the **old offence** of **'going equipped'**;
    - **Except** for the fact that the **new offence no longer** makes reference to *'while not at the place of abode'*.
- In essence this offence can now be committed **anywhere**.

E - Making Or Supplying Articles For Their Use In A Fraud
Either Way Offence
Penalty In The Crown Court – 10 Years Imprisonment And / Or A Fine
Penalty In The Magistrates Court – 12 Months Imprisonment And / Or A Fine

1 - Definition Of Making Or Supplying Articles For Their Use In A Fraud - Section 7 Fraud Act 2006

- A person commits an offence if they:
    - Either:
        - Make;
        - Adapt;
        - Supply; or
        - Offer to supply;
    - Any **article**;
    - Either:
        - **Knowing** that it is either:
            - **Designed**; or
            - **Adapted**;
        - For **use** either:
            - **In the course** of a fraud; or
            - **In connection** with fraud; or
        - **Intending** it to be used to either:
            - **Commit** a fraud; or
            - **Assist in the commission** of a fraud.

F - Obtaining Services Dishonestly
Either Way Offence
Penalty In The Crown Court – 5 Years Imprisonment And / Or A Fine
Penalty In The Magistrates Court – 12 Months Imprisonment And / Or A Fine

1 – Definition Of Obtaining Services Dishonestly - Section 11 (1) Fraud Act 2006

- A person commits an offence if they:
    - **Obtain services** for:
        - **Themselves**; or
        - **Another**;
    - By a **dishonest act**; and
    - The **services** are made **available** on the **basis** that **payment** either:
        - **Has** been made;
        - **Is** being made; or
        - **Will** be made; and
    - The **services** are **obtained without** either:
        - **Any payment** being made; or
        - **Payment** being made **in full**; and
        - When they **obtained** the **services** they:
            - **Knew** the **basis** upon which the services were made available (i.e. that they were **expected to pay**); and
            - They **intend** either:
                - **Not** to make **any payment**; or
                - **Not** to make **payment in full**.

Learning Point

- There must be an **'obtaining'** of the **services**.

Learning Point

- The **service** can be made available on the **internet**.

Learning Point

- This offence will be committed in the event of a **dishonest use of false credit card details**.

Learning Point

- This offence will be committed in the event of **trespassory entry into a premises to watch an event for which they would be expected to pay**.

G - Making Off Without Payment – "Bilking"
Either Way Offence
Penalty In The Crown Court – 2 Years Imprisonment
Penalty In The Magistrates Court – 6 Months Imprisonment And / Or A Fine

1 - Definition Of Making Off Without Payment – Section 3 Theft Act 1978

- An offence of **making off without payment** is committed:
    - When **payment on the spot** is required;
    - For either:
        - **Goods** supplied; or
        - **Services** done; and
    - A person **dishonestly makes off without payment**;
    - **Intending** to **avoid payment**.

- This offence is commonly known as **bilking.**

Exam Trip Up - Payment On The Spot

- This includes payment **at the time** - i.e. Collecting goods such as laundry.

Exam Trip Up - Legally Enforceable

- The **service** or **goods** must be **legally enforceable**.

H - Definition Of Blackmail – Section 21 Theft Act 1968
Indictable Only Offence
Penalty In The Crown Court – 14 Years Imprisonment

1 - Definition Of Blackmail – Section 21 Theft Act 1968

- A person commits an offence of **blackmail** if:
    - With a view to:
        - **Gain for themselves;** or
        - **Loss to another;**
    - They make an **unwarranted demand;**
    - **With menaces.**

2 - Defence To Blackmail – Section 21 Theft Act 1968

- **No offence** is committed if:
    - The person had **reasonable grounds** for the demand; and
    - The menace was a **proper way of enforcing** the demand.

For example:

- A demand from the electricity board saying pay up or we'll switch your lights off is fine.
- However a demand saying pay up or we'll punch your lights out is not!

Exam Trip Up

- It is not an offence to **blackmail** a person into **having sex** with you.

Exam Trip Up

- If the blackmail is **via mail:**
    - The **offence is complete** at the **time of posting;** and
    - The letter does **not have to be received.**

I - Definition Of Abstracting Electricity – Section 13 Theft Act 1968
Either Way Offence
Penalty In The Crown Court – 5 Years Imprisonment
Penalty In The Magistrates Court – 6 Months Imprisonment And / Or A Fine

- A person commits an offence if they **dishonestly** either:
    - **Use** electricity **without due authority;** or
    - Cause electricity to be:
        - **Wasted;** or
        - **Diverted.**

Exam Trip Up

- **Unauthorised use** of a **telephone is included in this offence.**

Exam Trip Up

- It is **not possible to steal electricity** therefore it is **not included in the burglary offence.**

Exam Trip Up

- **By-passing an electricity meter is included** in this offence.

Exam Trip Up

- Stealing a **pedestrian controlled vehicle is included** in this offence.

J – Handling Stolen Goods – Section 22 Theft Act 1968
Either Way Offence
Penalty In The Crown Court – 14 Years Imprisonment
Penalty In The Magistrates Court – 6 Months Imprisonment And / Or A Fine

1 - Definition Of Handling Stolen Goods – Part 1

- A person commits an offence when:
    - **Knowing** or **believing**;
    - The goods to be **stolen**;
    - They **dishonestly receive** the goods;
    - **Otherwise** than in the **course of stealing**.

2 - Definition Of Handling Stolen Goods – Part 2

- A person will also commit an offence if they:
    - **Dishonestly** either:
        - **Undertake** or **assist** in the stolen good's:
            - **Retention**;
            - **Removal**;
            - **Realisation**;
            - **Disposal**;
        - **- By** or for the **benefit** of **another person**; or
    - They **arrange** to do so.

Exam Trip Up

- Remember - **no theft no handling**.

Exam Trip Up

- Handling goods from **abroad** is an **offence** if it is an **offence in the other country**.

3 - When Are Goods Stolen?

- **Goods** are **stolen** if they are:
    - The **original** stolen goods; (e.g. a DVD);
    - They represent the **proceeds** of stolen goods; (Cash from the sale of the DVD); or
    - Goods subject to **blackmail**.
- **Goods cease to be stolen** when they have been **taken back into lawful possession**.

4 - Special Evidence – Section 27(3) Theft Act 1968

- If a person has been **convicted** in the **last 5 years** of a **theft offence**; and
- They have been found:
    - ☐ In **possession**;
    - ☐ Of **stolen goods**;
    - ☐ In the **last 12 months**;
- We can **presume** that they **knew** that these **goods were stolen**.

J – Taking A Vehicle Without Consent (TWOC)
Summary Only Offence
Penalty In The Magistrates Court – 6 Months Imprisonment And / Or A Fine

1 - Definition Of TWOC – Section 12 Theft Act 1968

- A person commits an offence of **TWOC** if they:
- Either **without**:
    - ☐ The **consent** of the **owner**; or
    - ☐ Other **lawful authority**;
- **TWOC** for either:
    - ☐ Their **own** use; or
    - ☐ **Another's** use;
- Or - **Knowing** the conveyance was **TWOC** either:
    - ☐ **Drives**; or
    - ☐ **Gets carried** in it.

2 - Definition Of A Conveyance? – Section 12(7) Theft Act 1968

- A **conveyance** includes anything:
    - ☐ **Constructed**; or
    - ☐ **Adapted**;
    - ☐ To **carry a person** by:
        - Land;
        - Sea (which includes, **rivers, lakes,** etc); or
        - Air.

Exam Trip Up

- For the offence of **allowing themselves to be carried** – It must be proven that the person **knew that it was stolen**.

Exam Trip Up

- If all persons in the vehicle **deny driving** - they are **all charged** with **being carried**.

K - Aggravated TWOC

Accident Causes Death – Indictable Only Offence
Penalty In The Crown Court – 14 Years Imprisonment

Basic Offence - Either Way Offence
Penalty In The Crown Court – 2 Years Imprisonment
Penalty In The Magistrates Court – 6 Months Imprisonment And / Or A Fine

1 - Definition Of Aggravated TWOC – Section 12(A) Theft Act 1968

- There must be a **TWOC** of a **mechanically propelled vehicle;** and
- **Between** the time:
    - The vehicle was **taken;** and
    - The **recovery** of the vehicle:
- There must be either:
    - An **act of dangerous driving** on:
        - A **road;** or
        - Other **public place;**
    - An **injury accident** - owing to the driving, an **injury is caused to any person;**
    - A **damage accident** - owing to the driving, **damage is caused to any property;** or
    - **Damage to the vehicle stolen.**

2 - Defence To Aggravated TWOC – Section 12(A)(3) Theft Act 1968

- It's a **defence** to prove that:
    - Any of the 4 consequences **happened before** the basic offence; or
    - The person was **not** in the immediate vicinity of the vehicle when the **consequence occurred.**

Exam Trip Up

- For **simple TWOC** you just need a **conveyance** which **need** *not* **be mechanically propelled** (e.g. a rowing boat).

- For **aggravated TWOC** you need a **mechanically propelled vehicle** (a rowing boat would not suffice).

    NB – For further guidance on what a mechanically propelled vehicle is see the standards of driving chapter under the Traffic section of the texbook.

Exam Trip Up

- If a person smashes the window of a car and returns to take the car later:

    ☐ This is **not aggravated TWOC.**

    ☐ This is **criminal damage** and **TWOC.**

    ☐ As the **damage** occurred *before* the **basic offence.**

Crime
Unit 11: Criminal Damage Offences

A – Criminal Damage
Either Way Offence
Penalty In The Crown Court – 10 Years Imprisonment
Penalty In The Magistrates Court – 6 Months Imprisonment And / Or A Fine

1 - Definition Of Straight Forward Criminal Damage – Section 1(1) Criminal Damage Act 1971

- The offence of **criminal damage** is committed by a person who:
    - Without lawful excuse;
    - Either:
        - **Destroys**; or
        - **Damages**;
    - Property;
    - Belonging to another;
    - Either:
        - **Intending** to do so; or
        - Being **(subjectively) reckless** in doing so.

2 - Definition Of Subjective Recklessness?

- In a nutshell, **subjective recklessness** means that:
    - You **foresee** a risk; and
    - Then go on to **take the risk anyway**.
- Under previous case law all you needed to prove was objective recklessness *(R v Caldwell* [1982] AC 341*)*.
- This has **now changed** to a **subjective test** following the House of Lords decision in the case of *R v G & R* [2003] 3 WLR 1060.

Exam Trip Up

- It's **not** an **offence**:
    - To **damage one's own property**;
    - **Unless**;
    - The owner **endangers a life** in doing so.

Police Pass OSPRE Part 1 Revision Crammer Textbook ©

Exam Trip Up

- It is **not** an **offence** to **damage wild**:
    - **Mushrooms;**
    - **Flowers;**
    - **Fruit;** or
    - **Foliage** on **any land**.

Exam Trip Up

- Criminal damage of:
    - **Less than £5000** is tried **summarily;**
    - **£5,000 or over** is an **either way offence.**

- Ensure that you look at the words surrounding the numbers.

- If the damage is:
    - £4999.99 or less it **must** be tried at the **Magistrate's Court;**
    - £5000 exactly or more and it can be tried at **either Magistrate's** or **Crown Court.**
    - Damage is caused by **fire** will irrespective of its value always be an **indictable only offence** triable in the **Crown Court.**

Exam Trip Up

- The offence can be **racially** or **religiously aggravated.**
- For an explanation of how an offence becomes racially or religiously aggravated, see the chapter on 'Offences against the Person'.

Exam Trip Up

- The damage caused does **not need to be permanent** in nature.
    - In the case of *Hardman v Chief Constable Avon and Somerset* [1986] Crim LR 330, a street artist using **water soluble paints** to paint on a pavement was held to criminal damage.
    - In the case of *Roe v Kingerlee* [1986] Crim LR 735, **smearing graffiti with mud** was held to be criminal damage.

Exam Trip Up

- If the **damage** does **not exceed £200** it can be dealt with by means of **fixed penalty notice.**

3 - Defences - Lawful Excuses

(i) - Consent – Section 5 Criminal Damage Act 1971

- The **defence** of **consent** will apply if:
    - ☐ **At the time** of the act;
    - ☐ The person causing the damage **honestly believed** that either:
        - The **owner** had provided their **consent**;
        - A person **entitled** to give **consent** had **done so**;
        - The **person who could have consented** to the damage taking place;
            - ☐ **Would have consented if they knew** of the:
                - **Damage**; and
                - **Circumstances.**

An Example Of Consent

- A person sees a bird trapped in a shed on a hot summer's day. They want to smash the window to let the bird out before it dies.

- In order to establish the defence of **consent** they must **before** smashing the window either:
    - ☐ **Approach** the **owner** of the shed or another **entitled to consent** to smashing the window and have reached an **honest belief** that they **consented** to them smashing the window to free the bird; or
    - ☐ **Not approach** the **owner** of the shed or another **entitled to consent** to smashing the window, but have reached an **honest belief** that **had they approached** such a person they **would have consented** to them smashing the window to free the bird.

(ii) - Protection – Section 5 Criminal Damage Act 1971

- It is a **defence** for a person to:
    - ☐ Either:
        - **Destroy**; or
        - **Damage**;
    - ☐ **Property**;
    - ☐ In order to **protect property belonging to:**
        - **Themselves**; or
        - **Another**;
    - ☐ Provided that:
        - The property was **in immediate need of protection**; and
        - The **means used were reasonable** in the circumstances.

An Example Of Protection

- You live in a block of flats. Water comes rushing down your walls from your neighbour's flat upstairs. You realise that the neighbour has left a tap running in their flat.

- You know that your neighbour is on vacation and is out of the country for the next fortnight and that they have not left a spare key with anybody.

- You would be covered by the protection defence if you ran upstairs and broke the door in order to gain entry to turn off the taps, as you will have:

    - **Damaged** the front door – **property**;

    - In order to **protect property** belonging both to:
        - **Themselves** – water damage to your own flat; or
        - **Another** – water damage to your neighbour's flat; and

    - Both your property and your neighbour's property were **in immediate need of protection**; and

    - The **means were reasonable in the circumstances**, as there was no spare key available to gain access without breaking down the door.

B - Definition Of Aggravated Criminal Damage – Section 1(2) Criminal Damage Act 1971
Indictable Only Offence
Penalty In The Crown Court – Life Imprisonment

- It is an offence for a person to:

    - **Destroy**; or
    - **Damage**;
    - **Property**;
    - **Belonging** either to:
        - **Themselves**; or
        - **Another**;
    - Either:
        - **Intending**; or
        - **Being (subjectively) reckless**;
      - to **cause** the **damage**; and
    - **At the time** of doing so they either:
        - **Intended** to **endanger life**; or
        - Were **(subjectively) reckless** as to whether **another's life would be endangered**.

Exam Trip Up

- There is **no** provision for the **defence** of a **lawful excuse** under this section.

Exam Trip Up

- It is essential to establish that:
    - **Criminal damage** was caused; and
    - There was a **danger to life**.

Exam Trip Up

- **Damage by fire** is **not included** – such action is covered by the separate offence of **arson**.

C - Arson - Section 1(3) Criminal Damage Act 1971
Indictable Only Offence
Penalty In The Crown Court – Life Imprisonment

- The offence of **arson** will be committed where:
    - **Property** is either:
        - **Destroyed;** or
        - **Damaged;**
    - By **fire**.

D - The Powers Of Fire Authority Personnel

- **Fire authority personnel** have various **powers** when attending to fires.
- These can be divided into **two categories** under Part 6 Fire and Rescue Services Act 2004:
    - **Emergency powers**; and
    - **Investigation powers**.

1 - Emergency Powers

- In the case of an **emergency**, it stands to reason that there are very wide powers available to fire personnel, including the **power to enter premises** to:
    - **Extinguish fire;**
    - **Prevent fire;**
    - **Protect life;** or
    - **Protect property**.
- This can be done via **force** if necessary.

2 - Investigatory Powers

- The obvious difference and exam trip up here is that the **power to investigate fires** does **not** include a **power to enter premises** by **force**.

- It will be permissible for:
  - ☐ A person **authorised (in writing)**;
  - ☐ To **enter premises** where there has **been a fire**;
  - ☐ At a **reasonable time**;
  - ☐ For the **purpose** of **investigating**:
    - What **caused** the fire; or
    - **Why** the **fire progressed** in the manner that it did.

- **Entry by force** is only permissible if a **Magistrate** has issued a **warrant**.

Exam Trip Up – Notification Obligations In Relation To Private Dwellings

- If the **fire** took place in a **private dwelling** the **authorised person** must:
  - ☐ **Provide** the **occupier**;
  - ☐ With **24 hours notice** of the **intention to enter**.

- This is why the police would be utilised to gain entry.

E – Definition Of Threats To Destroy Or Damage Property - Section 2 Criminal Damage Act 1971
Either Way Offence
Penalty In The Crown Court – 10 Years Imprisonment
Penalty In The Magistrates Court – 6 Months Imprisonment And / Or A Fine

- An offence is committed by a person who:
  - ☐ **Without lawful excuse**;
  - ☐ Makes a **threat** to **another**;
  - ☐ **Intending (offence complete)**;
  - ☐ For **them** to **fear** that the **threat** would be **carried out** to:
    - Either:
      - ☐ **Destroy**; or
      - ☐ **Damage**
    - **Any property**;
    - Belonging either to:
      - ☐ **Them**; or (e.g. – I'll smash your windows);
      - ☐ A **3rd party**; (e.g. I'll smash your friend's windows); **or**

(cont...)

- Either:
  - **Destroy**; or
  - **Damage**;
- Their **own property**;
- In a way they know is likely to **endanger the life of**:
  - **Them**; or
  - A **3rd person**.

Learning Point - Intention

- The offence is **complete**:
  - At the **time** the **threat** is **made**;
  - If the threatener *intended* the person to believe the threat would be carried out.
- The **person threatened** does **not need to believe** that the **threat will in fact be carried out**.

Exam Trip Up – Impossible Threats

- Even if it is **impossible to carry out the threat**, the offence will still be **complete** once the **intent** to cause the fear of the threat being carried out is **formed**.

  For example: Making a threat to throw a brick through a reinforced window.

F - Definition Of Having Articles With The Intent To Destroy Or Damage – Section 3 Criminal Damage Act 1971
Either Way Offence
Penalty In The Crown Court – 10 Years Imprisonment
Penalty In The Magistrates Court – 6 Months Imprisonment And / Or A Fine

- An offence is committed by a person who:
  - **Without lawful excuse**;
  - Has **anything**:
    - In their **custody**; or
    - Under their **control**;
  - **Intending (offence complete)** to:
    - **Use it**; or
    - **Cause** or **permit another** to use it;
  - To **destroy** or **damage** either:
    - Any **property belonging to another**; or
    - Their **own property** in a way likely to **endanger another's life**.

Learning Point - Intention

- **No destruction or damage of property is necessary** for the offence to be complete.
- The offence is **complete** once the **intention** to **destroy** or **damage property** is formed.

Conditional Intent

- It's enough if the person keeps an article **'just in case'**.

Custody or Control

- The concept of **custody** or **control** is **very wide**.
- Something kept in a **lock up garage** would suffice.

Causing or Permitting Use

- **Allowing** a **friend** to **use** the **article** with the **intent** to **destroy** or **damage property** will also be an offence.

G - Penalty And Removal Notices For Graffiti – Section 43 Anti Social Behaviour Act 2003

- An **authorised officer** from a **Local Authority**;
- May issue a **Penalty Notice**;
- If they have reason to **believe** that a person has **committed a relevant offence** by:
    - ☐ Painting;
    - ☐ Writing;
    - ☐ Soiling; or
    - ☐ Marking;
- A property.

Exam Trip Up

- It is **not permissible** to **issue** such a **notice** if the offence is **aggravated**:
    - ☐ Racially; or
    - ☐ Religiously.

H - Definition Of Contamination Or Interference With Goods – Section 38 Public Order Act 1986
Either Way Offence
Penalty In The Crown Court – 10 Years Imprisonment
Penalty In The Magistrates Court – 6 Months Imprisonment And / Or A Fine

1 - Contamination Or Interference With Goods – Intention Offence

- An offence will be committed by person who:
    - **Intends (offence complete)** to cause either:
        - **Public alarm or anxiety;**
        - **Injury to the public;** or
        - **Economic loss.**
    - By reason of people either:
        - **Shunning goods**; or
        - Taking steps to **avoid goods**;
    - That they have either:
        - **Contaminated or interfered with goods.**
        - **Appearance created that goods have been contaminated or interfered with.**
        - **Placed goods contaminated or interfered with near goods where they are sold, supplied, consumed, or used.**

Exam Trip Up – Focus Upon The Intention

- Two females are sitting in the café at Tesco's having a **private conversation.** For a **joke** one says to the other that she has contaminated the baby food stocked on the shelves with razors.
- Somebody **overhears** the conversation and complains to the manager of the store who takes steps to remove the goods.
- The female would **not commit** the offence as:
    - It was only a joke between friends;
    - She **lacked the mens rea** as she did **not intend** the outcome:
        - **Public alarm or anxiety;**
        - **Injury to the public;** or
        - **Economic loss.**

2 - Contamination Or Interference With Goods - Threats

- It is an offence to make **threats** to cause:
    - **Public alarm**; or
    - **Economic loss**.

Exam Trip Up

- Please note that **'injury'** is **not included** in the making threats offence.

3 - Contamination Or Interference With Goods – Possession

- It is an offence to **possess:**
    - **Materials** for **contaminating;**
    - **Goods** which have been **contaminated.**

Crime
Unit 12: Offences Against The Administration Of Justice

A - Perjury
Indictable Only Offence
Penalty In The Crown Court – 7 Years Imprisonment

1 - Definition Of Perjury – Section 1 Perjury Act 1911

- The offence of **perjury** is committed by:
    - Any person **lawfully sworn** as:
        - A **witness**; or
        - An **interpreter**;
    - In **judicial proceedings**;
    - Who **wilfully (deliberately)**;
    - Makes a **material (important) statement** in the proceedings which they either:
        - **Know to be false**; or
        - **Do not believe to be true.**

2 - Knowledge Checks

- To commit this offence, the defendant must be *lawfully* sworn.
- The **statement** must be **referred** to in **judicial proceedings** (court or tribunal).
- The **statement** can either be given:
    - **Orally**; or
    - In an **affidavit** (sworn statement).
- A **sworn statement** does *not* mean an MG11. This is a separate lesser offence.
- The statement must be **'material to proceedings'** and **not just of passing relevance.**
- To prove the offence it must be established that the defendant either:
    - **Knew** the statement to be **false**; or
    - Did **not believe** it to be **true.**
- **Corroboration** must be provided to prove perjury.

3 - Exam Trip Up – Purpose Of The Corroboration

- The corroboration:
    - **Is required** to **prove** the **falsity** of the statement; and
    - Is **not required** to **prove** either that:
        - The person **made the statement**; or
        - The person **knew it was false** or did **not believe it to be true**.

B – Aiding And Abetting Perjury

If The Principal Offence Is Contrary To Section 1 – Indictable Only Offence
Penalty In The Crown Court – 7 Years Imprisonment

Basic Offence - Either Way Offence
Penalty In The Crown Court – 2 Years Imprisonment
Penalty In The Magistrates Court – 6 Months Imprisonment

1 - Definition Of Aiding And Abetting Perjury – Section 7 Perjury Act 1911

- The offence of **aiding and abetting perjury** will be committed by any person who:
    - Either
        - **Aids;**
        - **Abets;**
        - **Counsels;** or
        - **Procures;**
        - The offence of perjury; or
    - **Incites** the offence of perjury.

C – False Statements
Either Way Offence
Penalty In The Crown Court – 2 Years Imprisonment And / Or A Fine
Penalty In The Magistrates Court – 6 Months Imprisonment And / Or A Fine

1 - Definition Of False Statements – Section 89 Criminal Justice Act 1967

- The offence of **providing a false statement** is committed by:
    - Any person who **wilfully (deliberately);**
    - Provides a **written material (important) statement;**
    - That is **tendered in criminal proceedings;**
    - That they either:
        - **Know to be false;** or
        - **Do not believe to be true.**

D – False Statements On Oath
Either Way Offence
Penalty In The Crown Court – 7 Years Imprisonment And / Or A Fine
Penalty In The Magistrates Court – 6 Months Imprisonment And / Or A Fine

1 - Definition Of False Statements On Oath – Section 2 Perjury Act 1911

- The offence of providing a false statement on oath is committed by:
    - Any person being **required** or **authorised** by **law**;
    - To make any **statement on oath**; and
    - Being **lawfully sworn otherwise than in judicial proceedings**;
    - Who **wilfully (deliberately)**;
    - Makes a **material (important) statement** for that purpose;
    - Which they either:
        - **Know** to be **false**; or
        - **Do not believe** to be **true**.

E – Perverting The Course Of Justice
Indictable Only Offence
Penalty In The Crown Court – Life Imprisonment And / Or A Fine

1 - Definition Of Perverting The Course Of Justice – Common Law Offence

- It is an offence to:
    - Do a **positive act (not an omission)**;
    - That is **intended** to **pervert the course of justice**.

2 - Learning Point

- To prove the offence it must be established that the defendant **intended** to **pervert the course of justice**.
- It will not be adequate to merely imply there was the intention to do so.

3 - When Is It Appropriate To Charge For This Offence?

- The case of *R v Sookoo* [2002] The Times 10th of April, established that a defendant who makes an **unsophisticated attempt to conceal their identity** should **not be charged** with the offence.
- However, if it is shown that there were **serious aggravating features**, for example a lot of police time being wasted, it will be **appropriate to charge**.

4 - Examples Of Perverting The Course Of Justice

- Admitting to a crime to ensure that the true offender escapes justice - *R v Devito* [1975] Crim LR 175
- Making a false allegation - *R v Goodwin* [1989] 11 Cr App R (S) 194;
- Giving another's personal details when reported for an offence - *R v Hurst* [1990] 12 Cr App R (S) 373.

F - Witness And Juror Intimidation
Either Way Offences
Penalty In The Crown Court – 5 Years Imprisonment And / Or A Fine
Penalty In The Magistrates Court – 6 Months Imprisonment And / Or A Fine

- There are **2 separate offences**:
    - Witness and juror intimidation in criminal proceedings;
    - Witness and juror intimidation in other court proceedings (non criminal).

1 – Definition Of Witness And Juror Intimidation In Criminal Proceedings – Section 51 Criminal Justice Public Order Act 1994

- An offence is committed by a person who:
    - **Does** to **another**;
    - An **act** which **intimidates another person**;
- With the **intention** of **intimidating** the **other person**;
- Whom they **know** or **believe** is **assisting** in the **investigation** of an offence as a:
    - **Witness**; or
    - **Juror**; and
- **Intends** to **cause** the **investigation** to be:
    - **Obstructed**;
    - **Perverted**; or
    - **Interfered with.**

    or

- An offence is committed by a person who:
    - Either:
        - **Does**; or
        - **Threatens** to do **to another**;
    - An **act** which **harms them**; and
    - The **act** was either:
        - **Intended** to **harm** them; or
        - **Intended** to make them **fear harm**;

- ☐ **Knowing** or **believing** that either:
    - ■ That **person**; or
    - ■ **Another**;
- ☐ Has either:
    - ■ **Assisted** in the **investigation** of an offence;
    - ■ Has **given evidence**; or
    - ■ Has acted as a **juror**; and
- ☐ Either **does** or **threatens** to do it **because** of their **knowledge** or **belief.**

Exam Trip Up

- ■ The Court of Appeal has confirmed that **'an act that intimidates'** does *not* have to result in **the victim actually being intimidated.**

Exam Trip Up

- ■ Doing **acts to third parties** in order **to intimidate another person** will result in the commission of this offence.

Exam Trip Up

- ■ The case of *DPP v Mills* [1997] QB 300, established that making **threats to another over the telephone** will constitute an offence.

Exam Trip Up

- ■ The offence will be committed where:
    - ☐ A **person** makes a **threat**;
    - ☐ *Via* **a third person**;
    - ☐ **Knowing** that the **threat will be passed on**; and
    - ☐ The ultimate recipient would be intimidated also counts.
- ■ For example - a person in prison asking a mate to carry out the threat on their behalf.

2 – Definition Of Intimidation Of Witnesses In Any Proceedings (Non Criminal) – Section 39 Criminal Justice And Police Act 2001

- ■ It is an offence for person to:
    - ☐ Do an **act**;
    - ☐ **After** the **commencement** of **relevant proceedings (any non criminal court except for the House of Lords);**
    - ☐ Which **intimidates another**; and
    - ☐ Is **intended** to **intimidate** another;

- ☐ Either **knowing** or **believing** the **other is** or **may** be a **witness** in any relevant proceedings; and
- ☐ In doing so **intends** to **cause** the **course of justice** to be:
    - **Obstructed;**
    - **Perverted;** or
    - **Interfered with.**

(i) - Definition Of A Witness

- **Witness** has a very wide meaning which includes:
    - ☐ Anyone who is able to provide:
        - **Information;**
        - A **document;** or
        - **Other thing;**
    - ☐ Which may be **used in evidence** in those proceedings.

(ii) - Learning Points

- This offence relates to **civil proceedings** such as:
    - ☐ A hearing to deal with a **breach of a community order;** or
    - ☐ An application for an **ASBO.**
- It is necessary to show that the **proceedings actually had begun by the time of the offence.**

H – Assisting Offenders
Either Way Offence
Penalty In The Crown Court – 10 Years Imprisonment
Penalty In The Magistrates Court – 6 Months Imprisonment And / Or A Fine

1 - Definition Of Assisting Offenders – Section 4 Criminal Law Act 1967

- An offence will be committed by any person who:
    - ☐ Either:
        - **Knows;** or
        - **Believes;**
    - ☐ **Another** person has **committed an offence;** and
    - ☐ Who **without** either:
        - **Lawful authority;** or
        - **Reasonable excuse;**
    - ☐ Does any **act** with the **intent** to **impede** either their:
        - **Arrest;** or
        - **Prosecution.**

2 - Permission Is Required To Prosecute

- NB – The **DPP's permission** is required to **prosecute**.

Exam Trip Up

- This offence must involve a **positive act**.
- Simply saying or doing nothing will not suffice.

Exam Trip Up

- This offence **cannot be attempted**.

Exam Trip Up

- Mere **suspicion** that somebody had committed an offence would be **inadequate**.
- It is necessary to show that the person either:
    - **Knew**; or
    - **Believed**.

I – Harbouring Offenders
Either Way Offence
Penalty In The Crown Court – 10 Years Imprisonment And / Or A Fine
Penalty In The Magistrates Court – 6 Months Imprisonment And / Or A Fine

1 - Definition Of Harbouring Offenders – Section 22 Criminal Justice Act 1961

- An offence is committed by any person who:
    - **Knowingly**;
    - Either:
        - **Harbours:**
            - An **escapee**; or
            - **Person unlawfully at large**; or
        - Gives **assistance** with the **intent** to:
            - **Prevent**;
            - **Hinder**; or
            - **Interfere**
        - with their **arrest**.

J - Escaping – Common Law Offence
Indictable Only Offence
Penalty In The Crown Court – Unlimited Penalty

- It is a offence to **escape from legal custody**.

Exam Trip Ups

- The case of *R v Moss and Harte* [1986] 82 Cr App R 116, established that this offence will **not be committed** by a prisoner who **escapes while in transit** either to or from prison.

- The person must have been held **lawfully** either:

  ☐ **Before** their conviction; or

  ☐ **After** their conviction.

- It was established in the case of *E v DPP* [2002] Crim LR 737, that the determination of whether a person was **'in custody'** is a **question of fact** for the jury to decide.

K – Assisting Escape
Indictable Only Offence
Penalty In The Crown Court – 10 Years Imprisonment

1 - Definition Of Assisting Escape – Section 39 Prison Act 1952

- An offence is committed by any person who either:

  ☐ **Aids** a prisoner to **escape**; or

  ☐ **Conveys** anything inside or outside of prison with a view to it coming into the possession of a prisoner.

Exam Trip Up

- The case of *R v Moss and Harte* [1986] 82 Cr App R 116, established that this offence will **not be committed** by a prisoner who **escapes while in transit** either to or from prison.

L – Wasting Police Time
Summary Only Offence
Penalty In The Magistrates Court – 6 Months Imprisonment And / Or A Fine

1 - Definition Of Wasting Police Time – Section 5 Criminal Law Act 1967

- It is an offence to:

  ☐ **Knowingly**;

  ☐ Make a **false report**;

  ☐ To *any* **person** which either:

    - Tends to **show** that:

      ☐ An **offence** has been **committed**;

      ☐ **They have material information about a police enquiry**; or

    - Would give rise to **apprehension for the safety** of:

      ☐ **Persons**; or

      ☐ **Property**.

2 - Permission Is Required To Prosecute

- The **permission** of the **DPP** is required to **prosecute**.

General Police Duties
Unit 1: Police

A - Policing Services and Jurisdiction

1 - Home Office Police Services - Section 30 Police Act 1996

- A member of a police force should have all the powers and privileges of a constable throughout England and Wales and the adjacent UK waters.

Exam Trip Up

- The Home Affairs Committee (1999) recommended that probationer constables are not attested until they have completed 6 months service.

Exam Trip Up

- The Police Reform Act 2002 removed the nationality bar that formerly prevented non-UK and Commonwealth citizens from joining the police.

Exam Trip Up

- Special Constables are appointed under section 27 and are required to be attested in the same way as Constables.

Exam Trip Up

- The Police Regulations 2003 require officers to provide a sample of hair or saliva in order to allow a DNA profile to be obtained.

2 - Serious Organised Crime Agency - Chapter 1 of the Serious Organised Crime & Police Act 2005

- The **Serious Organised Crime Agency (SOCA)** may:
    - **Institute criminal proceedings** in England and Wales or Northern Ireland;
    - Act in **support** of any activities of a **police force or law enforcement agency**, at the **request** of the **Chief Officer** or the **agency**;
    - Enter into other arrangements for **co-operating** with **bodies** or **people (UK or elsewhere)** which it considers appropriate in connection with the exercise of its relevant functions.

The Function Of The Serious and Organised Crime Agency

- The function of the **Serious Organised Crime Agency (SOCA)** is to:
    - **Prevent** and **detect** serious organised crime; and
    - **Contribute** to the **reduction** of such crime in other ways and to the **mitigation** of its **consequences.**
- SOCA also has a key function in relation to the **gathering, storing, analysing** and **disseminating** of **information** relevant to:
    - The **prevention, detection, investigation** or **prosecution** of offences; or
    - The **reduction of crime** in other ways or the **mitigation** of its **consequences.**

Serious and Organised Crime Agency - Agents or Constables?

- SOCA will **not** appoint its **own Constables**.
- SOCA's members can be **endorsed** with the **powers of a Constable**.
- SOCA is **not** a **police force**.
- Constables can be **seconded** to SOCA.
- Where a seconded officer does **not resign** from their "home" police service they will be treated as having been **suspended** from that office **until they return** to their "home" service.

3 - Special Constables - Section 30 Police Act 1996

- A Special Constable shall have **all the powers and privileges of a Constable:**
    - ☐ In the **police area** for which they are appointed; and
    - ☐ Where the **boundary** of that area includes the **coast**, in the **adjacent UK waters.**

Exam Trip Up

- Special constables have **jurisdiction** in **areas contiguous**, i.e. **next to their own force**.
- In the case of Special Constables in the City of London Police this includes areas contiguous to the Metropolitan Police district.

Exam Trip Up

- Special Constables have **all the powers and privileges of constables in other police areas** to which they are **sent** as part of a **mutual aid scheme.**

Exam Trip Up

- Special Constables are **subject to** the **complaints and conduct framework.**

B - Police and Trade Union Membership

- Where a person:
    - ☐ Was a **member** of a **trade union;**
    - ☐ **Before** becoming a **member** of the **police service;**
    - ☐ They may, with the **consent** of the **Chief Officer** of the police;
    - ☐ **Continue** to be a **member** of that **trade union** during their service.

Exam Trip Up

- If a constable who has previously been a trade union member but **relinquished that membership** prior to being attested as a constable then that person is **forbidden by law** from becoming a union member.

C - The Conduct, Complaints And Efficiency Framework Governing Unsatisfactory Performance - Police [Efficiency] Regulations 1999

1 - To Whom Does The Framework Apply?

- The framework applies to officers up to and including the rank of Chief Superintendent.

2 - To Whom Does The Framework Not Apply?

- The framework does not apply to:
    - ☐ Senior Officers (higher than C/Supt.);
    - ☐ Probationers;
    - ☐ Cadets; and
    - ☐ Civilian Police Staff.

3 - Why Is The Framework Necessary?

- The framework is necessary to:
    - ☐ To **address** issues of perceived **poor performance**.
    - ☐ Emphasis on **early identification of problems.**
    - ☐ Followed by **discussion** and **agreement** on **action** to be taken.
    - ☐ The officer is provided with an **opportunity to improve**.
    - ☐ **Monitoring period** followed by **review of performance** and **further agreement** and **action** as appropriate.
    - ☐ The final stage may involve **sanctions**, but the process is **ultimately developmental.**

4 - The Personnel involved in the Police [Efficiency] Regulations 1999 Process Governing Unsatisfactory Performance?

- **The Member**
    - ☐ The member of a Police Force in respect of whom proceedings are, or are proposed to be taken.

- **The Reporting Officer**
    - ☐ The person having immediate responsibility for the member concerned.
    - ☐ This person may be a Police Officer or a Civilian Member of Staff.

- **The Countersigning Officer**
    - ☐ The person who usually supervises the Reporting Officer.
    - ☐ This person may be a Police Officer or a Civilian Member of Staff.

Exam Trip Up

- While sworn officers and civilians may act as **reporting officers** and **countersigning officers**, when this function is carried out by a **civilian** they may only implement the various stages where the members **attendance** is in question – **as opposed to a purely performance related issues.**

Exam Trip Up

- The efficiency regulations **apply to SOCA agents.**

Exam Trip Up

- There is **no requirement** for the **Countersigning Officer** to have **direct responsibility** for the **member** concerned.

5 - The Procedure For Dealing With Unsatisfactory Performance

(i) - The Initial Process - Regulation 4

- **Reporting Officer** opines that members performance is **unsatisfactory** by:
    - ☐ **Internal observation** of the member; or
    - ☐ A **report** from a member of the **public.**
- If the matter relates to a **single event** or a stand alone act then **advice** may be given to the member.
- If a **course of conduct** or **pattern** is evident then **formal action** may be required.
- **Assistance** and **time** should be given to poorly performing member to **assist** in their **development.**
- If **improvement** in performance is noted then **no further action** may be taken.
- If **no improvement** is seen then the commencement of the **formal procedures** may be initiated.

(ii) - First Interview Procedure – Regulation 5

- The **Reporting Officer** sends a **notice in writing** to the member:
    - ☐ To attend at a **time** and **place** for an **interview** with either;
        - **Reporting Officer;**
        - **Countersigning Officer.**
    - ☐ Documenting the **reasons why** their **performance** is considered **unsatisfactory;**
    - ☐ Advising them that they may be **represented** by a **friend** (member of any police service).
- The **notice** will also be **sent to** the **Countersigning Officer.**

Exam Trip Up

- If a senior officer attends or is otherwise involved in the first interview then they are barred from appearing on a later inefficiency panel.

(iii) - The First Interview – Regulation 6

- The **Interviewing Officer** (Reporting or Countersigning Officer) shall:
    - ☐ **Explain** the **reasons** why the members performance is deemed **unsatisfactory;**
    - ☐ **Listen** to **representations** (by the **Member** or their **Friend** present);
- Then they shall:
    - ☐ **Inform** them in what respect they are considered unsatisfactory **(performance or attendance);**
    - ☐ **Warn** them of the **action required**; and
    - ☐ That the **action** must be **achieved** within a **reasonable time (3 - 6 months).**

(iv) - Action To Be Taken By The Interviewing Officer Following The First Interview – Regulation 7

- The Interviewing Officer shall, not later than **7 days** after the conclusion of the first Interview:
    - ☐ Prepare a **written record** of the interview; and
    - ☐ **Send a copy** to:
        - **The Member** (and their **Friend** if applicable) informing them that they may not later then **7 days** after the date on which the copy is **received by them:**
            - ☐ Submit **written comments**; or
            - ☐ Include **no comment,**
        - The **Senior Manager** (supervisor of the Countersigning Officer)
        - The **Personnel Officer** (police officer / civilian with HR responsibility); and
        - Either:
            - ☐ The **Reporting Officer** (if the **interview** was **conducted** by the **Countersigning Officer);**
            - ☐ The **Countersigning Officer** (if the **interview** was **conducted** by the **Reporting Officer).**

Exam Trip Up

- The **written record** produced by the **Interviewing Officer** need **not** be **verbatim account** of the first interview.

Exam Trip Up

- The **7 day period** to respond to the above record **begins** when the member **receives the copy** of the record.

Exam Trip Up

- The **Interviewing Officer** may make **recommendations** that the **member seeks assistance** in relation to any **welfare** or **health issues** raised.

Exam Trip Up

- If the member has not attended a first interview in relation to attendance issues, then a further written notice must be issued in accordance with reg. 7 (1A) (a) and (b) if the interviewing officer is satisfied that the members attendance is unsatisfactory. **In essence this is like having the first interview ex-parte.**

Exam Trip Up

- When the member is required to attend a **second interview** due to a **lack of progress** or improvement, then this further interview can **only relate to the behaviour that was subject to scrutiny in the first interview**.

(v) - Action To Be Taken Following A Failure To Improve By The Member – Regulation 8

- Where the **Reporting Officer** is of the opinion that:
    - A member, who had **previously been warned** that they were **required to improve** their **performance** or **attendance**;
    - Has **failed** to make a **significant improvement**;
- The **Reporting Officer** may **refer** the case to the **Countersigning Officer**; and
- The **Countersigning Officer**, may, after **consulting** with the **Personnel Officer**, require the member concerned to **attend a second interview.**

Exam Trip Up

- As in the first interview, the **power** for a **civilian manager** to require attendance at the further interview is limited to **attendance issues only**.

(vi) - Notification Requiring Attendance At A Second Interview – Regulation 9 Notices

- The countersigning officer shall **send a notice** to the **member** concerned:
    - **Requiring** them to **attend an interview** at a specified **time** and **place** with:
        - The **Countersigning Officer**; and
        - The **Personnel Officer**.
    - Stating:
        - The **reasons** why their **performance** or **attendance** is considered **unsatisfactory**; and
        - That **further action** will be **considered** in the light of the interview;
        - That they may be **represented** by a **friend**.
- The **notice** must also be **served** on:
    - The **Reporting Officer**;
    - The **Senior Manager**; and
    - The **Personnel Officer**.

(vii) - The Second Interview – Regulation 10

- The interview shall be **conducted** by:
    - ☐ The **Countersigning Officer**; and
    - ☐ The **Personnel Officer.**

- The **Countersigning Officer** shall:
    - ☐ **Explain why** the **Reporting Officer** is of the **opinion** that the member concerned has **failed to make a sufficient improvement;** and
    - ☐ Provide the **member** or their **friend** with the **opportunity** (one or both) to make **representations** in response.

- If the **Countersigning Officer** is satisfied that the **performance** or **attendance** is **unsatisfactory** during the period specified (**3 - 6 months**) then they shall:
    - ☐ **Inform** the **member** concerned in what **respect** his **performance** or **attendance** is considered **unsatisfactory**;
    - ☐ **Warn** the **member** that an **improvement** is **required**;
    - ☐ **Inform** the member of any **specific action** which they are **required to take** to **achieve** such an **improvement;** and
    - ☐ **Warn** the member concerned that, **if sufficient improvement is not made within a reasonable period** specified, they may be **required to attend** an **inefficiency hearing** at which the officers conducting the hearing will have the power if appropriate, to require the member to:
        - **Resign from the force;** or
        - **Order a reduction in rank.**

(viii) - Action To Be Taken Following The Second Interview – Regulation 11

- The **Countersigning Officer** shall, not later that **7 days** after the conclusion of the second interview:
    - ☐ In **consultation** with **Personnel Officer** - **prepare a written record** of matter discussed; and
    - ☐ **Send** a **copy** to the **member** and their **friend** (if applicable) in writing:
        - If a warning was given, confirming the **terms of the warning**; and
        - Informing him that they may no later that **7 days** after the date on which the copy is received by them either:
            - ☐ **Submit written comments;** or
            - ☐ **Indicate** that they have no **such comments,**

- If the **Countersigning Officer** receives any written **comments** in **response** - they shall ensure that they are **retained** with the record of the interview.

- The **Countersigning Officer** shall **send** a **copy** of the **interview record** and any **written comments** made by the member concerned to the:
    - ☐ **Reporting Officer;**
    - ☐ **Personnel Officer;**
    - ☐ **Senior Manager.**

Exam Trip Up

- There is **no need** for the **written record** to be a **verbatim account**.

Exam Trip Up

- The written record must be made in **consultation** with the **Personnel Officer.**

Exam Trip Up

- Where the officers **attendance is in issue**, the process above is, in effect, a **repeat performance of the 1st interview** and the hearing can be heard ex-parte.

(ix) - Assessment Of Performance Following The Second Interview – Regulation 12

- Not later than **14 days** after the date on which the period specified ends:
  - The **Countersigning Officer** shall, in **consultation** with the **Reporting Officer**, **assesses** the **performance** or **attendance** of the member concerned during that period; and
  - The **Countersigning Officer** shall **inform** the **member in writing whether** they are of the opinion that there has been **sufficient improvement** in that period.

(x) - Action To Be Taken When There Has Not Been A Satisfactory Improvement In Performance By The Member - Regulation 12

- If the **Countersigning Officer** is of the opinion that there has **not been a sufficient improvement**, the member concerned shall be **informed in writing** that he **may** be required to **attend**, at a time (not sooner that 21 days (not later than 56 days)), an **inefficiency hearing** to consider their performance.

Exam Trip Up

- An assessment must relate to the members performance or attendance during that assessment period.

Exam Trip Up

- If the **Countersigning Officer** is of the **opinion** that there has **not been a sufficient improvement**, they **must refer** the case to the **Senior Manager**, who then has the **discretion** to **direct an inefficiency hearing.**

(xi) - The Inefficiency Hearing – Regulation 13

- The **Personnel Officer** shall, not less that **21 days** before the date fixed for the hearing, **send** a **notice** to the **member** concerned:
  - **Requiring** them to **attend an inefficiency hearing** at a specified **time** and **place;**
  - Stating the **reasons why** their **performance** or **attendance** is considered **unsatisfactory;**

- ☐ Informing them that they may be represented by:
    - Counsel;
    - A solicitor; or
    - A friend.
- ☐ **Warning** that **sanctions** are available to officers conducting the hearing including:
    - Dismissal;
    - A requirement to resign; or
    - A reduction in rank.
- **Informing** the member that they **may call witnesses** to give evidence on their behalf - if within **7 days** of the **hearing** they give **notice** to the **Personnel Officer**.

Exam Trip Up

- The responsibility for **sending the notice** falls on the **Personnel Officer**.
- The notice must be sent (not necessarily received) not less than 21 days before the hearing.

Exam Trip Up

- The member **must** be afforded **legal representation** if the **sanctions** available to the hearing include:
    - ☐ **Dismissal**;
    - ☐ **Reduction in rank**; or
    - ☐ **Resignation**.
- If these **sanctions are not applicable** (e.g. only contemplating a fine, caution, etc) then there is **no requirement** for the member to be **legally represented**.

(xii) - Who Conducts The Inefficiency Hearing? – Regulation 14

Officers Below The Rank Of Superintendent:

Ordinarily:

Provincial Force	Assistant Chief Constable and 2 Superintendents
Metropolitan Force	Commissioner and 2 Superintendents
City of London Force	Commissioner and 2 Superintendents

If The Matter Arises From The Independent Police Complaints Commission:

Provincial Force	Assistant Chief Constable and 1 Superintendent and 1 Police Authority
Metropolitan Force	Commissioner and 1 Superintendent and 1 Police Authority

Officers Of The Rank Of Superintendent or Chief Superintendent:

Provincial Force	Assistant Chief Constable of own force and 2 external Assistant Chief Constables
Metropolitan Force	Chief Commander of own area and 2 Commanders from other areas
City Of London Force	Commander or Assistant Commissioner and 2 Assistant Chief Constables or Metropolitan Commanders

(xiii) - Documents Available To An Inefficiency Hearing – Regulation 14

- As soon as the **Chief Officer of Police** has been appointed as chairman, the **Personnel Officer** shall arrange for a **copy** of any **documentation:**
    - ☐ Which was available to the **Interviewing Officer** in relation to the **first interview;**
    - ☐ Which was available to the **Countersigning Officer** in relation to the **second interview;**
- To be **made available** to the **chairman;** and
- A **copy** of any such document shall be **sent** to the **member** concerned.

Exam Trip Up

- The **inefficiency hearing** will be held **in private** but may be held in **public** if **both** the **chair** and the **member agree.**

(xiv) - Postponement And Adjournment Of Inefficiency Hearings – Regulation 15

- The chair may **adjourn** or **postpone** an inefficiency hearing due to any:
    - ☐ An additional period of assessment;
    - ☐ Non-attendance for good reasons; or
    - ☐ Ill health.

(xv) - The Finding Of The Inefficiency Hearing – Regulation 16

- The chairman may at the conclusion of the hearing either:
    - ☐ **Defer** their **decision**; or
    - ☐ **State** their **finding.**

- If the performance is **unsatisfactory** they must **within 3 days send a copy of the findings** to :
    - ☐ The member;
    - ☐ The Senior Manager; and
    - ☐ The Personnel Officer.

- The copy sent to the member concerned shall be accompanied by a **notice in writing** informing them of their **right to request a review** under Regulation 19.

Exam Trip Up

- The decision need not be unanimous and may be based on a simple majority. – This will **not** be **indicated** in the finding.

(xvi) - The Sanctions – Regulation 17

- The powers of the chair include:
    - ☐ **Resignation;**
    - ☐ **Reduction in rank;** and
    - ☐ **Warning.**

Exam Trip Up

- Any **requirement** for the member to **resign cannot take effect before one month after the notice of the finding was received by the member.**

Exam Trip Up

- If the member has **not resigned by the required date**, then they will **automatically be dismissed.**

Exam Trip Up

- Any **reduction in rank** must take effect **"immediately"**.

Exam Trip Up

- Any **reduction in rank** will be **accompanied** by a **warning** that **sufficient improvement is still required within a specified period.**

(xvii) - The Review – Regulation 19

- A **request** for a **review** must be made:
    - ☐ To the **Reviewing Officer**;
    - ☐ **In writing**;
    - ☐ Within **14 days** of the date on which a **copy of the decision is received** by the member concerned;
    - ☐ **Unless** this period is **extended** by the **Reviewing Officer**.
- The **request** for a review shall state:
    - ☐ The **grounds** on which the review is requested; and
    - ☐ **Whether a meeting is requested**.

Exam Trip Up

- The review can take place after any of the 3 sanctions.

Exam Trip Up

- The request will be made to:
    - ☐ The **Chief Officer of Police** (regional forces); or
    - ☐ The **Assistant Commissioner** (Metropolitan force).
- The purpose of the review can be to consider:
    - ☐ The **finding**;
    - ☐ The **sanction**; or
    - ☐ **Both**.

Exam Trip Up

- The Reviewing Officer may:
    - ☐ **Confirm** the decision;
    - ☐ Impose a **different sanction**;
- They **cannot impose** a **more onerous sanction**.

D - Misconduct In A Public Office – Common Law
Indictable Only Offence
Penalty - Imprisonment At Large

- The case of *R v Wyatt* [1705] 1 SALK 380 established that:
    - It is a misdemeanour in **common law**;
    - For the holder of a **Public Office**;
    - To do anything that amounts to a:
        - **Malfeasance;** or
        - **Culpable misfeasance.**
- **Malfeasance** – requires some degree of wrongful motive or intention.
- **Culpable Misfeasance** – requires some form of wilful neglect of duty.

Exam Trip Up

- There must be some **connection** between the alleged **misconduct** and the **exercise** of the **public office**.
- Misconduct whilst off duty would not be covered by this offence.

E - Complaint and Conduct Matters - The Code of Conduct Schedule 1

- **Honesty and Integrity**
    - The public must have faith in the honesty and integrity of the police.
    - Officers should:
        - Be open and truthful in their dealings;
        - Avoid being improperly beholden to any person or institution; and
        - Discharge their duties with integrity.

- **Fairness and Impartiality**
    - The police have a responsibility to act with fairness and impartiality in all their dealings with the public and colleagues.

- **Politeness and Tolerance**
    - Officers should treat all persons with courtesy and respect, avoiding abusive or deriding attitudes or behaviour.
    - Officers must avoid:
        - Favouritism of an individual or group;
        - All forms of harassment, victimisation or discrimination; and
        - Overbearing conduct to a colleague, particularly to one junior in rank or service.

- **Use of Force and Abuse of Authority**

    ☐ Officers must never:

    - Knowingly use more force than is reasonable; or
    - Abuse their authority.

- **Performance of Duties**

    ☐ Police officers should be diligent and conscientious in their duties.

    ☐ Officers should attend work promptly when rostered for duty.

    ☐ If absent through sickness or injury, they should avoid activities which hinder their prompt return to such duty.

- **Lawful Orders**

    ☐ The police service is a disciplined body.

    ☐ Unless there is good and sufficient cause to do otherwise, officers must obey all lawful orders and abide by the provisions of Police Regulations.

    ☐ Officers should support their colleagues in the execution of their lawful duties, and oppose any improper behaviour.

- **Confidentiality**

    ☐ Information which comes into possession of the police service should be treated as confidential.

    ☐ This information should not be used for personal benefit and should not be disclosed to other parties, unless in the proper course of police duty.

    ☐ Officers should respect, as confidential, information about force policy and operations unless authorised to disclose it in their duties.

- **Criminal Offences**

    ☐ Officers must report any proceedings for a criminal offence taken against them.

    ☐ Conviction of a criminal offence or the administration of a caution may of itself result in further action being taken.

- **Property**

    ☐ Officers must exercise care to prevent the loss or damage to property (excluding their own property but including police property).

- **Sobriety**

    ☐ Officers must be sober whilst on duty. Officers should not consume alcohol whilst on duty unless authorised to do so or it becomes necessary for the proper discharge of police duty.

- **Appearance**
  - ☐ Officers should always be well turned out, clean and tidy whilst on duty, unless on duty which by its nature dictates otherwise.

- **General Conduct**
  - ☐ Whether on or off duty, police officers should not behave in a way which is likely to bring discredit upon the police service.

General Police Duties
Unit 2: Extending the Policing Family

Police Community Support Officers – Part 1 of Schedule 4 of the Police Reform Act 2002

- Police Community Support Officers (PCSO's) possess powers to:

Paragraph 1	Issue fixed penalty notices (FPN)
Paragraph 1A	Require a person's name and address
Paragraph 2	Detain
Paragraph 3	Require the name and address of a person acting in an anti-social manner
Paragraph 3A	Require a person's name and address: ROAD TRAFFIC OFFENCES
Paragraph 4A/4B	Disperse groups and remove young persons to a place of residence
Paragraph 5	Powers relating to alcohol consumption in designated public places
Paragraph 6	Confiscate alcohol
Paragraph 7	Confiscate tobacco
Paragraph 7A	Search and seizure powers:- alcohol and tobacco
Paragraph 7B	Seize and detain:- controlled drugs
Paragraph 8	Entry to save life or limb or prevent serious damage to property
Paragraph 8A	Entry to investigate licensing offences
Paragraph 9	Seize vehicles used to cause alarm
Paragraph 10	Deal with abandoned vehicles
Paragraph 11	Stop vehicles for testing
Paragraph 11B	Stop cycles
Paragraph 12	Control traffic for purposes of escorting an exceptional load
Paragraph 13	Carry out road checks

Paragraph 14	Cordoned areas
Paragraph 15	Stop and search in authorised areas - Section 44 Terrorism Act 2000
Paragraph 15A	Photographing of persons arrested, detained or given FPN

Investigating Officers – Part 2 of Schedule 4 of the Police Reform Act 2002

- **Investigating Officers** possess powers in relation to:

Paragraph 15 & 16	Safeguard applications for warrants and the execution of warrants
Paragraph 16	Search warrants
Paragraph 16A	Stolen goods warrants
Paragraph 16B	Misuse of Drugs Act 1971
Paragraph 17	Access to excluded and special procedure material
Paragraph 18	Entry and search after arrest
Paragraph 19	General power of seizure
Paragraph 20	Access and copying in the case of things seized by constables
Paragraph 21	Arrest a person at a police station for another offence
Paragraph 22	Transfer persons into the custody of investigating officer
Paragraph 22A	Powers in respect of detained persons
Paragraph 23	Require arrested person to account for certain matters (special warnings)
Paragraph 24	Extended powers of seizure
Paragraph 24A	Persons accompanying an investigating officer

Community Safety Accreditation Schemes – Accredited Employees - Schedule 5 Police Reform Act 2002

- **Accredited Employees** possess powers to:

Paragraph 1	Issue a fixed penalty notice (FPN)
Paragraph 2	Require the giving of a persons name and address
Paragraph 3	Require giving of the name and address of person acting in an anti-social manner
Paragraph 3A	Name and address – road traffic offences
Paragraph 4	Powers relating to alcohol consumption to designated public places
Paragraph 5	Confiscate alcohol
Paragraph 6	Confiscate tobacco
Paragraph 7	Deal with abandoned vehicles
Paragraph 8	Stop vehicles for testing
Paragraph 8A	Stop cycles
Paragraph 8B	Control traffic
Paragraph 9	Control traffic for purposes of escorting an exceptional load
Paragraph 9A	Photographing of persons given a FPN

General Police Duties
Unit 3: Human Rights

Convention Rights

A - Legitimate Limitations of Convention Rights

- Any **limitation** on a **convention right** must be:
    - ☐ Prescribed by **law**;
    - ☐ Intended to achieve a **legitimate objective**;
    - ☐ **Proportionate** to the end that it achieves.

1 - Prescribed By Law

- Any **powers** limiting convention rights must be **authorised by law**.

    For example - The ability to curtail an individual's right to privacy may be curtailed pursuant to the provisions embodied within the *Regulation of Investigatory Powers Act 2000*.

2 - Intended To Achieve A Legitimate Objective

- Any limitation must achieve a **legitimate goal**, as set out in the European Convention of Human Rights (ECHR) itself.

    For example - The legitimate goal of the prevention of crime.

3 - The Means Used Must Be Proportionate To The End Achieved

- The limitation adopted must be **proportionate** to the crime that it seeks to prevent.
- Put simply a sledgehammer should not be used to crack a nut.

B – The Definition Of Public Authorities Acting Unlawfully - Section 6 Human Rights Act 1998

- It is **unlawful**;
- For a **public authority**;
- To **act** in a way that is **incompatible** with a **Convention right**.

The Definition of A Public Authority - Section 6 Human Rights Act 1998

- A **public authority** includes:
    - A **court**;
    - A **tribunal**;
    - **Police**;
    - **Fire service**;
    - **Ambulance service**; and
    - Any **person** or **body** whose **functions** are of a **public nature**.

NB - **Not Parliament** or persons exercising functions in connection with **Parliamentary proceedings**.

Which Victims Can Bring Proceedings? – Section 7 Human Rights Act 1998

- **Victim**s eligible to bring proceedings include:
    - Any:
        - **Person**; or
        - **Organisation**;
    - That **believes** that:
        - A **public authority**;
        - Has acted **unlawfully**;
        - By **breaching** their **Convention rights**; and
    - Either:
        - They have **been directly affected** by the behaviour; or
        - They are **at risk of being directly affected** by the behaviour.

Time Limits Within Which A Victim Must Commence Proceedings - Section 7 Human Rights Act 1998

- The victim must **commence proceedings** either:
    - Within **1 year** of the act complained of; or
    - A **longer period** if:
        - The court considers it **equitable**;
        - Having regard to **all the circumstances**.

C - The Convention Rights

- The **convention rights** include:

    - Article 2 — Life
    - Article 3 — Freedom from torture
    - Article 4 — Freedom from slavery and forced labour
    - Article 5 — Liberty and security
    - Article 6 — Fair trial
    - Article 7 — No punishment without a crime
    - Article 8 — Private life
    - Article 9 — Freedom of thought
    - Article 10 — Freedom of expression
    - Article 11 — Freedom of assembly and association
    - Article 12 — Marriage
    - Article 13 — Effective remedy
    - Article 14 — Prohibition of discrimination
    - Article 15 — Derogation in times of emergency
    - Article 16 — Restrictions on political activities of aliens

The Right To Life – Article 2

- A **life may only be taken** by:

    - The **execution** of a **court order**;

    - The use of **force** which is **no more** than **absolutely necessary**:
        - To **defend** a person from **unlawful violence**;
        - To effect a **lawful arrest**;
        - To **prevent escape** from **lawful detention**;
        - To **lawfully quell** a:
            - **Riot**; or
            - **Insurrection**.

Freedom From Torture – Article 3

- No one shall be subjected to:

    - **Torture**; or

    - **Inhuman** or **degrading**:
        - **Treatment**; or
        - **Punishment**.

For example: **Interrogation techniques** such as **sleep deprivation, exposure to continuous loud noise** and **forcing suspects to adopt uncomfortable postures** has been held to be **degrading and inhuman**.

Freedom From Slavery And Forced Labour – Article 4

- **No one** shall be:
    - Held in **slavery** or **servitude**; or
    - Required to perform **forced** or **compulsory labour**.
- The following will **not contravene** the article:
    - Work done in the ordinary course of **detention**;
    - **Military service**;
    - **Service** exacted during an **emergency**; or
    - Work done as a **civic obligation**.

The Right To Liberty And Security – Article 5

- Everyone has the **right to liberty and security of person**.
- The **right to liberty and security** will **not be contravened** by:
    - A **lawful arrest**; and
    - Periods of **lawful detention**.

The Right To A Fair Trial – Article 6

- Everyone is entitled to:
    - A **fair** and **public hearing**;
    - Held within a **reasonable time**;
    - By an **independent** and **impartial tribunal** established by law.

No Punishment Without A Crime – Article 7

- It is **not possible** to:
    - Pass **retrospective legislation**; or
    - Impose a **heavier penalty** than that proscribed by law at the time the offence was committed.

The Right To A Private Life – Article 8

- People are entitled to **respect** for their:
    - **Private life**;
    - **Family life**;
    - **Home**; and
    - **Correspondence**.

- The privacy rights may be **curtailed** if it is in the **interests** of:
    - National security;
    - Public safety;
    - The economic wellbeing of the country;
    - Prevention of disorder or crime;
    - Protection of health or morals; or
    - Protection of the rights or freedoms of others.

Freedom Of Thought – Article 9

- Persons have the right to freedom of:
    - **Thought;**
    - **Conscience;**
    - **Religion.**

- The rights can only be **curtailed** if:
    - **Proscribed by law**; and
    - Are **necessary** in a democratic society in the **interests** of:
        - **Public safety;**
        - **Protection** of:
            - **Public order;**
            - **Health**; or
            - **Morals;**
    - For the **protection** of the **rights** and **freedoms** of **others.**

Freedom Of Expression – Article 10

- Persons have the right to the freedom of:
    - **Expression;**
    - **Opinion;**
    - **Information;** and
    - **Ideas.**

- The rights may only be **curtailed** if:
    - ☐ **Proscribed by law;** and
    - ☐ **Necessary** in a **democratic society** for:
        - National security;
        - Public safety;
        - Prevention of crime and disorder;
        - Protection of health or moral;
        - Protection of the reputation of others;
        - Preventing disclosure of confidential material;
    - ☐ Maintaining the authority and impartiality of the judiciary.

Freedom Of Assembly And Association – Article 11

- Everyone has the right to freedom of:
    - ☐ **Peaceful assembly**; and
    - ☐ **Association with others.**

- The rights may only be **curtailed** if:
    - ☐ Proscribed by law; and
    - ☐ It is necessary in a democratic society in the interests of:
        - National security;
        - Public safety;
        - Prevention of crime and disorder;
        - Protection of health and morals;
        - Protection of the rights and freedoms of others.

- The following can be **exempt:**
    - ☐ Armed forces;
    - ☐ Police; or
    - ☐ Persons involved in the administration of the state.

The Right To Marry – Article 12

- **Men** and **women** of **marriageable age** have the right to:
    - ☐ **Marry;** and
    - ☐ **Found a family.**

Prohibition Of Discrimination In Convention Rights – Article 14

- Everybody is entitled to **equal access** to the provisions of the **ECHR** regardless of their:
    - ☐ Sex;
    - ☐ Race;
    - ☐ Colour;
    - ☐ Language;
    - ☐ Religion;
    - ☐ Political or other opinion;
    - ☐ National or social origin;
    - ☐ Association with a national minority;
    - ☐ Property;
    - ☐ Birth; or
    - ☐ Other status.

Derogation In Times Of Emergency – Article 15

- A state can **derogate** from some of its **qualified obligations** under the convention during:
    - ☐ **Times of war;**
    - ☐ **Public emergencies** that threaten the life of the nation.

- A state can only derogate from article 2 (right to life) in relation to deaths during a lawful act of war.

- From articles 3 (torture), 4 (slavery & forced labour) or 7 (no punishment without a crime) can never be derogated from even in times of war.

General Police Duties
Unit 4: Police Powers & Trespass Offences

A - Section 4 Police Road Checks – Section 4 PACE 1984

1 –Stopping Vehicles

- It is possible to **stop vehicles** using section **163 Road Traffic Act 1988.**
    - A **Constable** or **PCSO** *must* be **in uniform** to use the Road Traffic Act 1988 power.
    - They may **stop:**
        - **All vehicles;** or
        - **Vehicles selected by specified criterion** e.g. blue vehicles, 4 male occupants, transit vans etc;
        - Within a **specified locality.**

2 – Permitted Reasons For Conducting The Road Check

- A **road check** may be conducted for any one of **4 reasons.** To **identify a person** who:
    - **Intends** to commit an **indictable offence;**
    - Has **committed** an **indictable offence;**
    - Is a **witnesses** to an **indictable offence;**
    - Is **unlawfully at large.**

Learning Point

- **3 out of the 4 reasons** are related to **indictable offences.**
- Remember: "P.P.W.":
    - **Pre** - P
    - **Post;** and - P
    - **Witness;** - W
    - To an **indictable offence.**
- Plus a person **unlawfully at large.**

Exam Trip Up

- For *P.P.W.* the officer's state of mind must be that of reasonable *belief.*
- For *unlawfully at large* the officer's state of mind must be that of reasonable *suspicion.*

3 - Authority For Section 4 Police Road Checks – Section 4(3) PACE 1984

The General Rule

- A **Superintendent** must authorise the road check.

The Exception To The General Rule – Emergencies

- In cases of **urgency - any officer** can authorise a road check.
- If so they must **as soon as practicable**:
    - Make a **written record** of the **time** at which **authorisation** is given;
    - **Inform** a **Superintendent**; and
    - **Superintendent** *may* **authorise** the road check **in writing**.

4 - Contents Of The Written Authorisation – Section 4(13) PACE 1984

- The **written authorisation** should include the:
    - **Name of Authorising Officer;**
    - **Purpose** of road check;
    - **Locality** of the road check.

5 - The Duration of the Authorisation – Section 4(11) PACE 1984

- The **authorisation period** is **7 days**.
- This period is **renewable** (not exceeding **7 days**).
- The authorisation may be for a:
    - **Continuous period;** or
    - **Specified time.**

6 - Notice Requirements – The Right To Request A Written Statement – Section 4(15) PACE 1984

- A **written statement** confirming the fact that the search took place;
- May be **requested** by **persons stopped**;
- For a period of up to **12 months** from date of the search.

B - Stop & Search – Section 60 CJPOA 1994

1 – Purpose Of The Search Power

- The **purpose** of the power is to:
    - **Prevent** either:
        - **Serious violence**; or
        - The **widespread carrying of weapons**;
    - That might lead to **serious injury**;
    - By empowering the police to **disarm** offenders.

2 – Who Provides The Authorisation To Stop & Search – Section 60(1) CJPOA 1994

- **Authorisation** must:
    - Be provided by an **Inspector**;
    - Who **reasonably believes** that **serious violence** will **result** if power **not authorised**.
- A **Superintendent** must:
    - Be **informed as soon as practicable**;
    - **In writing**;
    - Specifying the:
        - **Location**;
        - **Grounds**; and
        - **Period** of authorisation.

3 - The Duration Of The Power To Stop & Search – Section 60(1) CJPOA 1994

- The **duration** of the power is **24 hours**.
- The power is renewable for a **further 24 hours** where offences relating to **section 60 powers** are believed to take place.

For example:

The Cardiff City FC "Soul Crew" attend a football match against Birmingham City FC on a Saturday afternoon. A section 60 authorisation has been put in place by Superintendent Grey of BTP at Birmingham New Street station.

An incident takes place on Saturday and BTP receive further intelligence stating that the Soul Crew plan to descend on New Street station on the 09.00 train on Sunday morning.

Superintendent Grey can **renew** the power for a **further 24 hours** to **prevent serious violence** or **carrying of weapons**.

Exam Trip Up

- The **renewal** of the section 60 power must be provided by a **Superintendent**.

Exam Trip Up

- The renewal can only take place if:
    - ☐ **Violence;** or
    - ☐ **Carrying of weapons;**
- Has either:
    - ☐ **Taken place during** the **first 24 hours**; or
    - ☐ There are reasonable grounds to *suspect* that they **have taken place during the first 24 hours.**

4 - Notice Requirements – The Right To Request A Written Statement – Section 60(10A) CJPOA 1994

- A **written statement confirming** the fact that the **search took place;**
- May be **requested** by **persons searched** including:
    - ☐ **Pedestrians;**
    - ☐ **Drivers**
- For a period of up to **12 months** from date of the search.

5 - Who May Be Stopped and Searched? – Section 60(4) CJPOA 1994

- Either:
    - ☐ **Pedestrians;**
    - ☐ **Vehicles;**
    - ☐ All **occupants** of vehicles;
- May be **stopped and searched** for either:
    - ☐ **Offensive weapons;** or
    - ☐ **Dangerous instruments** (sharply bladed or pointed articles).
- **No grounds are required** by officers when an **authorisation is in place.**

C - Powers to Require The Removal Of Disguises - Section 60AA CJPOA 1994

- If an **Inspector** or above reasonably **believes:**
    - ☐ That **activities** may take place in any **locality** in their **police area** that are likely to involve the **commission of offences;** and
    - ☐ It is **expedient** to give an **authorisation** under this subsection in order to **prevent** or **control** the **activities;**
    - ☐ They may **authorise** that:
        - A **constable** have the **power** to **request** the **removal** of any **disguise;**
        - Used by any person **at any place within that locality;**
        - For a **specified period not exceeding 24 hours.**

- The **purpose** provision is to prevent those involved in intimidatory or violent protests using face coverings to **conceal** their **identity**.

Exam Trip Up

- This is **not simply** a **preventative power**.
- It can also be used when the **activities** are **under way**.

D - Powers Of Seizure – Section 60(6) CJPOA 1994

- A **constable** may **seize**:
    - Dangerous Instruments;
    - Offensive weapons;
    - Face coverings.

E - Face Coverings – Section 60AA(2) CJPOA 1994

1 – Power To Seize Face Coverings

- A **face covering** may only be **seized** if the **constable believes** that the coverings:
    - Are used:
        - **Wholly**; or
        - **Mainly**;
    - To **conceal identity**.

Exam Trip Up

- An officer **cannot search for concealment of a face covering**.

2 - Failure To Comply With A Requirement To Remove Items Used To Conceal Their Identity – Section 60AA(7) CJPOA 1994
Summary Offence Only
Penalty In The Magistrates Court – 1 Months Imprisonment And / Or A Fine

- A person commits an offence if they:
    - **Fail** to **remove** an **item worn** by them;
    - When **required** to do so by a **constable** in the exercise of their power under this section.

- It must be shown that:
  - The **requirement** was:
    - **Made**; and
    - **Understood**;
  - The **constable** that issued the requirement was in **uniform**;
  - The **constable** was **authorised** by a **section 60 authority**; and
  - The **constable** reasonable **believed** that the person concerned was **wearing the item to conceal their identity.**

Exam Trip Up

- This is an **absolute requirement** and **exceptions** such as "reasonable excuse or without good reason" **do not apply**.

Exam Trip Up

- Unlike section 60, there is **no specific power** under Section 60AA to **stop vehicles.**
- However, given that this is a power for **police officers in uniform**, then the **power** under **Section 163 Road Traffic Act 1988** could be used.

Exam Trip Up

- The further requirements in relation to **informing** a **Superintendent** are broadly similar to the Section 60 power.

Exam Trip Up

- The limitations on **geographical areas** and **time constraints** are similar to Section 60 powers.

Exam Trip Up

- "Item" is a very wide concept and would include **scarves, balaclavas** and **motorbike helmets.**
- The section is **not solely restricted to face coverings**. It extends to anything that could be **worn wholly or mainly for the purpose of concealing identity** e.g. swapping clothes.

F - Raves - Section 63 CJPOA 1994
Summary Only Offence
Penalty In The Magistrates Court - 3 Months Imprisonment And / Or Fine

1 – Definition Of A Rave

- A **rave** must take place:
    - [ ] **In the open air (20+ persons)**;
    - [ ] There must be:
        - **Amplified music**;
        - **At night**;
    - [ ] **Causing serious distress** to locals;
    - [ ] Due to **loudness, duration** and **time**; and
    - [ ] There is no public entertainments license in force.

2 – Who Provides Authorisation For The Direction – Section 63(2) CJPOA 1994

- **Authorisation** will be provided:
    - [ ] By a **Superintendent** (who need not be there);
    - [ ] Who **believes** that:
        - **2** or more – **making preparations**;
        - **10** or more – **waiting to gather**;
        - **10** or more – **attending a gathering**;
    - [ ] The **Superintendent** may give **directions** to:
        - **Leave land**; or
        - **Remove**:
            - [ ] **Vehicles**; or
            - [ ] **Property**.

3 – Failure To Comply With Directions Under Section 63 CJPOA 1994
Summary Only Offence
Penalty In The Magistrates Court – 3 Months Imprisonment And / Or A Fine

- It is an offence to:
    - [ ] **Fail to leave ASAP**;
    - [ ] **Re-enter** within **7 days** (Always 7 days with raves); or
    - [ ] Make **preparations** or **attend another gathering** within **24 hours**.

4 – Police Powers In Relation To Raves – Power Of Entry Exercisable At The Rave – Section 64 CJPOA 1994

- A **constable** can be authorised to:
  - [ ] **Enter land** to ascertain the situation;
  - [ ] Give **directions**;
  - [ ] **Seize equipment**; and
  - [ ] **Arrest**.

5 – Police Powers In Relation To Raves – Stopping Persons From Getting To A Rave – Section 65 CJPOA 1994

- A **police constable**;
- **In uniform**;
- May **stop** and **direct** a person **not to proceed** within a **5 mile exclusion zone** (from the perimeter);

6 - Defence In Relation To Raves – Section 63(7) CJPOA 1994

- A person will have a defence if they have a **reasonable excuse** for:
  - [ ] Not leaving; or
  - [ ] Re-entering.

G - Stop & Search - Section 1(2) PACE 1984

1 - Grounds To Stop & Search

- A **constable** may search:
  - [ ] Any:
    - **Person**; or
    - **Vehicle**;
    - Anything which is **in** or **on** a **vehicle**;
  - [ ] If they have **reasonable grounds** to **suspect** that they will find any:
    - **Stolen property**;
    - **Prohibited articles** (bladed or sharply pointed articles);
      - [ ] Items used in relation to **criminal damage offences**;
      - [ ] Items used in relation to **going equipped offences**,
    - **Offensive weapons**; and
    - **Fireworks**.
- The constable may **detain** a **person** or **vehicle** for the purpose of such a search.

Exam Trip Up

- The case of *R v Harrison* [1938] All ER 134 established that if the officer knows that there is **little or no likelihood** of **finding the articles sought**, the **power cannot be used.**

2 - Legitimate Sources Of Grounds To Suspect

- The **source** an officer's **grounds** to stop and search can include:
    - ☐ Personal observations of the searching officer or other officers;
    - ☐ Intelligence;
    - ☐ CHIS;
    - ☐ Members of the public; etc.

3 - Grounds To Suspect Based On Personal Characteristics - Code A Paragraph 2.6

(i) - The General Rule

- The grounds for a search of a person **cannot** be founded on **purely personal factors** - e.g. **age, colour** or **appearance.**

(ii) - The Exception To The General Rule

- It is permissible to based the grounds for a search on **personal factors** when those factors are related to:
    - ☐ Either:
        - ■ **Groups;** or
        - ■ **Gang members;**
    - ☐ Who **habitually carry:**
        - ☐ **Knives;**
        - ☐ **Weapons;** or
        - ☐ **Controlled drugs;** and
    - ☐ Who wear a **distinctive item of clothing** or **other means of identity.**

Exam Trip Up – Innocent Possession

- A constable who has **reasonable grounds** to **suspect** that a person is in **innocent possession** of:
    - ☐ Stolen articles;
    - ☐ Prohibited articles; or
    - ☐ Other items which give rise to a power of search;
- **Will be permitted to search;**
- Even though there would be:
    - ☐ **No power of arrest;** or
    - ☐ **No offences committed.**

4 – Location Of A Stop And Search

(i) - Places To Which The Public Have Access – Section 1(1) PACE 1984

- A **constable** may **stop and search** a person either:
    - In any place where at the time when they propose to exercise the power that the **public or any section of the public has access,** on **payment or otherwise,** as a **right** or by virtue of **express** or **implied permission;** or
    - In **any other place** to which people have ready access at the time when they proposes to exercise the power but which is **not a dwelling.**

(ii) - Searching A Garden Yard Or Land Connected To A Dwelling – Section 1(4) PACE 1984

- If a person who is to be searched is in:
    - A **garden;**
    - **Yard;** or
    - **Land connected to a dwelling;**
- Which is either:
    - **Occupied;** and
    - **Used as part of a dwelling;**
- The power to stop and search will **not apply;**
- **Unless;**
- The officer has **reasonable grounds** for **believing** that the person:
    - **Does not live there;** and
    - They are **not** there with the **permission** of any **person** who does **lives there.**

Exam Trip Up

- If the dwelling is **not occupied** then the **restriction** does **not apply.**
- The **same principle** applies to **vehicles parked** in areas that are not occupied.

5 - Duration Of The Search – Section 1 PACE 1984

- A **person** or **vehicle** may only be **detained** for **such time** as is **reasonably necessary** to permit a **search:**
    - **At the place** they were **first detained;** or
    - **Nearby.**

6 - Information To Be Provided By The Officer To The Person Searched - Code A Paragraph 3.8

- The **officer** conducting the search must **inform** the **person**:
    - ☐ They are being **detained** for the **purpose** of a **search**;
    - ☐ The **object** that they are being searched for;
    - ☐ The **officers name** (**except** in **terrorism** cases or if the officer believes it will put them in **danger** - then their **warrant number**);
    - ☐ The **police station** to which they are attached;
    - ☐ The **legal power** being used to authorise the search;
    - ☐ If they are **not in uniform**, their **warrant card** must be shown;
    - ☐ **Explanation** of the **purpose**, any **relevant reasonable suspicion** that is needed or the **relevant authority** used e.g. Section 60 CJPOA 1994, and
    - ☐ **Entitlement** of a **copy** of the **search record**.

7 - Consequences Of Failing To Notify The Person Searched

- The case of *Osman v DPP* [1999] The Times 28th September established that an **unreasonable failure** to **provide** the aforementioned **details** prior to a search will:
    - ☐ Make any subsequent **search unlawful**; and
    - ☐ The person being searched may use **reasonable force to resist the search.**

Exam Trip Up

- If the **purpose** for the search has **ceased**:
    - ☐ There is **no requirement to continue with the search**;
    - ☐ It will be necessary to fill out a **record** of the **stop**.

8 - Post Search Recording Obligations – Section 3 PACE 1984

- The **searching officer** must make a **record** of the search of the person or vehicle stating the:
    - ☐ **Object** being searched for;
    - ☐ **Grounds** for making the search;
    - ☐ **Date** and **time** when it was **conducted**;
    - ☐ **Date** and **time** when **stopped** if different;
    - ☐ **Place** where it was made;
    - ☐ Whether anything, and if so what, was **found**;
    - ☐ Whether any, and if so what, **injury** to a **person** or **damage** to **property** appears to the constable to have **resulted from the search**; and
    - ☐ **Identity** of the **constable** carrying out the search (name/warrant number provision);
    - ☐ The searched persons **self-defined ethnic background**;
    - ☐ The **vehicle registration number** and **description** should be recorded.

Exam Trip Up

- The **constable** must **ask** the **person searched** for their:
  - ☐ **Name;**
  - ☐ **Date of birth;** and
  - ☐ **Address.**

- However:
  - ☐ The person searched is under **no obligation** to provide these details; and
  - ☐ There is **no power to further detain** to obtain this information.

- If **no name** is **provided** - a **visual description** should be **recorded.**

9 - Providing Individuals With A Copy Of The Record – Section 1 PACE 1984

- A **copy** of any **record made at the time of the search** must be **given immediately** to the person searched.

- The following individuals shall be entitled to a **copy** of the **record** of the search **within 12 months of the search:**
  - ☐ The **person searched;**
  - ☐ The **owner** of a **vehicle searched;** or
  - ☐ The **person in charge** of a **vehicle searched.**

Exam Trip Up

- If the **object** and **grounds** for a **search** of the **vehicle** and **occupants** are the **same** then only **1 search record** needs to be completed.

- If **more than one person in the vehicle is searched** then **separate records** for each person must be completed.

10 - Searching Unattended Vehicles – Section 2 PACE 1984

- If an **unattended vehicle** is searched a **notice** should be prepared stating:
  - ☐ That a **constable has searched the vehicle;**
  - ☐ The **name** of the **police station** to which the **searching officer is attached;**
  - ☐ That an **application for compensation for any damage** caused by the search may be made to that police station; and

- The constable shall:
  - ☐ **Leave** the **notice inside the vehicle;**
  - ☐ **Unless** it is **not reasonably practical** to do so **without damaging the vehicle.**

Exam Trip Up

- The notice requirements apply to:
    - ☐ Searching anything **on** an unattended vehicle;
    - ☐ As well as the **vehicle** itself.

Exam Trip Up

- **If practicable** the officer must **leave the vehicle secure**.

H - Stop and Search Powers to Combat Terrorism

1 - Cordons - Section 33 of the Terrorism Act 2000

(i) – Authorising Cordons

- The police may set up **cordons** if it is considered **expedient** for the purposes of a **terrorist investigation**.
- The designation of a cordon may only be made:
    - ☐ By an officer of the rank of **Superintendent** or above;
    - ☐ Within an area that is **wholly** or **partly within their police area**.
- **Superintendents** from the **British Transport Police** or the **Ministry of Defence Police** can **authorise** in their **specific areas** of **jurisdiction**.
- An officer **below** the rank of **Superintendent** may make a designation if they considers it necessary by reason of **urgency**.

Exam Trip Up

- This power is **investigative** in its nature.

Exam Trip Up

- If the **Superintendent** makes the designation **orally,** they must **confirm** the designation **in writing as soon as reasonably practicable.**

Exam Trip Up

- If the designation is **made** by a **non Superintendent** ranked officer they must:
    - ☐ Make a **written record** of the **time** that the designation was made; and
    - ☐ **Inform** a **Superintendent.**
- The **Superintendent** can **confirm or cancel** the designation.
- If the designation is **cancelled** then a **record** must be made of:
    - ☐ The **cancellation;** and
    - ☐ The **reason** for cancelling.

(ii) - Demarcation Of The Cordoned Area – Section 33(4) Terrorism Act 2000

- If designation is made then the **cordoned area** must be **"de-marked"** by means of police tape etc.

(iii) - Duration Of The Designated Period - Section 35 (2), (3) & (5) Terrorism Act 2000

- The **designated period**:
  - **Begins** when the **order is made**; and
  - **Ends** at the **date specified in the order**.
- The **initial designation** cannot extend **beyond 14 days** from the **time of the order**.
- A **Superintendent** can **extend** the **designation** to an **overall limit of 28 days** beginning with the day on which the order was made.

(iv) - Police Powers In Relation To Cordoned Areas – Section 36 Terrorism Act 2000

- A **constable** in **uniform** may:
  - **Order** a person in a cordoned area to **leave immediately**;
  - **Order** a person immediately to **leave premises** which are **wholly or partly in or adjacent to a cordoned area**;
  - **Order** the **driver** or **person in charge** of a **vehicle** in a cordoned area to **move the vehicle from the area immediately**;
  - **Arrange** for the **removal of a vehicle** from a cordoned area;
  - **Arrange** for the **movement of a vehicle** within a cordoned area;
  - **Prohibit** or **restrict access** to a cordoned area by **pedestrians** or **vehicles**.

2 - Stop and Search Authorisations – Section 44 Terrorism Act 2000

(i) – Criteria In Which Authorisation May Be Provided

- An officer of or above the rank of:
  - **Assistant Chief Constable**;
  - **Commander**;
- May:
  - **Authorise** the use of **stop and search** powers within a **locality**;
  - For a period not exceeding **28 days**;
  - If they deem it:
    - **Expedient** to do so;
    - In order to **prevent acts of terrorism**.

(ii) - Post Authorisation Steps – Code A Paragraph 2.23 & Note 14A

- When authorisation is given, immediate steps must be taken to **send** a **copy** of the **authorisation** to the **National Joint Unit, Metropolitan Police Special Branch** who in turn will **forward** a **copy** to the **Secretary of State.**

- If the **Secretary of State** does **not confirm** the authorisation within 48 hours of it being given, **the authorisation runs out after 48 hours.**

- The **National Joint Unit** will **inform** the police force **within 48 hours** whether the **Secretary of State** has:
    - ☐ **Confirmed;**
    - ☐ **Cancelled;** or
    - ☐ **Reduced**
    - the period of authorisation.

(iii) - Conducting Searches

- The searching officer must be in **uniform.**
- The searching officer can stop and search:
    - ☐ **Pedestrians;** or
    - ☐ **Vehicles;** or
    - ☐ **Occupants of vehicles.**
- A **PCSO can** conduct a **search** under this power although they must be:
    - ☐ In the **company;** and
    - ☐ Under the **direct supervision;**
    - of a **constable**.
- It is permissible to search for any **articles used in connection with terrorism.**
- A **geographical limit** must be set on the search area, which could include a whole police area e.g. London.

Exam Trip Up

- Where **verbal authorisation** is given, it must be **confirmed in writing as soon as practicable.**

Exam Trip Up

- These powers are **preventative** rather than investigative measures.

I - Arrest

1 - Information To Be Given and Recorded on Arrest - Section 28 of the Police and Criminal Evidence Act 1984

(i) - The General Rule

- The following **information** must be **given** to a person either:
    - **Upon arrest**; or
    - **As soon as is practicable** after their **arrest**:
        - That they are **under arrest**;
        - The **grounds** for the **arrest**.
- **Failure** to do so will result in an **unlawful arrest**.
- The above **requirements apply regardless** of whether the facts of that the arrest is **obvious** or **otherwise**.

(ii) - The Exception To The General Rule

- It is **not necessary** to **inform** a person:
    - That they are **under arrest**; or
    - Of the **grounds** for their **arrest**;
- If it was **not reasonably practicable** for them to be so **informed** by reason of their having **escaped from arrest before the information was given.**
- This is the only circumstance when failure to give the arrestee the above facts would make the subsequent arrest lawful.

The Content Of The Information Provided

- The case of *Fox, Campbell and Hartley v UK* [1991] 13 EHRR 157 established that:

    "Any person arrested must be told in simple, non-technical language, that they can understand, the essential legal and factual grounds for their arrest so as to be able, if they see fit, to apply to a court to challenge its lawfulness"

- They must be informed of:
    - The suspected offence's:
        - **Nature**;
        - **Where** it was committed;
        - **When** it was committed.
    - **Why** their **arrest** is **necessary**.

- The case of *Wilson v Chief Constable of Lancashire Constabulary* [2000] 1 POLR 367, established that an arresting officers minimum obligation is to provide a suspect with:

    "...sufficient information as to the nature of an arrest to allow sufficient opportunity to respond."

- The case of *Christie v Leachinsky* [1947] AC 573 established that **colloquialisms** such as "you're nicked" **can be used** - **provided** the **arrestee knows** and **understands** its **meaning**.

2 - Record of Arrest - Code G Paragraph 4.1 & 4.4

- The **arresting officer** is required to **record**:
    - In their **pocket book**; or
    - By **other methods** used for recording information;
- The following information:
    - The **nature** and **circumstances** of the **offence** leading to arrest;
    - The **reason(s)** why the **arrest** was necessary;
    - The giving of the **caution;** and
    - Anything **said** by the person **at the time of arrest.**
- The **custody record** will serve as a **record** of the **arrest**.

3 - Caution Upon Arrest - Code C Paragraph 10.4

- A person must be **cautioned** on:
    - **Arrest;** or
    - **Further arrest.**
- The **exception** to the requirement to administer the **caution post arrest** are:
    - Where it is **impracticable** to do so by reason of the persons:
        - **Condition;**
        - **Behaviour**; or
    - Where they have **already been cautioned immediately before their arrest.**

J - Powers Of Arrest Without Warrant

1 - Constables Power Of Arrest Without Warrant – Section 24 PACE 1984

(i) Permitted Grounds For A Constable To Arrest Without Warrant

- A constable may **arrest without warrant:**
    - Anyone who is **about to commit** an offence;
    - Anyone who is in the **act of committing** an offence;
    - Anyone whom he has **reasonable grounds** for **suspecting to be about to commit** an offence;
    - Anyone whom he has **reasonable grounds** for **suspecting to be committing** an offence.
- If a constable has **reasonable grounds for suspecting** that an **offence has been committed**, they may arrest without a warrant anyone whom they have reasonable grounds to **suspect of being guilty of it.**

- If an **offence has been committed**, a constable may arrest without a warrant:
    - ☐ Anyone who is **guilty of the offence**;
    - ☐ Anyone whom they have **reasonable grounds for suspecting to be guilty of it**.

(ii) - The Test To Establish Reasonable Grounds to Suspect

- The term **"reasonable"** is **objective** in nature.
- Courts will consider in **all the circumstances**, whether, a **reasonable and sober person** might have found a **similar view** to that of the officer.
- The key test for establishing the lawfulness of an arrest without warrant is set out by the Court of Appeal in *Castorina v Chief Constable of Surrey* [1996] 160 LG Rev 241.

    This is a three stage test:
    - ☐ Did the **arresting officer suspect** that the person who was arrested was **guilty** of the offence (**Subjective Test**)?
    - ☐ If so, was there **reasonable cause** (i.e. reasonable grounds) for the **arresting officer's suspicion (Objective Test)**?
    - ☐ Was the **arresting officer's** exercise of their discretion **reasonable in all the circumstances?**

(iii) - Necessity Criteria

- With the adoption of SOCAP 2005 legislation, which has amended Section 24 of the Police and Criminal Evidence Act 1984, there is now an **additional requirement** that the power of arrest is exercisable only if the **constable** has **reasonable grounds for believing** that it is **necessary to arrest.**
- Therefore a constable needs to:
    - ☐ Show why they believed that an arrest rather than any other means of disposal was necessary; and
    - ☐ Point to the grounds on which the belief was based.

(iv) - Reasons Making Arrest Necessary

- Section 24 of the PACE 1984 sets out possible reasons that make an arrest **necessary**:

    - ☐ **C** – Protect a **child or vulnerable person**;
    - ☐ **O** – Prevent **obstruction of the highway**;
    - ☐ **P** – Prevent the person causing **physical injury to self, others or Suffering injury**;
    - ☐ **P** – Prevent **public decency offences**;
    - ☐ **L** – **Loss or damage to property**;
    - ☐ **A** – **Address** of person in question **cannot be readily ascertained**;
    - ☐ **N** – **Name** of person in question **cannot be readily ascertained**;
    - ☐ **E** - To allow the **effective and prompt investigation of offences**;
    - ☐ **D** – To avoid the **disappearance of the person in question** and therefore **hinder a prompt investigation**.

Exam Trip Up

- There is **no** specific and absolute **requirement** under the Human Rights Act 1998 for **all arrests** to be *'necessary'*.

2 - Arrest Without Warrant By Others - Section 24A PACE 1984

- A **person other than** a **constable** may **arrest without warrant:**

    - Anyone who is **in the act** of **committing** an **indictable offence**;

    - Anyone whom they have **reasonable grounds** for **suspecting** to be **committing** an **indictable offence.**

    - Where an **indictable offence** has been **committed:**

        - Anyone who is **guilty** of the offence; or

        - Anyone whom they have **reasonable grounds** for *suspecting* to be **guilty** of it.

- The person making the arrest *must* have **reasonable grounds** for *believing* that:

    - It is **necessary to arrest** the person to **prevent** them from:

        - **Causing physical injury** to:

            - **Themselves**; or

            - **Others**;

        - **Suffering physical injury**;

        - **Causing loss** of or **damage** to **property**; or

        - **Making off** before a **constable** can **assume responsibility** for them; and

    - It appears to the person making the arrest that it is **not reasonably practicable for a constable to make the arrest instead.**

Memory Aid

- Remember **non constables** need a "**P.A.L.**"

    - P – Physical Injury;
    - A – Assume Responsibility; and
    - L – Loss or Damage to Property.

3 - Other Powers of Arrest Without Warrant

(i) - Absentees And Deserters – Section 186 Army & Air Force Act 1955 & Section 105 Navy Discipline Act 1957

- There is a power of arrest without warrant for **service personnel** where:
    - A **constable** has **reasonable cause** to **suspect** a person has either:
    - **Deserted**; or
    - **Absent without leave.**
- Where absentees or deserters have been **arrested**:
    - They must be **taken directly** to a **Magistrates Court**; and
    - The appropriate **service authority contacted**.
- Magistrates Courts may **remand until** they can be **collected** by a **military escort**.
- If the **escort is likely to be provided soon after the persons appearance at court**, the **Magistrates**:
    - **May remand to a police station**; and
    - **Must issue a certificate** which **must** be **given** to the **escort**.

(ii) - Breach Of The Peace

(iii) - Fingerprinting and Samples (see chapters in Evidence and Procedure)

(iv) - Failure To Answer Bail (see chapters in Evidence and Procedure)

(v) - Cross Border Arrest Without Warrant

- The Criminal Justice and Public Order Act 1996, sections 136-140 makes provisions for:
    - Officers from one part of the UK to go to another part of the UK and arrest someone with an offence committed within their jurisdiction; and
    - Power of search on arrest.

K - Powers of Search and Seizure Under Warrant

1 - Application For A Warrant – Section 15 of the PACE 1984

- Where a **constable** applies for any such warrant, it shall be their duty to **state**:
    - The **ground** on which they make the application;
    - The **enactment** under which the warrant would be issued; and
    - If the application is for a warrant authorising **entry and search** on **more than one occasion**:
        - The **ground** on which they applied for such a warrant; and
        - Whether they **seek a warrant authorising**:
            - **An unlimited number of entries,** or
            - If not - the **maximum number of entries desired**;
    - To **specify** the **matters** set out below; and
    - To **identify**, so far as is practicable, the:
        - **Articles** sought; or
        - **Persons** sought.
- The matters set out above are:
    - If the application relates to **one or more sets of premises specified** in the application **each set of premises which it is desired to enter and search**; and
    - If the application relates to any **premises occupied or controlled** by a person specified in the application:
        - As **many sets of premises** which it is desired to enter and search as it is **reasonably practicable** to specify;
        - The person who is in **occupation or control** of those premises and **any others which it is desired to enter and search;**
        - Why it is **necessary** to search more premises than those specified; and
        - Why it is **not reasonably practicable** to **specify all the premises which it is desired to enter and search.**

2 - Definition Of Premises – Section 23 PACE 1984

- **Premises** include any:
    - **Place;**
    - **Vehicle;**
    - **Vessel;**
    - **Aircraft;**
    - **Hovercraft;**
    - **Offshore installation or a renewable energy installation;**
    - **Tent or moveable structure.**

3 - The Form Of Application – Section 15(3)&(4) PACE 1984 & Code B Paragraph 3.4

- An **application** for such a warrant shall:
    - Be made **ex parte;** and
    - Supported by an **information in writing.**
- The constable **shall answer on oath** any question that the JP or Judge hearing the application asks them.
- The details of the **extent of the proposed search** should be made clear in the application.

4 - Authorisation To Lodge The Application - Code B Paragraph 3.4

- Applications for warrants must be made with the **written authority** of an **Inspector**.
- In cases of **urgency** where **no Inspector** is **"readily available"** then the **senior officer on duty** may **authorise** the application.

5 - Terms Of The Warrant

- A warrant shall authorise an **entry on one occasion only unless it specifies that it authorises multiple entry.**
- If it specifies that it authorises **multiple entries**, it must also specify whether:
    - The number of entries authorised is **unlimited;** or
    - **Limited** to a **specified maximum.**

6 - Execution of Warrants – Section 16 PACE 1984

- A warrant may **authorise persons to accompany constables** in its execution.
- The **accompanying person** has the **same powers of search and seizure** as the **constable** provided they are:
    - **In the company** of a constable; and
    - **Under the supervision** of a constable.
- **Entry** and **search** must take place within **3 months of issue.**
- Under the SOCAP Act 2005 amendment, under Section 16(3B) of PACE 1984, where a **warrant authorises multiple entries**, any **subsequent entries** must be **authorised in writing** by an **Inspector** or above.
- **Failure to comply** with the requirements of Section 16 PACE 1984 make entry and seizure **unlawful** e.g. not leaving a copy of the warrant.

Action To Be Taken When The Occupier Is Not Present

- Section 16(6) states that where:
    - The **occupier** of such premises;
    - Is **not present**;
    - **At the time** when a constable seeks to **execute** such a warrant;
    - But **some other person** who **appears** to the **constable** to be **in charge of the premises is present**;
    - The **constable** shall **supply them** with a *copy* of it.

Exam Trip Up

- Watch for the exam trip up when the **nosy neighbour** comes and watches the search.
- The neighbour:
    - Is **not in charge**; and
    - Therefore should **not be supplied with a** *copy*.

Exam Trip Up

- Under s. 16(7):
    - If there is **no person present**;
    - Who **appears** to the constable to be **in charge of the premises**;
    - The constable shall **leave** a *copy* of the warrant in a **prominent place on the premises.**
- The **original warrant** must *not* be **left** with:
    - The **occupier**;
    - **Any other person**; or
    - **On the premises itself.**

7 - Returning The Warrant – Section 16(1) & (10A) PACE 1984

- After a **warrant**:
    - Has been **executed**; or
    - Is **void** due to expiry of the time limit - 3 months from it's date of issue;
- It must be **returned** to:
    - The **designated officer** for the local justice area in which a **Justice of the Peace issued** the warrant; or
    - To an **appropriate officer** of the court where it was **issued** by a **judge**.

L - Search Warrants for Indictable Offences – Section 8 PACE 1984

1 – The Forms Of Warrants

- Section 8 warrants have been amended by SOCAP Act 2005, and a constable can apply for **two different types of warrant**, namely:
    - **Specific premises warrant** – one set of premises to be searched; or
    - **All premises warrant** – search all premises under the occupation and control of a person where it is not practicable to specify all such premises at the time of the application.

2 - Criteria For Granting A Warrant – Section 8(1) PACE 1984

- The constable applying for the warrant **must have reasonable grounds for believing that material which is likely to be of substantial value to the investigation of the offence is on the premises specified.**

    All property seized must fall within the above description.

    Any material which is **solely for intelligence purposes cannot be seized** under a **Section 8 warrant**.

3 - Who May Apply For And Execute A Warrant? - Section 8(2) PACE 1984

- The **power to apply for** and **execute warrants** under Section 8 of PACE 1984 can be conferred on a person designated as an **Investigating Officer** under the Police Reform Act 2002.

4 - Extent Of Entry Authorised By A Warrant - Section 8(1A) PACE 1984

- The warrant **may authorise entry on more than one occasion.**
- If **multiple entries** are authorised these may either be:
    - **Unlimited**; or
    - **Limited** to a **maximum**.

M - Powers Of Entry, Search and Seizure Without A Warrant

1 - Power To Search After Arrest For Indictable Offences – Section 18 PACE 1984

- A **constable**;
- May:
    - **Enter**; and
    - **Search**;
- Any **premises**:
    - **Occupied**; or
    - **Controlled**;

- By a person who is **under arrest** for an **indictable offence;**
- If they have **reasonable grounds** for **suspecting** that there is **on the premises evidence**, other than items subject to **legal privilege**, that relates:
    - ☐ To **that offence**; or
    - ☐ To some **other indictable offence** which is either:
        - **Connected** with that offence; or
        - **Similar** to that offence.
- If they have obtained the authorisation of an **Inspector** or above.

2 - Post Authorisation Obligations – Section 18(7) PACE 1984

- The **Inspector** must:
    - ☐ Make a **written record** of the **authorisation**; and
    - ☐ Outline the:
        - **Grounds** of the search; and
        - The **evidence** that is being **sought.**

Exam Trip Up

- Section 18(5) allows for a search to **take place prior to the arrested person being conveyed to a police station or given street bail.**

Exam Trip Up

- If a person is **re arrested whilst in custody** then the Section 18 power is **re created for each indictable offence.**

Exam Trip Up

- The power to search should only be to the extent that is **reasonably required** for the **purpose of discovering such evidence.**

Exam Trip Up

- The **occupied** or **control** provision must be **factual**. A suspicion or belief is inadequate.

N - Search of Premises After Arrest – Section 32 PACE 1984

- A **constable** shall have the power to:
    - [ ] **Enter;** and
    - [ ] **Search;**
- **Any premises** in which the person was either:
    - [ ] **When they were arrested;** or
    - [ ] **Immediately before being arrested;**
- For an **indictable offence;**
- If the **constable** has **reasonable grounds** for **believing** that there is **evidence** relating to the **offence for which they were arrested.**
- The **constable** may **search:**
    - [ ] **Any dwelling in which the arrest took place** or in which the **person arrested was immediately before his arrest;** and
    - [ ] Any parts of the premises which the occupier of any such dwelling **uses in common with occupiers of any other dwellings comprised in the premises.**

O - Powers To Search A Person After Arrest For Other Offences - Section 32 PACE 1984

- A **constable** may **search;**
- A **person arrested** at a **place other than a police station;**
- If they have **reasonable grounds** for **believing** that the arrested person may present a **danger** to:
    - [ ] **Themselves;** or
    - [ ] **Others.**
- A constable shall also have power in any case to **search** the **arrested person** if they have **reasonable grounds** to **believe** that the person has in their **possession** anything:
    - [ ] Which they might use to **assist them to escape** from lawful custody; or
    - [ ] Which might be **evidence** relating to an offence.
- The **constable** may only search to the extent that is **reasonably required** for the purpose of **discovering any such thing or evidence.**
- The **constable** may only:
    - [ ] Remove:
        - **Outer clothing;**
        - **Jacket;** or
        - **Gloves;**
    - [ ] Search of a person's **mouth;**
    - in a **public place.**

Exam Trip Up

- A section 32 search may only take place outside a police station.

P - Power of Entry - Section 17 PACE 1984

- A constable may enter and search any premises for the purpose:
    - Of **executing**:
        - An **arrest warrant**; or
        - A **commitment warrant**;
    - Of **arresting** a person for an **indictable offence**;
    - Of **arresting** a person for an offence under:
        - Section 1 Public Order Act 1936 (Prohibition of Uniforms);
        - Section 6 to 8 or 10 of the Criminal Law Act 1977 (Land offences);
        - Section 4 Public Order Act 1986 (Fear or provocation of violence);
        - Section 4 (Unfit to Drive) or 163 (Fail to Stop) of the Road Traffic Act 1988;
        - Section 27 of the Transport and Works Act 1992;
        - Section 76 of the Criminal Justice and Public Order Act 1994 (failure to comply with interim possession order);
    - **Arresting** any **child** or **young person** who is **unlawfully at large from secure accommodation**;
    - **Recapturing** a person **unlawfully at large** whom they are **pursuing**; or
    - **Saving life** or **limb** or **preventing serious damage to property**.

Q - General Powers of Seizure - Section 19 PACE 1984

- A **constable** may **seize anything** which is **on premises**;
- If they have **reasonable grounds** for **believing**:
    - Either:
        - That it is **evidence** in relation to an **offence** which they are **investigating** or **any other offence**; and
        - That it has been **obtained** in **consequence** of the **commission of an offence**; and
    - That it is **necessary** to **seize it** in order to **prevent it** being:
        - **Concealed**;
        - **Lost**;
        - **Damaged**;
        - **Altered**; or
        - **Destroyed**.

- A **constable** may require any **information** which is:
    - ☐ **Stored** in any **electronic form**; and
    - ☐ Accessible from the premises to be produced in a **form in which it can be taken away**; and
    - ☐ Either:
        - **Visible and legible**; or
        - From which it can readily be **produced in a visible and legible form**;
- If they have **reasonable grounds for believing**:
    - ☐ Either:
        - That it is **evidence** in relation to:
            - ☐ An offence which they is **investigating**; or
            - ☐ **Any other offence**; or
        - It has been obtained in consequence of the **commission of an offence**; and
    - ☐ That it is necessary to do so in order to prevent it being:
        - **Concealed**;
        - **Lost**; or
        - **Destroyed**.
- The **constable** must be **lawfully** on the **premises**.

Exam Trip Up

- Watch out for questions involving a constable who is **not on premises lawfully** and has been **asked to leave** by the occupiers.
- They are a **trespasser** at that point and **cannot seize items** subject to section 19 PACE 1984 powers.

R – Trespass Intending To Obstruct, Disrupt, Or Intimidate - Section 68 CJPOA 1994
Summary Only Offence
Penalty In The Magistrates Court – 3 Months Imprisonment And / Or A Fine

1 – Criteria Of The Offence

- It is an offence of **aggravated trespass** if:
- In relation to a **lawful activity** which persons are either:
    - ☐ **Engaged in**; or
    - ☐ **About to engage in**:
- Either:
    - ☐ **On land**; or
    - ☐ **Adjoining land**;

- A person **trespasses** on land;
- To do something **intending** to have the effect of:
    - ☐ **Intimidating;**
    - ☐ **Obstructing;** or
    - ☐ **Disrupting;**

    - Them from **engaging in their activity.**

Learning Points

- The person must be a **trespasser.**
- They must **intent** to **"spoil the day"** only - e.g. hunt saboteurs, environmentalists.
- **Land** does **not** include a **road.**
- The offence **can** take place **inside buildings.**
- The offence is **complete** once the **intent** is **formed.**
- There is **no need** for a **result.**

2 - Police Powers – Section 69(1) CJPOA 1994

- The **senior police officer** present at the scene may **direct persons to leave the land** provided they **believe** either:
    - ☐ A person:
        - **Is** committing;
        - **Has** committed; or
        - **Intends** to commit;

        - An offence of **aggravated trespass;** or
    - ☐ **2 or more** persons are **trespassing** on the land with the **common purpose** of:
        - **Intimidating;**
        - **Obstructing;** or
        - **Disrupting;**

        - A **lawful activity.**

3 - When Is The Offence Complete?

- An offence will be **complete** if after a **direction** a person:
    - ☐ **Fails to leave ASAP;** or
    - ☐ **Returns** within **3 months.**

4 - Defence – Section 69(3)&(4) CJPOA 1994

- A person will have a **defence** if either:
    - They are **not a trespasser**; or
    - They have **reasonable grounds** for:
        - Failing to leave; or
        - Re-entering.

S - Collective Trespass: Two Or More Persons Trespassing For The Purpose Of Residence - Section 61 CJPOA 1994
Summary Only Offence
Penalty In The Magistrates Court – 3 Months Imprisonment And / Or A Fine

1 – Definition Of The Offence

- The **senior police officer present at the scene** may **direct** persons to:
    - **Leave land;** and
    - **Remove** any **vehicles** or **property on the land;**
- If they **believe** either that:
    - **2 or more** persons are **trespassing;**
    - Their **common purpose** is to **reside** there;
    - They have been **asked to leave;** and
    - **Any** of those persons have either:
        - **Caused damage;**
        - Used **threatening, abusive, insulting words** or **behaviour** towards occupiers family or employees; or
        - **6 or more vehicles.**

2 - The Definition Of Vehicles - Section 61(9) CJPOA 1994

- The definition of a **vehicle** includes:
    - **Shells;**
    - **Chassis** with or without wheels – count them all!

3 - The Definition Of Damage (As Per The Definition Of Criminal Damage In The Criminal Damage Act 1971)

- The definition of **damage** includes:
    - **Oil spillages;**
    - **Pollution (defecating, urinating etc).**

4 - Those That Become Trespassers Subsequently

- If an individual initially **enters land lawfully** and **subsequently becomes a trespasser**;
- The police can only give **directions from the time that they become a trespasser**.
- Once a direction has been made, a **constable** can communicate that direction.

T - Failure to Follow Directions to Leave – Section 61(4) CJPOA 1994
Summary Only Offence
Penalty In The Magistrates Court – 3 Months Imprisonment And / Or A Fine

- A person commits an offence if:
    - **Knowing** that:
        - A **direction** has been **given**; and
        - The **direction applies to them**:
    - They either:
        - **Fail to leave the land as soon as reasonably practicable**; or
        - Having **left**:
            - **Re-enters** the **land**;
            - As a **trespasser**;
            - Within the period of **3 months** beginning with the day on which the direction was given.

W - Trespassing For The Purpose Of Residence with Vehicle(s) When An Alternative Site Is Available – Section 62A CJPOA 1994
Summary Only Offence
Penalty In The Magistrates Court – 3 Months Imprisonment And / Or A Fine

- A Senior Police Officer;
- Present **at the scene**;
- May **direct** the person:
    - To **leave the land**; and
    - To **remove** any **vehicle** and **other property** they **have with them** on the land;
- If they **reasonably believe** that any of the following **conditions** are satisfied in relation to **a person on land**:
    - That the **person** and **one or more others** are **trespassing** on the land;
    - That the trespassers have **at least one vehicle on the land**;
    - That the trespassers have a **common purpose to reside on the land for any period**;

- ☐ It **appears** to the **officer** that:
    - ■ The person has **one or more caravans**:
        - ☐ **In their possession**; or
        - ☐ **Under their control**
        - on the land; and
    - ■ That there is a **suitable pitch** on a **relevant caravan site** for each of those caravans;
- ☐ That the **occupier** of the land or **person acting on their behalf** has **asked** the **police** to **remove the trespassers** from the land.

Exam Trip Up

- ■ The **senior officer** (**any officer rank**) must have reasonable belief that:
    - ☐ **2 persons** are trespassing;
    - ☐ **1 vehicle**;
    - ☐ **Common purpose to reside on land**; and
    - ☐ They have been **asked to leave the land by police on the owners behest**.

- ■ If they have a **caravan** then there is a **further duty** on the senior officer to make **enquires** with the **local authority** with regards to a **suitable pitch** for any **caravans**.

- ■ If the above conditions are satisfied then the **direction to leave** and **remove property is a lawful one**.

Exam Trip Up

- ■ The officer making the direction **need not be in uniform**.

V - Failure to Comply with Direction To Leave Under Section 62A – Section 62B CJPOA 1994
Summary Only Offence
Penalty In The Magistrates Court – 3 Months Imprisonment And / Or A Fine

1 – Definition Of The Offence

- ■ A person commits an offence if:
    - ☐ They **know** that a **direction** under section 62A(1) has been given which applies to them; and
    - ☐ Either:
        - ■ They **fail to leave** the relevant land **as soon as reasonably practicable**; or
        - ■ They **enter any land** in the area of the relevant **local authority** as a **trespasser before** the **end** of the **relevant period** with the **intention of residing** there.

Memory Aid

- This power has **two strands:**
    - The first is a **failure to leave**; or
    - The second is **entering any land** in the **same local authority area within 3 months** with the **purpose of residing** at that location.

2 - Defence

- The **defence** to the above offence is that:
    - They were **not a trespasser**; or
    - They had **reasonable grounds** to fail to leave or to return; or
    - They were:
        - **Under 18** when the direction was given; and
        - **Living with their parents or guardians.**

W - Causing or Permitting A Nuisance – Section 547(1) Education Act 1996
Summary Only Offence
Penalty In The Magistrates Court – Fine Only

- A person will be guilty of an offence if they are:
    - **Present on:**
        - **School premises;**
        - **School land;**
    - **Without lawful authority;** and
    - Either:
        - **Causes;** or
        - **Permits;**
    - Either a:
        - **Nuisance;** or
        - **Disturbance;**
    - To the **annoyance of persons who lawfully use those premises** (whether or not any such persons are present at the time).

Exam Trip Up

- This offence can take place even if **no persons are present** at the relevant time i.e. after school time.

Exam Trip Up

- The offender must be on the premises **without lawful authority** and has **caused or permitted nuisance or disturbance.**

Exam Trip Up

- The school must be a local authority or grant maintained school, **not an independent school.**

Exam Trip Up

- The **police or other relevant person** may enter and **remove offenders** from school premises even if **no offences are still being committed at that time.**

General Police Duties
Unit 5: Harassment, Anti-Social Behaviour & Communication Offences

A - Harassment - Section 1 & 2 PHA 1997

1 - The Definition Of Harassment

- A person will commit an offence of **harassment** if they:
    - Pursue a **course of conduct (on at least 2 occasions)**;
    - That amounts to an act of **harassment (causing alarm** or **distress)**;
    - Which they **either:**
        - **Know; (subjective awareness);** or
        - **Ought to have known**; (objective test);
    - Would amount to an **act of harassment.**

2 - Learning Point - The Objective Test

- The **"reasonable person"** test must be satisfied in determining whether they **ought to have known** that the conduct amounted to harassment - i.e. If a **reasonable person** in possession of the same information would **think** that the **actions would amount to harassment** – the objective test is satisfied.

3 – Establishing A Course Of Conduct

- In the case of *R v Kelly* [2003] Crim LR 45, several calls made to a mobile phone over a very short period of time were found to be a harassing course of conduct.

    The phone calls were not even answered, with the victim later listening to the messages left by the defendant on the voicemail facility, replaying each message one after the other.

    The victim was found to be **harassed by the conduct as a whole** rather than each individual telephone call or voicemail message.

Exam Trip Up

- There is **no requirement** for the **course of conduct** to be of the **same nature** - e.g. A course of conduct could involve sending alarming letters and damaging property!

Exam Trip Up

- In the case involving **racially** or **religiously aggravated** offences, the **aggravating feature** of the harassment must be proved in **both or all instances** of the **course of conduct.**

Exam Trip Up

- There is **no requirement** that any person feels **harassed, alarmed** or **distressed.**
- It is simply a matter of the offender **pursuing a course of conduct which would lead to this consequence.**

Exam Trip Up

- It is only to establish either:
    - ☐ **Harassment;**
    - ☐ **Alarm**; or
    - ☐ **Distress.**
- Not all three.

Exam Trip Up

- The case of *DPP v Dziurzynski* [2002] 166 JP 545 established that:
    - ☐ A **company cannot be harassed** as they are not a legal person; but
    - ☐ **Employees** of the company **can be harassed.**
- For example - An animal rights group target a high street retailer for their sale of fur coats. That retailer as a legal entity cannot feel harassed, although the lady working in the Fur coat department or the manager can.

4 - Penalties For Harassment & Powers Of Arrest

(i) - Simple Harassment – Sections 1 & 2 PHA 1997

- The **simple harassment** offence is a **summary only** offence - **6 months imprisonment** and or a **fine.**
- As such only a **constable** can **arrest** if the necessary criteria apply.

(ii) - Aggravated Harassment – Section 32(1)(A) CDA 1998

- The **racially** or **religiously aggravated** offence is **triable ether way:**
    - ☐ **2 years imprisonment** and or a **fine** if tried on **indictment;**
    - ☐ **6 months imprisonment** and or **fine** if tried **summarily** and
- As such has an **"any person" can arrest** if the necessary criteria apply.

5 - Defences To The Offence Of Harassment - Section 1(3) PHA 1997

- **No offence** will be committed if the **course of conduct** was carried out either:
    - ☐ For the **purpose** of:
        - **Preventing crime;**
        - **Detecting crime;**
    - ☐ Under a **rule of law;**
    - ☐ The conduct was **reasonable.**

B – Putting People In Fear Of Violence

1 - The Definition Of Putting People In Fear Of Violence - Section 4 PHA 1997

- A person commits an offence if they:
    - Cause another to **fear**;
    - On **at least 2 occasions**;
    - That **violence** will be **used against them**;
    - And the person:
        - **Knows (subjectively aware)**; or
        - **Ought to know (objective test)**;
    - That their **course of conduct**:
        - Will cause them **fear**;
        - On *each* occasion.

2 – Establishing A Course Of Conduct

- The case of *Mohammed Ali Caurti v DPP* [2002] Crim R 131, established that:
    - The **course of conduct**;
    - Has to **cause** a person to **fear**;
    - On **at least 2 occasions**;
    - That **violence** would be **used against** *them* (rather than against a member of their family).
- The victim **must fear violence on** *each* **occasion** for the offence to be made out.

Exam Trip Up

- The **violence** in this offence **can be in the future**, as long as the **fear** of it is **in the present tense** - i.e. **on the occasion of the threat**.

Exam Trip Up

- The **course of conduct** must cause the victim to fear that violence *will* rather than *might* be used.
- The classic exam trip up with regard to this circumstance is causing the victim to be seriously frightened of what *might* happen in the future. This is **not enough!** (*R v Henley* [2002] Crim LR 582).

3 - Penalties For Putting People In Fear Of Violence

(i) - Standard Offence – Section 4 PHA 1997

- The sentencing power for the standard offence is:
    - **5 years imprisonment** and or a **fine** for offences tried on **indictment**; and
    - **6 months imprisonment** and or a **fine** for offences tried **summarily**.

(ii) - Aggravated Offence - Section 32(1)(A) CDA 1998

- The sentencing power of the racially or religiously aggravated offence has been increased by the Crime and Disorder Act 1998 to:
    - **7 years imprisonment** and or a **fine** for offences tried on **indictment**; and
    - **6 months imprisonment** and or a **fine** for offences tried **summarily.**

Racially Aggravated Offence Of Putting People In Fear Of Violence - Section 28(1)(a) Crime and Disorder Act 1998

- An offence is **racially aggravated** if:
    - Either:
        - **At the time** of the offence;
        - **Immediately before** committing the offence; *or*
        - **Immediately after** committing the offence;
    - The offender **demonstrates towards the** *victim* of the offence;
    - **Hostility;**
    - **Based** on the victim's:
        - **Membership**; or
        - **Presumed membership**;
    - Of either a:
        - **Racial** group; or
        - **Religious** group.

The Timing Of The Hostility Displayed

- The **timing of the hostility** may be either:
    - *Before* the offence; or
    - *During* the offence;
    - *After* the offence.

Exam Trip Up

- However, for displays following the offence the hostility:
    - **Must** take place *immediately* **afterwards**; and
    - **Not** *sometime* after.

Exam Trip Up

- In the case of *DPP* v *M* [2004] 1 WLR 2758:
    - The words *'bloody foreigners'* was held to amount to an expression of hostility based on a person's membership or presumed membership of a racial group.

4 - Defences To The Offence Of Putting People In Fear Of Violence - Section 4 PHA 1997

(i) - General Defences

- **No offence** will be committed if the course of conduct was carried out either:
    - For the **purpose** of:
        - **Preventing crime;**
        - **Detecting crime;**
    - Under a **rule of law;**
    - The conduct was **reasonable** for the **protection** of either:
        - **Themselves;**
        - **Another;** or
        - **Property.**

(ii) - Defence For Specified Persons On Specified Occasions – Section 12 PHA 1997

- A defence will be established if **certification** has been provided by the **Secretary of State** that:
    - A **specified person**;
    - On a **specified occasion**;
    - Who was acting on **behalf of the crown**;
    - Acted in relation to:
        - **National security;**
        - **The economic well being of the UK;**
        - **Prevention or detection of serious crime.**

C – Bomb Threats – Placing Or Sending Articles - Section 51 Criminal Law Act 1977
Either Way Offence
Penalty In The Magistrates Court – 6 Months Imprisonment And / Or A Fine
Penalty In The Crown Court – 7 Years Imprisonment And / Or A Fine

- A person commits an offence if they either:
    - ☐ **Place** an **article** anywhere; or
    - ☐ **Send** an **article** by:
        - **Post**;
        - **Rail**; or
        - **Other** means;
    - ☐ With the **Intent (offence complete)**;
    - ☐ To cause another to **believe** it is likely to **explode** or **ignite**;
    - ☐ Thereby **causing**:
        - **Personal injury**; or
        - **Damage** to **property**.
- The **article** must be:
    - ☐ **Placed**; or
    - ☐ **Sent**.
- **Intent Offence** - The offence will be **complete** once the **intent** is formed. There is **no need** for a **result**.

Exam Trip Ups

- The offence only applies to articles placed or sent **in the UK**.
- **Bogus** packages are **covered** by the offence.

D – Communicating Bomb Threats - Section 51(2) CLA 1977
Either Way Offence
Penalty In The Magistrates Court – 6 Months Imprisonment And / Or A Fine
Penalty In The Crown Court – 7 Years Imprisonment And / Or A Fine

- A person will commit an offence if they:
    - ☐ **Communicate information** which they either:
        - **Know**; or
        - **Believe**;
    - ☐ To be **false**;
    - ☐ With the **Intent (offence complete)**;
    - ☐ To **induce any person** to **believe** that either of the following are **in any place**:
        - A **bomb**; or
        - Anything liable to **explode**.

E - Compare And Contrast With The Provisions Of Section 114 Anti Terrorism, Crime And Security Act 2001
Either Way Offence
Penalty In The Magistrates Court – 6 Months Imprisonment And / Or A Fine
Penalty In The Crown Court – 7 Years Imprisonment And / Or A Fine

- A person is guilty of an offence if they:
    - ☐ **Place** any **substance** or **other thing** in **any place**; or
    - ☐ **Send** any **substance** or **other thing** from **one place to another** by:
        - Post;
        - Rail; or
        - Any other means;
    - ☐ With the **intent (offence complete)**;
    - ☐ To **induce** in a person **anywhere in the world (not just the UK)**;
    - ☐ A **belief** that it is likely to be (or contain) a **noxious substance** or other **noxious thing** capable of:
        - Endangering human life; or
        - Creating a serious risk to human health.

    For example - Sending fake anthrax "white powder" packages by post.

F – The Definition Of Threats Involving Noxious Substances Or Things – Section 114(2) Anti Terrorism Crime & Security Act 2001
Either Way Offence
Penalty In The Magistrates Court – 6 Months Imprisonment And / Or A Fine
Penalty In The Crown Court – 7 Years Imprisonment And / Or A Fine

- A person is guilty of an offence if they:
    - ☐ **Communicate** any **information** which they:
        - Know; or
        - Believe;
        - To be **false**;
    - ☐ With the **intent** to induce in a person **anywhere in the world**;
    - ☐ A **belief** that a **noxious substance** or other **noxious thing** is likely to be **present** (whether **at the time** the information is communicated or **later**) **in any place**; and
    - ☐ Thereby either:
        - Endangering human life; or
        - Creating a serious risk to human health.

Summary Table

Offence	Threat Type	Location	Intent	Example
Section 51(1) Criminal Law Act 1977	Bomb Threat only	UK	Specific Intent	Bomb at School or city centre
Section 114 A.C & S Act 2001	Broader concept (C.B.R.N. threat or any article)	Anywhere	Specific Intent	White powder parcels

Offence	Threat	Location	Victim	Future Threat	Intent
Section 51(2) CL Act 1977	Direct or Indirect	UK	None	No	Specific intent
Section 114 ACS Act 2001	Direct or Indirect	World	None	Yes	Specific Intent

G – Interfering With Mail - Section 84 Postal Services Act 2000
Summary Only Offence
Penalty In The Magistrates Court – 6 Months Imprisonment And / Or A Fine

- A person commits an offence if they:
    - Without reasonable excuse either:
        - Intentionally delays or opens a postal packet in the course of its transmission by post;
        - Intentionally opens a mail bag; or
        - Intending to act to a persons detriment:
            - Opens a postal packet;
            - Which they know or reasonably suspect;
            - Has been incorrectly delivered to them.

H – Sending Prohibited Articles By Post – Section 85 Postal Services Act 2000
Either Way Offence
Penalty In The Magistrates Court – A Fine
Penalty In The Crown Court – 1 Years Imprisonment

- It is an offence to either **send** or **procure** to be sent;
- A **posted packet** which contains:
    - **Explosives**;
    - **Dangerous substances**;
    - **Noxious substances**;
    - **Filth**;
    - **Unprotected sharp instruments**;
    - **Noxious living creatures**;
    - **Anything likely to injure other postal packets or persons on postal business**;
    - **Indecent or obscene** Prints, Painting, Photographs, Lithographs, Engravings, Files, Books, Cards or Articles; or
    - Anything which is **grossly offensive or indecent** (on the outside cover).

I – Malicious Communications - Section 1 Malicious Communications Act 1988
Summary Only Offence
Penalty In The Magistrates Court – 6 Months Imprisonment And / Or A Fine

1 – Definition Of The Offence

- A person commits an offence if they:
    - **Send** to another:
        - A **letter**; or
        - **Other article**;
    - Which conveys a **message** which is either:
        - **Indecent**;
        - **Grossly offensive**;
        - A **threat**; or
        - Contains **information** which they **know** to be **false**.
    - Which they **intend (offence complete)** to cause:
        - **Distress**; or
        - **Anxiety**;
    - To either:
        - The **recipient**; or
        - **Another**.

2 - Defence

- A person who **sent** the letter or article will have a **defence** if they can establish on the **balance of probability** that it was sent:
    - To **reinforce a demand** which they had **reasonable grounds** for making; and
    - The threat was the **proper means** of **reinforcing the demand**.

For example - A gas company **threatening** to cut off the gas if a bill is not paid by a deadline may well cause the recipient **distress** or **anxiety**. However, there would be **reasonable grounds** for making the threat in the circumstances and the warning letter would be an **appropriate means** of issuing the threat.

J – Sending Prohibited Articles By Post – Section 85 Postal Services Act 2000
Either Way Offence
Penalty In The Magistrates Court – A Fine
Penalty In The Crown Court – 1 Years Imprisonment

- A person commits an offence if they **send** by **post** a **postal packet** which either:
    - **Encloses:**
        - Any **creature, article,** or **thing:**
            - Which is likely to **injure:**
                - Other **postal packages;** or
                - A **postal worker.**
        - Any **indecent** or **obscene** print, painting, photograph, lithograph, engraving, cinematograph film or other record of a picture, book, card or written communication; or
        - Any **indecent** or **obscene article**; ot
    - Has **on the:**
        - **Packet;** or
        - **Cover** of the packet;
    - Any:
        - **Words;**
        - **Marks;** or
        - **Designs;**
    - Which are of an **indecent** or **obscene** character.

K - Threats To Kill - Section 61 OAPA 1861
Either Way Offence
Penalty In The Magistrates Court – 6 Months Imprisonment And / Or A Fine
Penalty In The Crown Court – 10 Years Imprisonment

1 – Definition Of A Threat To Kill

- A person commits an offence if they:
    - Without lawful excuse;
    - Make a **threat to kill** to a:
        - Person; or
        - 3rd Person;
    - Intending (offence complete);
    - The other to **fear** the **threat** would be **carried out**.

2 - Learning Point - When Is The Offence Complete?

- The offence is **complete** once the **intent to cause fear is formed**.
- **No result** is required.
- The **threat does not have to be believed** by the other person.

3 - Lawful Excuses

For example - A **police firearms team** would have a **lawful excuse** to threaten to kill an armed hostage taker in their sights if they did not come peacefully.

Exam Trip Up – The Threat Need Not Be To Kill The Person Who Hears The Threat

- A tells B they intend to kill C – Offence complete.

L - The Anti Social Behaviour Order (ASBO) – Section 1 Crime & Disorder Act 1998

1 - Criteria For Ordering An ASBO

- An application for an order may be made by:
    - The **local authority**; and
    - The **Chief Officer of police**;
- In relation to a person aged **10 or over**;

- If it appears that:
    - They have **behaved** in a manner that **caused** or was **likely to cause**:
        - **Harassment, alarm** or **distress (HAD)**;
        - To **one** or **more** persons;
        - **Not of the same household** as themselves; and
    - The order is **necessary** to **protect persons** in the **area** from **further anti-social acts** by them.

2 – Who May Lodge An Application For An ASBO?

- An **application** for an **ASBO** can be made by:
    - The **Chief Officer of Police**;
    - The **Local Authority**;
    - The **Chief Constable of the British Transport Police**;
    - Any **Social Landlord** who provides or manages any houses or hostels in a local government area; or
    - Any **Housing Trust**.
- **Criminal Courts** may also make an **application** where a defendant has been **convicted** of an **offence**.
- These **"bolt on"** type ASBO's are made by the **court** on it's **own volition**, regardless of any prior application made by an external agency.
    - The ASBO can only be made **in addition** to any:
        - **Sentence**; or
        - **Conditional discharge**.

3 - Applying For An ASBO

- An application must be made:
    - **Between** the:
        - **Police**; and
        - **Local authority**;
    - To a **magistrates court** in the **area** where the anti social behaviour is **taking place**.

4 - The Extent Of An Order – Section 1(B)(a) Crime & Disorder Act 1998

- An **ASBO** may protect:
    - Persons in the **local government area**; and
    - Persons in an **adjoining local government area** as specified in the application.

5 - Consultation

- If an application for an **adjoining area** is made the **relevant persons** in that area must be **consulted**.

6 - The Duration Of An ASBO – Section 1(7) Crime & Disorder Act 1998

- An **ASBO** will **last 2 years**.

- However the applicant and defendant (where the both consent) may have the ASBO **discharged** before the 2 years have expired.

7 - Conditional Discharges And ASBO's

- A court **cannot impose a conditional discharge** on a defendant following an ASBO application.

8 - Ex Parte ASBO's

- An application **can** be made **ex-parte**.

9 - Appeals

- The **Crown Court** may:
    - Make such orders as may be necessary; and
    - Make incidental or consequential orders as appear to be just.

Exam Trip Up

- The case of *Lonergan v Lewes Crown Court* [2005] EWHC 457 established that a **curfew condition** is an **acceptable provision** in an **ASBO** if it is imposed to:
    - **Prevent** anti social behaviour; and
    - **Protect** the **public** from further instances of such behaviour.

- The **curfew condition** does **not have to run** for the **duration** of the **ASBO**.

Exam Trip Up

- *In the case of (On the application of Stanley) v Metropolitan Police Commissioner, Brent London Borough and the Secretary of State for the Home Department [2005]:*
    - It was established that **publicity** is also a possible **provision** with regards to the imposition of an ASBO.
    - The **publishers** of the information (i.e. the police) must show a **link** between the **publicity** and the **practical effectiveness** of the **ASBO**.

Exam Trip Up

- The case of *R (On application of the Chief Constable of West Midlands Police) v Birmingham Magistrates' Court* [2003] Crim LR 37 established that:
    - **Chief Constables** may **delegate** their responsibility with regards to ASBO applications at court to **any officers judged suitable**.
    - **Local authorities** may also make arrangements for the **contracting out** of their **ASBO functions** subject to an **order** by the **Secretary of State**.

10 - Breach Of An Anti-Social Behaviour Order – Section 1(10) CDA 1998

- If a person subject to an ASBO:
    - **Without reasonable excuse;**
    - Does **anything** which they are **prohibited** from doing by the terms of their **ASBO**;
    - They are guilty of an offence and liable:
        - On **summary conviction**:
            - To **imprisonment** for a term not exceeding **six months**; or
            - **A fine**; or
            - **Both**; or
        - On conviction **on indictment**:
            - To **imprisonment** for a term not exceeding **five years**; or
            - **A fine**; or
            - **Both**.

M - Failing To Comply With A Requirement To Give A Name And Address – Section 50(2) Police Reform Act 2002
Summary Only Offence
Penalty In The Magistrates Court – A Fine Only

- Any person who is acting in an **anti-social manner**;
- Who either:
    - **Fails to give their name and address** when required to do so; or
    - **Gives a false or inaccurate name or address** in response to a requirement;
- Is guilty of an offence.

Key Points

- A **constable** or **PCSO** may request the details.
- An offence is committed if a person **either**:
    - **Fails** to give details; or
    - Gives **false** details.
- NB - It does **not have to be both!**

When Is The Offence Complete?

- For the offence to be **complete**:
    - The **person** must have **heard** and **understood** the **requirement**; and
    - The **constable** or **PCSO heard** and **understood** the **response**.

General Police Duties
Unit 6: Public Order

A – Riot – Section 1 Public Order Act 1986
Indictable Only Offence
Penalty In The Crown Court - 10 Years Imprisonment And / Or A Fine

1 – The Definition Of A Riot

- A **riot** involves:
    - **12 or more** persons;
    - **Present together** with a **common purpose (only offence)**;
    - Who either **uses** or **threatens violence** to either a:
        - **Person;** or
        - **Property;** and
    - Either:
        - **Intended** to use or threaten violence; or
        - Was **aware** that their conduct may have been violent;
    - Provided their **conduct taken together** would cause a **hypothetical person of reasonable firmness present to fear for their safety.**
- **Only** the **user** of violence is **guilty;** and
- The person of reasonable firmness <u>**need not**</u> be present.

Exam Trip Up

- There is **no need** for the **12 or more** persons to use or **threaten violence simultaneously.**

Exam Trip Up

- It is **immaterial whether all of the 12 or more** persons **intend** to use violence or are **aware** that their conduct may be violent.
- A person may be guilty of riot even if some of the 12 or more co-rioters are not guilty because they lack the necessary mens rea.

Exam Trip Up

- There is **no need** for:
    - A **pre determined plan;** or
    - The **common purpose to be unlawful** e.g. Buying a Harry Potter book.

2 - The Location Of A Riot – Section 1(5) Public Order Act 1986

- The offence can **take place anywhere:**
    - A **public** place; or
    - A **private** place.

3 - Defences To The Offence Of Riot – Section 6 Public Order Act 1986

- There are **2 defences** - either:
    - **Non Self Induced Intoxication ("Slip it in");** or
    - **Medicine.**

Exam Trip Up

- The **consent** of the **Director of Public Prosecutions** is required.

An Example Of A Riot

It is 8.30 am on the morning of the release of the new Harry Potter book. An impatient crowd of 20 fans have gathered outside WH Smiths, waiting for the store to open to enable them to buy a copy of the book.

The manager, who is inside the store behind a locked glass door, explains to the crowd that they only have 5 copies of the book in stock. As a result the crowd become restless.

John, who is part of the assembled crowd, breaks ranks, beats the glass door and shouts to the manger that if he is not let in first he will beat the manager up.

- The offence of **riot** has been committed by John because:
    - There were **more than 12 persons present**;
    - They all have the **common purpose** of purchasing a copy of the book;
- John both:
    - **Used violence against property;**
    - **Threatened violence against the manager;** and
- The collective behaviour of the group would have **caused a hypothetical person of reasonable firmness to fear for their safety.**

B – Violent Disorder – Section 2 Public Order Act 1986
Either Way Offence
Penalty In The Magistrates Court – 6 Months Imprisonment And / Or A Fine
Penalty In The Crown Court – 5 Years Imprisonment And / Or A Fine

1 – Definition Of Violent Disorder

- An offence of **violent disorder** will be committed by each of **3 or more** persons;
- Present **together**;
- Who either:
    - **Use**; or
    - **Threaten**;
- **Unlawful violence** on:
    - **Persons**; or
    - **Property**;
- That would **cause a hypothetical person of reasonable firmness present to fear for their safety.**
- The person of reasonable firmness **need not** be present.
- There **need not** be a **common purpose**.

2 - The Location Of Violent Disorder - Section 2(4) Public Order Act 1986

- The offence can **take place anywhere**:
    - A **public** place; or
    - A **private** place.

3 - The Defences To Violent Disorder – Section 6 Public Order Act 1986

- There are **2 defences** - either:
    - **Non Self Induced Intoxication ("Slip it in")**; or
    - **Medicine**.

Exam Trip Up

- There is **no need** for the **violence to be used simultaneously.**

Exam Trip Up

- Where there are only three defendants and one of those defendants have been acquitted then if the jury is satisfied that others not charged were taking part in the violent disorder, then the jury may convict the remaining persons standing trial - *R v Warton* [1989] 154 JP 201.

An Example Of Violent Disorder

Tom and Dick, who are friends, get into an argument with their enemy Harry. All 3 start fighting in a deserted alleyway. **All 3** individuals will be guilty of **violent disorder** because:

- There were **3 persons present** together;

- They have **used violence** against **persons (each other)**;

- Their actions would have **caused a hypothetical person of reasonable firmness to fear for their safety had they been present.**

- The fact they were fighting against each other is irrelevant as there is **no need for a common purpose.**

C – Affray – Section 3 Public Order Act 1986
Either Way Offence
Penalty In The Magistrates Court – 6 Months Imprisonment And / Or A Fine
Penalty In The Crown Court – 3 Years Imprisonment And / Or A Fine

1 - The Definition Of Affray

- **Affray** involves a minimum of **1 person**;

- Who either:
    - **Uses**; or
    - **Threatens** to use;

- **Unlawful violence**;

- On **persons (only)** <u>present</u> at the scene;

- Provided the conduct would **cause a hypothetical person of reasonable firmness present to fear for their personal safety.**

- A reasonable person <u>**need not**</u> be present.

2 - Who Is Guilty Of Affray?

- **Only** the person who:
    - **Uses**; or
    - **Threatens**;
    - The **violence** will be **guilty** of affray.

- Words alone will **not do.**

- There must also be <u>**actions.**</u>

3 - The Location Of An Affray - Section 3(5) Public Order Act 1986

- The offence can **take place anywhere**:
    - A **public** place; or
    - A **private** place.

4 - Defences To Affray - Section 6 Public Order Act 1986

- There are **2 defences** - either:
    - **Non Self Induced Intoxication** ("Slip it in"); or
    - **Medicine**.

Exam Trip Up - The 'Hypothetical Person Present Test'

- The case of *R v Sanchez* (1996) 160 JP 321 established:
    - It is necessary to prove that:
        - The **defendant's conduct**;
        - Would have **caused** a **hypothetical person present at the scene**;
        - To **fear** for their **personal safety**.
    - This is **more** than simply being **threatened** with **violence**.

An Example Of An Affray

Bill attacks Ben in a deserted alleyway, punching him in the face. Ben is a professional boxer. He is not fearful for his safety, as he knows that he is capable of effectively defending himself.

- An offence of **affray** has been committed because:
    - Bill has **used violence** against Ben.
    - It is **irrelevant** that **Ben did not fear for his personal safety**.
    - All that is required is that a **hypothetical person of reasonable firmness would have feared for their safety had they been present**.

Summary Table
Riot, Violent Disorder & Affray

Attribute	Riot	V Disorder	Affray
Minimum Number Of Persons	12	3	1
Present Together	Yes	Yes	N/A
Common Purpose	Yes	Not required	N/A
Unlawful Violence	Person or property	Person or property	Person only present
Reasonable Person	Need not be present	Need not be present	Need not be present
Who Is Guilty?	The user of violence	The user or threatener	The user or threatener: Must be words & actions
Intoxication Defence	Provisions apply	Provisions apply	Provisions apply
Private or Public	Anywhere	Anywhere	Anywhere
Arrest	Indictable	Indictable	Indictable

D - Fear of Provocation of Violence - Section 4 Public Order Act 1986
Summary Only Offence
Penalty In The Magistrates Court – 6 Months Imprisonment And / Or A Fine

1 – Definition Of The Offence

- A person is guilty of an offence if they either:
    - **Use towards another words** or **behaviour** that are:
        - Threatening;
        - Abusive;
        - Insulting; or

- **Distributes** or **displays** to **another person:**
    - Any:
        - Writing;
        - Sign; or
        - Visible representation;
    - Which is:
        - Threatening;
        - Abusive; or
        - Insulting;
- With *intent* (**offence complete**) to:
    - To **cause** them to **believe**;
    - To **provoke** them to **believe**; or
    - **Result** in them being likely to **believe**;
- That **immediate unlawful violence** will be **used** against either:
    - Them; or
    - Another.

2 - The State Of Mind Of The Defendant

- The defendant must either:
    - **Intend** their words or behaviour to be insulting etc; or
    - **Be aware** that their words or behaviour may be insulting etc.

3 - When Is The Offence Complete?

- The offence is **complete** when the **intent is proved**.
- The **result** is **not important!**

4 - The Location Of The Offence - Section 4(2) Public Order Act 1986

- The offence can be committed either in:
    - Public; or
    - Private.

5 - The Dwelling Defence – Section 4(2) Public Order Act 1986

- The offence is **not complete** if:
    - ☐ Both parties;
    - ☐ Are in:
        - A dwelling; or
        - Different dwellings.

Exam Trip Up

- **Communal landings** do **not** form part of a dwelling.

6 - The Definition Of A Dwelling – Section 8 Public Order Act 1986

- The list includes:
    - ☐ Houses;
    - ☐ Flats;
    - ☐ Caravans;
    - ☐ House Boats;
    - ☐ Tents;
    - ☐ Tree Houses; etc.

- In essence **any structure** that persons can **live in.**

Examples Of The Dwelling Defence In Operation

- Tarzan would not commit the offence if he threatened Jane with unlawful personal violence whilst they are both in their tree house.

- Livingstone lives in a tent below Tarzan's tree house. If Tarzan threatened Livingstone with unlawful personal violence from the window of his tree house whilst Livingstone was inside his tent, there would be no offence - as both Tarzan and Livingstone would be within their own respective dwellings when the threat was made.

- As per last example, but this time, Christopher Biggins, who is strolling through the jungle, overhears the altercation between Tarzan and Livingstone. If as a result Christopher Biggins feared that:
    - ☐ Immediate unlawful violence;
    - ☐ Would be used against any person including:
        - Livingstone;
        - Himself (Biggins);
        - Anybody else;
    - ☐ Then the offence would be complete.

Exam Trip Up

- This offence can be committed when a **telephone call** is made to a person provided:
    - ☐ **One of the persons is not in a dwelling; and**
    - ☐ **A threat of immediate violence is made.**

7 - The Aggravated Offence – Section 31(1)(a) Crime & Disorder Act 1998
Either Way Offence
Penalty In The Magistrates Court – 6 Months Imprisonment And / Or A Fine
Penalty In The Crown Court – 2 Years Imprisonment And / Or A Fine

- The offence can be **religiously** or **racially** aggravated.

E - Intentional Harassment, Alarm or Distress - Section 4A Public Order Act 1986
Summary Only Offence
Penalty In The Magistrates Court – 6 Months Imprisonment And / Or A Fine

1 – Definition Of The Offence

- A person commits an offence, if with **intent to cause:**
    - ☐ **Harassment;**   H
    - ☐ **Alarm; or**   A
    - ☐ **Distress;**   D

- They either:
    - ☐ **Use threatening, abusive or insulting words or behaviour;**
    - ☐ **Use disorderly behaviour;** or
    - ☐ **Display any threatening, abusive or insulting writing, sign or visible representation;**

- Thereby **causing (result) a person:**
    - ☐ **Harassment;**   H
    - ☐ **Alarm; or**   A
    - ☐ **Distress.**   D

Learning Point

- There are **two elements** to the **section 4(A) offence** which **differ** from the **section 4 offence.**
    - ☐ Section 4A requires that:
        - Not only must the offender have the requisite intent to cause the consequence;
        - The offender must also bring about the result of H.A.D.
        - The result is the important aspect.

    - ☐ There are **more defences available:**
        - Dwelling defence; plus
        - 2 statutory defences.

2 - The Dwelling Defence – Section 4A(2) Public Order Act 1986

- The offence is **not complete** if:
  - Both parties;
  - Are in:
    - A dwelling; or
    - A different dwelling.

Exam Trip Up

- **Communal landings** do **not** form part of a dwelling.

3 - The Statutory Defences – Section 4A(3)(a)&(b) Public Order Act 1986

- There are also two additional defences to the offence under section 4A POA 1986:
  - The defendant:
    - Was inside a dwelling; and
    - They had no reason to believe that a person outside the dwelling could hear or see what was offensive; or
  - The defendant's conduct was reasonable.

4 - The Location Of The Offence - Section 4(A)(2) Public Order Act 1986

- The offence can be committed in a:
  - Public place; or
  - Private place.

Exam Trip Up

- **Posting inflammatory letters** through letter boxes is **not an offence** under this particular section.

5 - The Aggravated Offence – Section 31(1)(b) Crime & Disorder Act 1998
Either Way Offence
Penalty In The Magistrates Court – 6 Months Imprisonment And / Or A Fine
Penalty In The Crown Court – 2 Years Imprisonment And / Or A Fine

- The offence can be **religiously** or **racially** aggravated.

F - Harassment, Alarm or Distress – Section 5 Public Order Act 1986.
Summary Only Offence
Penalty In The Magistrates Court – Fine

1 – Definition Of The Offence Of Harassment, Alarm or Distress

- It is an offence to:
    - Either:
        - Use threatening, abusive or insulting words or behaviour;
        - Use disorderly conduct; or
        - Display any threatening, abusing or insulting writing, sign, or visible representation;
    - Within the sight or hearing of a person likely to be caused:
        - Harassment;   H
        - Alarm; or   A
        - Distress.   D

2 - The Location Of The Offence - Section 5(2) Public Order Act 1986

- The offence can be committed in a:
    - **Public** place; or
    - **Private** place.

3 - The State Of Mind Of The Defendant

- The defendant must either:
    - **Intend** their words or behaviour to be insulting etc; or
    - **Be aware** that they may be.

Exam Trip Up

- **E-mailing** between dwellings is **not** an **offence** under this section of legislation.

4 - The Dwelling Defence - Section 4(2) Public Order Act 1986

- The offence is **not complete** if:
    - Both parties;
    - Are in:
        - A dwelling; or
        - A different dwelling.

Exam Trip Up

- **Communal landings** do **not** form part of a dwelling.

5 - The Statutory Defences – Section 5(2) & (3) Public Order Act 1986

- There are also **3 statutory defences:**

  - **The defendant was:**
    - **Inside a dwelling; and**
    - They had **no reason to believe that a** person outside the dwelling could hear or see what was offensive;

  - The conduct was **reasonable;**

  - They had **no reason to believe** that there was any person within **sight or hearing** who was likely to be caused H.A.D.

Exam Trip Up

- The case of *Holloway v DPP* [2004] EWHC 2621 established that in relation to harassment, alarm or distress there **needs to be a person within whose sight or hearing the conduct takes place.**

- The circumstances of this case were that the person was filming children in a playground using a **long range lens**.

- He was initially convicted, however his conviction was quashed on appeal as in the circumstances **no person was within the sight or hearing of the conduct** could be harassed, alarmed or distressed.

6 - The Aggravated Offence – Section 31(1)(c) Crime & Disorder Act 1998
Summary Only Offence
Penalty In The Magistrates Court – Fine Only

- The offence can be **religiously** or **racially aggravated**.

Summary Table

Offence	Action	Nature	Purpose
Section 4	<ul><li>Words</li><li>Behaviour</li><li>Writing</li><li>Sign</li><li>Visual Representation</li></ul>	<ul><li>Threatening</li><li>Abusive</li><li>Insulting</li></ul>	Intent to cause, provoke, or generate a belief of immediate unlawful violence
Section 4A	<ul><li>Words</li><li>Behaviour</li><li>Writing</li><li>Sign</li><li>Visual Representation</li></ul>	<ul><li>Threatening</li><li>Abusive</li><li>Insulting</li><li>Disorderly</li></ul>	Intent to cause:<ul><li>Harassment;</li><li>Alarm;</li><li>Distress.</li></ul>
Section 5	<ul><li>Words</li><li>Behaviour</li><li>Writing</li><li>Sign</li><li>Visual Representation</li><li>Conduct</li></ul>	<ul><li>Threatening</li><li>Abusive</li><li>Insulting</li><li>Disorderly</li></ul>	<ul><li>Intend for their words or behaviour to be insulting etc; or</li><li>Be aware that they may be.</li></ul>

Offence	Against	Result Required	Venue	Defences
Section 4	<ul><li>Them</li><li>Another</li></ul>	No Offence complete once the intent is formed	<ul><li>Public</li><li>Private</li></ul>	Dwelling defence only
Section 4A	<ul><li>Them</li><li>Another</li></ul>	Yes<ul><li>Harassment</li><li>Alarm</li><li>Distress</li></ul>	<ul><li>Public</li><li>Private</li></ul>	<ul><li>Dwelling defence</li><li>Plus 2 others</li></ul>
Section 5	Within the sight or hearing of a person likely to be caused HAD	No	<ul><li>Public</li><li>Private</li></ul>	<ul><li>Dwelling Defence</li><li>Plus 3 others</li></ul>

General Police Duties
Unit 7: Firearms

A – The Definition Of A Firearm - Section 57 Firearms Act 1968

- A **firearm** is:
    - A **lethal barrelled weapon** of any description;
    - **Capable** of **discharging** a:
        - **Shot**;
        - **Bullet**;
        - Other **missile (e.g. a dart from a blowpipe)**;
    - And includes:
        - A **prohibited weapon** that is:
            - **Lethal**; or
            - **Non Lethal**;
        - A **component part** of any weapon that is:
            - **Lethal**; or
            - **Prohibited**;
        - **Accessories** which **diminish**:
            - **Noise** caused by firing; or
            - **Flash** caused by firing.
- The questions you must always ask yourself at exam time is:
    - Has it got a **barrel?**
    - Does anything get **shot** out of it?
    - Can it **kill** you?
- If the answer is **"yes"** then you have a **firearm** in your hands.

    For example - Blow pipes, starting pistols, air pistols, etc. (even when they are not working).

Exam Trip Up - What Is Not A Firearm?

- The following are **not** a **firearm**:
    - Bottle of bleach;
    - Fingers held under a jacket; (It has been held that an unsevered hand cannot be possessed and cannot be an imitation firearm - *R v Bentham* [2005] UKHL 18);
    - An empty bottle of washing up liquid bottle filled with acid.

B - The Definition of A Prohibited Weapon – Section 5 Firearms Act 1968

- The following are **prohibited weapons:**
    - ☐ **Automatic weapons;**
    - ☐ **Self loading or pump action weapons;**
    - ☐ **Most handguns;**
    - ☐ **Gas powered air weapons;**
    - ☐ **CS gas canisters;**
    - ☐ **Grenades;** and
    - ☐ **Mortars.**
- Put simply - Any **weapons** that **should be in the hands of a soldier!**

Exam Trip Up

- The **authority** of the **Secretary of State** must be obtained before a prohibited weapon can be:
    - ☐ **Possessed;**
    - ☐ **Acquired;**
    - ☐ **Bought;**
    - ☐ **Sold**; or
    - ☐ **Transferred.**

Exam Trip Up

- Any **air weapon designed** or **adapted** to use a **self contained gas cartridge system** is covered under this section.

Exam Trip Up

- Any **firearm** that **discharges** any **noxious liquid, gas or other thing** will be prohibited.

Exam Trip Up

- An **electric stun gun** has been held to be a prohibited weapon as it discharges an electric current - *Flack v Baldry* [1988] IWLR 393.
- A stun gun **continues** to be such a device **even if it is not working** - *R v Brown* [1992] The Times 27th March.

C - The Definition Of A Component Part - Section 57(1)(b) Firearms Act 1968

- Put simply - **If a gun cannot be operated without a specific part** that part will be a **component part.**
- **Component parts** include:
    - ☐ **Triggers;**
    - ☐ **Barrels;** or
    - ☐ **Stocks.**

D - The Definition Of Accessories Which Diminish Flash Or Noise - Section 57(1)(c) Firearms Act 1968

- The case of *R v Buckfield* [1998] Crim LR 673, established that:
    - If a person is found in **possession** of a:
        - Silencer; or
        - Anti flash device;
    - Which has been **manufactured**;
    - For a weapon in their **possession**;
- Then under the act it is a **firearm**.

Accessories Which Diminish Flash Or Noise That Are Manufactured For A Different Weapon - Section 57(1)(c) Firearms Act 1968

- If a:
    - **Silencer**; or
    - **Anti flash device**;
- Is **made for a different weapon**;
- The **prosecution** will have to prove:
    - That it **could be used with the weapon in their possession**; and
    - They had **possession for that purpose**.

E - When Does A Firearm Cease To Be A Firearm? – Section 8 Firearms (Amendment) Act 1988

- A **firearm** may **cease** to be so if:
    - It is **de-activated** by proving:
        - It bears a **mark**:
            - **Approved** by the **Secretary Of State**;
            - **Denoting** the fact that it has been **de-activated**;
            - By an **approved company**, and
        - The **company** has **certified in writing** that the **work has been carried out** in an approved manner for rendering it incapable.

F - The Definition Of A Shotgun - Section 1(3)(a) Firearms Act 1968

- A **shotgun** is a:
    - **Smooth bore** gun (not an air weapon or revolver) which:
        - Has a **barrel** not less than **2 feet (24 inches)**;
        - Whose **bore** does not exceed **2 inches**, and
        - Whose **magazine** (if any) does not hold more than **2 cartridges**.

Memory Aid

- Remember "**The Rule of Two's**"!
    - **Barrel** not less than **2 feet**
    - **Bore** not more than **2 inches**, and
    - **Magazine** not more than **2 cartridges**.
    - **2 x 2 x 2!**

G - The Definition Of Air Weapons - Section 1(3)(b) Firearms Act 1968

- In summary **air weapons** include any:
    - **Air rifle;**
    - **Airgun;** or
    - **Air pistol;**
    - Which either:
        - Are **not** of a type **declared** to be **especially dangerous;** or
        - **Uses** or is **designed** or **adapted** for use with a **self contained gas cartridge system.**

H - The Definition Of Especially Dangerous Air Weapons – Section 1 Firearms Act 1968

- An **air weapon** is **especially dangerous** when:
    - An **air pistol's** kinetic energy exceeds **6ft per lb;**
    - An **air weapon's** kinetic energy exceeds **12 ft per lb,** or
    - When **disguised** as **another object.**

Memory Aid

- Remember the "**Double Rule**":

    "**Six, twelve** and it can **double** as something else"

    6 x DOUBLED = 12

Exam Trip Up

- Watch out for questions involving an underwater spear gun – They are **not especially dangerous.**

I - Firearm Ammunition Exemptions - Section 1 Firearms Act 1968

- The following are **exempt** from the requirement for a **section 1 certificate:**
    - **Cartridges** containing **5 or more shots**, not bigger than **0.36 inch;**
    - **Ammunition** for an **air weapon,** and
    - **Blanks** not more than **1 inch** in diameter.

Memory Aid

- Basically - If it is going to hurt me badly – a certificate is required!

J – Possession Of A Firearm Or Ammunition Without A Certificate - Section 1 Firearms Act 1968

1 - The Definition Of The Offence

- It is an offence for a person to:
    - Either:
        - **Possess;**
        - **Purchase;** or
        - **Acquire:**
    - Either a:
        - **Firearm;**
        - **Imitation firearm;** or
        - **Ammunition;**
    - **Without** a **certificate**; or
    - In the case of **ammunition** - quantities **in excess** of the **authorised amounts.**

Key Points

- It is a **strict liability** offence.
- No "**Mens rea**" is required.
- Simple **possession** makes the **offence complete**.
- "Sawn off shotguns" – **aggravated** offence.

2 - Definition Of Possession

- **Possession** is a **very wide concept** within the Firearms Act.
- It is possible for one person to be in possession, even though some other person has physical control.
- It is therefore possible for more than one person to be in possession of the same article.

For example:

One person owns a firearm but the weapon is kept in a friend's firearms cabinet at his home.

The two persons mentioned would be in possession and control of the weapon.

3 - Definition Of Has With Them

- **Has with them** is a **narrower concept than possession**, and is seen in some of the aggravated firearms offences (e.g. Sec. 18).

- Has with them means that the firearm is **"readily accessible"**.

- For example the firearm could be:
    - On the defendants person;
    - In a holdall carried with the defendant;
    - In a car boot or in a car parked near by.

- However, it would not be with them if it was left at home or in a car two miles away.

4 - Exempt Persons Or Organisations

- The following persons or organisations are **exempt** from the requirement to hold a **certificate**:
    - Police permit holders;
    - Crown servants (services / visiting services);
    - European permit holders;
    - Athletic purposes;
    - Auctioneers;
    - Carriers;
    - Warehouse staff;
    - Authorised dealers;
    - Slaughterers;
    - Ship / aircraft equipment;
    - Proof houses;
    - Antiques;
    - Theatrical / museum use.

Memory Aid

- *"A Mars a day helps you work, rest and play"*.

- All of these exemptions relate to environments surrounding:
    - Work;
    - Rest; or
    - Play.

K - Borrowing Rifles On Private Premises - Section 16 Firearms Act 1968

- Where a **rifle** is **borrowed** on **private premises**:
- Either the:
    - ☐ **Certificate holder**;
    - ☐ **Agent**;
    - ☐ **Servant**
- Must be **present**.

L - Criminal Use Of Firearms

- The following sections of the **Firearms Act 1968** relate to specific offences:
    - ☐ **Possession with intent to endanger life (s16)**.
    - ☐ **Possession with intent to cause fear of violence (s16a)**.
    - ☐ **Using a firearm to resist arrest (s17(1))**.
    - ☐ **Possession of a firearm while committing or being arrested for a schedule 1 offence (s17(2))**.
    - ☐ **Having a firearm with intent to commit an indictable offence or resist arrest (s18)**.

Key Point

- ☐ **All** of the offences **apart** from the **s16** offence relate to <u>**both**</u>:
    - **Firearms**; or
    - **Imitation firearms**.

Memory Aid

- ☐ Remember the **"Intent / Result Rule"**
    - **All** offences **apart** from **s17(2)** are **intent** offences.
    - Therefore all that is required is:
        - ☐ To have a **firearm**;
        - ☐ With the **intent** to **do something nasty**.

M - Possession Of A Firearm Whilst Committing Or Being Arrested For A Schedule 1 Offence - Section 17(2) Firearms Act 1968

1 – Definition Of The Offence

- A person commits an offence if:
    - **At the time** of:
        - **Committing**; or
        - **Being arrested for**;
    - A **schedule one offence**;
    - They have in their **possession** a:
        - **Firearm**; or
        - **Imitation firearm**.

Schedule 1 Offences

- **Schedule 1 offences** include:
    - Rape and other serious sexual offences;
    - Criminal damage;
    - Theft – NB – not handling;
    - Robbery;
    - Blackmail;
    - Burglary;
    - TWOC;
    - Assaults (not section 18 OAPA 1861);
    - Child abduction; and
    - Aiding and abetting any of the above.

Memory Aid

- Remember "**D.A.R.T**":
    - Damage   -   D
    - Assaults   -   A
    - Rape   -   R
    - Theft   -   T

Exam Trip Up

A previous exam question used the **DART** mnemonic in relation to **schedule 1 offences**. The example given was a **section 18 assault**.

This is **not** a **DART offence** as the sentencing power for a section 18 assault is life imprisonment.

As the sentencing power is already at the maximum it is not possible for the aggravating circumstance to increase the penalty.

2 - Lawful Authority

- **No offence** is committed where:
    - ☐ A person who is **being arrested** for a **schedule 1 offence**;
    - ☐ **At the time of arrest**;
    - ☐ Has **lawful authority** for the **possession** of the weapon.

For example: No offence would be committed where a defendant is arrested sometime after the offence and at that time they are shooting at a rifle range or shooting rabbits in a field.

Summary Table

Offence	"Possession" or "Has with him"	Firearm or Imitation Firearm	Intent or Result	Miscellaneous Matters
Section 16 Possession with intent to endanger life.	Possession	Firearm	Intent	Must provide the means for the threat. Conditional threat will do. Ammunition is covered.
Section 16A Possession with intent to cause fear of violence.	Possession	Firearm Imitation Firearm	Intent	Must provide the means for the threat.
Section 17(1) Using a firearm to resist arrest.	"Has with him"	Firearm Imitation Firearm	Intent	Component Parts/Silencers/Flash Eliminators are not included. Arrest must be lawful.
Section 17(2) Possession of a firearm while committing or being arrested for a schedule 1 offence.	Possession	Firearm Imitation Firearm	Result	No need to be convicted of D.A.R.T. offence or even to prove the elements of the offence.
Section 18 Having a firearm with intent to commit an indictable offence or resist arrest.	Has with him	Firearm Imitation Firearm	Intent	Broader than Sec. 17 offence. No need for arrest to be lawful.

M – Firearms In A Public Place - Section 19 Firearms Act 1968

- A person commits an offence if:
    - Without:
        - Lawful authority; or
        - Reasonable excuse;
    - They **have with them** in a **public place**;
- Either:
    - **Loaded Shotgun,**
    - A **firearm,** whether **loaded** or **unloaded**, together with suitable **ammunition**;
    - **Loaded** or **unloaded air weapon**; or
    - **Imitation firearm.**

Exam Trip Up

- **Previously section 19:**
    - **Made no reference to an imitation firearm;** and
    - The offence would only be committed in relation to an **air weapon** when it was **loaded.**
- This has now **changed.**

Exam Trip Up

- **Age** is **not a consideration** with regards to this offence.

N - Trespassing With Firearms

- There are **2 offences** for **trespassing with firearms**:
    - Trespassing with a firearm **in a building** – Section 20(1) Firearms Act 1968
    - Trespassing with a firearm **on land** - Section 20(2) Firearms Act 1968

Exam Trip Up

- **Firearms, imitation firearms** or **air weapons** are all covered under section 20 Firearms Act 1968.

Exam Trip Up

- **Trespassing** with an **imitation firearm** or **air weapon** is a **summary only** offence.

1 - Trespassing With A Firearm In A Building – Section 20(1) Firearms Act 1968

- A person commits an offence if:
  - They either:
    - **Enter**; or
    - **Are in**;
  - Any:
    - **Building**; or
    - **Part of a building**;
  - As a **trespasser**; and
  - **Without reasonable excuse** (burden of proof lies on them);
  - They **have with them** either a:
    - **Firearm**; or
    - **Imitation firearm**.

Learning Points

- Once the **permission** has been **withdrawn** the **offence is complete**.
- **Entering** or **being in** a building will suffice.
- If the **defendant** raises the defence of a **reasonable excuse** must discharge the **burden of proof** on the **balance of probabilities**.

2 – Trespassing With A Firearm On Land - Section 20(2) Firearms Act 1968

- A person commits an offence if:
  - They either:
    - **Enter**; or
    - **Are on**;
  - **Any land** (including **land covered by water**);
  - As a **trespasser**;
  - **Without lawful excuse** (the burden of proof lies on them); and
  - They have with them a:
    - **Firearm**; or
    - **Imitation firearm**.
- The person does **not** have to have firearm on them at the time of entry.

O - Persons Prohibited From Possessing Firearms – Section 21 Firearms Act 1968

Memory Aid

Remember: **3 + 3 = 5**

Sentence	Prohibition
3 years or more	At any time - permanent
3 months to 3 years	5 years
Licence or Order with a condition not to possess	Duration of the order

Exam Trip Up

- The prohibition relates to the **sentence issued** at court not time served.
- For example:
- If the defendant was sentenced to 5 years imprisonment for robbery, but only served 2.5 years then in those circumstances they would be prohibited from possession of firearms for life.

Exam Trip Up

- The prohibition does **not** relate to **imitation firearms**.
- Restrictions only relate to **all firearms** and **ammunition**.

P - Firearms: Police Powers In Relation To Persons - Section 47 Firearms Act 1968

- If a **constable** has **reasonable cause** to **suspect** that a person:
    - Is in **possession** of a **firearm** in a **public place;** or
    - Is **committing** or **about to commit** a **relevant offence elsewhere** than a **public place;**
- The **constable** may:
    - Require them to **hand over** the **firearm** and **ammunition** for examination; or
    - **Search** them and **detain** them to do so.
- Anyone **failing to hand over the firearm or ammunition** commits an **offence**.

Q - Firearms: Police Powers In Relation To Vehicles - Section 47(4) Firearms Act 1968

- A **constable** may **stop and search** a vehicle if:
    - They have **reasonable grounds** to **suspect** that either:
        - There is:
            - A **firearm**;
            - In a **vehicle**;
            - In a **public place**; or
        - A **vehicle** is:
            - Being **used** or **about to be used**;
            - For a **relevant offence**;
            - **Elsewhere** than in a **public place**.

Learning Point

- There are two powers in essence provided under section 47 Firearms Act 1968:
    - A constable may require may **require a person in a public place to hand over a firearm for examination.**

        For example: A stop search in the High Street, for the purposes of detecting offences.

    - A **power to examine a weapon from a person elsewhere than in a public place** – provided the officer has **reasonable cause to suspect** the person is **committing** or **about to commit** a relevant offence (Section 18/20 Firearms Act 1968 offences).

        For example: A police officer is told that two persons are in possession of a firearm within a dwelling and are conspiring to commit an armed robbery at a nearby 24 hour garage. Section 47 gives the power to **enter** and **search**. However, this section does **not** give the power to **arrest**.

R - Constables Power To Demand A Firearms Certificate – Sections 47 & 48 Firearms Act 1968

- A **constable** may **demand a certificate** from any person they **believe** is **in possession** of a:
    - **Firearm**;
    - **Ammunition**; or
    - **Shotgun**.
- Where the person **fails** to:
    - **Produce** a certificate;
    - **Allow** the certificate to be **read**; or
    - **Show** they are **exempt**;
- The **constable** may:
    - **Seize** and **detain** the person; or
    - **Demand** the persons **name** and **address** (immediately).

General Police Duties
Unit 8: Weapons Offences

A – Offensive Weapons In A Public Place – Section 1 Prevention of Crime Act 1953
Either Way Offence
Penalty In The Magistrates Court – 6 Months Imprisonment And / Or A Fine
Penalty In The Crown Court – 4 Years Imprisonment And / Or A Fine

1 – Definition Of The Offence

- A person commits an offence if they:
    - **Without** either:
        - **Lawful authority**; or
        - A **reasonable excuse**;
    - Have **with them**;
    - In a **public place**;
    - Any **offensive weapon**.

2 - The Definition Of Lawful Authority

- The following may have a **lawful authority**:
    - **Police**;
    - **Armed services**.

3 - The Definition Of A Reasonable Excuse

- The following may amount to a **reasonable excuse**:
    - **Workers** carrying **tools** of their trade;
    - **Security guards** may have a reasonable excuse if an **attack is anticipated**.
- **I forgot I had it!** – Is **not** a reasonable excuse.

4 - Carrying Weapons As A General Precaution

- It is **unlawful** possession to retain a weapon on a **"just in case"** basis.
- However, if an **attack** is **anticipated** which is unlawful then possession would be **lawful**.

5 - The Burden Of Proof

- The **prosecution** must initially prove the **possession**.
- It will then be up to the **defendant** to prove their **lawful excuse** on the **balance of probability**.

6 - Has With Them

- The offence is a **strict liability** offence - **no intent** is required.
- Possession itself is adequate.

An Example Of Innocent Articles Used Offensively

- Where a builder hits a customer as a result of an argument over "shoddy work" with a **lump hammer:**
    - Whilst the offence of assault is made out;
    - He is **not** in possession of an offensive weapon;
    - As the builder **formed the intention** to use the hammer **after it came into their possession.**

7 - The Definition Of An Offensive Weapon – Section 1(4) Prevention of Crime Act 1953

- An offensive weapon will include:
    - Any **article** either:
        - **Made:** Items **specifically designed to cause injury** – e.g. knuckle duster, flick knife etc.
        - **Adapted:** The item must be **physically adapted** - e.g. broken bottle, shards of glass in potato.
        - **Intended:** Although the article has an **innocent purpose if properly used**, the defendants **intention to use it in an offensive manner** makes the article an offensive weapon.

            The article could be **anything,** as long as the **intention** is to use it **cause injury**, which includes shock and stress - e.g. Using a walking stick to hit somebody over the head.
    - For **causing injury.**

B – Having Blades Or Sharply Pointed Articles In A Public Place – Section 139(1) Criminal Justice Act 1988
Either Way Offence
Penalty In The Magistrates Court – 6 Months Imprisonment And / Or A Fine
Penalty In The Crown Court – 2 Years Imprisonment And / Or A Fine

1 – Definition Of The Offence

- It is an offence to:
    - Have an **article**;
    - Which either;
        - Has a **blade;** or
        - Is **sharply pointed;**
    - In a **public place.**

2 - The Definition Of A Blade

- **Folding** pocket knifes:
    - With a **blade less than 3 inches** long are **exempt;**
    - Unless the **blade locks** – such items are **not exempt.**

3 - Defence – Section 139(4)&(5) CJPOA 1988

- A **defence** will be established if the defendant had:
    - **Good reason**;
    - **Lawful authority**; or
    - The blade or sharply pointed article was used for:
        - **Work**;
        - A **religious reason**; or (e.g. Sikhs carrying a kirpan)
        - As part of a **national costume** (e.g. Kilt with a knife in the sock).

C – Having Blades Or Sharply Pointed Articles On School Premises
Either Way Offence
Penalty In The Magistrates Court – 6 Months Imprisonment And / Or A Fine
Penalty In The Crown Court – 2 Years Imprisonment And / Or A Fine

1 – Definition Of The Offence - Section 139(A)(1) Criminal Justice Act 1988

- It is an offence to:
    - Have an **article** which either:
        - Has a **blade**; or
        - Is **sharply pointed**;
    - On school premises.

2 - Defence - Section 139(A)(1) Criminal Justice Act 1988

- A **defence** will be established if the defendant had:
    - **Good reason**;
    - **Lawful authority**; or
    - The blade or sharply pointed article was used for:
        - **Work**;
        - A **religious reason**; or (e.g. Sikhs carrying kirpan)
        - As part of a **national costume** (e.g. Kilt with knife in sock).

3 - The Definition Of School Premises – Section 4 Education Act 1996

- The definition of **school premises** includes:
    - **Primary schools**;
    - **Secondary schools**.
- The definition does **not** include:
    - **FE Institutions**;
    - **HE Institutions**.
    - **School dwellings -** i.e. headmasters or caretakers address.

D – The Power Of Entry And Search – Section 139(B) Criminal Justice Act 1988

- A constable;
- Who has **reasonable grounds** to **suspect**;
- That an **offence** under **section 139(A)** either:
    - **Is** being committed; or
    - **Has** been committed:
- May:
    - **Enter premises** (by **force** if necessary); and
    - **Search** (using **reasonable force**) either:
        - **Premises**; or
        - **Persons**.

The Power Of Seizure

- If the constable **suspects** that any **persons in the premises** are in **possession** of either:
    - **Sharps**; or
    - **Offensive weapons**;
- The constable may:
    - **Seize**; and
    - **Retain**
    - what they find.

New Powers For Teaching Staff To Search Pupils As Introduced By The Violent Crime Reduction Act 2006

- There is now an additional power which enables a **member of staff** to **search pupils** if they:
    - Have **reasonable grounds** to **suspect**;
    - That the **pupil** is **in possession** of either a:
        - **Knife**;
        - **Bladed article**; or
        - **Offensive weapon**.

Exam Trip Up – The Permitted Location Of A Search

- The member of staff may only search the pupil if either:
    - **Both teacher** and **pupil** are *on* **school premises**; or
    - If *off* school premises – the **pupil is under the control of member of staff**. i.e. school trip etc.

Exam Trip Up - Who May Conduct The Search?

- Only either of the following may conduct the search:
    - ☐ The **headmaster**; or
    - ☐ A **member of staff authorised** by the **headmaster**;

Exam Trip Up - Action To Be Taken In Relation To Any Item Recovered During The Search

- Any **item recovered** must be **delivered** to a **constable** as soon as practicable.

E - Trespassing With A Weapon Of Offence – Section 8(1) Criminal Law Act 1977
Summary Only Offence
Penalty In The Magistrates Court – 3 Months Imprisonment And / Or A Fine

1 – Definition Of The Offence

- A person who is:
    - ☐ On *any* **premises**;
    - ☐ As a **trespasser**;
    - ☐ After having **entered** as a **trespasser**;
    - ☐ Is guilty of an offence if:
        - Without:
            - ☐ **Lawful authority**; or
            - ☐ **Reasonable excuse**;
    - They:
        - ☐ Have **with them on** the **premises**;
        - ☐ *Any* **weapon of offence**.

2 - Definition Of A Weapon Of Offence – Section 8(2) Criminal Law Act 1977

- This is the **same** definition as per the **"weapon of offence"** relating to **aggravated burglary**.
- This is:
    - ☐ An **article**;
    - ☐ Which is either:
        - **Made**; or
        - **Adapted**;
    - ☐ For either:
        - **Causing injury** to or **incapacitating** a person; or
        - **Intended** by the person having it with them **for that use**.

3 - Definition Of Premises – Section 12 Criminal Law Act 1977

- **Premises** includes any:
    - ☐ **Buildings**;
    - ☐ **Part of a building** under separate occupation;
    - ☐ **Adjacent land** used or intended to be used in connection with that land;
    - ☐ **Fixed structure** or any **movable structure**;
    - ☐ **Vehicle** or **vessel designed** or **adapted** for **residential purposes**.

Exam Trip Up

- This offence **differs** from the **trespass offence** in the **Firearms Act**.
- In this legislation the person:
    - ☐ Must have *entered* as a trespasser; and
    - ☐ *Not* subsequently became one.

F - Manufacture, Sale or Hire of Weapons - Section 1 (1) Restriction of Offensive Weapons Act 1959
Summary Only Offence
Penalty In The Magistrates Court – 6 Months Imprisonment And / Or A Fine

- It is an offence for any person to:
    - ☐ **Manufacture**;
    - ☐ **Sell**, or **offer** or **expose** for **sale**;
    - ☐ **Hire**, or **offer** or **expose** for **hire**;
    - ☐ **Lend**; or
    - ☐ **Give**;

    - ☐ Any:
        - **Flick** knife; or
        - **Gravity** knife.

G - Sale of Knives And Articles To Under 18's - Section 141A Criminal Justice Act 1988
Summary Only Offence
Penalty In The Magistrates Court – 6 Months Imprisonment And / Or A Fine

- It is an offence to:
    - ☐ **Sell**;
    - ☐ To any person **under 18**;

- Any:
    - **Knife**;
    - **Knife blade**;
    - **Razor blade**;
    - **Axe**; or
    - **Any other article** which:
        - Has a **blade** or which is **sharply pointed**; and
        - Is **made** or **adapted** for **use** for **causing injury** to the person.

Exemptions

- This **offence** does **not apply** to:
    - **Folding pocket knives** with a **cutting edge not greater** than **3 inches** or **7.62cm**; or
    - **Razor blades in a cartridge** where **not more than 2mm of blade is exposed**; e.g. "Gillette" or "Wilkinson Sword" type razor cartridges.

H - Unlawful Marketing of Knives - Section 1 Knives Act 1997
Either Way Offence
Penalty In The Magistrates Court – 6 Months Imprisonment And / Or A Fine
Penalty In The Crown Court – 2 Years Imprisonment And / Or A Fine

1 - Definition Of The Offence

- A person is guilty of an offence if:
    - They **market** a knife;
    - In a way which:
        - **Indicates**, or **suggests**, that it is **suitable for combat**; or
        - Is otherwise **likely to stimulate** or **encourage violent behaviour** involving the **use of the knife as a weapon**.

2 - Definition Of Marketing - Section 1(4) Knives Act 1997

- "Marketing" includes **selling, offering** or **exposing for sale** or **hire** and **possessing** it **for those purposes**.

3 - Definition Of Suitable For Combat - Section 1(3) Knives Act 1997

- "Suitable for combat" means use as a weapon **for inflicting injury** or causing them to **fear injury**.

4 - Definition Of Violent Behaviour - Section 10 Knives Act 1997

- "Violent behaviour" means an **unlawful act inflicting injury** or **causing** a person to **fear injury**.

5 - Fear

- Names such as "killer", "special forces" etc on the packaging or advertisement relating to the knife may give an indication that the knife is suitable for combat.

6 - Defences - Sections 3 & 4 Knives Act 1997

- A **defence** will be established where the **knife** was **marketed**:
    - For **use by armed forces** of any country;
    - As an **antique** or **curio**;
    - It was **reasonable** for the knife to be **marketed in that manner**; or
    - There are **no reasonable grounds for believing the knife would be used unlawfully.**

- It is also a **defence** to prove that they did **not know** or **believe** that the **way** that the **knife** was **marketed** or **published** indicated that it was:
    - **Suitable for combat**, or would **stimulate** or **encourage violent behaviour**; or
    - They took **reasonable precautions** and **exercised due diligence** to **avoid committing** the offence.

I - Crossbows - Section 1 - 3 Crossbows Act 1987
Summary Only Offence
Penalty In The Magistrates Court – 6 Months Imprisonment And / Or A Fine

- It is an offence for a person:
    - **Under 18** years;
    - To **have with them** either:
        - A **crossbow capable of discharging a missile**;
        - **Parts which can be assembled to form a crossbow capable of discharging a missile**;
    - **Unless**;
    - They are **supervised** by a person aged **21 or over**.

- It is also an offence to:
    - Either:
        - **Sell**; or
        - **Hire**;
    - Either:
        - A **crossbow**; or
        - **Part** of a **crossbow**;
    - To a person aged **under 18**;
    - **Unless** they have **reasonable grounds** for **believing** they are **18 years or over**.

- It is also an offence for a person **under 18 years** to:
    - Either:
        - **Buy**; or
        - **Hire**;
    - Either:
        - A **crossbow**; or
        - **Part** of a **crossbow**.

Exam Trip Up

- The offences relate to **"has with them"** situations and **not possession.**
- This is a much narrower definition.

Exam Trip Up

- The offences only apply to crossbows which are capable of firing a missile or parts that can be so assembled with a **"draw weight" 1.4kg or more.**

Exam Trip Up

- The use of the crossbow **differs** from a similar provision in the Firearms Act where it becomes an offence if the projectile goes beyond the boundary of a dwelling.
- This is **not** the case under the **Crossbow Act.**
- If the **bolt** goes **beyond the boundary** there is **no offence** in the context of this act.

Exam Trip Up

- An **under 18** must be **accompanied** by a person who is **21 years or over** in **public** or **private**.

J - Powers Of Search And Seizure – Section 4 Crossbow Act 1987

- If a **constable suspects** with **reasonable cause** that a person is **committing**, or **has committed** an offence, the constable may:
    - **Search** that **person** for a crossbow or part of a crossbow:
    - **Search** any **vehicle**, or **anything in** or **on any vehicle**, in or on which the constable **suspects** with reasonable cause there is a crossbow, or part of a crossbow, connected with the offence.

Exam Trip Up

- There is **no mention** of a **uniform proviso** with regard to this search power.

Exam Trip Up

- **Crossbows** or **parts of a crossbow** may be **seized** by the constable.

Exam Trip Up

- The constable may **enter any land other than a dwelling** under this power.

General Police Duties
Unit 9: Civil Disputes

A – Non Molestation Orders - Section 42 FLA 1996

1 - Nature Of A Non Molestation Order

- A **Non Molestation Order** is an order that prohibits a person (**respondent**) from **molesting**:
    - Another person **associated** with the respondent; or
    - A **relevant child**.

2 - Definition Of Molestation

- "**Molesting**" includes conduct ranging from physical violence to non physical intentional harassment such as stalking, nuisance calls etc.

3 - Definition Of Associated Persons – Section 62 FLA 1996

- **Associated persons** can include:
    - Spouses, ex spouses, civil partners and ex partners;
    - Cohabitants and ex cohabitants;
    - Persons who live or have lived in the same household other than as the others employee, tenant, lodger or boarder;
    - Blood relatives;
    - They have agreed to marry one another, even if that agreement has been terminated;
    - Relatives of any of the above.

4 - Who May Apply For A Non-Molestation Order?

- The court may make a **Non Molestation Order**:
- Of its **own motion**;
- On the **application** of:
    - An **associated person**; or
    - A **relevant child**.

- A person under 16 **cannot** apply for such an order **without the leave of the court**.
- If the child satisfies the court that they have **sufficient understanding** to make the application, **they may be granted such leave**.

5 - Criteria For Granting A Non Molestation Order – Section 42 FLA 1996

- The court will grant a **Non Molestation Order** where:
    - The parties are **associated**;
    - An **act** of **molestation** has taken place; and
    - There is the need to **secure** the:
        - **Health**;
        - **Safety**; and
        - **Well being**;
    - Of the:
        - **Applicant**; or
        - **Relevant child**.

6 - Attaching Powers Of Arrest To The Order – Section 47 FLA 1996

- If the court makes either a:
    - **Non Molestation Order**; or
    - **Occupation Order**; and
- It appears to the court that the **respondent** has either:
    - **Used**; or
    - **Threatened**;
- **Violence** against either:
    - The **applicant or**
    - **A relevant child,**
- The court shall **attach** a **power of arrest** to one or more provisions of the order;
- **Unless**;
- It is satisfied that in all the **circumstances** of the case the **applicant** or **relevant child** will be **adequately protected without a power of arrest.**

Exam Trip Up

- If a **power of arrest** is **not attached** to the order then in the event of further acts of molestation the applicant will be required to go to court to seek a **warrant for arrest.**
- If a **power of arrest is attached** to the order a **constable can arrest the respondent without a warrant** in the event of a further act of molestation.

Exam Trip Up

- The arrestee must be **brought before a court** within **24 hours of arrest**, not including Christmas Day, Good Friday or a Sunday.

B - Trade Disputes

1 - Picketing - Section 220 of the Trade Union and Labour Relations Act 1992

(i) - Lawful Picketing Activities

- It is **lawful** for a person;
- In **contemplation** or **furtherance** of a **trade dispute**;
- To **attend**:
    - **At or near their own place of work**; or
    - If they are an **official of a trade union** - at or near the place of work of a member of the union **whom they are accompanying** and **whom they represent**;
- For the **purposes** of either:
    - **Peacefully obtaining** or **communicating information**; or
    - **Peacefully persuading** any person to either:
        - **Work**; or
        - **Abstain from working**.

(ii) - Ambiguities In Determining The Picketers Place Of Work

- If a person works or normally works:
    - **Otherwise** than at **any one place**; or
    - At a place the **location** of which is such that **attendance** there for a purpose mentioned above is **impracticable**;
- Their place of work for the purpose of the act shall be any **premises of his employer from which**:
    - **They work**; or
    - **Their work is administered**.

(iii) - Picketers Who Have Become Unemployed

- In the case of a **worker not in employment** where:
    - Their **last employment** was **terminated** in **connection with a trade dispute**; or
    - The **termination** of their employment was one of the **circumstances giving rise to a trade dispute**;
- Their **former place of work** shall be treated as being their **place of work**.

Exam Trip Up

- Lawful picketing **does not include** instances where the **business has moved since dismissing the workers** - i.e. *New* premises cannot be picketed.

Exam Trip Up

- The Code Of Practice states a number of **6 pickets**, although this is **not legally enforceable**.
- If large numbers of pickets are present there is a possible presumption of intimidation etc.

Exam Trip Up

- There is **no absolute right to picket** – i.e. danger of crime or public disorder.

Exam Trip Up

- **Pickets cannot enter private land to picket.**

Exam Trip Up

- **Dispersal Orders** under the Crime and Disorder Act **do not apply to picketing**.

Exam Trip Up

- **Conspiracy** charges **do not apply** to union officials if the charge is one of a minor nature and related to a **trade dispute** e.g. Obstruction of the Highway

2 - Intimidation Or Annoyance By Violence or Otherwise – Section 241 Trade Union and Labour Relations (Consolidation) Act 1992
Summary Only Offence
Penalty In The Magistrates Court – 6 Months Imprisonment And / Or A Fine

- A person commits an offence when:
    - With a view to **compelling** another person to either:
        - **Abstain** from doing or to do any act which that person has a **legal right** to do; or
        - **Abstain** from doing, **wrongfully and without legal authority**;
    - Either:
        - Uses **violence** or **intimidates** that **person, their spouse, civil partner or child, or injures his property,**
        - **Persistently follows that person** about from place to place,
        - **Hides any tools, clothes or other property owned or used by that person**, or deprives him or hinders him in the use thereof,
        - **Watches or besets the house** or **other place** where the **person resides, works, carries on a business or happens to be**, or the **approach to any such house** or **place**, or
        - **Follows** that person with **2 or more other persons** in a **disorderly manner** in or through any **street or road.**

Exam Trip Ups

- Section 241 is a **specific intent** offence.
- With regards to **disorderly manner** - there is **no need for either the threat or use of violence**.
- The offence can still be committed if the **victim is on strike** and the **intention is to return to work**.

General Police Duties
Unit 10: Regulation of Investigatory Powers Act 2000

A - RIPA And Article 8 Of The Human Rights Act 1998 – The Right To Private Life

- The **Article 8 right to a private life** formed the basis for the introduction of the Regulation of Investigatory Powers Act 2000.
- RIPA regulates situations where a **public authority infringes the privacy rights of an individual.**
- RIPA is a **Human Rights Act compliant** piece of legislation.

B - Part 1 and Part 2 of RIPA 2000

- Part's 1 & 2 of RIPA deal with differing situations:
    - **Part 1 - Interception of Communications.**
    - **Part 2 - Covert Surveillance.**

C - Possible Consequences Of A Breach Of Parts 1 & 2

- The following **consequences** may follow within **1 year** of a **breach**:
    - Evidence can be excluded as unfair;
    - Criminal offences;
    - Police Conduct Regulations proceedings;
    - Cases may be referred to the Investigatory Powers Tribunal.

D - Part 1 Interception of Communications

- There are **2** basic offences:
    - **Unlawful Interception of Public Communications - Section 1(1) RIPA 2000.**
    - **Unlawful Interception of Private Communications - Section 1(2) RIPA 2000.**

E - Unlawful Interception of Public Communications – Section 1(1) RIPA 2000
Either Way Offence
Penalty In The Magistrates Court – Fine Only
Penalty In The Crown Court – 2 Years Imprisonment And / Or A Fine

- It is an offence for a person:
    - **Intentionally;** and
    - **Without lawful authority;**
    - To **intercept** in any place **in the UK;**
    - Any **communication;**
    - In the **course** of its **transmission;**
    - By means of a **public:**
        - **Postal service;** or
        - **Telecommunication system.**

F - Interception Of A Communication In The Course Of Its Transmission – Section 2 RIPA 2000

1 – What Amounts To An Interception?

- An interception involves a **third party** getting involved in the transmission. This may include either:
    - **Modifying** or **interfering** with either a:
        - **System;**
        - **Operation;** or
    - **Monitoring** transmissions:
        - To make the **communication available;**
        - To a **person other than** the:
            - **Sender;** or
            - **Intended recipient**
        - *While* the communication is being **transmitted.**

Examples of intercepting communications include:
- Telephone taps;
- Opening mail;
- Reading mail;
- E-mail still in <u>inboxes</u> (still stored!)

2 - Communications Not Covered By The Act

- The following communications are **not covered** by RIPA:
    - Interception of any communication broadcast for **general reception** - e.g. TV, Radio.
    - Interception of **traffic data.**

3 - Who Will Bring A Prosecution?

- The **Director of Public Prosecutions (DPP)** must decide whether to bring a prosecution.

G - Unlawful Interception of Private Communications – s1(2) RIPA 2000
Either Way Offence
Penalty In The Magistrates Court – Fine Only
Penalty In The Crown Court – 2 Years Imprisonment And / Or A Fine

1 – Definition Of The Offence

- It is an offence for a person:
    - **Intentionally**; and
    - **Without lawful authority** (conduct may be exempt under s1(6));
    - To **intercept**;
    - In any place in the **UK**;
    - Any **communications**;
    - In the **course** of its **transmission**;
    - By means of a **private telecoms system.**

2 - The Meaning Of A Private Telecoms System – Section 2(1) RIPA 2000

- A **private telecoms system** means a system:
    - **Attached:**
        - **Directly;** or
        - **Indirectly;**
    - **To a public telecoms system;**
    - Which has **apparatus** comprised in it which is located in the **UK**; and
    - Which is **used for attaching** the private telecoms system to the public telecoms system.

    For example: An **office payphone** - although it forms part of an internal system it is ultimately attached to the public system.

3 - The Section 1(6) RIPA 2000 Exemptions

- Some interception of communications are **exempt** where the **interceptor**:
    - Has a **right to control** of the operation;
    - Has the **right to use** the system; or
    - Has **consent** for such a purpose.

    For example: An insurance company monitoring calls for quality assurance or training purposes.

4 - Is Private Post Covered By s1(2) RIPA 2000?

- **Private post** is **not covered** by this section.

    For example: The interception of mail from a **solicitor's private DX mail system** will **not** breach the act.

5 - Who Will Bring A Prosecution?

- The **Director of Public Prosecutions (DPP)** must decide whether to bring a prosecution.

Summary Table

Type	Mens Rea	Without Lawful Authority	Intercept Communication In The UK	In The Course Of Transmission	Medium	Not Covered	Who Brings Prosecution	Exemption
Public	Intent	Yes	Yes ■ Modify ■ Interfere ■ Monitor	Yes	Postal Service Telecom System	General Reception Traffic Data	DPP	N / A
Private	Intent	Yes	Yes ■ Modify ■ Interfere ■ Monitor	Yes	Private Telecoms System	Post	DPP	Right To Control Right To Use Consent

6 - When Is The Interception Of A Private Communication Permitted?

- An **interception** will be **permitted** of a **private** communication where:
    - There is **lawful authority** to intercept – **section 1(5) RIPA 2000**;
    - There is **section 3 RIPA 2000 authorisation**;
    - There is **section 4 RIPA 2000 authorisation**;
    - The interception is in accordance with a **section 5 RIPA 2000 Interception Warrant**.

1 - Lawful Authority To Intercept Communications – Section 1(5) RIPA 2000

- This will involve **conduct in accordance with any** other **statutory power** for the purpose of:
    - **Obtaining information;** or
    - **Taking possession** of any:
        - **Document;** or
        - Other **property;**
    - In relation to any **stored communication.**

    For example: The police would have **lawful authority** to seizing **mobile** and obtain a **court order** under **PACE 1984** to view information it contains.

2 - Section 3 RIPA 2000 Authorisation

- An **interception warrant** is **unnecessary** where either:
    - **Both** the **sender** and the **recipient consent** to the interception.
    - The interceptor had **reasonable grounds to believe** that **both** the **sender** and **recipient** have **consented.**
    - **Either** the **sender** or **recipient** has **consented** and surveillance by means of interception has been **approved.**

        For example: A blackmail demand situation or monitoring abusive calls.

    - The interception is **by** or **on behalf** of a **service provider.**

        For example: The royal mail opening mail to check the recipient's details to enable them to return the mail to the sender.

3 - Section 4 RIPA 2000 Authorisation

- Certain **authorities** may need to intercept communications in specific situations.

    For example: The prison service is permitted to intercept communications to or from prisoners in **prison.**

4 - Section 5 RIPA 2000 Interception Warrants

(i) – Circumstances In Which An Interception Warrant May Be Issued

- The **Secretary of State;** or
- In **urgent cases** - a **senior official authorised** by the **Secretary of State;**
    - May issue **interception warrants;**
    - If they **believe** the warrant is necessary either:
        - To prevent or detect **serious crime;**   S
        - For the purposes of **international mutual assistance;**   I
        - In the interests of **national security;**   N
        - To **safeguard the economic wellbeing of the UK;**   S

Memory Tip

- Remember: **S.I.N.S.**

☐ Serious Crime.	S	(3 months)
☐ International mutual assistance.	I	(6 months)
☐ National security.	N	(6 months)
☐ Safeguarding economic wellbeing.	S	(6 months)

(ii) - Additional Considerations For The Secretary Of State When Issuing Interception Warrants - Section 5 RIPA 2000

- The **Secretary of State** must also consider:
    - ☐ Whether the information sought **could be obtained using less intrusive means** than by an interception warrant.

(iii) - Who May Lodge An Application For An Interception Warrant? – Section 5 RIPA 2000

- **Chief Officer** of Police;

- **Director General** of other agencies.

    e.g. S.O.C.A., HM Customs, MI5, MI6 etc.

(iv) - The Duration Of An Interception Warrant – Section 9 RIPA 2000

- The **duration** of an interception warrant **depends** on **who issued** the warrant:
    - ☐ **Serious crime** interception warrants **(S)** - Up to **3 months**.
    - ☐ **Other** interception warrants **(I.N.S.)** – Up to **6 months**.
    - ☐ **Serious or other interception warrants obtained urgently** - Up to **5 days**.

Summary Table

Individuals Capable Of Granting An Interception Warrant	When You must Apply To Them	When will they grant an application	Must they consider less intrusive means	Duration Of Warrant	Who May Apply
Secretary Of State	Always – unless an urgent situation	S I N S	Yes	S. – 3 Months I.N.S. – 6 Months	Chief Officer Of Police Director General Of Other Agencies
Senior Official Appointed By The Secretary Of State	Only in urgent situations	S I N S	Yes	S.I.N.S - 5 Days	Chief Officer Of Police Director General Of Other Agencies

(v) - Unauthorised Disclosures - Section 19 RIPA 2000
Either Way Offence
Penalty In The Magistrates Court – 6 Months Imprisonment And / Or A Fine
Penalty In The Crown Court – 5 Years Imprisonment And / Or A Fine

- Where an interception warrant has been issued or renewed, it shall be the **duty** of every **specified person** to **keep secret**:
    - The **existence** and **content** of the **warrant**;
    - The **details** of the **issue** or **renewal** of the **warrant**;
    - The **existence** and **content** of any requirement to provide **assistance** with giving effect to the warrant;
    - Everything in:
        - The **intercepted material**; or
        - Any **related communication**.
- **Failure** to do so is an **offence**.

(vi) - Who Is A Specified Person? – Section 19(5) RIPA 2000

- The following are **specified persons**:
    - **Crown officials**;
    - Members of **SOCA**;
    - Personnel of the:
        - Police;
        - Postal service;
        - Telecoms industry.
- i.e. everybody after that warrant has been signed.

(vii) Defence For Specified Persons – Section 19(5) RIPA 2000

- A **specified person** will have a **defence** if they **could not have reasonably been expected** after first becoming aware of the matter disclosed **to take steps to prevent disclosure**".

H - Covert Human Intelligence Sources (CHIS)

1 – Definition Of A CHIS – Section 26(8) RIPA 2000

- A **CHIS** is someone who:
    - The **police ask** to:
        - **Establish** or **maintain** a **relationship** with another person;
        - For the **covert purpose** of:
            - **Obtaining information**;
            - **Providing access to information**; or
    - **Covertly discloses** information obtained by the use of such a relationship.

2 - What Is A Covert Purpose? – Section 26(9) RIPA 2000

- A **covert purpose** will exist where:
    - ☐ **One** of the parties;
    - ☐ Is **unaware** of:
        - The **CHIS purpose** of the relationship; or
        - The fact that the **information** gained will **subsequently be disclosed** to the police.

- A lay explanation of a **CHIS** is:
    - ☐ A person whether a **police officer** or **not**;
    - ☐ Who **hides** their true **identity**;
    - ☐ In a **relationship** with another person or persons;
    - ☐ At the **request** of the **police**;
    - ☐ To **gather information** for the police.

    Examples of CHIS include:
    - ☐ A police informant;
    - ☐ An undercover police officer; or
    - ☐ Proactively tasking a member of the public.

An Example Of A CHIS Relationship With A Member Of The Public

- Mrs Smith has seen ongoing suspect activity at a house in her street. There are people coming and going to the property at all hours. She thinks that her neighbour is a drug dealer.
- Mrs Smith **unilaterally** contacts DS Bradshaw to provide information in relation to the activities.
- She will not become a CHIS at this point as she has **volunteered** the information.
- DS Bradshaw attends Mrs Smith's property at a later date and **tasks** her to:
    - ☐ **Take index numbers** of vehicles calling at her neighbours;
    - ☐ Contact the police if a **red BMW vehicle** is seen at the address;
    - ☐ **Speak to neighbours to take numbers** on her behalf; or
    - ☐ Covertly establish a **relationship** with the suspect neighbour.
    - ☐ Mrs Smith **now becomes a CHIS.**

3 - CHIS Authorisation – Section 30 RIPA 2000

- The following must provide **CHIS authorisation**:

(i) - The General Rule

- A **Superintendent** or above must provide **authorisation**;
- **Unless**;
- It is *not* **reasonably practicable** for them to do so.

(ii) – The Exception To The General Rule

- If it is *not* **reasonably practicable** for the **Superintendent** to provide **authorisation**;
- Due to **urgency** of the situation;
- An **Inspector** may provide authorisation instead.

4 - What Form Must The CHIS Authorisation Take? – Section 30 RIPA 2000

- The **form of authorisation depends** on the **rank** of the authorising officer:
  - A **Superintendent's** authorisation **may** be:
    - **Verbal**; or
    - **In writing.**
  - An **Inspector's** authorisation **must** be **in writing**.

5 - The Duration Of The CHIS Authorisation – Section 43(3) RIPA 2000

- The **duration** of the **CHIS authorisation** depend on:
  - The **rank** of the authorising officer;
  - The **manner** in which authorisation was provided; and
  - The **age** of the person subject to the CHIS:
    - **Superintendent in writing** - 12 months
    - **Superintendent orally** - 72 hours
    - **Inspector in writing** - 72 hours
    - **Superintendent in writing for persons under 18** - 1 month.

Summary Table

Rank Of Authorising Officer	Circumstances In Which Each Officer Must Be Approached	Method Of Authorisation	Duration Of The CHIS
Superintendent	Always for adults– Unless it is not practical due to urgency.	In Writing	12 months
		Verbal	72 hours
	Always for juvenile CHIS – no exception	Always in writing	1 month
Inspector	Only in instances of urgency	Only in writing	72 hours

6 - The Use Of A CHIS – Section 29 RIPA 2000

- The **authorising officer** must only authorise any CHIS if they:
    - **Believe** it is necessary:
        - For the **purpose** of either:
            - Preventing or detecting **crime**;
            - Preventing **disorder**;
            - Protecting **health**;
            - Collecting **taxes**;
        - In the interest of **national security, public safety** or the **economic well being** of the UK;
        - For any **purpose specified** by the **Secretary of State**;
    - And that to do so is **proportionate** to what is being sought to be achieved.

I - Covert Surveillance – Section 26 RIPA 2000

- There are **2 forms** of **covert surveillance**:
    - **Directed** surveillance;
    - **Intrusive** surveillance.
- The differing forms of surveillance will be **authorised by different individuals.**

1 - Directed Covert Surveillance – Section 26 RIPA 2000

(i) – Circumstances In Which Covert Surveillance Will Be Directed

- Covert surveillance will be **directed** where:
    - ☐ The surveillance is **covert** (subjects are **unaware** of it!);
    - ☐ For the purpose of a **specific investigation or operation**;
    - ☐ Which is likely to result in the obtaining of **private information** about a person (Article 8 HRA);
    - ☐ **Whether** or **not** the **person** has been **specifically identified prior** to the **investigation.**

(ii) - When Will Authorisation Not Be Required For Directed Covert Surveillance?

- **Authorisation** will **not** be **required** where:
    - ☐ The covert surveillance is in <u>immediate</u> response to:
        - Events; or
        - Circumstances;
    - ☐ Where it would <u>not</u> be reasonably practicable to seek prior authorisation.

    For example - Where an officer in pursuit of a suspect spontaneously conceals themselves behind an object as an **immediate response** to events.

(iii) - Authorising Directed Surveillance – Section 28 RIPA 2000

- The following must provide **authorisation** for **directed** surveillance:

(a) - The General Rule

- A **Superintendent** or above must provide authorisation;
- **Unless**;
- It is <u>not</u> reasonably practicable.

(b) - The Exception To The General Rule

- If it is **not reasonably practicable** for the **Superintendent** to provide **authorisation**;
- Due to **urgency** of the situation;
- An **Inspector** may provide authorisation instead.

(iv) - What Form Must The Directed Surveillance Authorisation Take?

- The **form of authorisation** depends on the **rank** of the authorising officer:
    - ☐ A **Superintendent's** authorisation **may** be **verbal or in writing.**
    - ☐ An **Inspector's** authorisation **must** be **in writing.**

(v) - The Duration Of Directed Surveillance Authorisation – Section 43 RIPA 2000

- The **duration** of **directed** surveillance authorisation **depends** on:
    - The **Rank** of the authorising officer; and
    - The **manner** in which authorisation was provided.
        - **Superintendent** in **writing** - 3 months
        - **Superintendent orally** - 72 hours
        - **Inspector** in **writing** - 72 hours

Exam Trip Up

- If the **material sought** is:
    - **Subject to legal privilege**;
    - **Confidential personal information**; or
    - **Journalistic material**;
- The only person who can **authorise** the directed surveillance in these **Chief Officer**.

2 - Intrusive Covert Surveillance – Section 26 RIPA 2000

(i) – When Is Covert Surveillance Intrusive?

- Covert surveillance is **intrusive** where:
    - The surveillance is **covert** (i.e. the subject is **unaware** of it);
    - It is carried out in relation to **activities taking place in** any:
        - **Residential premises** - (includes hotel rooms); or
        - **Private vehicle**; and
    - Either:
        - Involves the **presence of an individual CHIS** on the premises or in the vehicle; or
        - Is carried out by means of a **surveillance device** (bug / camera etc).

(ii) - Authorising Intrusive Surveillance – Section 32 RIPA 2000

- Generally only the **Secretary of State** can **authorise** surveillance by the:
    - **Intelligence services**;
    - **Armed forces** etc.
- Authorisation by either the:
    - **Police**; or
    - **Military Police** (exam trip up!);

- Must be provided by **Senior Authorising Officers** including:
    - ☐ **Chief Constable;**
    - ☐ **Commissioner;**
    - ☐ **Provost Marshall (PM).**

- The authorising person may only give authorisation if they **believe** that it is **necessary and proportionate** to do so:
    - ☐ In the interests of **national security**;
    - ☐ For the purpose of **preventing or detecting serious crime**, or
    - ☐ For the purpose of **safeguarding the economic well-being of the UK.**

(iii) - Notifying The Surveillance Commissioner Of Intrusive Surveillance – Section 35 RIPA 2000

- Any authorisation must be:
    - ☐ **Notified** to a **Surveillance Commissioner;**
    - ☐ In **writing;**
    - ☐ As soon as is reasonably practicable.

- The authorisation **will not take effect** until the **Surveillance Commissioner** has:
    - ☐ **Approved;** and
    - ☐ Given **written notification** to that effect.

Summary Table - Directed & Intrusive Surveillance

Type Of Covert Surveillance	Authorising Officer	Circumstances In Which They Will Be The Authorising Officer	Form Of Authorisation	Duration
Directed	Superintendent	Always – Unless not practical due to urgency	In writing / Verbally	3 months / 72 hours
Directed	Inspector	Only in instances of urgency	Only in writing	72 hours
Intrusive	Secretary Of State	Authorisation to: Intelligence / Armed Forces	Must Notify Surveillance Commissioner in writing ASAP who must approve in writing	Open ended
Intrusive	Chief Authorising Officer Of Police	Authorisation to: Police / Military Police	Must Notify Surveillance Commissioner in writing ASAP who must approve in writing	Open ended

General Police Duties
Unit 11: Sporting Events

A - The Definition Of A Designated Football Match – Part 2 Football Spectators Act 1989

- A **Designated Football Match** includes:
    - Only **Association Football Matches** - i.e. **Soccer**;
    - In simple terms this is a **"Big Game"**:
        - **Premiership**;
        - **Conference**;
        - Games involving sides from outside England and Wales (This includes Scottish teams); and
        - Internationals.

B – Offences At Designated Football Matches - Sections 2, 3 & 4 Football Offences Act 1991
Summary Only Offences
Penalty In The Magistrates Court – Fine Only

- **3 offences** of misbehaviour may take place at a **designated football match**:
    - Entering the Playing Area;   E
    - Throwing;   T
    - Chanting.   C

1 – Throwing – Section 2 Football (Offences) Act 1991

- It is an offence to **throw anything** at:
    - The **playing area**;
    - Areas **adjacent** to the **playing area** where **spectators** are **not** **admitted**; or
    - Any area at which **spectators are present**;
- **Without** either:
    - **Lawful authority**; or
    - **Reasonable excuse**.

An Example Of A Lawful Authority

- A paramedic on standby at a game who throws a medical implement to a colleague on the pitch to enable them to treat an injured player would have a **lawful authority** to do so in the circumstances.

An Example Of A Reasonable Excuse

- If a ball is kicked out of play and is thrown back onto the playing area by a spectator they would have **reasonable excuse** to do so in the circumstances.

2 – Entering The Playing Area – Section 4 Football (Offences) Act 1991

- It is an offence to **enter** either:
    - ☐ The **playing area**; or
    - ☐ Any area **adjacent** to the **playing area** where **spectators** are **not** normally allowed;
- **Without** either:
    - ☐ **Lawful authority**; or
    - ☐ **Reasonable excuse**.

An Example Of A Lawful Authority

- A physiotherapist entering the playing area to treat an injured player will have **lawful authority**.

An Example of a Reasonable Excuse

- Supporters getting crushed by a crowd surge would have a **reasonable excuse** to enter the playing area to escape the surge.

3 – Chanting – Section 3 Football (Offences) Act 1991

- It is an offence to **chant** in a manner that is either:
    - ☐ **Indecent**;
    - ☐ **Racist**.
- **Religious** chanting is **not** an offence.

(i) - The Definition Of Chanting – Section 2(a) Football (Offences) Act 1991

- **Chanting** - involves the **repeated** uttering of:
    - ☐ **Words**; or
    - ☐ **Sounds**.
- An offence is committed on the **second utterance**.
- It is possible to chant either:
    - ☐ **Alone**; or
    - ☐ **In concert** with others.

(ii) - The Definition Of Racist Chanting – Section 2(b) Football (Offences) Act 1991

- Chanting of a **racist** nature involves:
    - **Words** or **conduct** that are:
        - Threatening;
        - Abusive; or
        - Insulting;
    - To a person by means of their:
        - Colour;
        - Race;
        - Nationality; or
        - Ethnic origins.

Summary Table - Offences At Designated Football Matches

Offence	Prohibited Activity	Where	Defences
Section 2	Throwing anything	<ul><li>Playing area;</li><li>Areas adjacent to the pitch where supporters are not allowed;</li><li>Areas where spectators are present</li></ul>	<ul><li>Lawful authority;</li><li>Reasonable excuse.</li></ul>
Section 3	Chanting:<ul><li>Indecent</li><li>Racist</li><li>On at least 2 occasions</li><li>Alone or in concert</li></ul>	At a Designated Football Match	None
Section 4	Entering	<ul><li>Playing area</li><li>Areas adjacent to the pitch where supporters are not allowed</li></ul>	<ul><li>Lawful authority</li><li>Reasonable excuse</li></ul>

C - For How Long Will A Football Ground Be Designated? - Section 9 Sporting Events (Control Of Alcohol) Act 1985

- The **"time limits"** for a **designated sporting event** depend on the circumstances:

1 - The General Rule

- As a **general rule** the time limits are:
  - ☐ **2 hours before** the **start** of the match; and
  - ☐ **1 hour after** the **end** of the match.

2 - Delayed Matches

- Where a match is **delayed** the time limit is:
  - ☐ **2 hours before** the **advertised start time**; and
  - ☐ **1 hour after** the **end** of the match.

3 - Postponed Matches

- Where a match is **cancelled** the time limit is:
  - ☐ **2 hours before** the **advertised start time**; and
  - ☐ **1 hour after** the **advertised start time**.

Summary Table - Duration During Which A Football Ground Will Be Designated

Situation	Start Of Designated Time	End Of Designated Time
General Rule Match On Time	2 hours before the *actual* start time	1 hour after the actual *end*
Match Delayed	2 hours before the *advertised* start time	1 hour after the actual *end*
Match Postponed	2 hours before the *advertised* start time	1 hour after the *advertised start* time

D – Alcohol On Coaches And Trains Carrying Passengers To A Designated Sporting Event – Section 1 Sporting Events (Control Of Alcohol) Act 1985
Summary Only Offence
Penalty In The Magistrates Court – 3 Months Imprisonment And / Or A Fine

- It is an offence for any person who is either:
    - [ ] The **operator** of the vehicle; or
    - [ ] A **servant** or **agent** of the operator;
    - [ ] A person who has **hired** a vehicle; or
    - [ ] The hirers **agent** or **servant**;
- To **knowingly**:
    - [ ] **Cause**; or
    - [ ] **Permit**;
- **Alcohol** to be **carried** on a:
    - [ ] **Public Service Vehicle (PSV)**; or
    - [ ] **Train**;
- Whose **principal purpose** is to carry passengers **to** or **from** a **designated sporting event**.
- The following will also be liable under s1:
    - [ ] Any person who has **intoxicating alcohol in their possession** whilst **on** such a **vehicle**;
    - [ ] Any person who is **drunk** whilst **on** such a **vehicle**.

The Definition Of A Designated Sporting Event?

- A **designated sporting event** includes:
    - [ ] Any and all sporting events **designated**.
    - [ ] It does **not only** apply to **football** matches.
    - [ ] It can include events **designated outside the UK**.

E – The Definition Of Alcohol On Other Vehicles Carrying Passengers To A Designated Sporting Event - Section 1A Sporting Events (Control Of Alcohol) Act 1985
Summary Only Offence
Penalty In The Magistrates Court – 3 Months Imprisonment And / Or A Fine

- It is an offence for any person who is:
    - Either:
        - The **driver**;
        - The **keeper** (or their **servant** or **agent**);
        - A person to whom the vehicle is **made available** (by loan or otherwise)
    - To **knowingly**:
        - **Cause**; or
        - **Permit**;
    - **Alcohol** to be **carried** on a **vehicle** which:
        - Is **not** a PSV;
        - Is adapted to carry **more than 8 passengers**;
        - Is being used for the **principle purpose** of carrying:
            - **2 or more passengers**;
            - **To** or **from** a **designated sporting event**.
- The following will also be liable under section 1A:
    - Any person who has **intoxicating alcohol in their possession** whilst **on** such a **vehicle**;
    - Any person who is **drunk** whilst **on** such a **vehicle**.

F - Alcohol At Designated Sports Grounds - Section 2 Sporting Events (Control Of Alcohol) Act 1985
Summary Only Offence
Penalty In The Magistrates Court – 3 Months Imprisonment And / Or A Fine

1 – Definition Of The Offence

- A person will commit an offence if whilst:
    - **Entering** or **trying to enter** a **designated sports ground**; or
    - **Inside** a **designated sports ground** from an **area** where the event can be **directly viewed**;
    - They are either:
        - **Drunk**;
        - Have **alcohol** in their **possession**; or
        - Have an **article** in their **possession**.

2 - Definition Of An Article? - Section 2 Sporting Events Act 1985

- An **article** is an item:
    - ☐ **Capable** of causing **injury;** or
    - ☐ **Capable** of **holding** any **drink** which **when empty** is either:
        - ■ **Discarded,** or
        - ■ **Returned.**

3 - What Is Exempt? – Section 2(3) Sporting Events Act 1985

- **Exempt items** include:
    - ☐ **Medicine containers;**
    - ☐ Items **not discarded or returned when they are empty** that will be **taken home** (e.g. hip flasks, cool boxes, etc)

4 - When Can Alcohol Be Consumed In A Designated Sports Ground? - Section 2 Sporting Events Act 1985

- Alcohol **may** only be consumed within a **designated sports ground** when the **event cannot be directly viewed.**

    For example:

    It is not an offence to watch the event **on TV** in a hospitality box or bar within a stadium provided there is **no direct view** onto playing area.

    If there any windows overlooking the pitch from the hospitality box they would have to be drawn throughout the match while the game would be watched on TV).

G - Football Banning Orders and Detention Powers - Football Spectators Act 1989
Breach Of A Football Banning Order - Summary Only Offence
Penalty In The Magistrates Court – 6 Months Imprisonment And / Or A Fine

- There are **2 types** of **football banning order:**
    - ☐ Following a **conviction** at court for a **relevant offence** – section 14(a);
    - ☐ Following a **complaint** by the Chief Officer of Police – section 14(b).

1 - Football Banning Orders On Conviction At Court For A Relevant Offence - Section 14(a) Football Spectators Act 1989

- ☐ This section relates to a **banning order**, which is made after a **court convicts** an individual for a **relevant offence**:
    - POA 1986 **(Exam trip up – not section 4(a))**;
    - OAPA 1861;
    - Football Offences; etc.
- ☐ The court has a **duty** to pass a **ban** if:
    - There are **reasonable grounds** to **believe**;
    - That an order would help **prevent further violence** or **disorder**;
    - **At** or **in connection** to a **regulated football match** (big games).
- ☐ The **ban** is **in addition to any sentence** passed on conviction.
- ☐ Bans **can** be applied even if the court gives a defendant a:
    - **Conditional discharge;** or
    - **Absolute discharge.**

2 - Football Banning Orders On A Complaint By The Chief Officer of Police - Section 14(b) Football Spectators Act 1989

(i) – Nature Of The Application

- **Applications** are lodged by the **Chief Officer of Police** in the area in which the person resides.
- The application is made at a **Magistrates court**.

(ii) - The Grounds For Granting A Section 14(b) Order

- The **Chief Officer** making the application must:
    - ☐ Honestly **believe** that making the order will **prevent violence**.
- The evidentiary burden must be discharged on the **"balance of probability"**.
- **Evidence** of bad character to support the application may be provided by establishing that the subject of the ban has **previously:**
    - ☐ **Caused** or **contributed** to any:
        - **Violence;** or
        - **Disorder;**
    - ☐ In the:
        - **UK;** or
        - **Elsewhere.**

3 - The Duration Of Football Banning Orders – Section 14F(3),(4)&(5) Football Spectators Act 1989

(i) - The Duration of A Banning Order Made Under Section 14(a) Football Spectators Act 1989

- A **banning order** may be made for between **6-10 years** if an **immediate custodial sentence** is passed by the court.

- If a **custodial sentence is not passed** a banning order may be made for between **3-5 years**.

- Once the banning order has existed for **two thirds** of its time the defendant can **apply** for the ban to be **terminated** by the court.

(ii) - Duration Of The Banning Order Under Section 14(b) Football Spectators Act 1989

- The **duration** of such a banning order is between **2 and 3 years**.

- The recipient can again **apply** for the banning order to be **terminated** once **two thirds** of the order has been completed.

Summary Table - The Duration Of Football Banning Orders

Section 14 (a)	Section 14 (a)	Section 14 (b)
Immediate custodial sentence for a relevant offence	Non custodial sentence for a relevant offence	Application by the Chief Officer of Police
Between 6 – 10 years	Between 3 – 5 years	Between 2 – 3 years

4 - The Scope Of Football Banning Orders – Section 14E(3) Football Spectators Act 1989

- **Conditions** may be attached to a **football banning order**:
    - The recipient can be banned from a **designated venue** for **football matches only**.
    - The recipient must be required to **surrender their passport**:
        - In connection with **regulated football matches**;
        - **Outside the UK**;
        - **Unless**;
        - There are **exceptional circumstances**.

Exam Trip Up

- Look out for the **trick question** with regards to going to watch a **pop concert!**

5 - The Effect Of A Football Banning Order - Section 14E(2) Football Spectators Act 1989

- The **effect** of a banning order is that the person initially has to **report to the police station specified** within *five* days of the day on which the order is made.

- This requirement is **suspended** in the case of a person **detained in legal custody**.

H - Powers Of Detention During A Control Period Of Persons Not Subject To A Football Banning Order - Section 21A Football Spectators Act 1989

1 – Control Periods

- The **control period** will last during the **5 day period prior to a regulated game** *outside* **England & Wales**:
    - Club game (e.g. Man Utd v Celtic);
    - International;
    - World cup;
    - European cup;
    - Champions League etc.

2 – Purpose Of The Powers

- This power is used in **ports or airports**:
    - When **known offenders**;
    - Who are **not** subject to a football banning order;
    - Are **attempting to travel abroad**.

3 - Police Powers Of Detention During A Control Period – Section 21A(1) - (3) Football Spectators Act 1989

- During any **control period**:
    - A police **constable** in **uniform** who:
        - Has **reasonable grounds** for **suspecting**:
            - That any **British Citizen**;
            - Has at **any time**;
            - **Caused** or **contributed** to any **violence** or **disorder** in:
                - The **UK**; or
                - **Elsewhere**; and

- Has **reasonable grounds** for **believing**:
    - That a **football banning order** would:
        - Help to **prevent violence** or **disorder**;
        - At or in **connection** with any **regulated football match**;
- The **constable in uniform** may **detain** a person in **custody**;
- For a maximum period of **4 hours**.
- An **Inspector** may authorise a further **2 hours** – permitting detention to a maximum of **6 hours**.
- They have **until the expiry of this period** to decide whether to **issue a notice in writing** which may order the recipient to either:
    - **Appear** before a **magistrates court** within **24 hours**; and
    - In the interim the person can be required to:
        - Not leave **England or Wales**; or
        - Surrender their **passport**.

4 - Purpose Of The Notice

- The **notice** is in essence an **application** to the court for a **section 14(b) banning order**.

5 - The Consequences Of A Failure To Comply With Police Constables Request – Section 21C Football Spectators Act 1989

- If a person **fails to comply** with a request, they will be:
    - **Arrested**;
    - Brought before a court within **24 hours**;
    - Required to **surrender their passport**.

I - Ticket Touts
Summary Only Offence
Penalty In The Magistrates Court – Fine Only

1 – Definition Of The Offence - Section 166 CJPOA 1994 (Football only!)

- It is an offence for:
    - An **unauthorised person** to:
        - Sell;
        - Offer; or
        - Expose for sale;
    - A **ticket** for a **designated football match**;
    - Either:
        - In a **public place**; or
        - In **any place** in the **course of a business**.

2 - Who Is An Unauthorised Person?

- An **unauthorised person** will be:
    - Anyone who does *not* **have written permission** from:
        - The **home club**; or
        - The **organiser**.

3 - What If The Ticket Is A Fake?

- A **ticket** means anything which **purports** to be a ticket.
- It includes:
    - **Genuine tickets**; and
    - **Forgeries**.

Exam Trip Up

- The classic examination trip up relates to offering a ticket which is surplus to requirements to a friend:
    - In a **public place** or a **place where the public has access - offence**.
    - In a **private place - no offence**.

4 - Unauthorised Selling Of Tickets For Designated Football Matches On The Internet - Violent Crime Reduction Act 2006

- It is an offence for:
    - A **service provider** established **in the U.K**;
    - To either:
        - **Sell**; or
        - Otherwise **dispose**;
        - A **ticket** for a **Designated Football Match**;
        - If they are **not authorised** to do so;
        - **Regardless** of **where** sale or disposition takes place.

Exam Trip Up

- This provision does **not apply** to **internet service providers** based **outside the U.K.**

General Police Duties
Unit 12: Licensing Offences

A – The Licensing Objectives

- The **licensing objectives** include:
    - [ ] The **prevention** of **crime** and **disorder**;
    - [ ] Ensuring **public safety**;
    - [ ] The **prevention** of **public nuisance**; and
    - [ ] The **protection** of **children** from harm.

B – The Definition Of Licensable Activities – Section 1 Licensing Act 2003

- **Licensable activities** include:
    - [ ] The **supply by retail of alcohol**;
    - [ ] The **supply of alcohol by or on behalf of a club to a member of a club** (otherwise than by sale or retail);
    - [ ] The provision of **regulated entertainment**; and
    - [ ] The provision of **late night refreshment**.

C - Distinguishing Sale By Retail And Supply To A Member

- As **members clubs** are organisations **jointly owned by the members** themselves in equal shares.
- If alcohol is supplied to a member in the club bar in return for cash, it is **not a sale by retail**.
- It is a release by the other members of their interest in the alcohol supplied amounting to a **supply of alcohol by or on behalf of a club to a member of a club.**
- If however a members guest is sold alcohol in the club bar this would be an instance of the **supply by retail of alcohol.**

D - The Definition Of A Late Night Refreshment

- A **late night refreshment** involves:
    - [ ] The **supply** of either:
        - **Hot food**; or
        - **Hot drink**;
    - [ ] To the **public**;
    - [ ] For **consumption** either:
        - **On** the premises; or
        - **Off** the premises;
    - [ ] Between **11pm – 5am.**

E – The Definition Of Supplies Exempt From Being Late Night Refreshments

- **Exemptions** include:
    - The **supply of food or drink free of charge to a registered charity**;
    - Provision by way of a **vending machine**;
    - **Supplies to guests** at:
        - Hotels;
        - Guest houses;
        - Camp sites; etc.

F – The General Exemptions To Licensable Activities – Sections 173 - 175 Licensing Act 2003

- **Exemptions** include activities:
    - Aboard an **aircraft, hovercraft** or **railway** engaged on a **journey**;
    - Aboard a **vessel** engaged in an **international journey**;
    - At an **approved wharf** at a **designated port** or **hover port**;
    - At an **examination station** at a **designated airport**;
    - At **premises** which at the time are **permanently** or **temporarily occupied** for the purposes of the **armed forces of the crown**;
    - A **premises** covered by a **national security exemption**; and
    - At such **other place as may be prescribed.**

G – The Police Power Of Entry To Investigate Licensable Activities – Section 179(1) Licensing Act 2003

- Where either:
    - A **constable**; or
    - Other **authorised person**;
- Has reason to **believe** that any **premises are being or about to be used for a licensable activity**;
- They may **enter** the premises (**with force if necessary**);
- With a view to **checking** whether the **activity either**:
    - **Is authorised,** or
    - **Will be authorised.**

H - The Police Powers Of Entry To Investigate Licensing Offences – Section 180 Licensing Act 2003

- A **constable** may:
    - Enter **(by force if necessary)**; and
    - **Search**;
- Any premises in respect of which they have reason to **believe** that a **Licensing Act 2003 offence** either:
    - **Has been committed**; or
    - **Is about to be committed.**

I – Premises Licences

1 - The Definition Of A Premises Licence – Section 11 Licensing Act 2003

- A **premises licence** is a licence granted in respect of:
    - Any **premises**;
    - Which **authorises** the premises to be **used**;
    - For **one** or **more licensable activities**;
    - Which **lasts until** it is either:
        - **Revoked**; or
        - **Surrendered.**

2 - Persons Eligible To Apply For A Premises Licence – Section 16 Licensing Act 2003

- The following aged **over 18** may **apply for a premises licence:**
    - A person who carries on, or proposes to carry on, a **business** which involves the **use of the premises for licensable activities** to which the application relates;
    - A **recognised club**;
    - A **charity**;
    - The **chief officer of police** of a police force in England & Wales;
    - The **proprietor** of an **educational institution**;
    - A **health service body**;
    - An individual applying under any **statutory function or prerogative.**

3 - Where To Lodge A Premises Licence Application – Section 17(3)&(4) Licensing Act 2003

- An **application** must be made:
    - To the **relevant licensing authority** (**council** of the area in which the premises in question is located);
    - On a **proscribed form**;
    - Accompanied by a **fee.**

J – Personal Licences – Section 111 Licensing Act 2003

1 - The Definition Of A Personal Licence

- A **personal licence** is:
    - A **licence**;
    - **Granted** by a **licensing authority** for the area in which the applicant is normally resident;
    - To an **individual**;
    - That either **authorises** them to either:
        - **Supply** alcohol; or
        - **Authorise the supply** of alcohol;
    - **In accordance with the licence** granted to the premises.

2 - The Definition Of Alcohol – Section 191 Licensing Act 2003

- **Alcohol** includes:
    - **Spirits**;
    - **Wine**;
    - **Beer**;
    - **Cider**;
    - Any other fermented, distilled, or spirituous liquor.

- **Alcohol** does **not** include:
    - **Alcohol below 0.5% at the time of sale or supply**;
    - **Perfume**;
    - **Flavoured essences**;
    - **Medicinal alcohol**;
    - **Denatured, menthyl, or naphtha alcohol**; or
    - **Liqueur confectionary.**

3 - The Duration Of A Personal Licence – Section 115 Licensing Act 2003

- A **personal licence** will **last** for a period of **10 years**;
- **Unless** it is:
  - ☐ **Revoked**;
  - ☐ **Suspended**; or
  - ☐ **Surrendered**.
- At the **expiry** of the **10 year period** the **personal licensee** may **apply for a review**.

K – Club Premises

1 - The Criteria For A Club To Be A Qualifying Club – Section 61 Licensing Act 2003

- For a club to be deemed a **qualifying club** the following criteria must be evident:
  - ☐ No one may be admitted as a member without an interval of **at least 2 days** after their nomination or application for membership;
  - ☐ Persons becoming members without prior notification or application may not be admitted as a member without an interval of **at least 2 days** between their becoming members and admission;
  - ☐ The club is **established** and is **conducted in good faith**;
  - ☐ The club has **at least 25 members**;
  - ☐ No **alcohol** is **supplied**, or is **intended to be supplied**, to members on the premises except **by or on behalf of the club.**

2 - Club Premises Certificates

- A **Club Premises Certificate** is very **similar** to a **Premises Licence**.
- It **permits qualifying club activities** to take place including:
  - ☐ The supply otherwise than by retail of sale of alcohol to club members;
  - ☐ The sale by retail of alcohol to the guests of members;
  - ☐ The provision of regulated entertainment.

3 - Police Powers Of Entry Of Clubs Making An Application For A Club Premises Certificate – Section 96(2) Licensing Act 2003

- Where a **club** makes the following types of **application** in relation to a **club premises certificate:**
  - ☐ Application for **issue**;
  - ☐ **Variation** of an existing certificate;
  - ☐ **Review** of a certificate after its expiry;
- The **chief officer of a force** may **authorise** a **constable** to:
  - ☐ **Enter** the premises; and
  - ☐ **Inspect** the premises.

4 - When May The Constable Enter? – Section 96(3) & (4) Licensing Act 2003

- A **constable** may **enter:**
  - At a **reasonable time of day;**
  - **Within 14 days** of the lodging of the application;
  - Provided that they have supplied the club with **48 hours notice.**
- **Obstructing** a constable in the exercise of this power is a **summary offence.**

5 - Constables Additional Powers Of Entry To Clubs – Section 96 Licensing Act 2003

- Where a club has a **valid club premises certificate;**
- A **constable** may:
  - **Enter** (by **force** if necessary); and
  - **Search;**
- The **premises** if they have **reasonable cause** to **believe:**
  - That the offence of **supplying;** or being **concerned in the supply;** or making an **offer to supply** a **controlled drug** either:
    - **Has** been committed;
    - **Is** being committed;
    - **Is** about to be committed; or
  - That there is **likely to be a breach of the peace** there.

L – The Definition Of Permitted Temporary Activities – Section 100 Licensing Act 2003

- **Licensable activities** that **do not have** either a valid:
  - **Premises licence;** or
  - **Club premises certificate;**
- **May** be carried out on a **temporary basis** (e.g. a bar in a marquee);
- Provided a **licensing authority** has **issued** a **temporary events notice.**
- A **temporary events notice** may only last for a **maximum of 96 hours.**

M – The Definition Of Unauthorised Licensable Activities – Section 136 Licensing Act 2003
Summary Only Offences
Penalty In The Magistrates Court – 6 Months Imprisonment And / Or A Fine

- A person will commit an offence if either:
    - They either:
        - **Carry on**; or
        - **Attempt to carry on**;
    - A **licensable activity**;
    - Either **on** or **from** any **premises**;
    - **Otherwise than in accordance with an authorisation**; or
    - They **knowingly allow** a **licensable activity** to be carried on.

N – Exposing Alcohol For Unauthorised Sale – Section 137 Licensing Act 2003
Summary Only Offences
Penalty In The Magistrates Court – 6 Months Imprisonment And / Or A Fine

- A person commits an offence if they:
    - On any **premises**;
    - **Expose for sale by retail**;
    - Any **alcohol**;
    - In circumstances where the **sale by retail** of the alcohol on those premises would be an **unauthorised licensable activity**.

O - Defences To Unauthorised Licensable Activities And Exposing Alcohol For Unauthorised Sale – Due Diligence – Section 139 Licensing Act 2003

- It is a **defence** to prove on the **balance of probabilities** that either:
    - Their **act was due to** either:
        - A **mistake**;
        - **Reliance on information** given to them;
        - The **act** or **omission** of **another person**; or
        - Some other cause beyond their control; *and*
    - They **took all reasonable precautions** and **exercised all diligence** to avoid committing the offence.

P – Allowing Disorderly Conduct – Section 140 Licensing Act 2003
Summary Only Offences
Penalty In The Magistrates Court – Fine Only

1 – The Definition Of The Offence

- It is an offence for:
    - A **specified person**;
    - To **knowingly**;
    - **Allow disorderly conduct**;
    - **On licensed premises**.

2 – The Definition Of Specified Persons – Section 140 Licensing Act 2003

- **Specified persons** include:
    - In respect of **premises**:
        - Any **person who works at the premises** in a **capacity** which **authorises them to prevent the conduct**;
        - The **holder** of the **premises licence**;
    - In respect of **clubs**:
        - The **designated premises supervisor**;
        - Any **member or officer** of the club **present at the time in a capacity which enables them to prevent it**;
    - In the case of **temporary activities**:
        - The **premises user** in relation to the **temporary event notice**.

Q – The Definition Of Selling Alcohol To A Drunk – Section 141 Licensing Act 2003
Summary Only Offences
Penalty In The Magistrates Court – Fine Only

- A **specified person** commits an offence if:
- Whilst on **relevant premises**;
- They **knowingly**:
    - **Sells** or **attempts to sell** alcohol to a person who is drunk; or
    - **Allows alcohol to be sold** to such a person.

R – Obtaining Alcohol For A Drunk – Section 142 Licensing Act 2003
Summary Only Offences
Penalty In The Magistrates Court – Fine Only

1 – The Definition Of The Offence

- A person commits an offence if they:
    - On **relevant premises**;
    - **Knowingly** either:
        - **Obtains** alcohol; or
        - **Attempts to obtain** alcohol;
    - For **consumption on those premises** by a **person who is drunk**.

2 – The Definition Of Relevant Premises – Section 159 Licensing Act 2003

- **Relevant premises** includes:
    - **Licensed premises**;
    - Premises with a **club certificate**; or
    - Premises used for a **permitted temporary activity**.

S – Failure To Leave Licensed Premises – Section 143 Licensing Act 2003
Summary Only Offences
Penalty In The Magistrates Court – Fine Only

1 – The Definition Of The Offence

- An offence is committed by:
    - A person who is either:
        - **Drunk;** *or*
        - **Disorderly**;
    - Who **without reasonable excuse** either:
        - **Fails to leave relevant premises** when **requested** to do so by a:
            - **Constable**;
            - **Authorised person**; or
        - **Enters** or **attempts to enter relevant premises** after they have been requested not to enter by a:
            - **Constable**; or
            - **Authorised person**.

2 - The Definition Of An Authorised Person – Section 143(2) Licensing Act 2003

- **Authorised persons** will include:
    - Any person who **works at the premises** in a capacity which **authorises them to sell alcohol;**
    - In the case of **licensed premises**:
        - The premises **licence holder**; and
        - The **designated supervisor;**
    - In the case of **clubs**:
        - Any **member or officer present** on the premises in a **capacity which enables them to make such a request;**
    - In the case of **temporary activities**:
        - The **premises user** under the temporary events notice.

T - The Police Duty To Help Expel Disorderly Persons – Section 3 Licensed Premises Act 1980

- On being **requested** to do so by any of the **authorised persons;**
- A **constable** must either:
    - **Help expel** the disorderly or drunk person from the premises; or
    - **Help prevent** such a person **entering.**
- Note the duty remains one of **assisting the authorised person** (as under previous law) rather than simply doing it oneself.

U – Exclusion Orders From Licensed Premises – Section 2(1) Licensed Premises (Exclusion of Certain Persons) Act 1980
Summary Only Offences
Penalty For A Breach In The Magistrates Court – 1 Months Imprisonment And / Or A Fine

1 - When May Persons Be Excluded From Licensed Premises?

- A person may be **excluded, by Court Order**, from licensed premises where:
    - They have **committed on licensed premises;**
    - Any **offence** involving:
        - **Violence;** or
        - **Threat of violence.**

2 – The Scope Of Exclusion Orders

- The Exclusion Order may **prohibit** the offender from:
    - ☐ **Entering** any **specified premises** (which will be set out in the Order);
    - ☐ **Without** the **express consent** of:
        - The **licensee;** or
        - The **licensee's agent.**

3 – The Duration Of An Exclusion Order

- Such **exclusion orders** may remain in force for any period between **3 months – 2 years.**

4 - The Power To Expel A Person In Breach Of An Exclusion Order - Section 3 Licensed Premises (Exclusion of Certain Persons) Act 1980

- Either:
    - ☐ The **licensee;** or
    - ☐ Their **servant / agent;**
- May **expel** any persons who:
    - ☐ Has **entered**; or
    - ☐ Whom they reasonably **suspects** of having **entered;**
    - ☐ **The premises in breach** of an exclusion order.
- A **constable** shall **on demand help to expel** any person whom the **constable** reasonably **suspects** of having **entered in breach** of an exclusion order.

V – The Definition Of Selling Alcohol To Children – Section 146 Licensing Act 2003
Summary Only Offences
Penalty In The Magistrates Court – Fine Only

- Either a:
    - ☐ **Person;** or
    - ☐ **Club;**
- Commits an offence if they either:
    - ☐ **Sell alcohol;** or
    - ☐ **Supply alcohol;**
- To a person **under 18.**

W – The Definition Of Selling Alcohol To Children On Licensed Premises – Section 147 Licensing Act 2003
Summary Only Offences
Penalty In The Magistrates Court – Fine Only

- Any **persons who works** at **premises** that are either:
    - ☐ **Licensed** ;
    - ☐ Have a **club premises certificate**; or
    - ☐ Are used for **permitted temporary activity**;
- In a **capacity** which **authorises them to prevent the sale**;
- Commits an offence if they:
    - ☐ **Knowingly**;
    - ☐ **Allow** the **sale** or **supply** of **alcohol**;
    - ☐ **On** the **premises**;
    - ☐ To a person **under 18.**

X – The Definition Of Selling Liqueur Confectionary – Section 148 Licensing Act 2003
Summary Only Offences
Penalty In The Magistrates Court – Fine Only

- It is an offence to:
    - ☐ **Sell;**
    - ☐ **Liqueur confectionary**;
    - ☐ To a person **under 16** years of age.

Y – The Definition Of Purchasing Alcohol By Children – Section 149 (1) Licensing Act 2003
Summary Only Offences
Penalty In The Magistrates Court – Fine Only

- A person **under 18** commits an offence if they:
    - ☐ Either:
        - **Buy alcohol;**
        - **Attempt to buy alcohol**; or
    - ☐ If they are a **club member:**
        - **Alcohol** is **supplied** to them at their order by or on behalf of the club; or
        - They **attempt to have alcohol supplied** to them or to their order by or on behalf of the club.

Z – The Definition Of Purchasing Alcohol For Children – Section 149(3) Licensing Act 2003
Summary Only Offences
Penalty In The Magistrates Court – Fine Only

- A person commits an offence if they:
    - Either:
        - Buy alcohol;
        - Attempt to buy alcohol;
    - For a person under 18.
    - Or if they are a **club member**:
        - They **make arrangements** on behalf of a person under 18 for the supply of alcohol to them or to their order by the club; or
        - They **attempt to make arrangements** on behalf of a person under 18 for the supply of alcohol to them or to their order by the club.

AA – Purchasing Alcohol For A Child in Licensed Premises – Section 149(4) Licensing Act 2003
Summary Only Offences
Penalty In The Magistrates Court – Fine Only

1 – The Definition Of The Offence

- A person commits an offence if they:
    - **Buy** or **attempt to buy alcohol** for the **consumption on relevant premises** by a person **under 18** years old; or
    - Where they are a **club member**:
        - By some **act** or **default** of them, **alcohol is supplied to them,** or **to their order**, by the club **for consumption by a person under 18 years of age; or**
        - They attempts such supply.

2 - Defence

- Where a person had **no reason to suspect that the child was under 18** years of age.

3 - Exception - Table Meals – Section 150(4) Licensing Act 2003

- No offence is committed in the following circumstances:
    - ☐ The **relevant person** is **18 or over**;
    - ☐ The **child** is **16 or 17** years of age;
    - ☐ The **alcohol** is:
        - Beer;
        - Wine; or
        - Cider;
    - ☐ Its purchase or supply is **for consumption at a table meal** on the premises;
    - ☐ The **child** is **accompanied** at the meal **by a person aged 18 years or over**.

BB – Consumption Of Alcohol By A Child – Section 150 (1) Licensing Act 2003
Summary Only Offences
Penalty In The Magistrates Court – Fine Only

1 - The Definition Of The Offence

- A person **under 18** years of age commits an offence if they:
    - ☐ **Knowingly**;
    - ☐ **Consume alcohol;**
    - ☐ **On relevant premises.**

2 - Exception – Section 150(4) Licensing Act 2003

The **table meal exception** applies.

CC – Sending Child to Obtain Alcohol – Section 152 Licensing Act 2003
Summary Only Offences
Penalty In The Magistrates Court – Fine Only

1 - The Definition Of The Offence

- A person commits an offence if they:
    - ☐ **Knowingly sends an individual under 18 years** of age to obtain:
        - **Alcohol sold** or to be sold on relevant premises for consumption on the premises; or
        - **Alcohol supplied** or to be supplied by or on behalf of a club for such consumption.

2 - Exceptions – Section 152(4) Licensing Act 2003

- ☐ **Test purchases** are exempt.

- ☐ The offence will not be committed where the person **under 18** years of age on the premises in a capacity which **involves delivery of alcohol**.

DD - Confiscating Alcohol From Children – Section 1 Confiscating of Alcohol (Young Persons) Act 1997

- Where a **constable** (who **need not be in uniform**);

- Reasonably **suspects** that a person in a **relevant place** is in **possession of alcohol**, and that either:

    - ☐ They are **under 18** years of age; or

    - ☐ They **intend that any of the alcohol should be consumed by a person under 18** years of age in that or any relevant place; or

    - ☐ A person **under 18** years of age **who is, or has recently been, with them has recently consumed alcohol** in that or any relevant place.

- The **constable** may require them to:

    - ☐ **Surrender** anything in his possession which is, or the **constable** reasonably **believes** to be, **alcohol** or a **container for such alcohol, (which the constable may dispose)**; and

    - ☐ To **state** their **name** and **address**.

Exam Trip Up

- Watch out for questions involving a **constable**:

    - ☐ **Searching persons** at:
        - *On* **licensed premises**;
        - *Off* **licensed premises**.

    - ☐ **Searching persons** who:
        - Have **initially** gained **access lawfully to a licensed premises**; and
        - **Later** became a **trespasser**.

- The **power to confiscate alcohol** does *not apply* in any of the aforementioned circumstances.

EE - Failure To Comply With A Request To Surrender – Section 1(3) Confiscation Of Alcohol (Young Persons) Act 1997
Summary Only Offences
Penalty In The Magistrates Court – Fine Only

- It is an offence to **fail to** comply with a request to **surrender without a reasonable excuse.**

- The constable may only require the surrender of **sealed containers** if they:
  - Reasonably **believe** that the person:
    - Either:
      - **Is;** or
      - **Has been;**
    - Either:
      - **Consuming alcohol;** or
      - **Intents to consume alcohol.**

The Definition Of A Relevant Place – Section 1(6) Confiscation Of Alcohol (Young Persons) Act 1997

- A **relevant place** includes any:
  - **Public place (not licensed premises);** or
  - Place, **other than a public place**, to which that person has **unlawfully gained access.**

- Therefore this would include a **place to which the public has access on payment** - e.g. Cinema, Bowling Alley etc.

FF – The Power To Close Premises – Section 160 Licensing Act 2003

- Following an application by a **Superintendent** or above;

- Where there **is or is expected to be any disorder** in their area;

- A **Magistrates Court** for that area may make an **order** requiring:
  - **All premises situated at or near the place of that disorder** and
  - In respect of which a **temporary event notice** has effect,
  - To be closed for a period **not exceeding 24 hours.**

- A **constable** may **use such force as is necessary to close such premises.**

- It is an offence to **knowingly contravene the order.**

Exam Trip Up

- Under s. 164(1) of the Licensing Act 2003:
    - Where a **closure order** has been made;
    - The **responsible officer must:**
        - Firstly:
            - **Apply** to the relevant **justices**;
            - *As soon as reasonably practicable* after the order was made;
            - To enable the **justices** to **consider:**
                - The **order;** and
                - Any **extension** to it.
        - Secondly - **notify** the relevant **licensing authority.**

Duration Of A Closure Order

- A closure order will **expire 24 hours after the notice was served** on the relevant person.

Exam Trip Up

- The legislators have allowed for the fact that **most areas do** *not* **have a court sitting on a Sunday** by:
    - **Allowing the senior police officer to** *extend* **the existing closure order;**
    - By **serving a new written notice** on the relevant person - (section 162).
- This extension will last for **another 24 hours**, allowing the responsible officer to attend court on the Monday.

For Example:

- If the **original closure order**:
    - **Commenced** at 10pm on Saturday; and
    - **Expired** at 10 p.m. on a Sunday;
- The **further extended period of 24 hours commences** when the **previous order expires**.
- However, the **written notice** *must:*
    - Be *served* on the relevant person (licensee);
    - *Before* the existing closure order *expires* (see section 162(3) and (4)).

Exam Trip Up

- In order to **extend a closure order** the **senior police officer** would still reasonably have to *believe* that it is **necessary:**
    - ☐ In the **interests of public safety;** or
    - ☐ To **prevent excessive noise.**

- Therefore:
    - ☐ If the **senior police officer** (**Inspector** in cases of **urgency**);
    - ☐ Had **no reason** to **believe** that there would have been **further problems on the Sunday;**
    - ☐ They could *not* have closed the **premises** down.

- The **senior police officer** would **still have to attend court** on the Monday to **report on the facts of the closure order** served on the Saturday.

General Police Duties
Unit 13: Information Offences

A - Unauthorised Access To Computers – Section 1 Computer Misuse Act 1990
Summary Only Offence
Penalty In The Magistrates Court – 6 Months Imprisonment And / Or A Fine Only

1 – The Definition Of The Offence

- A person is guilty of an offence if:
    - They **cause** a **computer** to **perform** any **function** with **intent** to **secure access** to **any program** or **data** held in **any** computer;
    - The **access** they intend to secure is **unauthorised;** and
    - They **know at the time** when they cause the computer to perform the function that that is the case.

2 – Learning Point

- The **intent** a person has to have to commit an offence **need not be directed** at:
    - **Any particular program or data**;
    - **A program or data of any particular kind;** or
    - **A program or data held in any particular computer**.
- This is an offence of **"specific intent"**.

Exam Trip Up

- The **access** must be **unauthorised** rather than unauthorised use of data.

Exam Trip Up

- Even an **attempt** to **log on** to a computer with the requisite **intent** will **suffice** with regards to this offence.

Exam Trip Up

- **Reading material** off the computer screen will **not suffice.**
- With the advances in technology a **mobile phone or MP3** player may fall within the boundaries of this offence.

Exam Trip Up

- Due to the summary nature of this offence it **cannot be attempted**.
- However the substantive offence covers a multitude of actions from switching on the computer to many acts that would ordinarily be classed as "merely preparatory".

2 - Unauthorised Access to Computers with Intent – Section 2 Criminal Misuse Act 1990
Either Way Offence
Penalty In The Magistrates Court – 6 Months Imprisonment And / Or A Fine
Penalty In The Crown Court – 5 Years Imprisonment And / Or A Fine

- A person is guilty of an offence if:
    - They **commit** an **offence** under **Section 1**;
    - With **intent** to either:
        - **Commit an offence** to which this section applies; or
        - **Facilitate the commission** of such an offence (**themselves or another**); and
    - The offence they **intend** to **commit** or **facilitate** either:
        - Carries a **sentence fixed by law**; or
        - A person who has attained the **age of 21** (**18 year in England and Wales**) and has **no previous convictions** may be sentenced to imprisonment for a term of **5 years**.

Exam Trip Up

- It is **immaterial** for the purpose of this section whether the **further offence** is to be committed:
    - On the **same occasion** as the **unauthorised access** offence; or
    - On **any subsequent occasion**.

Exam Trip Up

- A person may be guilty under this section even though the **commission of the further offence is impossible**.

    For example: An offender attempting to access the bank details of a person who they believed were customers at a specific bank, where it transpires that person did not hold an account with the said bank.

Exam Trip Up

- The offender **must have** the required **intent at the time** of the:
    - **Access**; or
    - Other *actus rea*.

Exam Trip Up

- The **intended further offence**:
    - Does **not** have to be **committed** at the **same time**; and
    - **May be committed in the future**.

For example: An offender who works for a credit card company and accesses the account details of customers at work and then at a later date uses their details either themselves, or passes on their details to an associate, in order to obtain property by fraud.

C - Unauthorised Modification of Computer Material – Section 3 Computer Misuse Act 1990
Either Way Offence
Penalty In The Magistrates Court – 6 Months Imprisonment And / Or A Fine
Penalty In The Crown Court – 5 Years Imprisonment And / Or A Fine

1 – Definition Of The Offence

- A person is guilty of an offence if:
    - They do any **act** which **causes** an **unauthorised modification** of the **contents** of any **computer**; and
    - At the time of the act they have the:
        - **Requisite intent**; and
        - **Requisite knowledge**.

2 - Definition Of The Requisite Intent – Section 3(2) Computer Misuse Act 1990

- The **requisite intent** is an **intent to cause a modification of the contents of any computer** to either:
    - **Impair the operation of any computer;**
    - **Prevent or hinder access to any program or data held in any computer;** or
    - **Impair the operation of any such program or the reliability of any such data.**

- The **intent need not** be **directed** at:
    - **Any particular computer;**
    - **Any particular program or data;** or
    - **A program or data of any particular kind;** or
    - **Any particular modification;** or
    - **A modification of any particular kind.**

3 - Definition Of The Requisite Knowledge - Section 3(4) Computer Misuse Act 1990

- The **requisite knowledge** is **knowledge** that any **modification** they **intend** to **cause** is **unauthorised.**

Learning Aid

- The offence requires both **intent** and **knowledge.**

Exam Trip Up

- Intentionally implanting or sending a virus would fall within the remit of this offence.

Police Pass OSPRE Part 1 Revision Crammer Textbook ©

Exam Trip Up

- It is immaterial if any unauthorised modification or intended affect is **permanent or temporary**.

Exam Trip Up

- For the purposes of the Criminal Damage Act 1971 a modification of the contents of a computer shall not be regarded as damaging any computer or computer storage medium **unless** its effect on that computer or computer storage medium **impairs its physical condition**.

4 - Definition Of Data – Section 1 Data Protection Act 1998

- **Data** means information which:
    - Is being **processed** by means of **equipment operating automatically** in **response to instructions**;
    - Is **recorded** with the **intention** that it should be **processed by means of such equipment**;
    - Is **recorded** by means of a **relevant filing system**; or
    - Does not fall within the above but forms part of an **accessible record**.

5 - Definition Of An Accessible Record – Section 68(1) Data Protection Act 1998

- **Accessible records** include any:
    - **Health record;**
    - **Educational record;** or
    - Any **record** which is **accessible** as a **public record**.

6 - Definition Of A Relevant Filing System

- A **relevant filing system** means:
    - Any **set of information** relating to **individuals**;
    - That although the **information is not processed** by means of **equipment operating automatically** in response to instructions given for that purpose;
    - **The set is structured**, either by **reference to**:
        - **Individuals;** or
        - **Criteria relating to individuals**;
    - In such a way that:
        - **Specific information;**
        - **Relating to a particular individual;**
        - **Is readily accessible.**

7 - Definition Of Personal Data

- **Personal data** includes any **data** which relates to a **living individual** who can be **identified** either:
    - [ ] **From the data;** or
    - [ ] From those data and other information which is in the **possession of, or is likely to come into the possession of, the data controller**, and includes:
        - Any **expression of opinion** about the individual; and
        - Any **indication of the intentions of the data controller or any other person in respect of the individuals**.

8 - Definition Of Sensitive Personal Data - Section 2 Data Protection Act 1998

- Sensitive personal data includes:
    - [ ] The **racial or ethnic origin** of the subject;
    - [ ] Their **political opinions**;
    - [ ] Their **religious beliefs** or beliefs of a similar nature;
    - [ ] Whether they are a **member of a Trade Union**;
    - [ ] Their **physical** or **mental health** or condition;
    - [ ] Their **sexual life**;
    - [ ] The **commission or alleged commission** by them of an **offence**; or
    - [ ] Any **proceedings for any offence committed** or **alleged to have been committed by them**;
    - [ ] The **disposal of such proceedings**; or
    - [ ] The **sentence of any court in such proceedings**.

General Police Duties
Unit 14: Diversity, Discrimination and Equality

A - Discriminatory Behaviour Outside Of The Workplace And The Code Of Conduct For Police Officers

- Where acts amounting to discrimination take place **outside the workplace**, the **employer** and **employees may** still be caught within the framework of the legislation.

- The case of *Chief Constable of Lincolnshire v Stubbs* [1999] IRLR 81, established that where police officers engage in inappropriate sexual behaviour towards a colleague at a **work related function**, a tribunal may be entitled to hold that that function was a **natural extension of the workplace** and so hold the Chief Officer liable for the acts of their officers at that function.

B - The Race Relations Act 1976

1 - Discrimination On The Grounds Of Race – Section 1 Race Relations Act 1976

- The Section 1 Race Relations Act 1976 makes it unlawful to **discriminate against others** on the grounds of **race** in relation to the **areas** of:
    - **Employment;**
    - **Training and education;**
    - The **provision of:**
        - **Goods;**
        - **Facilities;** and
        - **Services.**

2 - Definition Of Racial Grounds - Section 3 Race Relations Act 1976

- Discrimination will be **racial** when it is on the grounds of a person's:
    - **Colour;**
    - **Race;**
    - **Nationality;** or
    - **Ethnic or National origins.**

Exam Trip Up

- "**Nationality**" includes citizenship acquired at birth.

Exam Trip Up

- **"Ethnic group"** is a broad definition which may include any group with a shared culture or history.

3 - The Race Relations (Amendment) Act 2000

- This act covers the functions of **public authorities**.
- The provisions of the amended act and the 2003 regulations make it:
  - Unlawful for a **public authority** to:
    - **Discriminate against; or**
    - **Harass;**
  - A person on the **grounds** of **race** in carrying out any of its **functions**.
- The term **public authority** should be viewed in similar terms to that of the **Human Rights Act**.

Limited Exemption

- The public authority discriminates against a person on the grounds of **nationality or ethnic/national origins** and, in doing so, is **properly** acting on behalf of a **Minister of the Crown** in relation to **immigration** or **nationality functions**.

4 - Race Equality Schemes

- **Police Forces, Chief Officers** and **Police Authorities** are under a statutory duty to publish a **Race Equality Scheme**.
- These schemes must include details of:
  - Those **functions and policies** that they have assessed as being relevant to the performance of their duties;
  - Their arrangements for **assessing** and **consulting** on the likely impact of those proposed policies on the **promotion of race equality**;
  - **Monitoring policies** for **adverse impact** on the promotion of race equality;
  - **Publishing** the **results** of such assessments and consultation;
  - Ensuring **public access** to the to information and services; and
  - **Training staff.**

5 - Extension of Police Liability

- Both:
  - The **Police Authorities; and**
  - **Chief Officers;**
- Are liable for **acts done by** *them* to a police **constable**.

Exam Trip Up

- **Chief Officers will also be *vicariously liable*** for racially **discriminatory acts by constables** under their:
    - ☐ **Direction**; and
    - ☐ **Control**.

C - The Sex Discrimination Act 1975

1 - Discrimination On The Grounds Of Sex – Section 1 Sex Discrimination Act 1975

- The act makes it **unlawful** to **discriminate** on the grounds of a persons:
    - ☐ **Sex**; or
    - ☐ **Martial status**.
- The legislation applies equally in favour of **both**:
    - ☐ **Men**; and
    - ☐ **Women equally**.
- The legislation does **not** operate **equally** in respect of **married or single people**.
- An employer may provide **greater benefits for married employees**.
- The legislation now treats constables as being in the **employ** of their **Chief Officer** for the purposes of making the **Chief Officer vicariously liable for unlawful acts done in the performance of the constable's role.**

D - The Disability Discrimination Act 1995

1 - Discrimination On The Grounds Of Disability – Section 1 Disability Discrimination Act 1995

- The act as amended by the 2005 Act makes it unlawful to discriminate against people on the grounds of their **disability.**

2 - Definition Of A Disability - Section 1 Disability Discrimination Act 1995

- A person will be disabled for the purposes of the Act if:
    - ☐ They have a;
        - **Physical** impairment; or
        - **Mental** impairment;
    - ☐ Which has a **substantial and long term adverse effect** upon their **ability to carry out normal daily functions.**

3 - Making Reasonable Adjustments To Accommodate The Disability – Section 6 Disability Discrimination Act 1995

- Employers are required to make **"reasonable adjustments"** to prevent disabled people from being put at a **substantial disadvantaged** when compared with others "able" bodied persons.

- The act allows a defence of **justification** to employers.

- Persons subject to mental illness are protected by this act, as are persons with specific medical complaints such as cancer, HIV or diabetes.

E - Forms Of Discrimination

1 - Direct Discrimination – The "But For" Test

- **Direct discrimination** can best be summarised as:
    - One person being **treated less favourably** than another person; and
    - The **reason** for their **less favourable treatment** was based upon their **membership** of a protected **group** (race, sex etc).

- i.e. they would not have been treated less favourably **"but" for** the fact that they were a member of that particular group.

- It must be shown that the treatment was made on the **grounds** of or by reason of the person **belonging** to a **protected group** or having such **characteristics.**

2 - Indirect Discrimination

- **Indirect discrimination** arises where:
    - A condition is applied to **all relevant people**; but
    - Persons belonging to the **protected group** are **disproportionately disadvantaged** than other persons to which the condition applies;
    - Because their **characteristic** makes them **less able to comply** with the condition.

- For example, the case of *Walker J.H. Ltd v Hussain* [1996] IRLR 11, established that requiring all employees to work on certain days would possibly put people of a certain nationality, sex or religious belief at a disadvantage.

- **Indirect Discrimination** will occur if:
    - A **person** or **organisation** applies equally a:
        - **Provision;**
        - **Criterion;** or
        - **Practice;** and
    - That provision, criterion or practice puts people in the **protected group** at a **disadvantage when compared to others;** and
    - The organisation or person (x) **cannot** show their actions to be a **proportionate means** of achieving a **legitimate aim.**

The Burden Of Proof In Discrimination Claims

- The case of *Wong v Igen Ltd* [2005] EWCA Civ 142, endorsed that:
    - The employee must make an initial case of discrimination by showing facts which could in the absence of explanation amount to less favourable treatment on the prohibited ground.
    - Once this initial case is made out by the employee and there is no adequate explanation then the burden moves onto the employer.

3 - Harassment

(i) - Racial Harassment – Section 3A & 4 Race Relations Act 1976

- The Race Relations Act 1976 contains a specific definition of **racial harassment** which:
    - Prohibits **harassment**;
    - On the grounds of **race** or **ethnic** or **national origin**;
    - Which either:
        - **Violates** the persons **dignity**; or
        - Creates an **environment** that is:
            - **Intimidating**;
            - **Hostile**;
            - **Degrading**;
            - **Humiliating**; or
            - **Offensive**.

(ii) - Sexual Harassment

- The case of *Wadman v Carpenter Farrer Partnership* [1993] IRLR 374, defined **sexual harassment** as:
    - Either:
        - **Unwanted conduct** of a **sexual nature**; or
        - Other **conduct based on sex**;
    - **Affecting** the **dignity** of persons at work.

(iii) - The Manner Of Harassment

- The harassment may be as a result of either:
    - **Verbal** communication;
    - **Written** communication;
    - Physical **gestures (e.g. exposure)**;
    - Physical **contact (e.g. groping)**.

(iv) – Harassment As Criminal Conduct

- Harassment is also a criminal offence and if the psychological shock of such behaviour is sufficient it may amount to an offence of assault.

4 - Victimization

- A person is subject to **victimization** if:

    - They are **treated less favourably** than another person is or would be treated in the same circumstances;

    - With regard to any **action covered by the discrimination acts** because the person:

        - **Brought proceedings** against any person under any of the acts;

        - Has given **evidence** or **information** in connection with **proceedings** under those acts;

        - **Otherwise did anything under or by reference to the acts** with regard to any person;

        - Has **alleged that** any person has done anything which would amount to a **contravention of those acts**; or

        - Because the **discriminator knows or suspects that the person victimised has done or intends to do anything set out above.**

- The above points are referred to as **"Protected Acts"**

- The case of *Aziz v Trinity Street Taxis Ltd* [1989] QB 463 established that in proving victimisation - the victim must prove that:

    - Their **less favourable treatment**;

    - Occurred **as a result** of their **involvement** in the **protected action**.

F – Defences - Genuine Occupational Qualifications (GOQ's)

- The **GOQ** defence only applies to:

    - **Recruitment**;

    - **Refusing employment**; and

    - **Affording access to promotion, training** etc.

- The principle behind this defence is that **certain roles/occupations** may well have a **legitimate reason** why certain protected groups **may not carry out the role**.

- Such occasions are generally concerned with:

    - **Preserving decency and privacy** (e.g. masseur);

    - **Authenticity** (e.g. actor/actresses); or

    - **The provision of personal services.**

G - Positive Action

- This is sometimes required to **encourage under represented groups** to apply for certain **employment** or **training opportunities** for **legitimate reasons**.

- **Positive action** should not be confused with **"positive discrimination"** or **"affirmative action"** which is illegal in the UK.

- Therefore an attempt to recruit female police officers into a specialist role by excluding male applicants has been held to be unlawful - *Jones v Chief Constable of Northamptonshire Police* [1999] The Times, 1st November.

H - Maternity and Paternity Rights

- Women and men have the following rights in relation to pregnancy and childbirth:
    - ☐ Rights to unpaid time off work;
    - ☐ Protection against dismissal;
    - ☐ Rights to maternity & paternity pay;
    - ☐ Rights to maternity & paternity leave, and
    - ☐ Rights to return to work;
    - ☐ Parental leave rights.

General Police Duties
Unit 15: Terrorism

A – Definition Of Terrorism - Section 1 Terrorism Act 2000

- **Terrorism** is defined as:

- The **use** or **threat** of **action** where:

    - The **action** falls within any of the following **acts:**

        - **Involves serious violence against a person;**
        - **Involves serious damage to property;**
        - **Endangers a persons life**, other than the person committing the act;
        - **Creates a serious risk to the health or safety of the public or a section of the public;** or
        - Is designed **seriously to interfere** with or **seriously to disrupt an electronic system;** *and*

    - The **use** or **threat** is **designed** to either:

        - **Influence the:**
            - **Government;** or
            - An **international governmental organisation;** or
        - **Intimidate** the **public** or a **section** of the **public;** *and*

    - The **use** or **threat** is made for the **purpose** of **advancing a:**

        - **Political cause;**
        - **Religious cause;** or
        - **Ideological cause.**

Exam Trip Up

- The definition includes both:
    - **International** terrorism; and
    - **Domestic** terrorism.

Exam Trip Up

- The definition is **very broad** in nature and could be considered with other offences such as:
    - **Blackmail;**
    - **Threats to kill;** or
    - **Contamination** offences.

Exam Trip Up

- The definition encompasses **broad actions** and **threats** which **may not be overtly violent**, although will have a serious impact for the community at large e.g. contamination of goods or a utility supply.

Exam Trip Up

- Where the activity involves the **use of firearms or explosives**, there is **no further need** to show that the behaviour was designed to:
    - ☐ **Influence the government**; or
    - ☐ **Intimidate the public**.

Exam Trip Up

- The act can take place in:
    - ☐ The **UK**; or
    - ☐ **Elsewhere**.

B – Proscribed Organisations

(i) - The Activities Of A Proscribed Organisation - Part II Terrorism Act 2000 As Amended By The Terrorism Act 2006

- The **activities** of a **Proscribed Organisation** include:
    - ☐ **Unlawful glorification** of the **commission or preparation** of **acts of terrorism**; or
    - ☐ **Acts** carried out in a manner that ensures that the **organisation** is **associated** with **statements containing** such **glorification**.

(ii) - Definition Of Glorification – Section 3(5A) Terrorism Act 2000

- "**Glorification**" includes any form of:
    - ☐ **Praise**; or
    - ☐ **Celebration**.

(iii) - Definition Of A Statement - Section 3(5C) Terrorism Act 2000

- A "**statement**" includes any:
    - ☐ **Communication**;
    - ☐ Either **with** or **without words**;
    - ☐ Consisting of:
        - ■ **Sounds**;
        - ■ **Images**; or
        - ■ **Both**.

C - Terrorist Offences Arising Out Of Proscribed Organisations
All Indictable Only Offences
Penalty In The Crown Court – 10 Years Imprisonment

(i) - Section 11(1) Terrorism Act 2000

- **Belonging** or **professing to belong** to a proscribed organisation;

(ii) - Section 12(1) Terrorism Act 2000

- **Inviting support** for a proscribed organisation;

(iii) - Section 12(2) & (3) Terrorism Act 2000

- **Arranging** or **managing** (or **assisting** in doing so);
- A **meeting** of **three or more people**;
- In **public** or **private**;
- Which the **defendant knows** is:
    - To **support** a proscribed organisation;
    - To **further** the activities of a proscribed organisation;
    - To be **addressed by a person** who **belongs or professes to belong** to a proscribed organisation; or
    - **Addressing** a **meeting** to:
        - **Encourage support** for a proscribed organisation; or
        - **Further its activities**.

D - Finance Based Terrorism Offences Under The Terrorism Act 2000
All Indictable Only Offences
Penalty In The Crown Court – 14 Years Imprisonment

- The main offences include:
    - **Inviting** another to provide money or other property (section 15(1));
    - **Providing** money or other property (section 15(3));
    - **Receiving** money or other property (section 15(2));
    - **Possessing** money or other property (section 16(2));
    - **Arranging** for money or other property to be made available; (section 17)
- The mens rea for the above offences requires the defendant to either:
    - **Intend**; or
    - Have **reasonable cause to suspect**;
    - That the money **may be used for the purposes of terrorism** (sections 15, 16(2) and 17):
- **Using** money or other property for the **purposes of terrorism** (section 16(1));
- **Concealing, moving** or **transferring** any **terrorist property** (section 18).

E - Information Received During The Course Of Business In Relation To Financial Terrorism Offences - Section 19 Terrorism Act 2000
Indictable Only Offence
Penalty In The Crown Court – 5 Years Imprisonment

- Where a person either:
    - **Believes;** or
    - **Suspects**
- That another person has **committed** an **offence** under **sections 15 to 18;** and
- **Bases** that **belief** or **suspicion** on **information** which comes to their **attention** in the **course** of a:
    - Trade;
    - Profession;
    - Business; or
    - Employment;
- They **must disclose** to a **constable** as soon as **reasonably practicable** that **belief or suspicion**, and the **information** on which it is based.

Exam Trip Up

- Under section 19 of the Act:
    - Where a person:
        - **Believes;** or
        - **Suspects;**
    - That **another person** has **committed** an **offence** under *any* of **sections 15 - 18;** and
    - **Bases** that **belief** or **suspicion** on **information** which **comes** to their **attention in the course of a:**
        - Trade;
        - Profession;
        - Business; or
        - Employment;
    - They must disclose to a constable as soon as is reasonably practicable:
        - That:
            - **Belief;** or
            - **Suspicion;** and
        - The **information** on which it is **based.**

Exam Trip Up

- Although:
  - Banks; and
  - Other **financial institutions** are required to disclose activities they become aware of;
- The requirement extends **further** to *any* person who forms the **suspicion** or **belief in the course of a:**
  - Trade;
  - Profession;
  - Business; or
  - Employment.
- Therefore watch for the exam trip up when *any* **business person** such as **shopkeeper, landlord,** etc becomes suspicious of terrorist activity.
- They also have a **positive obligation to report**.

Exam Trip Up

- The requirement under section 19 **only applies** where the suspicion or belief has arisen **during** *the course of* **the** person's *work*.
- The classic exam trip up involves a person who **comes by the information** *during non-work activities.*
- Although there may be a moral or civic obligation there is *no* **legal duty of disclosure placed upon individuals who become suspicious of terrorist activities during their general day-to-day life.**

Exam Tip Up

- The offences under sections 15 – 18 apply to:
  - Either:
    - Providing;
    - Receiving;
    - Possessing; and
    - Using;
  - Either:
    - Money; or
    - *Property;*
  - Which may be **used for the purposes of terrorism**.

- Therefore, this could possibly manifest itself in the guise of:
    - **Passports**;
    - **Other official documents**; or
    - **Cash.**

F - Offences Under The Terrorism Act 2006

- Offences under the Terrorism Act 2006 are grouped into **3 categories**:
    - **Encouragement** of terrorism;
    - **Preparation of terrorist acts and training**; and
    - Offences involving **radioactive devices** and **materials** and **nuclear facilities** and **sites**.

1 - Encouragement Offences

(i) - Publishing – Section 1(2) Terrorism Act 2006
Either Way Offence
Penalty In The Magistrates Court – 1 Years Imprisonment And / Or A Fine
Penalty In The Crown Court – 7 Years Imprisonment And / Or A Fine

- An offence will be committed under section 1(2) where a person:
    - **Publishes** a **statement**;
    - To **encourage** the:
        - **Commission**;
        - **Preparation**; or
        - **Instigation**;
    - Of either:
        - **Acts of terrorism**; or
        - **Convention offences.**

Definition Of Convention Offences – Section 1(2) Terrorism Act 2006

- **"Convention offences"** include offences in relation to:
    - Explosives;
    - Hostage taking;
    - Hijacking;
    - Terrorist funds; and
    - C.B.R.N. offences (Chemical, Biological, Radioactive and Nuclear).

(ii) - Dissemination – Section 2(1) Terrorism Act 2006
Either Way Offence
Penalty In The Magistrates Court – 1 Years Imprisonment And / Or A Fine
Penalty In The Crown Court – 7 Years Imprisonment And / Or A Fine

- An offence will be committed under section 2(1) where a person:
    - **Engages** in the **dissemination** of **terrorist publications**.

Exam Trip Up

- These offences can be committed by **electronic means**.

Exam Trip Up

- It is necessary to prove the **glorification** of the **acts of terrorism**.

2 - Preparation of Terrorist Acts and Terrorist Training Groups

- An offence will be committed where a person either:
    - **Makes preparations** for terrorist acts (section 5(1));
    - **Provides** either **instruction** or **training** in any **skills** mentioned for the commission or preparation of acts of terrorism or convention offences (section 6(1));
    - **Receives instruction** or **training in any of the skills** mentioned for the commission or preparation of acts of terrorism or convention offences (section 6(2));
    - **Attends a place used for terrorist training** (section 8(1)).

Penalties

- The section 5(1) offence is an indictable only offence with a maximum penalty in the Crown Court of life imprisonment.

- The 3 other offences are either way offences with a maximum penalty in the Crown Court of 10 years imprisonment and or a fine and a maximum penalty in the Magistrates Court of 1 years imprisonment and or a fine.

Exam Trip Up

- The **preparation** offence does not have to relate to any:
    - Particular act of terrorism;
    - Acts of a particular description; or
    - Acts in general.

Exam Trip Up

- The **instruction** offence is very broad and can include any act which may be used for the purposes of terrorism.

Exam Trip Up

- The **terrorist training** offence (s.8(1)), can take place:
    - In the **UK**; or
    - **Elsewhere**.

3 - Offences Involving Radioactive Devices etc.
Indictable Only Offences
Penalty In The Crown Court – Life Imprisonment

- Offences under this heading include:
    - **Making** and **possession** of **devices** or **materials** (section 9(1));
    - **Misuse** of **devices** or **materials** and **misuse** and **damage** of **facilities** (sections 10(1) and (2));
    - **Terrorist threats relating to devices**, **materials** or **facilities** (sections 11(1) and (2));
    - **Trespassing etc. on nuclear sites.**

G - Disclosure Of Information – Section 38B Terrorism Act 2000
Either Way Offence
Penalty In The Magistrates Court – 6 Months Imprisonment And / Or A Fine
Penalty In The Crown Court – 5 Years Imprisonment And / Or A Fine

1 – Definition Of The Offence

- Where a person has **information**;
- Which they either:
    - **Know**; or
    - **Believe**
- Might be of **material assistance in:**
    - In **preventing** the **commission** by another person of an **act of terrorism**; or
    - In **securing** the:
        - **Apprehension**;
        - **Prosecution**; or
        - **Conviction**;
    - **Of another person** in the **UK**;
    - For an **offence** involving the:
        - **Commission**;
        - **Preparation**; or
        - **Instigation**
    - of an **act of terrorism**.

Exam Trip Up

- ☐ The person commits the offence if they **do not disclose the information as soon as is reasonably practicable**.

2 - To Whom Must The Disclosure Be Made? – Section 38B(3) Terrorism Act 2000

- **Disclosure** should be made:
    - ☐ In **England and Wales**, to a **constable**;
    - ☐ In **Scotland**, to a **constable**; or
    - ☐ In **Northern Ireland**, to a **constable** or a member of **Her Majesty's forces**.

H - Powers To Stop Search & Seize - Section 43 Terrorism Act 2000

- **Section 43** gives a **constable** the **power** to:
    - ☐ **Stop and search** a person whom they **reasonably suspects** to be a **terrorist** to discover whether they have in their possession anything which **may constitute evidence** that they are a terrorist; and
    - ☐ **Seize** and **retain** anything which they **discover** in the course of the search which they **reasonably suspect may constitute evidence** that the person is a terrorist.
    - ☐ A person who has powers of a constable in one part of the UK may exercise these powers anywhere in the UK.
- Schedule 5 to the 2000 Act provides for **searches** for the **purposes** of **terrorist investigations**.
- These **warrants** include **specific premises warrants** and **all premises warrants**.

I - Control Orders – Sections 1 – 4 Prevention of Terrorism Act 2005

(i) - The Function Of Control Orders

- The Act provides for the making of **control orders** imposing **obligations** on those **suspected** of being involved in terrorism-related activity.
- **Control orders** are **preventive orders** designed to **restrict** or **prevent further involvement** in such activity.
- They can be made against **any individual**, whether they are:
    - ☐ A **UK citizen;** or
    - ☐ **Otherwise.**
- The obligations on a person subject to such an order can cover a **wide spectrum**, provided that are necessary for the sole purposes of **preventing or restricting further involvement** in such terrorism-related activity.

- For example - **restrictions on:**
  - ☐ **Possessing property;**
  - ☐ **Movement;**
  - ☐ **Home address;**
  - ☐ **Communications;** or
  - ☐ **Associations.**

(ii) - Consultation Obligations – Section 8(2) Prevention of Terrorism Act 2005

- Where it appears to the **Secretary of State** that:
  - ☐ There is **terrorist related activity** by a person; and
  - ☐ An **offence** may have been committed;
- Then they must **consult** the **Chief Officer of the police force** before either **making or applying for a control order.**

(iii) - Action To Be Taken Once A Control Order Is Made – Section 8(4) Prevention of Terrorism Act 2005

- If a **control order** is **made** against a person:
  - ☐ The **Secretary of State** must **inform** the **Chief Officer** that the **order** has been **made;** and
  - ☐ The **Chief Officer** has a duty to make sure that the **investigation into the persons conduct with a view for prosecution for terrorist offences** is kept under **review throughout the duration of the control period.**
- Control orders are subject to full hearings by the **High Court** and there is a **right of appeal** on a **point of law** from the court's decision.

(iv) - Contravention Of A Control Order – Section 9 Prevention of Terrorism Act 2005
Either Way Offence
Penalty In The Magistrates Court – 1 Years Imprisonment And Or A Fine
Penalty In The Crown Court – 5 Years Imprisonment And Or A Fine

- A person who **without reasonable excuse, contravenes an obligation** imposed on them by a control order is guilty of an offence.

Exam Trip Up

- The contravention of *any* **obligation** will suffice.
- There **must** be the **absence** of a **reasonable excuse.**

(v) - Arrest and Detention Pending a Control Order – Section 5 Prevention of Terrorism Act 2005

- A **constable** may **arrest** and **detain** an individual if:
  - ☐ The **Secretary of State** has made an **application** to the court for a **derogating control order** to be made against the individual; and
  - ☐ The **constable considers** that the individual's **arrest** and **detention** is **necessary** to ensure that he is available to be **given notice of the order** if it is made.

Exam Trip Up

- The arrested person must be taken to a **designated place** that the constable considers most appropriate **as soon as practicable after arrest**.

Exam Trip Up

- The detainee can be detained at that location for **48 hours after arrest** and this can be extended for a **further 48 hours by order of a court**.

Exam Trip Up

- The detainee will be in **police detention** for the purposes of PACE 1984.

Traffic
Unit 1: Standards Of Driving

A - Definitions

1 - Definition Of A Mechanically Propelled Vehicle

- A **mechanically propelled vehicle (MPV)** includes any vehicle powered by:
    - ☐ Petrol;
    - ☐ Gas;
    - ☐ Diesel;
    - ☐ Electricity; or
    - ☐ Steam.

2 – Definition Of A Motor Vehicle – Section 185(1) Road Traffic Act 1988

- A **motor vehicle** is defined as:
    - ☐ An **MPV**;
    - ☐ Which is:
        - **Intended;** or
        - **Adapted**
    - ☐ For use **on a road**.
- Examples that are **not** motor vehicles include:
    - ☐ Off road scrambler bikes;
    - ☐ Drag racers;
    - ☐ Fork lift trucks.

Exam Trip Up

- The Road Traffic Act 1988 expressly states that:
    - ☐ **Neither:**
        - **Electronically assisted pedal cycles;** or
        - **Invalid carriages;**
    - ☐ Are either:
        - **Motor vehicles;** or
        - **Mechanically propelled vehicles.**

3 - Definition Of A Road – Section 192(1) Road Traffic Act 1988

- The definition of a **road** includes any:
    - ☐ **Highway**;
    - ☐ **Road** to which the **public have access**; and
    - ☐ **Bridges** over which a **road passes**.

4 - Definition Of A Highway

- The definition of a **highway** is **wide** and includes:
    - ☐ **Public footpaths**;
    - ☐ **Public bridleways**; and
    - ☐ **Public carriageways**.

B – Causing Death By Dangerous Driving
Indictable Only Offence
Penalty In The Crown Court - 14 Years Imprisonment, Plus Obligatory Disqualification & Compulsory Re-Testing

1 - Definition Of Causing Death By Dangerous Driving - Section 1 Road Traffic Act 1988

- A person commits an offence of **death by dangerous driving** if they:
    - ☐ **Unlawfully**;
    - ☐ **Cause** the **death**;
    - ☐ Of another **human being**;
    - ☐ By **driving** an **MPV dangerously**;
    - ☐ On a:
        - **Road**; or
        - Other **public place**.

2 – Definition Of Driving

- There is no statutory definition of driving.
- Whether or not a person is driving is:
    - ☐ A question of fact;
    - ☐ Determined by whether the person had control of:
        - Movement; and
        - Direction;
    - - Of the vehicle.

Exam Trip Up

- There must be admissible evidence of the aforementioned factors.
- A mere suspicion, no matter how strong will be insufficient to prove that driving had taken place.

3 - The Cause Of Death

- The driving does **not** need to be the **sole** or **major cause of the death**.
- It need only be a **contributory cause of death** which was **more than a mere trifling cause of death**.

4 - The State Of The Vehicle

- Regard can be had for anything:
    - **Attached** to the vehicle; or
    - **Carried in** or **on** the vehicle; or
    - The **manner** in which it was:
        - Carried; or
        - Attached.

C – Dangerous Driving
Either Way Offence
Penalty In The Crown Court - Two Years Imprisonment And / Or A Fine
Penalty In The Magistrates Court - Six Months Imprisonment And / Or A Fine Plus Obligatory Disqualification & Compulsory Re-Testing

1 - Definition Of Dangerous Driving - Section 2 Road Traffic Act

- A person commits an offence of **dangerous driving** if they:
    - Drive an **MPV**;
    - **Dangerously**;
    - On either:
        - A **road**; or
        - Other **public place**.

Exam Trip Up

- The **same standards** apply to **all drivers** irrespective of their experience.

Exam Trip Up

- It is **not** a **defence** for the driver to assert that they **did not intend** to drive dangerously.

2 - Definition Of Dangerous – Section 2A(1) Road Traffic Act 1988

- Driving will be deemed to be **dangerous** where:
    - The persons driving **falls far below** the **standards** of a **competent** and **careful** driver; and
    - It would be **obvious to a competent and careful driver** that either:
        - **Driving that way** would be **dangerous;** or
        - **Driving** the vehicle in it's **current state** would be **dangerous.**

3 - What Must The Danger Relate To?

- The **danger** must relate to either:
    - **Injury** to any **person;** or
    - **Serious damage** to **property.**

4 - Current State Of The Vehicle

- **Current state** of the vehicle implies something **different** to its **original state.**
- For example – if a tractor was **manufactured** with a **spike** attached to its front the dangerous spike formed part of its **original state.**

D - Careless And Inconsiderate Driving
Summary Only Offence
Penalty In The Magistrates Court – Fine & Discretionary Disqualification

1 - Definition Of Careless And Inconsiderate Driving - Section 3 Road Traffic Act 1988

A person commits an offence of **careless and inconsiderate driving** if they:
- **Drive** an **MPV;**
- On either:
    - A **road;** or
    - Other **public place;**
- **Without** either:
    - **Due care and attention;** or
    - **Reasonable consideration** for other road users.

2 - Definition Of Due Care And Attention

- **Due care and attention** refers to driving which falls **below** the **standards** expected of a **driver** who is:
    - **Competent;** and
    - **Careful.**

3 - Definition Of Reasonable Consideration

- An absence of reasonable consideration will involve persons *actually* being **inconvenienced by the driving.**

- For example – it will be necessary to prove that a person driving through a puddle **actually splashed** and therefore **inconvenienced** a passer by.

E - Causing Death By Careless Driving Whilst Under The Influence Of Drink Or Drugs
Indictable Only Offence
Penalty In The Crown Court - Fourteen Years Imprisonment & Obligatory Disqualification (Minimum Of 2 Years)

1 - Definition Of Causing Death By Careless Driving Of A MPV Whilst Under The Influence Of Drink Or Drugs - Section 3A Road Traffic Act 1988

- It is an offence to:
    - **Cause** the **death** of another human being;
    - By **driving** an **MPV**;
    - On either:
        - A **road**; or
        - Other **public place**;
    - **Without** either:
        - **Due care and attention;** or
        - **Reasonable consideration;** and
    - They are **unfit** through **drink** or **drugs.**

2 - Definition Of Causing Death By Careless Driving Of A Motor Vehicle Whilst Under The Influence Of Drink Or Drugs - Section 3A Road Traffic Act 1988

- It is an offence to:
    - **Cause** the **death** of another human being;
    - By **driving** a **motor vehicle**;
    - On either:
        - A **road**; or
        - Other **public place**;
    - **Without** either:
        - **Due care and attention;** or
        - **Reasonable consideration;** and
- The proportion of **alcohol** in their **breath/blood/urine exceeds the limit**; or
- **Within 18 hours** after that time they are **required to provide a specimen** for analysis and **without reasonable excuse – they fail to provide.**

Exam Trip Up

- The requirement is for a **specimen** for **analysis.**
- This does **not** mean a **road side breath test**.
- This pat of the offence relates to a **motor vehicle.**

Exam Trip Up

- The **request** must be made **within 18 hours after the** *act* **of driving that caused the death** not 18 hours after the death.

F - Failing To Stop – Police Reform Act 2002 Section 59(1)
Summary Only Offence
Penalty In The Magistrates Court – A Fine

- A person that fails to comply with an order under subsection (3)(a) is guilty of an offence.

Exam Trip Up

- The order relates to the person driving.

Exam Trip Up

- If there is to be a prosecution it is necessary to display that the order was properly given - i.e. that the person giving the order had the authority to do so.

Exam Trip Up

- The stopping must be for a sufficient duration to enable the officer to exercise whatever additional powers are appropriate - *Lodwick v Sanders* [1985] 1 All ER 577.

Traffic
Unit 2: Drink Driving

A - Drink Drive Offences

- There are **2 offences**:
    - ☐ Unfitness through drink or drugs – Section 4 RTA 1988
    - ☐ Driving over the prescribed limit – Section 5 RTA 1988

B - Unfitness Through Drink Or Drugs
Summary Only Offence
Penalty In The Magistrates Court - 6 Months Imprisonment And / Or A Fine Plus Obligatory Disqualification

1 - Definition Of The Offence - Section 4(1) RTA 1988

- It is an offence for a person to:
    - ☐ Either:
        - **Drive**;
        - **Attempt** to drive; or
        - Be **in charge**;
    - ☐ Of a **MPV**;
    - ☐ Either on a:
        - **Road**; or
        - **Public place**;
    - ☐ If they are **unfit** through:
        - **Drink**; or
        - **Drugs**.

2 – Police Powers Of Entry For Section 4 Offences – Section 17(c)(iiia) PACE 1984

- A **constable** may **arrest** if they:
    - ☐ Have **reasonable cause**;
    - ☐ To **suspect** that a person:
        - **Is**; or
        - **Has**;
    - committed an offence under the act; and
    - ☐ The **constable may enter** any place they suspect the person to be.

3 - Matters Disregarded By The Court – Section 4(4) RTA 1988

- The court may **disregard** any:
    - ☐ **Damage** to the **vehicle**; or
    - ☐ **Injury** to the defendant (in charge of the vehicle).

4 - Evidence By Lay Witnesses

- Evidence of any impairment may be given by any lay witness and does not require expert testimony.
- Lay witnesses cannot however give evidence as to the defendant's ability to drive.

Exam Trip Up

- The case of *DPP v Robertson* [2002] RTR 383, established that if a person provides a negative breath test and is then seen staggering away etc and the officer suspects that the driver is unfit - then the section 4 powers of arrest can be utilised.

Exam Trip Up

- It is **not necessary** to show any quantity of alcohol or drugs in the defendant's system.
- If the real world you are going to proceed to prove the quantity of alcohol or drugs.
- However strictly speaking and for the purposes of the exam:
    - ☐ This is **not necessary**; and
    - ☐ **Evidence by a lay or expert witness will suffice.**

5 - Police Powers To Require A Person To Supply A Preliminary Breath Test – Section 6(1) – (4) RTA 1988

- If a **constable** has **reasonable grounds** to **suspect**:
    - ☐ That a person is either:
        - **Driving**;
        - **Attempting** to drive; or
        - In **charge**;
    - ☐ Of a **motor vehicle** on either a:
        - **Road**; or
        - **Public place**;
    - ☐ And they either:
        - Have alcohol in their body; or
        - Have committed a moving traffic offence;
- The constable may **require a specimen of breath.**

C - Driving Over The Prescribed Limit
Summary Only Offence
Penalty In The Magistrates Court - 3 Months Imprisonment And / Or A Fine, Plus Discretionary Disqualification

1 – Definition Of The Offence - Section 5(1)(a) RTA 1988

- It is an offence for a person:
  - To either:
    - **Drive**;
    - **Attempt** to drive;
    - Be **in charge**;
  - Of a **motor vehicle**;
  - On either a:
    - **Road**; or
    - **Public place**;
- After consuming so much **alcohol** that the proportion of it in their **breath/blood/urine exceeds the limit**.

D – Police Powers To Request A Specimen Of Breath Following An Accident? – Section 6(5) RTA 1998

- If an **accident** occurs;
- Owing to the presence of a **motor vehicle** on a:
  - **Road**; or
  - **Public place**;
- A **constable** may **require** any person they **believe** were:
  - **Driving**;
  - **Attempting** to drive;
  - **In charge**;
- Of the vehicle at the time of the accident to provide a **specimen of breath**.

E - Police Powers Of Entry Following An Accident To Request A Specimen Of Breath – Section 6E(1) RTA 1998

- A **constable** may:
  - Following an **accident**;
  - Where they **suspect** the accident involved **injury to any person**;
  - **Enter** any **place**;
  - That they **suspect** the **driver to be**;
  - To ask for a **breath test**.

Summary Table
Sections 4 & 5 RTA 1988

	Unfit – Section 4	Over Prescribed Limit – Section 5
Driving	Driving, attempting, in charge	Driving, attempting, in charge
Vehicle	Mechanically propelled vehicle	Motor vehicle
Where	Road or public place	Road or public place
Uniform	No	Yes
Power to arrest or request breath test	A constable may arrest	Breath teat where a constable suspects: ■ Has alcohol in their body or has committed a moving traffic offence; ■ Has had alcohol in their body and still has alcohol in their body; ■ Has committed a moving traffic offence
Offence	Unfit through drink or drugs	Breath, blood, urine exceeds the prescribed limit
Arrest	Is committing or has been committing	■ Positive breath test ■ Failed breath test and constable suspects alcohol in their body
Entry	Yes – where they are suspected to be	Conditional: ■ To require breath test ■ Arrest after an injury accident
Defence	No likelihood of driving whilst they remained unfit	No likelihood of driving whilst they remained over the limit

Exam Trip Ups Relating To Drink Drive - Section 7(A) RTA 1988

- Due to the procedural difficulties encountered where suspected **drivers are injured in accidents and are incapable of providing their consent to the taking of a sample -** the following provisions now apply:

    - **Samples** can be **lawfully taken without consent.**

    - The **driver must subsequently provide their permission** for the **sample to be tested** at the laboratory.

    - Any **failure by the driver to give their permission** will result in the commission of an **offence.**

- The medical professional taking the sample must **not** be the professional in charge of the defendant's care or welfare.

- It must appear to the constable that the person has been **"involved"** in an accident. This is a **far wider concept than suspicion** only.

F - The Location In Which Evidential Samples Of Breath Can Be Taken - Section 154 – SOCPA 2005

- **Evidential samples** may be taken at:
    - ☐ A **police station**;
    - ☐ A **hospital**;
    - ☐ **At or near** a place where the relevant **breath test**:
        - ■ **Has been administered** to the person concerned; or
        - ■ **Would have been administered** but for their failure to cooperate.

G - Unreliable Evidentiary Breath Samples Taken Away From The Police Station

- If an **evidential breath sample taken away from the police station** provides an **unreliable result**;
- The defendant can be:
    - ☐ **Arrested**; and
    - ☐ **Conveyed** to a **police station**;
- In order to **obtain another sample of breath**.

H - Faulty Intoxilizers At Police Stations

- In the case of *DPP v Denny* [1990] RTR 417, it was established that:
    - ☐ If the **intoxilizer is faulty** at the **initial police station**;
    - ☐ The defendant can be **transferred to another police station where another intoxilizer is available**;
    - ☐ **Even though 2 samples have already been given on the inaccurate machine.**
    - ☐ NB – If the suspect only provides 1 sample then they will be guilty of a failure to provide.

Exam Trip Up

- When a **fault** occurs which leads to a **blood specimen being unsuitable** the **prosecution may not use the original breath specimen** to prove that the person was over the limit.

Exam Trip Up

- Once consent is provided by the suspect to provide a sample of blood it is **for the doctor to determine which part of the body the blood will be taken from**.
- This reinforces the fact that **consent may not be accompanied by any "conditions"** laid down by the suspect.
- Any insistence upon a different course of action by the suspect will amount to a refusal.

Exam Trip Up

- Breath or blood (not both).
- Cannot revert to breath if blood is chosen.

I - Samples Of Urine – Learning Points – Section 7(3)(a) – (c) RTA 1998

- **Samples of urine** can be **taken** by an **officer**.
- **2 distinct samples** must be taken from **2 separate acts of urination** (as opposed to 2 samples taken during 1 act of urination).
- The **hour** within which the specimens must be produced **begins from the time that the request is made** and not between the 1st and 2nd samples being provided.
- The suspect must be given the **opportunity to provide the urine within the hour long period**.

Exam Trip Up

- Moving traffic offence = no need to suspect alcohol.
- An officers "reasonable cause to suspect" may arise from the observations of another officer.

J - Section 10 RTA 1988 (As Amended By SOCPA 2005)

- A person may now be detained at a police station (post arrest) if:
  - A **constable believes**;
  - That were the person **driving an MPV on a road**;
  - Then they would **commit an offence under sections 4 or 5 RTA 1988**.
- Where the sample has been provided otherwise than at a police station:
  - The driver can be:
    - Arrested; and
    - Taken to a police station; and
    - Detained at a police station.

For example: If the initial breath sample was taken at a hospital and the officers have reasonable grounds for believing that the person would drive. In such situations the power of arrest could take place at the hospital, but only applies where it would not be prejudicial to their proper care and treatment.

K - Legal Limits Of Blood Breath And Urine In Samples – Section 11(2) RTA 1998

- Breath   :   **35 micrograms** in **100 millilitres** of breath.
- Blood   :   **80 milligrams** in **100 millilitres** of blood.
- Urine   :   **107 milligrams** in **100 millilitres** of urine.

Memory Aid

- Note how the figures in each instance all **add up to 8.**
    - ☐ 3 + 5 = **8**
    - ☐ 8 + 0 = **8**
    - ☐ 1 + 0 + 7 = **8**

Exam Trip Up

- Questions in recent years have related to the **words surrounding the numbers** – you need to learn parrot fashion whether each figure relates to:
    - ☐ **Micrograms;** or
    - ☐ **Milligrams.**

Traffic
Unit 3: Accidents

A – Reportable Accidents

1 - The Definition Of A Reportable Accident – Section 170 RTA 1988

- A **reportable accident** will arise when the presence of a **mechanically propelled vehicle**;

- On a **road** or other **public place causes an accident** whereby either:

    - ☐ **Injury** is caused to a **person other than the driver**; or

    - ☐ **Damage** is caused to either:

        - Another vehicle;

        - An animal (not inside that vehicle or trailer); or

        - **Property** that is either:

            - ☐ Constructed on;

            - ☐ Fixed to;

            - ☐ Growing on; or

            - ☐ Forms part of either:

                - The **road**; or

                - **Areas adjacent** to the road.

2 - Definition Of An Animal – Section 170(8) RTA 1998

- An **animal** will include any:

☐	Cattle;	C
☐	Horse;	H
☐	Ass;	A
☐	Mule;	M
☐	Pig;	P
☐	Sheep;	S
☐	Dog; or	D
☐	Goat.	G

B – Driver's Responsibilities Following A Reportable Accident – Section 170(2) RTA 1998

- The **driver** must:
    - **Stop**; and
    - **If required** by any **person having reasonable grounds** for doing so, **provide:**
        - The **driver's name** and **address**;
        - The **name** and **address** of the **owner** of the vehicle;
        - The **identification mark** of the vehicle.
    - If the driver **does not give their name and address** they must **report** the accident.

Exam Trip Up

- The driver is only obliged to **stop and remain for such time as to allow interested individuals to request the drivers details**.
- The driver does **not need to make their own enquiries** to find such interested persons.

Exam Trip Up

- The case of *DPP v Bennett* [1993] RTR 175 established that it is **permissible to supply the address of your solicitor** when exchanging details.

Exam Trip Up

- The case of *Cawthorn v DPP* [2000] RTR 45 established that a driver will still be **obliged to report an accident even when they were not in the vehicle at the time of the accident** - e.g. the driver leaves the vehicle to pop a letter in a post box and the car runs off down a hill, crashing into a wall.

C - Reporting The Accident - Section 170(3) RTA 1998

- When the **driver does not provide their name and address** at the time of the accident:
    - They must **report** the accident;
    - **As soon as possible;**
    - Within a **maximum period of 24 hours;**
    - To either:
        - A **police officer;** or
        - At a **police station in person.**

Exam Trip Up

- Whilst there is a maximum prescribed period of 24 hours within which to report, this does not mean that the driver can leave reporting to the last minute when they have had ample opportunity to report the matter sooner. The driver must report the matter as **soon as is reasonably practicable** in the circumstances.

D - The Offence Of Failing To Stop Or Report An Accident – Section 170(4) RTA 1988
Summary Only Offence
Penalty In The Magistrates Court - 6 Months Imprisonment And / Or A Fine, Plus Discretionary Disqualification

- A person commits an offence if following an accident they either:
    - **Fail** to **stop**; or
    - **Fail** to **report** the accident.

Exam Trip Up

- The court of Appeal in the case of *R v Clark* [2003] 2 Cr App R 23, held that a **failure** to either **stop** or **report** an accident would **not** however amount to the offence of **perverting the course of justice**.

- This is because the offence requires a **positive act** rather than an omission to act.

E - Production Of Insurance Documents – Section 170 RTA 1988

- **At the time** of the accident the driver shall **produce their insurance documentation** either to:
    - A **constable;** or
    - To **any person having reasonable grounds.**
- If they are **unable to do so at the time** of the accident the driver will have a **7 day period** to **produce** the documents **at a police station specified.**
- **Failure** to do so will be an **offence.**

Traffic
Unit 4: Insurance

A – Offence Of Having No Insurance
Summary Only Offence
Penalty In The Magistrates Court - Fine, Plus Discretionary Disqualification

1 – Definition Of The Offence Of Having No Insurance – Section 143(2) RTA 1988

- It is an offence to either:
    - **Use**;
    - **Cause**; or
    - **Permit**;
- A **motor vehicle**;
- On either a:
    - **Road**; or
    - **Public place**;
- **Without insurance**.

2 - Defence To The Offence Of Having No Insurance – Section 143(3) RTA 1988

- A driver with no insurance will have a **defence** where:
    - The vehicle did **not belong to them** and was **not** in their possession **under a contract of hire or loan**;
    - They were using the vehicle **during the course of their employment**;
    - They **neither knew nor had reason to believe** that there was no insurance.

3 – Factors That Do Not Render A Policy Of Insurance Void – Section 148(2)(a) – (h) RTA 1998

- Breach of the following does **not make the policy of insurance void**:
    - The drivers age or mental condition;
    - The vehicle's condition;
    - The number of persons carried in the vehicle;
    - The weight or characteristics of goods carried;
    - The times or areas in which the vehicle is used;
    - The power or value of the vehicle;
    - Carrying any apparatus;
    - Carrying any identification of the vehicle.

B - Police Powers To Demand Production Of Insurance Documents – Section 165(1) – (5) RTA 1988

- A **constable** or **vehicle examiner** can request any of the following to provide:
    - ☐ **Their name** and **address**;
    - ☐ The **name** and **address** of the **vehicle owner**;
    - ☐ The **certificate of insurance** of that vehicle (and any test certificate)
- A person **driving** a motor vehicle on a road;
- A person whom thy reasonably believe to have been the **driver when an accident occurred** owing to their presence on a road or public place; or
- A person who they reasonably believe to have **committed an offence** in relation to the use of the vehicle on the road.
- **Failure** to produce the documents is an **offence.**

C – Defence - Insurance Documents Not Produced At The Time Of the Request - Section 165(4)(a) – (c) RTA 1988

- A **driver who does not produce their insurance documents at the time of the request** will have a **defence** provided either:
    - ☐ Their insurance documents are **produced within 7 days** at a specified police station;
    - ☐ Their insurance documents are **produced as soon as was reasonably practicable;**
    - ☐ It was **not practicable to produce the insurance documents before the proceedings began.**

Traffic
Unit 5: Safety Measures

A – Seat Belt Offences
Summary Only Offences
Penalty In The Magistrates Court – Fine Only

1 - Seat Belt Offences For Persons Aged 14 Or Over – Section 14(3) RTA 1988

- It is an offence for:
    - A person **aged 14 or over**;
    - To either:
        - **Drive** a **motor vehicle**;
        - **Ride** as a **front passenger**;
        - **Ride** in the **rear seat** of a motor car or a passenger car;
    - Without wearing an adult seatbelt.

Exam Trip Up

- There is no offence of aiding and abetting this particular offence.

Exam Trip Up

- Only the person not wearing the seatbelt will be guilty.

    For example: A driver wearing a belt who allows a passenger in his car who is not wearing a belt will not be guilty of the offence. Only the non belt wearing passenger will be guilty.

2 - Seat Belt Offences For Persons Under 14 – Section 15(1) RTA 1988

- A child **under 14** sitting in the **front seat** of a vehicle **must wear a seatbelt**.
- A child **under 14** sitting in the **rear seat** of a vehicle **must wear a seatbelt unless:**
    - They are aged **under 12** years and it is a **small child** (under 150cm);
    - **No seat belt is fitted in the rear**; and
    - The **seat in the front** has a belt but it is **occupied**.
- The **driver** will **commit an offence (not the child)** if they drive in such circumstances **without a reasonable excuse**.

B – Riding A Motorcycle Without Protective Headgear
Summary Only Offence
Penalty In The Magistrates Court – Fine Only

1 – Definition Of The Offence - Section 16 RTA 1988

- It is an offence for a person to **ride a motorcycle without protective headgear;**
- **Except** for:
    - **Mowing machines;**
    - **Sikhs wearing a turban;**
    - Situations where the motorcycle is being **pushed – NB not straddled.**

2 - Who Is Guilty Of The Offence If There Are Un-Helmeted Passengers? – Section 16(4) RTA 1988

(i) - The General Rule

- **Only the person failing to wear the helmet is guilty.**
- A helmeted driver will not be responsible for an un-helmeted passenger.
- Only the un-helmeted passenger will be guilty in such circumstances.

(ii) - The Exception To The General Rule

- If the **passenger** is **under 16** both the helmeted driver and the un-helmeted passenger will be guilty.

C - Passengers On Motorcycles – Section 23 RTA 1988
Summary Only Offence
Penalty In The Magistrates Court – Fine Plus Discretionary Disqualification

- Only **1 passenger** may be carried.
- They must be:
    - **Sitting astride;**
    - **On a secured seat;**
    - **Behind the driver.**
- Failure to do so will result in:
    - The **driver** committing an **offence.**
    - The **passenger** committing the offence of **aiding and abetting.**

D - Obstructing The Highway – Section 137 Highways Act 1980
Summary Only Offence
Penalty In The Magistrates Court – Fine Only

- An offence is committed by any person who:
    - Without lawful:
        - Authority; or
        - Excuse;
    - Wilfully obstructs a highway.

E – Obstructing A Road – Regulation 103 Road Vehicles (Construction And Use) Regulations 1986
Summary Only Offence
Penalty In The Magistrates Court – Fine Only

- An offence is committed by any **person in charge** of either:
    - A **motor vehicle**; or
    - **Trailer**;
- Who either:
    - **Causes**; or
    - **Permits**;
- It to **stand on a road**;
- So as to cause an **unnecessary obstruction of the road**.

F – Obstructing A Street – Section 28 Town Polices Clauses Act 1847
Summary Only Offence
Penalty In The Magistrates Court – 14 Days Imprisonment And / Or A Fine

- An offence is committed by any person in any **street** who:
    - To the **obstruction, annoyance** or **danger** of either:
        - Residents; or
        - Passengers;
    - Either:
        - **Wilfully interrupts** any **public crossing**; or
        - Causes any **wilful obstruction** in any **public footpath**.

G – Parking Heavy Vehicles On Verges – Section 19 RTA 1988
Summary Only Offence
Penalty In The Magistrates Court – Fine Only

- It is an offence to **park** a **heavy commercial vehicle (over 7.5 tonnes);**
- **Wholly** or **partly** either:
    - On the **verge** of a road;
    - Between **carriageways;**
    - On a **footway;**
- **Unless** it was **parked** either:
    - With the **permission of a constable in uniform**; or
    - For the **purpose** of either:
        - Saving life;
        - Putting out fire;
        - An emergency; or
    - It was there for **unloading**; and
    - It could **not otherwise** have been unloaded; and
    - It was **never unattended.**

H – Leaving A Vehicle In A Dangerous Position
Summary Only Offence
Penalty In The Magistrates Court – Fine Plus Discretionary Disqualification

- An offence is committed by a **person in charge** of a **vehicle** or **trailer;**
- Who either:
    - **Causes;** or
    - **Permits;**
- It to **remain at rest on a road** in either:
    - Such a **position;**
    - Such **condition;** or
    - Such **circumstances;**
- As to involve a **danger of injury to other road users.**

I - The Removal And Immobilisation Of Parked Vehicles – Regulation 4 Removal And Disposal Of Vehicles Regulations 1986

- Where a vehicle is permitted to remain at rest on a road either:
    - In **contravention of a prohibition or restriction;**
    - In a position or circumstances that will **obstruct or cause danger;**
    - **On any land in open air** and appears to have either been:
        - **Abandoned;** or
        - **Broken down;**
- A **constable** may **arrange for it to be removed** from that road to **another position** either:
    - **On that road;** or
    - **On another road.**

J - Police Powers To Remove Vehicles From The Road – Regulation 3 Removal And Disposal Of Vehicles Regulations 1986

- A **constable** may require:
    - The **owner** of a vehicle;
    - The **driver** of a vehicle; or
    - The person either in **charge or control** of the vehicle;
- Which has either:
    - **Broken down** on a road; or
    - Been **permitted to remain at rest on a road;**
- To **remove** the vehicle either:
    - **To a road;** or
    - **Off the road;**
- If it is either:
    - In a **position** or **condition** likely to **cause obstruction** or **danger;** or
    - In **contravention** of a **restriction** or **prohibition.**

K - Abandoning Motor Vehicles – Section 2(1) Refuse Disposal (Amenity) Act 1978
Summary Only Offence
Penalty In The Magistrates Court – Fine Only

- An offence is committed by any person who **without lawful authority** either:
    - **Abandons** on any **land in the open air;** or **any highway** either:
        - A **motor vehicle;** or
        - **Anything which formed part of a motor vehicle** and was removed from it whilst dismantling the vehicle on land; or
    - **Abandons** on such land **anything** (not a motor vehicle) **brought there for the purpose of abandoning it.**

L – The Removal Of Abandoned Motor Vehicles – Section 3 Refuse Disposal (Amenity) Act 1978

- The **local authority** has a **duty to remove** any **motor vehicle**:
    - ☐ **Abandoned**;
    - ☐ **Without lawful authority**;
    - ☐ On either:
        - Any **land in the open air**;
        - Any **highway**.

M – Tampering And Getting Onto Motor Vehicles – Section 25 Road Traffic Act 1988
Summary Only Offence
Penalty In The Magistrates Court – Fine Only

- A person will commit an offence if in relation to a **motor vehicle** on either a:
    - ☐ **Road**; or
    - ☐ **Local authority parking place**;
- They either:
    - ☐ **Get onto the vehicle**; or
    - ☐ **Tamper** with the **brakes** or other **mechanism**;
- **Without** either a:
    - ☐ **Lawful authority**; or
    - ☐ **Reasonable excuse**.

Exam Trip Up

- This offence can only be committed on the **road** or in a **Public Authority car park**.
- No other type of car park will do.

Exam Trip Up

- The offence only relates to **motor vehicles**.
- The offence cannot be committed against a trailer.

N – Holding Or Getting Onto A Vehicle In Motion – Section 26 RTA 1988
Summary Only Offence
Penalty In The Magistrates Court – Fine Only

- A person commits an offence if:
    - For the **purpose of being carried**;
    - They **without** either:
        - **Lawful authority**; or
        - **Reasonable excuse**;
    - Either:
        - **Take hold of**; or
        - **Get onto**;
    - A **motor vehicle** or **trailer** which is:
        - **In motion**; *and*
        - **On a road**;
    - For the **purpose** of **being drawn**.

O - Builders Skips
Summary Only Offence
Penalty In The Magistrates Court – Fine Only

1 – Obtaining Permission To Deposit A Skip - Section 139(1) Highways Act 1980

- A **skip** can only be **deposited** with the **written permission** of the **Highways Authority**.

2 – When Will An Offence Be Committed? - Section 139(4) Highways Act 1980

- The **owner** of the skip and the **offender** will be guilty in the event of the following:
    - Placing the skip **on a highway without permission**;
    - The skip **not** being **properly lit during darkness**;
    - The skip does **not bear** the **owners name** and **telephone number**;
    - The skip is **not removed as soon as possible after it is filled**;
    - There is a **failure to comply with any condition** of the Highway Authority.

3 - Defence For The Owner Of The Skip - Section 139(6) Highways Act 1980

- The **owner** may have a **defence** where:
    - The offence arose due to the **action** or **default of another**; and
    - They had taken **all reasonable precautions** and **exercised due diligence to prevent the offence**.

3 - Police Powers In Relation To Skips - Section 140(3) Highways Act 1980

- A **constable** in **uniform** may require the **removal of a skip in person.**
- Failure to do so is an offence.

P - Road Works – Section 65(5) New Roads And Street Works Act 1991

- **Work sites** must be properly:
    - ☐ **Guarded;**
    - ☐ **Signed**; and
    - ☐ **Lit.**
- It is an **offence to remove** any of the above **without** either:
    - ☐ **Lawful authority**; or
    - ☐ **Reasonable excuse.**

Traffic
Unit 6: Construction and Use

A - Defective Tyres – Regulation 27 Road Vehicles (Construction and Use) Regulations 1986

- A **tyre** is **defective** when:
    - It is **unsuitable for use**;
    - It is **under inflated** or **over inflated**;
    - It has a **cut in excess of 25mm** or **10% of its section width** (whichever is greater) and is deep enough to **reach the ply or cord**;
    - It has a **lump, bulge** or **tear** caused by failure of the structure;
    - **Ply** or **cord** is **exposed**;
    - It is **not maintained** in a condition **fit** for its use;
    - It has a **defect** that might cause **damage** to the **road** or to **persons**;
    - The **base of a groove in a tread is not visible** because either:
        - The grooves of the **tread** of the tyre do **not have a depth** of at least **1.6 mm** throughout a **continuous band** measuring at least ¾ **of the breadth of the tread** round the entire **outer circumference**; or
        - If the grooves of the original tread did not extend beyond ¾ of the breadth of the tread, **any groove** which showed in the original tread does **not have a depth of** at least **1.6 mm.**

B - Brakes – Regulations 15 - 18 Road Vehicles (Construction and Use) Regulations 1986

- The regulations stipulate that:
    - **Every part** of every **braking system**; and
    - The **means of operation** fitted to a vehicle;
    - Shall be **maintained** in a good and efficient **working order.**

C - Breach Of Brake Or Tyre Requirements – Section 41A RTA 1988

- A person will commit an offence if they:
    - **Fail to comply** with regulations as to **breaks** or **tyres**; or
    - **Uses on a road** a motor vehicle or trailer which does **not comply** with the regulations;
    - **Causes or permits another to use on a road** a motor vehicle or trailer which does **not comply** with the regulations.

D - Silencers – Regulations 54 and 57 Road Vehicles (Construction and Use) Regulations 1986

- Every **vehicle propelled** by an **internal combustion engine**:
  - ☐ Must be fitted with an **exhaust system** including a **silencer**; and
  - ☐ The **exhaust gases** from the engine must not escape without **passing through** the **silencer**.

E - Mirrors – Regulation 33 Road Vehicles (Construction and Use) Regulations 1986

- With certain exceptions every:
  - ☐ **Passenger** vehicle;
  - ☐ **Goods** vehicle;
  - ☐ **Dual purpose** vehicle;
- First used on or **after 1st June 1978;**
- Must be equipped with:
  - ☐ An **interior rear view mirror**; and
  - ☐ At least one **exterior mirror** fitted to the **off side**.
- If the **interior rear view mirror** is **obscured** the driver must have an **exterior rear view mirror** attached to the **near side** of the vehicle.

F - Quitting – Regulation 107 Road Vehicles (Construction and Use) Regulations 1986

- It is an offence to **leave a motor vehicle unattended on a road;**
- **Unless** both:
  - ☐ The **engine** has been **stopped**; and
  - ☐ The **brake** has been **set**.

F - Stopping Engines – Regulation 98 Road Vehicles (Construction and Use) Regulations 1986

- The **driver** of a vehicle when **stationary** shall **stop** the action of any machinery attached to or forming part of the vehicle so far as is necessary to **prevent:**
  - ☐ **Noise;** or
  - ☐ **Exhaust emissions**.
- **Exceptions** include vehicles stationery due to:
  - ☐ **Traffic;**
  - ☐ The need to **examine machinery** following its **failure;**
  - ☐ The need to **work the vehicle** for a purpose **other than driving** the vehicle; or
  - ☐ **Vehicles propelled by** gas produced **in plant** carried on the vehicle.

G - Using A Motor Vehicle In Dangerous Condition – Section 40A Road Traffic Act 1988
Summary Only Offence
Penalty In The Magistrates Court - Fine Plus Discretionary Disqualification

- A person is guilty of an offence if:
    - They:
        - **Use;**
        - **Cause;** or
        - **Permit;**
    - **Another** to **use** a:
        - **Motor vehicle;** or
        - **Trailer;**
    - **On a road** when either:
        - The **condition** of the vehicle or trailer or its accessories/equipment;
        - The **purpose** for which it is used;
        - The **number** of **passengers** carried by it;
        - The **manner** in which **passengers** are carried;
        - The **weight, position** or **distribution** of its load; or
        - The **manner** in which the **load** is **secured;**
    - Is such that its use involves a **danger** to **any person.**

Learning Point

- The existence of **danger** is a **question of fact** for the Magistrates or the jury.

Exam Trip Up

- The offence does **not cover mechanically propelled vehicles.** The offence only applies to **motor vehicles.**

I - Breach Of Weights Requirements For Goods And Passenger Vehicles
Summary Only Offence
Penalty In The Magistrates Court – Fine

1 – Definition Of The Offence – Section 41B(1) RTA 1988

- A person will commit an offence if they either:
    - **Fail to comply** with the regulations in relation to **weights** applicable to:
        - A **goods vehicle;**
        - A **motor vehicle** or trailer adapted to carry **more than 8 passengers;** or
    - **Uses on a road** a vehicle that does not comply with the requirements; or
    - **Cause or permit another to use on a road** a vehicle that does not comply with the requirements.

2 - Defence To Breach Of Weights Requirements - Section 41B(2) RTA 1988

- It is a **defence** to prove that:
  - At the time the vehicle was being used on a road:
    - It was **proceeding to the nearest weighbridge to be weighed**; or
    - It was **proceeding from a weighbridge** to the **nearest point at which it was reasonably practicable to reduce the weight** to the relevant limit **without causing an obstruction** on the road; or
  - If the vehicle was **not more than 5% overweight**:
    - The **limit was not exceeded at the original time of loading**; and
    - **No** person has **subsequently added the weight**.

J - Using, Causing or Permitting Use of Vehicle Without Test Certificate - Section 47(1) Road Traffic Act 1988
Summary Only Offence
Penalty In The Magistrates Court – Fine Only

- A person commits an offence if they:
  - Either:
    - Use; or
    - Cause or permit to be used;
  - On a road;
  - At any time;
  - A motor vehicle;
  - To which there is no test certificate been issued within the appropriate time (12 months or less as may be prescribed).

Exam Trip Up

- Vehicles **provided** (as opposed to **used**) for **police purposes** are **exempt** if they are **maintained** in an **approved workshop**.

Exam Trip Up

- An **exemption** exists where a person is **taking the motor vehicle either to or from a testing centre.**
- This only applies when the test has been **previously arranged** with the testing centre.

K - Using, Causing Or Permitting Use Of Goods Vehicles Without Test Certificate - Section 53(2) Road Traffic Act 1988
Summary Only Offence
Penalty In The Magistrates Court – Fine Only

- An offence will be committed by:
    - ☐ Any person who at **any time after** the **relevant date**;
    - ☐ Either
        - **Uses;** or
        - **Causes** or **permits** to be used;
    - ☐ **On a road;**
    - ☐ A **goods vehicle** of a **class required** to have submitted for a **goods vehicle test;** and;
    - ☐ **At the time** of doing so there is **no test certificate in force.**

Road Traffic
Unit 7: Forgery and Falsification Of Documents – Sergeants Syllabus Only

A - Forgery Of Non Registration Documents
Either Way Offence
Penalty In The Crown Court – 2 Years Imprisonment And / Or A Fine
Penalty In The Magistrates Court – A Fine Only

1 – Definition Of The Offence – Section 173(1) RTA 1988

- An offence of **forgery** will be committed by:
    - Any person who with the **intent** to **deceive** either:
        - **Forges, alters,** or **uses** a **relevant document** or **thing;**
        - **Lends,** or **allows another to use** a **relevant document** or **thing;** or
        - **Makes** or **has in their possession** any **relevant document** or **thing** so closely **resembling** a relevant document or thing as to be **calculated to deceive.**

2 - Definition Of A Relevant Document Or Thing - Section 173(2) RTA 1988

- A **relevant document** or **thing** may include:
    - Licences;
    - Test certificates;
    - Insurance documents;
    - Certificates of exemption for seatbelts;
    - Haulage permits; or
    - Goods vehicles plates.

Exam Trip Up

- Forgery means making a false document in order that it may be used as genuine.

Exam Trip Up

- It is necessary to establish an intention to deceive.

B - Forgery Of Registration Documents – Sections 44 - 45 Vehicle Excise and Registration Act 1994
Either Way Offence
Penalty In The Crown Court – 2 Years Imprisonment And / Or A Fine
Penalty In The Magistrates Court – A Fine Only

- A person will be guilty of an offence of **forging registration documents** if they carry out any of the following in respect of a vehicle registration document:
    - ☐ **Forge it;**
    - ☐ **Fraudulently alter it;**
    - ☐ **Fraudulently use it;**
    - ☐ **Lend** it or **allow another to use it** to do any of the above.

C - Forgery Of Documents Relating To PSV's
Either Way Offence
Penalty In The Crown Court – 2 Years Imprisonment
Penalty In The Magistrates Court – A Fine Only

1 – Definition Of The Offence – Section 65(2) Public Passenger Vehicles Act 1981

- An offence will be committed by any person who with **intent** to **deceive** either:
    - ☐ **Forges;**
    - ☐ **Alters;**
    - ☐ **Uses;**
    - ☐ **Lends** to another or **allows** another to **use;**

    - a **relevant document** or **thing**; or

    - ☐ Either:
        - **Makes;** or
        - Has in their **possession;**

    - any **document** or **thing** so **closely resembling** a **document** or **thing** as to be **calculated to deceive.**

2 - Definition Of A Relevant Document Or Thing Relating To PSV's - Section 65(1) Public Passenger Vehicles Act 1981

- A **relevant document** or **thing** may include any of the following:
    - ☐ **Licences;**
    - ☐ **Certificates of fitness;**
    - ☐ **Certificates of type;**
    - ☐ **Operators disc certificates of competence.**

D - Forgery Relating To Goods Vehicles – Section 38 Goods Vehicles (Licensing Of Operators) Act 1995
Either Way Offence
Penalty In The Crown Court – 2 Years Imprisonment And / Or A Fine
Penalty In The Magistrates Court – A Fine Only

- A person will be guilty of an offence if:
    - With **intent to deceive** they carry out any of the following in respect of a **document** or **thing**:
        - Forge it;
        - Alter it;
        - Use it;
        - Lend it or allow it to be used;
        - Have **in their possession** a **document** or **thing** so **closely resembling** a **document** or **thing** as to be **calculated to deceive**.

E - Misuse Of Parking Documents Or Apparatus – Section 115 Road Traffic Regulations Act 1984
Either Way Offence
Penalty In The Crown Court – 2 Years Imprisonment And / Or A Fine
Penalty In The Magistrates Court – A Fine Only

- A person shall be guilty of an offence if with **intent to deceive** they either:
    - **Use, lend** or **allow** to be used:
        - Any **parking device** or **apparatus** designed to be used in connection with parking devices;
        - Any **ticket issued** by a **parking meter, parking device** or **apparatus;**
        - Any **authorisation** by a **certificate** or **other means of identification**; or any **permit or token**; or
    - **Makes** or has in their **possession** anything **so closely resembling any such thing** as to be **calculated to deceive;** or
    - **Knowingly** makes a **false statement** for the **purposes of procuring the grant or issue** or any such **authorisation**.

F - Making False Statements – Section 174 RTA 1988

- An offence will be committed by a person who either:
    - **Knowingly** makes a **false statement** for the **purpose** of:
        - Obtaining a **licence;**
        - **Preventing** the **granting** of a **licence;**
        - **Procuring** a **provision** or **condition** on a **licence;**
        - Obtaining an **international road haulage permit**; or
        - **Securing** the **entry** or **retention** of the name of any person on the **register of approved instructors; or**

☐ In **supplying information** or **producing documents** to achieve such an outcome either:

- **Knowingly** or **recklessly** makes a **false statement**;

- **Knowingly** or **recklessly** makes **use of a false document**;

- **Knowingly produces a false statement** or **evidence** in a **declaration**;

- **Wilfully** makes a **false record** in a **document required to be kept**;

- With **intent** to deceive **makes use of a false record in a document required to be kept**; or

- **Makes use of a false statement** or **withholds information** for the **purpose of the issue of insurance**.

Exam Trip Up

- There is **no need** to prove that the person **gained** from their actions – *Ocean Accident etc Co. v Cole* [1932] 96 JP 191.

G - Police Powers In Relation To Documents Obtained Falsely or Forged Documents – Section 176 RTA 1988

- A **constable** may **seize** a document if they have **reasonable cause** to **believe** that a document produced to them was either:

    - **Forged**; or

    - **Falsely obtained**.

Traffic
Unit 8: Notices Of Intended Prosecution - Sergeants Syllabus Only

A - Issuing Notices Of Intended Prosecution - Section 1 Road Traffic Offenders Act 1988

- **Prior** to a defendant being **prosecuted** for **certain traffic offences** they must have either:
    - Been **warned** of the possibility of **prosecution at the time of the offence**; or
    - Been **served** with a **summons** or **charged within 14 days of the offence**; or
    - **Received within 14 days of the offence** a **notice** setting out the possibility of prosecution. This will be sent to either:
        - The **driver** of the vehicle (e.g. a boy racer); or
        - The **registered keeper** of the vehicle (e.g. the parent who owns the car that the boy racer was using).

B - Who Will Issue The Warning Or Notice?

- The **warning** or **notice** must be **issued** by the **'prosecutor'**.
- This will normally be the **police.**

Exam Trip Up

- The case of *Swan v Vehicle Inspectorate* [1997] RTR 187 established that if the **person issuing** the warning is **not empowered** to make a decision whether or not to prosecute (e.g. a vehicle examiner) the **warning will be deemed not to have been issued.**
- The case of *Gibson v Dalton* [1980] RTR 410 established that if a *verbal* **notice of intended prosecution** is issued it is necessary to prove that the defendant **understood** the notice.
- As a result it will be common practice to **follow up a verbal notice of intended prosecution with a written notice of intended prosecution**.

Exam Trip Up

- Where jurisdiction falls between two counties a court in either county could hear the case.
- For example - a driver committing an offence in Somerset, returns home to Dorset and fails to give their details to the officer as required.

C - Offences Requiring A Notice Of Intended Prosecution To Be Issued – Schedule 1 Road Traffic Offenders Act 1988

- The following offences will **require a notice of intended prosecution** to be issued:
    - Dangerous, careless, or inconsiderate driving;
    - Dangerous, careless, or inconsiderate cycling;
    - Failing to comply with traffic signs and directions;
    - Leaving a vehicle in a dangerous position; and
    - Speeding offences under sections 16 and 17 of the Road Traffic Regulation Act 1984

D - Exceptions Where It Will Not Be Necessary To Issue A Notice Of Intended Prosecution For Such Offences - Section 2(1) Road Traffic Offenders Act 1988

- There is **no need to issue a notice of intended prosecution** for such offences if:
    - Either:
        - **At the time of the act**; or
        - **Immediately afterwards**;
    - An **accident** occurred;
    - Owing to the **presence** of the **vehicle** concerned **on a road.**

Exam Trip Up

- It is **not necessary** for the **accident** to be **reportable** in nature.
- Any accident will suffice.

Exam Trip Up

- The accident must happen on a **road.**

Exam Trip Up – Drivers Unaware Of Minor Accidents

- If the **driver** is **unaware an accident has happened** because it is **so minor**, it **will be necessary to issue a notice of intended prosecution.**
- For example – In the case of *Bentley v Dickinson* [1983] RTR 356, a driver of a HGV was unaware they had clipped and damaged an object whilst going around a corner. In such circumstances it was necessary to issue a notice of intended prosecution.

Exam Trip Up – Drivers Who Cannot Remember An Accident Due To Its Severity

- The case of *DPP v Pidhajeckyj* [1991] RTR 136, established that where an **accident is so severe that the driver does not remember it happening**, it will **not** be **necessary to issue a notice of intended prosecution.**

E - Service Of A Notice Of Intended Prosecution

- The case of *Hosier v Goodall* [1962] 1 All ER 30, established that it will be sufficient to serving a notice of intended prosecution personally on a:
    - Partner; or
    - Spouse
- The case of *Phipps v McCormick* [1972] Crim LR 540, established that where a person is on holiday or in hospital, service at their last known address will suffice even if the police are aware the person was absent.
- If neither the defendant nor the registered keeper of the vehicle have any fixed abode, it is necessary to attempt to effect personal service.
- If it is not possible to effect personal service in such circumstances – service is dispensed with.

Traffic
Unit 9: Fixed Penalty System - Sergeants Syllabus Only

A - Definition Of A Fixed Penalty - Section 52 Road Traffic Offenders Act 1988

- A fixed penalty means:
    - A **notice**;
    - Offering the **opportunity** to **discharge** any **liability** for the **conviction** of an **offence** to which the notice relates;
    - By **payment** of a **fixed penalty**.

B – Circumstances In Which A Fixed Penalty May Be Issued

- The system envisages two situations:
    - Firstly where the **driver** is **present**; and
    - Secondly:
        - Where the driver is **absent**; *and*
        - There is a **statutory vehicle** to which the **notice** can be **attached**.

C - Issuing Fixed Penalties When The Driver Is Present

1 – When May A Fixed Penalty Be Issued? - Section 54(1) Road Traffic Offenders Act 1988

- A **constable in uniform**;
    - **May issue a fixed penalty** if they have reason to **believe** that a person;
    - Either:
        - **Is committing**; or
        - **Has committed**;
    - A **fixed penalty** offence.

2 – Prerequisites To Be Satisfied Before The Fixed Penalty Is Issued - Section 54(3) Road Traffic Offenders Act 1988

- The constable can only issue the fixed penalty if all of the following criteria are satisfied:
    - The person **produces for inspection** by the constable their:
        - **Licence**; *and*
        - Its **counterpart**;
    - The constable is satisfied, on inspection that the person would **not be liable to disqualification;** and

- ☐ The person **surrenders** their:
    - ■ **Licence;** *and*
    - ■ **Its counterpart;**

- ■ If the person **cannot satisfy all of the criteria** - the constable may issue a **notice** requiring them to **surrender** their **licence** and its **counterpart** within **7 days**.

3 - Production Of A Notice, Licence And Its Counterpart To A Police Station Within 7 Days - Section 54(5) Road Traffic Offenders Act 1988

- ■ The person **must produce:**
    - ☐ The **notice;**
    - ☐ Their **licence;** and
    - ☐ Its **counterpart;**
- ■ To:
    - ☐ A **constable;** or
    - ☐ **Authorised person;**
- ■ At a police station.

4 – Action To Be Taken Following A Production - Section 54(5) Road Traffic Offenders Act 1988

- ■ If the person:
    - ☐ Is **not subject to a disqualification** if convicted; and
    - ☐ **Surrenders their licence;**
- ■ The constable or authorised person **must issue a fixed penalty**.

Exam Trip Up

- ■ The **constable** must be **in uniform** to issue a fixed penalty.

Exam Trip Up

- ■ If the person surrenders their licence at a police station, they can only be given a fixed penalty if it does not take them to 12 points or above.

Exam Trip Up

- ■ If the **offence** is **endorsable,** the fixed penalty can only be given if:
    - ☐ The person **surrenders** their **licence;** and
    - ☐ It does **not take them to 12 points or more.**

D - Procedure When The Driver Is Not Present - Section 62(1) Road Traffic Offenders Act 1988

- If a **constable** has reason to **believe** that a **fixed penalty offence** either:
    - ☐ **Is being committed**; or
    - ☐ **Has been committed**;
- By a **statutory vehicle**;
- The **constable** may **affix** a **fixed penalty notice** to the **vehicle**;
- **Unless**;
- The offence involves an **obligatory endorsement** (basically means points on your licence).

Exam Trip Up

- The **constable** need not be **in uniform** to issue the fixed penalty.

E - Removing Or Interfering With Fixed Penalty Notice On Vehicle – Section 62(2) Road Traffic Offenders Act 1988
Summary Only Offence
Penalty In The Magistrates Court – Fine Only

- A person is guilty of an offence if:
    - ☐ They either:
        - **Remove**; or
        - **Interfere** with;
    - ☐ Any **notice fixed** to a **vehicle**;
    - ☐ **Unless**;
    - ☐ They do so with the **authority** of the:
        - **Driver**;
        - **Person in charge** of the vehicle; or
        - **Person liable** for the fixed penalty.

F - Making False Statements In Relation To A Notice To An Owner - Section 67 Road Traffic Offenders Act 1988
Summary Only Offence
Penalty In The Magistrates Court – Fine Only

- A person commits an offence if:
    - ☐ In **response** to a **notice** to the owner;
    - ☐ They either:
        - **Knowingly**; or
        - **Recklessly**;
    - ☐ Provide a **statement** which is **false** in a material particular.

G - Conditional Offers – Section 75 Road Traffic Offenders Act 1988

1 - Purpose Of A Conditional Offer

- The advent of **automatic devices for detecting speeding offences** precipitated the need to be able to issue a ticket in a way previously unavailable, namely by sending a **notice** to the alleged offender on **behalf** of the **Chief Constable**.

2 – Contents Of A Conditional Offer - Section 75(1), (6), (7) & (8) Road Traffic Offenders Act 1988

- The **notice** must:
    - Outline the **offence** alleged;
    - State the **amount** of the **fixed penalty**;
    - State that **no proceedings** can take place for **28 days following** the date the **offer** was issued
    - Indicate that if the following **conditions** are fulfilled any **liability to conviction** shall be **discharged:**
        - **Within 28 days** the offender makes **payment** for the **fixed penalty** to the **fixed penalty clerk**; and
        - Where there is an **obligatory endorsement**, at the **same time** the offender **delivers** their **licence** and **counterpart** to that clerk; and
        - The **clerk** is **satisfied** that if convicted, the offender would **not be liable to disqualification.**